'The History of Ashanti K
the whole country itse

and Other Writings

A reading and writing lesson in the Seychelles, from left to right Kokofuhene Osei Asibe, Government Interpreter Timothy Korsah and Asantehene Agyeman Prempeh. The photograph was taken before 1904 when Korsah returned to the Gold Coast. (Collection Professor A. Adu Boahen)

FONTES HISTORIAE AFRICANAE, NEW SERIES
SOURCES OF AFRICAN HISTORY
6

'The History of Ashanti Kings and the whole country itself'

and Other Writings

by
Otumfuo, Nana Agyeman Prempeh I

edited by
A. ADU BOAHEN
EMMANUEL AKYEAMPONG
NANCY LAWLER
T. C. McCASKIE
IVOR WILKS

Published for THE BRITISH ACADEMY
by OXFORD UNIVERSITY PRESS

OXFORD
UNIVERSITY PRESS

Great Clarendon Street, Oxford OX2 6DP
United Kingdom

Oxford University Press is a department of the University of Oxford.
It furthers the University's objective of excellence in research, scholarship,
and education by publishing worldwide. Oxford is a registered trade mark of
Oxford University Press in the UK and in certain other countries

© The British Academy, 2003

The moral rights of the author have been asserted

Database right The British Academy (maker)

First published 2003
Reprinted 2003, 2005, 2006
Paperback edition 2008
Reprinted 2014

All rights reserved. No part of this publication may be reproduced,
stored in a retrieval system, or transmitted, in any form or by any means,
without the prior permission in writing of The British Academy,
or as expressly permitted by law, or under terms agreed with the appropriate
reprographics rights organization. Enquiries concerning reproduction
outside the scope of the above should be sent to the Publications Department,
The British Academy, 10 Carlton House Terrace, London SW1Y 5AH

You must not circulate this work in any other form
and you must impose this same condition on any acquirer

British Library Cataloguing in Publication Data
Data available

Library of Congress Cataloging in Publication Data
Data available

ISBN 978-0-19-726415-7

Contents

List of Plates and Figures	viii
Preface	ix

PART I: ESSAYS

CHAPTER ONE: Agyeman Prempeh before the Exile, *T. C. McCaskie*
Introduction	3
Kinship, Royalty and the Birth of Agyeman Prempeh	3
Agyeman Prempeh's Childhood	6
Agyeman Prempeh, Yaa Kyaa, and Civil War	9
Agyeman Prempeh, Asante, and the British	15

CHAPTER TWO: Agyeman Prempeh in the Seychelles, 1900–1924, *A. Adu Boahen*
Introduction	21
Daily Life at Le Rocher: Asante in Microcosm	23
Education, Christianity, and Modernity	26
Agyeman Prempeh, Asante, and Repatriation	29
Homecoming	40

CHAPTER THREE: Agyeman Prempeh's Return from Exile, 1924–1931, *Emmanuel Akyeampong*
Introduction	43
Our King is Back! But What Kind of King?	44
British Colonial Rule in Asante	47
Renegotiating 'Kingship' in Colonial Asante: Agyeman Prempeh, 1924–31	49
Conclusion	55

CHAPTER FOUR: Agyeman Prempeh as Author: Textual History, *Ivor Wilks*
Literacy in Asante before the Exile	57
Literacy and the Exiles	59
History of the Text of *HAK*	62
Genesis of the New Edition	66
Establishing a Text of *HAK*	68
HAK, A Related Text, and Other Pieces	69

PART II: THE SEYCHELLES WRITINGS *transcribed and presented by Nancy Lawler, T. C. McCaskie and Ivor Wilks*
Conventions ... 83

CHAPTER FIVE: Historical Pieces
  The Arrival of Ankyewa Nyame at Asantemanso ... 85
  Ankyewa Nyame and the Gathering of the Clans (*Mmusua*) ... 86
  The Reigns of Akyampon Tenten, Twum, Antwi, and Kwabia Anwanfi ... 89
  The Reign of Oti Akenten ... 91
  Osei Tutu at Denkyira ... 93
  The First Domaa War ... 96
  The Reign of Obiri Yeboa ... 97
  Osei Tutu Succeeds Obiri Yeboa ... 100
  Osei Tutu Defeats the Domaa ... 101
  Reorganisation of the Kumase Army ... 102
  The Defeat of Asiedu Papaa Kesee ... 103
  The Dispute with Denkyira ... 104
  Okomfo Anokye and the Preparations for the Denkyira War ... 105
  The Denkyira War ... 107
  The Elmina Tribute ... 109
  The War with Adanse ... 110
  The Denkyira Rebellion ... 110
  The Attack on Kaase ... 111
  The Attack on Tafo ... 111
  The Attack on Amakom ... 112
  Osei Tutu and the Succession ... 113

CHAPTER SIX: Ethnographic Pieces
  Introduction ... 115
  The Akan "Cities" ... 115
  The *Ntɔrɔ* and Soul-Washing ... 116
  The Calendar ... 117
  The Origins of Apafram ... 118
  The Origins of *Atɔperɛ* and the Adanse-Denkyira Conflict ... 119
  The "Reserve" Asantehenes ... 122
  The Funeral of an Asantehene ... 123
  The Division of Revenues ... 125
  The Akwamu Factor in the Rise of Asante ... 125

CHAPTER SEVEN: Office Lists and Genealogies
  Office Lists: Introduction ... 127
  The Genealogies ... 129

The Pre-Asante Rulers	129
The Descendants of Manu	131
The Census of "Royals"	138

CHAPTER EIGHT: Memoirs
Introduction	147
The Petition of 1913	147
The Memoir of 1922–23	150
History and Apologia	159

CHAPTER NINE: Reporting to the Living, Accounting for the Dead
Agyeman Prempeh's Report of 1925	175
The Disposition of the Dead	182
The Matter of the "Brass Pan"	185

PART III: WORKS CITED   193

PART IV: CONCORDANCE   197

List of Plates and Figures

PLATES

FRONTISPIECE:
A Reading and Writing Lesson in the Seychelles   ii

Plates 1–6: "The History of Ashanti Kings and the whole country itself", Facsimile Pages 1 – 6	72–77
Plates 7–10: "King Otti Akenten . . . King Obi Yaeboa", Facsimile	78–81
Plate 11: 'Palaver and Submission of King Prempeh', 1896	167
Plate 12: 'Embarkation of King Prempeh', 1896	168
Plate 13: Asantehene Agyeman Prempeh at Elmina Castle, 1896	169
Plate 14: The Asante Exiles in the Seychelles, 1904	170
Plate 15: Asantehene Agyeman Prempeh on his way home, 1924	171
Plate 16: Akwamuhene Asafo Boakye on his way home, 1924	172
Plate 17: Frederick Prempeh on his way home, 1924	173
Plate 18: Agyeman Prempeh being installed as 'Kumasihene', 1926	174

FIGURES

Figure 1: Textual Correlations, *HAK* exemplar and present edition	71
Figure 2: Relationships of the Pre-Asante Rulers	130
Figure 3: Pedigree of the 18th and 19th Century Asantehenes and Asantehemaas	132

Preface

The members of the editorial committee wish to express their gratitude to the late Asantehene, Otumfuo Opoku Ware II, and to his successor, Otumfuo Osei Tutu II. The former gave, and the latter continues to give, inestimable support for the publication of the writings of Asantehene, Otumfuo Nana Agyeman Prempeh.

Kwaku Dua Asamu was born in 1872, and was enstooled as Asantehene Nana Kwaku Dua III in 1888. He was, however, to become better known as Nana Agyeman Prempeh. He was taken prisoner and exiled by the British in 1896, returned from exile in 1924, and was made "Kumasihene" in 1926. He died in 1931. Our primary concern in this work is to make available texts written by, or at the dictation of, Nana Agyeman Prempeh, for the most part during his exile. A secondary concern is to provide sufficient editorial assistance to make the texts accessible to the non-Akan specialist. This has been done particularly through the medium of the Concordance (Part IV), which functions both to index Agyeman Prempeh's writings, and to identify, so far as is possible, persons and places mentioned in them. Care has been taken, however, not to anticipate the use scholars may make of these texts and thereby to preempt their interpretations. This volume is not, in other words, intended to be exegetical in character.

The history of the texts, and the editorial procedures employed to aid the reader, are discussed at length in Chapter Four. While some have been reordered in accordance with what can be deduced about their genesis and subsequent history, no corrections or emendations have been made to the writing itself. The reader may consult, at the British Academy Website www.britac.ac.uk/pubs/src/fha/ashanti, digitalised photographic copies of original texts with which we have worked; namely, "The History of Ashanti Kings and the Whole Country Itself," "King Otti Akenten", and "King Obi Yaeboa."

The matter of the transliteration of Twi names and terms remains a subject of debate. For the most part we have followed the Ghanaian practice of publishing English language material, including newspapers, in standard English orthography. This matter is fully discussed at the beginning of Part IV. The reader will note in particular that we have rendered the Twi "*Pɛrɛmpɛ*" as "Prempeh." This is the form that the Asantehene chose, signing himself "Agyeman Prempeh," or "Edward Prempeh,"and it is, moreover, the form that is used today by those descended from him. Although several of us in the past have used "Prempe" as a compromise, in this study we have decided to follow his own practice.

It is hoped that a reconstituted editorial board will, in time, be similarly enabled to make available to a wider public the lengthy compilation of Asante historical material put together in the 1940s by a committee working under the chairmanship of Asantehene, Otumfuo Sir Osei Agyeman Prempeh II. A difference between the work of Agyeman Prempeh and his successor may be noted here. The former drew upon the knowledge of nineteenth century informants whose lives had been lived in an independent Asante; the latter enjoyed no such privilege.

A. Adu Boahen
Emmanuel Akyeampong
Nancy Lawler
T. C. McCaskie
Ivor Wilks

PART I
ESSAYS

CHAPTER ONE

Agyeman Prempeh Before the Exile

T. C. McCaskie

INTRODUCTION

This chapter deals with the period between Agyeman Prempeh's birth in 1872 and his exile from Asante in 1896. It recounts his childhood, adolescence and young manhood. Two themes are interwoven with this biography. One is the context of kinship and family, a matter that the Asante held to be central to the shaping of every individual, but especially so when the person concerned was, like Agyeman Prempeh, a member of the ruling dynasty. The other is the immensely complex politics of the last decades of the nineteenth century, a period of unprecedented change for Asante during which polity and people moved from independence through civil war to incorporation into the British Empire. That said, the account given here advances no claims to comprehensiveness as a history of Asante in the later nineteenth century. Rather and simply, it is a profile of Agyeman Prempeh who lived through the events of these years, latterly at the very heart of them. This then is a life and times, and as far as possible in that order.[1]

KINSHIP, ROYALTY AND THE BIRTH OF AGYEMAN PREMPEH

Agyeman Prempeh was the fourth born of eight children produced by the marriage between the Kumase royal Oyoko woman Yaa Kyaa and the

---

[1] Asante history is richly documented and extensively analysed, and especially so for the years covered in this chapter. Accordingly, I have adopted two conventions to reduce the number of footnotes to manageable proportions. First, sources and context for much of the argument made here can be found in one or the other of five books: T.J. Lewin, *Asante before the British: the Prempean years 1875–1900* (Lawrence KS, 1978); T.C. McCaskie, *State and Society in Precolonial Asante* (Cambridge, 1995) and *Asante Identities: History and Modernity in an African Village 1850–1950* (Edinburgh and Bloomington IN, 2000); W. Tordoff, *Ashanti under the Prempehs 1888–1935* (Oxford, 1965); and I. Wilks, *Asante in the Nineteenth Century: the structure and evolution of a political order* (Cambridge, 1975: reprinted with a new *Preamble*, 1989). Second, footnotes are provided for direct quotation and where the argument relies on primary material not previously cited or on supplementary published work of particular relevance.

Ayebiakyerehene Kwasi Gyambibi, one of the many sons of the Asantehene Kwaku Dua (1834–67). Agyeman Prempeh was born some five years after the death of Kwaku Dua, but in a fundamental sense he owed his existence to his paternal grandfather. In brief, the marriage between Yaa Kyaa and Kwasi Gyambibi was authorised by the Asantehene Kwaku Dua as a part of his overall dynastic strategy. Thus Agyeman Prempeh was quite literally the outcome of his paternal grandfather's design. This matter requires contextual explanation, for the circumstances of his birth were the key determination in shaping the course of Agyeman Prempeh's life.[2]

In Asante matrilineality was fundamental; it assigned kinship belonging and defined royal status through female lines of descent. Patrilineality by comparison was secondary, but this is not to say that it was negligible; it transmitted intangible characteristics of personhood through male lines of descent. This patrilineal bequest was memorialised—and the virtues passed down by it were reinforced—through the recurring use of names in alternate generations. In historically important male descent lines, "great names" (*aboadenfɔ*) and bynames (*nkwadaadin*) of the mighty dead were conferred upon children in an attempt to conduce a "reincarnation" (*kra pa*). Efforts to combine and so maximise the advantages inhering in particular lines of female and male descent were articulated most saliently in marriage strategies. The rules at work in marriage were qualified by a principle and an understanding.

The principle was that Asante kinship organisation was structurally exogamous; marriages might be contracted only between persons of different matrilineages. The understanding was that Asante people held the view that there were optimum conditions for realising the inherited benefits of descent through marriage; repetitive marital alliances between close descendant generations, as and when these did not contravene kinship prohibitions, were the best means of strengthening the desirable legacies of both female and male lines of descent. Thus, the most valued alliance was exogamous cross-cousin marriage. This was supremely the case within the ruling dynasty of Asante in Kumase. Necessarily, an Asantehene had to belong to the royal Oyoko lineage segment that was matrilineally descended from the ancestress Manu in the seventeenth century. Ideally, he should also be a patrilineal grandson of a previous Asantehene. In practice, and bearing in mind all of the considerations just described, such a person was born to an exogamous cross-cousin marriage between a female Oyoko royal (like Yaa Kyaa) and a son of an Asantehene (like Kwasi Gyambibi).

However, there was an obdurate problem in this arrangement. Kumase royal matriliny was vested in a unitary and highly compact descent structure,

---

[2] See T.C. McCaskie, "*Konnurokusɛm*: kinship and family in the history of the *Oyoko Kɔkɔɔ* dynasty of Kumase*," in *Journal of African History*, 36, 3 (1995), 357–89.

but dynastic patriliny was dispersed across competing "houses" that traced their individual lines of descent from different Asantehenes. In fact, Asante kingship in the eighteenth and early nineteenth centuries was dominated by the claims of two such patrilineal "houses" in a pattern of (agreed but often unstable) alternation. These were descended in the male line from the first Asantehene Osei Tutu (d. 1717) or his successor the second Asantehene Opoku Ware I (c. 1720–50). Challenges to this arrangement were viewed as being temporary or aberrant deviations from a sedimented norm that was symbolised in the naming of the Golden Stool for its first two holders—*Osei ne Opoku sika dwa*.

This was the normative situation when the long lived and ruthlessly ambitious Kwaku Dua—who became the ninth Asantehene in 1834 in unusual circumstances—decided to engineer the insertion of his own male descendants into the affairs of the dynasty as a third "house." He pursued this goal by directed use of political power and partisan management of the strategy of exogamous cross-cousin marriage. He began by eliminating the senior males of the "houses" of Osei Tutu and Opoku Ware I. This was accomplished by the late 1850s, whereupon he proceeded to marry off all available senior royal women of childbearing age to his own sons. He hoped to achieve three related objectives. First, he planned to secure numbers of patrilineal grandsons, any one of whom might be eligible to succeed to the Golden Stool. Second, he intended that the number of such grandsons would be sufficient to insure against early deaths by leaving enough survivors to embed his "house" at the centre of the dynasty. Third, he tried to create a genealogical monopoly over the future by making royal wives unavailable to males from any "house" other than his own.

These were the arrangements that led to the birth of Agyeman Prempeh. His mother Yaa Kyaa was the elder of two daughters of the reigning Asantehemaa Afua Kobi. Kwaku Dua first gave her in marriage to his son the Somihene Kwasi Abayie. Of the five children born to this marriage, two were sons: Agyeman Kofi (born c. 1860) and Kwabena Kyeretwie (born c. 1863). Then in 1867 Kwasi Abayie died and his young widow was immediately remarried to his paternal brother Kwasi Gyambibi. Of the eight children born to this marriage, two were again sons: Agyeman Prempeh (born 1872) and Agyeman Badu (born 1874). In addition, Yaa Kyaa's younger sister Akua Afriyie was also married to two sons of Kwaku Dua in succession. Of her ten children who survived infancy, three were patrilineal grandsons of Kwaku Dua: Kwasi Berko was born in the 1860s while his younger half-brothers Kwaku Dua and Fredua Agyeman were born around 1880.

It is evident that Kwaku Dua's dynastic strategy succeeded structurally, in that the senior Oyoko women of childbearing age produced for him a total of seven patrilineal grandsons who were also royals of the Golden Stool. But it foundered temporally, in that establishing the political conditions that made it possible was prolonged to the point where its implementation occurred too late in Kwaku Dua's reign. Thus when Kwaku Dua himself died in 1867 the eldest of his patrilineal grandsons eligible to succeed him as Asantehene was a child of about seven. In the event, and in a widespread reaction against Kwaku Dua's authoritarianism and policies, the claims of his eldest grandson Agyeman Kofi were easily set aside on the grounds of age. The new Asantehene was Kofi Kakari (1867–74), one of three sons of the Asantehemaa Afua Kobi and so brother to Yaa Kyaa. The prevailing view among Kwaku Dua's sons and their supporters—albeit one not shared by Kofi Kakari—was that the new Asantehene was a "caretaker" pending the maturation of his predecessor's royal grandsons. This line of argument reasoned that Kofi Kakari's father the counselor Kofi Nti was a commoner of no patrilineal distinction, and so was unqualified to fill the role of founder of a "house" within the royal dynasty. Among those who acquiesced in the election of Kofi Kakari, no doubt many looked beyond his tenure in office to the future emergence, once Kwaku Dua's stranglehold over the marriages of royal women weakened with the passage of time, of a suitable candidate for the Golden Stool from the established "houses" of Osei Tutu or Opoku Ware.

AGYEMAN PREMPEH'S CHILDHOOD

Agyeman Prempeh's childhood was mediated and conditioned by the matters just described. He was junior to Agyeman Kofi in his grandfather's dynastic design, but the instrumental intent of that policy gave decisive shape to his identity. The crucial matter of naming, to which reference has already been made, is illustrative. Situating (but anglicizing) his own place in the royal genealogies, Agyeman Prempeh recorded that Yaa Kyaa gave birth to "a boy named Kwakudua Asamu whose surname is Prempeh. This surname Prempeh was a nickname given to him by the Chief Justice called Kodjoe Fofie." Elsewhere he offered additional comment. "My birthday name is Kwesi as I was born by my mother on the Sabbath Day." However, he continued,

> Ashanti people set store in using of names or Big Names as they are known by us. From starting in life I was called Kweku Duah in fond memory of the King of that name who is my ancestor. It is thought a respectful thing to those who went before. The old people said I was growing like him in every way and so they called me with his name.[3]

That is, the child Agyeman Prempeh's close kin addressed him by the "great name" of Kwaku Dua. This was done as a mark of commemorative respect for

---

[3] Old Manhyia Palace, Kumase, Correspondence of the Asantehene Agyeman Prempeh, No. 17, 12/28, E. Prempeh to DC (Kumase), dd. Kumase, 23 June 1928.

the patrilineal line to which both belonged and to encourage the reincarnated manifestation of the grandfather in the grandson. Although direct evidence is lacking, it is logical to assume that others of Kwaku Dua's patrilineal grandsons were called by his name and for the same reasons. In a like manner, Asamu was a byname conferred upon the Asantehene Kwaku Dua (or perhaps inherited by him from his own patrilineal forebears). The name denoted "the born warrior" (*sa*, "war": *mu*, impl. "a capacity for doing something") and it was assigned to Agyeman Prempeh to direct his development by encouraging aspiration.

How then did Kwasi called Kwaku Dua Asamu become Agyeman Prempeh? As noted, he claimed that the byname ("surname") Prempeh was given to him by the Kumase Akyeamehene Kwadwo Fofie Baakompra, head of the royal counselors. A sobriquet of this sort was familiar, used to identify someone by his or her appearance or behaviour. The name Prempeh connoted a plumpness and smooth lightness of skin admirable in Asante eyes. Hence Agyeman Prempeh's peers recalled his "great beauty" as a youth.[4] But such appellations were never unequivocal in that they embraced a range of possible derivations, associations and readings. Some traditions argue that the name Prempeh referenced the word *pem(ɛ)*, a term that denoted bulk or substance but in the sense of a stateliness lightly and confidently borne. Many accounts suggest that the byname was meant to call up thoughts of the *prempe* drum, introduced by the first Asantehene Osei Tutu. This would make Prempeh cognate with Asamu in its allusion to war, for the drum played "I desire it much" to signal an intention to fight and conquer. More resonantly, the *prempe* drum was said to be "fat" (round in shape) and "light" (high in pitch), making it analogous to those physiological attributes possessed by Agyeman Prempeh.

In tradition these readings are commingled with a historically situated explanation in the layered manner characteristic of royal naming practices. It is said that just before Agyeman Prempeh was born the Asantehene Kofi Kakari arbitrated a dispute between the chiefs of Kokofu and Dadease over subjects at Asiwaa. He asked them via Kwadwo Fofie Baakompra to reconcile on the grounds that they were brother members of the Oyoko clan. The Kokofuhene refused. Kofi Kakari then confiscated the disputed subjects and awarded them to Dadease. As a "thank offering" (*aseda*) the Dadeasehene returned two of these subjects to the Asantehene. One was a boy nicknamed Prempeh in commemoration of the honorific bestowed upon the Dadeasehene in the Gyaman war of 1818–19 for "pushing forward" against the enemy in response to the signal from the *prempe* drum. Kofi Kakari was greatly taken with the name Prempeh because he saw it as a punning admonition to remind the Kokofuhene

---

[4] *Ibid.*, "Otumfuo. The Potential of Ashanti Nation (with Notes on Royalty) by Bema Owusu Ansah," 1937.

of his temerity in "pushing forward" against royal advice to settle with Dadease. Thus, it is said that when Yaa Kyaa's third son was born immediately after these events Kwadwo Fofie Baakompra and others nicknamed the boy Prempeh, the name then on everyone's lips.[5] We may conclude by noting that the praise name Agyeman is uncomplicated in meaning and reference. It denoted "a defender of the nation" and was a title accorded to Kwaku Dua and then assigned to or assumed by his grandson Agyeman Prempeh.

Little is known in detail of the childhood of Agyeman Prempeh. But it is known that it was a time in which he cemented lifelong affective ties with some of his closest kin. By far the most significant figure then and throughout his life—a congruence here between personal feelings and the normative expectations of Asante society—was his formidable mother Yaa Kyaa. The bond between the two of them that was forged in Agyeman Prempeh's childhood was severed only by Yaa Kyaa's death in exile in the Seychelles in 1917, and even then she lived on in attentive filial remembrance. This was the most enduringly important relationship of Agyeman Prempeh's life. In childhood he also became close to his maternal aunt Akua Afriyie, and among his mother's other twelve children he developed intimate ties with his younger full siblings Agyeman Badu (next born after himself) and Ama Adusa (last born), as well as an easygoing friendship with his uterine elder brother Kwabena Kyeretwie. These relationships were defined by reciprocal amity—"If you are loved by someone, then in turn you love that person" as the Asante proverb has it. As was the Asante norm in pre-adolescent childhood (*mbofraase*), interaction between the son Agyeman Prempeh and his father Kwasi Gyambibi was relatively formal, a distancing underscored by the boy's royal status. None the less, the two were evidently on good terms and it is said that the child accorded "all due honour and respect" to his non-royal parent.[6]

Tradition recounts that as Agyeman Prempeh grew he became a member of a loose circle of male friends. This was a *kuo*, a fellowship of boys, youths and younger men united together in interdependent sociability. A group of this sort was structurally indeterminate, but recruits to its ranks often forged relationships with fellow members that continued throughout life. In boyhood Agyeman Prempeh associated with a *kuo* in the Bogyawe quarter of Kumase, close by the palace, that was dominated by young royal servants (mainly hammock bearers) from the village of Suame. A leading light in the affairs of this group was Yaw Daani of Suame, a patrilineal great-grandson of the Asantehene Osei Kwame (1777–1803). Yaw Daani's junior brother Kwaku Firi

---

[5] Manhyia Record Office, Kumase, K.22, "Enquiry into the Constitutional Position of Dadease", Testimony of Dadease Akyeamehene Kofi Ba Ankoma (on behalf of Dadeasehene Kofi Adaakwa and Stool Elders), dd. Kumase, 8 January 1939.
[6] Old Manhyia Palace, Kumase, "Otumfuo. The Potential of Ashanti Nation (with Notes on Royalty) by Bema Owusu Ansah", 1937.

was "nanny" (ɔbagyegyeni) to Yaa Kyaa's children, and most probably this was the connection that first brought Agyeman Prempeh into the orbit of the Suame group. At this time, around 1880, Yaw Daani was a man approaching thirty who was well known for his forceful and bold personality. For whatever reason, self-interested or otherwise, he decided to take Agyeman Prempeh under his wing. As the association deepened, the boy came to regard the man as a mentor and confidant. In due course, Yaw Daani was to marry the royal Akosua Nsia (a daughter of Agyeman Prempeh's aunt Akua Afriyie), and become head of the royal hammock bearers after playing a part in a revealing passage in Agyeman Prempeh's adult life.[7]

AGYEMAN PREMPEH, YAA KYAA, AND CIVIL WAR

Agyeman Prempeh grew up in tumultuous times. As an infant he was carried off to safety when the Asante royal family decamped to Breman and Kwapra to avoid capture during the first but very brief British occupation of Kumase in 1874. This was a portent of the future, for Agyeman Prempeh's young life coincided with an ever rising tide of British meddling in Asante affairs. But more immediately in the early 1880s Asante suffered internal "confusions" (mmasammasa) that spiralled out of control into civil war and unstable rule by a succession of juntas. This is the most complicated and best-documented period in nineteenth-century Asante history. As far as is possible comment here is restricted to the parts played in it by Agyeman Prempeh and—crucially—his mother Yaa Kyaa.

The Asantehene Kofi Kakari was removed from office and sent into internal exile in 1874 as a result of the British invasion and because of maladministration in his handling of fiscal affairs. He was replaced by his younger full brother the Asantehene Mensa Bonsu (1874–83). There is a suggestion of preemption in this changeover, with opponents of the "house" of Kwaku Dua allying with critics of the discredited Kofi Kakari to forestall any groundswell of opinion in favour of the fourteen year old Agyeman Kofi. Be that as it may, it is recalled that Mensa Bonsu's accession was made conditional on his recognition of Kwaku Dua's eldest grandson as heir-apparent. The new Asantehene inherited a depleted polity. Military and fiscal problems encouraged secession among resentful tributaries and disaffected provincials. Mensa Bonsu was an able man, but his autocratic behaviour exacerbated these difficulties. He

---

[7] I.K. Agyeman Papers, Kumase, "Notes on the History of the Ashanti Kings by the Secretary of the Asanteman Council: Being a Record of Talks held by Otumfuo the Asantehene Osei Agyeman Prempeh II with the Queen Mother and Council Members", dd. Kumase, February–March 1942. It should be noted that *HAK* records that Yaw Daani's marriage was to Akosua Nsia's younger sister Akosua Manhyia.

alienated office holders and commoners alike. In 1883, with provincial revolt threatening Kumase, he was removed from office and sent into internal exile like his brother before him.

Policy failures brought about the destoolments of Kofi Kakari and Mensa Bonsu, but it is significant in light of the reputation of both as dynastic "caretakers" that their inability to control events was widely attributed to intrinsic personal defects. Kofi Kakari was said to be congenitally spendthrift and motivated by his insecure need to buy popularity; Mensa Bonsu was held to be incurably acquisitive and driven on by his appetites for gold and women. In short, the brothers were suspect by nature because of their unexalted patrilineal ancestry. No doubt members and supporters of the "house" of Kwaku Dua encouraged this view. It was also said that the Asantehemaa Afua Kobi's faulty upbringing of her sons had encouraged their weaknesses. In consequence she too was forced to abdicate. Her replacement in office was her elder daughter Yaa Kyaa, mother of four of Kwaku Dua's grandsons. Whether or not Yaa Kyaa conspired to supplant her mother she was now Asantehemaa, constitutionally the most important figure during an interregnum and charged with mobilising the election of a new ruler.

It was non-office holding Kumase "youngmen" (*nkwankwaa*) and commoners who initiated the forced removal of Mensa Bonsu.[8] Such people had suffered exaction and worse at the hands of the deposed ruler and his office holders. Radicals among them now contemplated abolition of the office of Asantehene. This was a minority view and its defeat was ensured by a compact that Yaa Kyaa struck with *nkwankwaa* leaders headed by Yaw Daani, Agyeman Prempeh's *kuo* associate. Yaa Kyaa offered wealth and office and in return Yaw Daani mobilised popular support to encourage or pressure office holders to enstool one of her sons as Asantehene.[9] In truth, the majority in Kumase needed little persuasion. Yaa Kyaa's sons quite literally incarnated continuity with the reign of Kwaku Dua. That era of confident power lay in a past unsullied by the parlous reigns of Kofi Kakari and his brother, but it was within the grasp of memory and might be restored by one of Kwaku Dua's grandsons. Yaa Kyaa now concluded an agreement (*nhyehye*) in fulfilment of Kwaku Dua's wish that his eldest grandson Agyeman Kofi—now about twenty-three—should become Asantehene and restore Kumase authority and Asante unity.

These goals proved hard to realise. Rebellious disaffection within Asante was compounded when the deposed Kofi Kakari challenged for the Golden

---

[8] For the *nkwankwaa* leaders who overthrew Mensa Bonsu see Old Manhyia Palace, Kumase, "Record of the Evidence Submitted about the Abolition of Nkwankwaahene in Asante", dd. Kumase, 1–5 and 20–3 December 1935: Testimonies of Domakwaehene and Akyeamehene Kwasi Apea Nuama (4 December), Tafohene Yaw Dabanka (4 December), Gyaasehene Saaman Akyampon (21 December) and Boakye Nimaako of Saawua and Kumase (22 December).
[9] *Idem.*

Stool. There followed the "war of promises" (*bohyeε adε sa*) between partisans of Kofi Kakari and Agyeman Kofi. Yaa Kyaa prevailed due to her own steely determination and the ruthlessness of her supporters. Kofi Kakari was captured. Then on 28 April 1884 Agyeman Kofi became Asantehene and assumed the stool name Kwaku Dua Kumaa ("the younger"). But in early June he suddenly died. Smallpox was the probable cause but rumours circulated that he had been poisoned by one of Kofi Kakari's concubines.[10] Whatever occasioned Kwaku Dua Kumaa's death it sealed Kofi Kakari's fate. On 24 June he was done away with by Yaa Kyaa's agents.[11]

The Asantehemaa now strove to weld together a constituency to support the claims to the Golden Stool of one of her surviving sons. Her goal, she later recalled, was "to have a King on the throne in order to obtain peace and have an end of the rebellion."[12] It is clear that her preferred candidate was Agyeman Prempeh, but he was only twelve years old. So her nominee to succeed Kwaku Dua Kumaa was her second son Kwabena Kyeretwie, an amiable man fond of carousing but lacking gravity or support. He was rejected, as Yaa Kyaa surely knew he would be. But she had now run out of stalking horses and resorted instead to the tactic of showing Kumase that there was no alternative to Agyeman Prempeh. To drive home her point she mooted the candidacy of her cousin Kwasi Kyisi, son of the second marriage of her mother Afua Kobi's third youngest (of five) sisters. He was an obscure, middle-aged man known only for a misplaced vanity about his remote descent from the long dead "caretaker" Asantehene Kusi Obodom (d. 1764). But the matter of Kwasi Kyisi resolved itself when he died in August 1884. The Asantehemaa now openly revealed her hand. Taking Agyeman Prempeh with her, she went in public procession to ask the oracular shrine of *taa kwadwo* at Asokwa to name the next Asantehene. The reply, or so she claimed, was "the handsome one" (*ɔhofεfo*), a nickname for Agyeman Prempeh. The boy was smeared in white clay (*hyire*) as a token of victory, and with his mother by his side, he was formally presented to the assembled Kumase office holders. But doubts persisted about his age and the succession crisis dragged on in debate and indecision.[13]

By late 1884 the failure to provide leadership had deepened unrest and turmoil in provincial Asante. This was particularly the case in areas that had

---

[10] The woman alleged to have poisoned Kwaku Dua Kumaa was Akosua Antwiwaa Ababio, and the motive was revenge. She was a sister of the Akuroponhene Safo Anwoma, a major supporter of Kofi Kakari who was killed by Kumase forces in August 1883.
[11] Authoritative tradition recounts that he was strangled with his own chewing stick by the *nkwankwaa* leader Asamoa Kyekye acting on Yaa Kyaa's instructions.
[12] National Archives of the Seychelles, Victoria, Mahé, "Political Exiles: Ashanti", C/SS/2, vol. II, Elizabeth Ya Echiah and others to Governor, dd. Ashanti Camp, Le Rocher, 16 October 1913.
[13] Ashanti Social Survey Papers, Centre of West African Studies, University of Birmingham, "A Report on The Tano Fetish at Asukwa with a History of Its Doings by J.C. Frimpong", dd. Kumase, 1945.

supported Kofi Kakari or wanted to throw off central government authority. Generalised revolt in Manso Nkwanta and Atwoma threatened to cut off Kumase's food supplies. Yaa Kyaa's attempt to impose a military solution went awry at the battle of Ofuase when her forces suffered a catastrophic defeat and rebels killed key Kumase office holders. Central government was crippled and the Asantehemaa now lacked resources to retrieve the situation. Kumase was an open city and the Saamanhene Akyampon Panin of Saawua, an extremely wealthy provincial warlord and erstwhile supporter of Kofi Kakari, occupied it. He marginalised Yaa Kyaa, usurped control of the government, and earned the nickname "boulder" (*bokokuroko*) because he sat on and "squashed" (*moamoa*) Kumase under his weight.[14] Throughout 1885 intense politicking took place between Yaa Kyaa, Akyampon Panin and other provincial power brokers. The objective was to restore legitimacy to central government. The sticking point remained the question of the succession. Who would be Asantehene? Who could occupy the Golden Stool with an authority sufficient to reimpose order, achieve reconciliation and rebuild Asante? Most pointedly, who would select, appoint and have influence over the new ruler?

Akyampon Panin needed someone who could challenge Yaa Kyaa's son Agyeman Prempeh for the Golden Stool. In 1886 he and his associates threw their support behind Yaw Twereboanna, another of Kwaku Dua's patrilineal grandsons but one with a contentious past. This centred on his mother Yaa Afere, younger sister of the Asantehemaa Afua Kobi and aunt to Yaa Kyaa. In the late 1850s she was convicted of adultery and divorced from her husband. In line with his dynastic strategy Kwaku Dua remarried her immediately to his son Asabi Boakye by whom she had five children. The first of these was Yaw Twereboanna, born about 1860. When he was still a small child his mother was arraigned before Kwaku Dua on a charge of publicly abusing her sister Afua Kobi. The Asantehene reminded Yaa Afere that she had already appeared before him on an adultery charge, admonished her for being troublesome (*wo ha adwene dodo*), and ordered her to reconcile with the Asantehemaa. Yaa Afere angrily refused and went on to upbraid Kwaku Dua. This was contempt of the Golden Stool (*animtiaabu*), a capital offence. Kwaku Dua was incensed. He swore before his office holders that Yaa Afere was a disgrace (*w'anim aguase*) and imposed a punishment that in Asante thinking exceeded even the death penalty. Yaa Afere, her children and her uterine descendants were excluded (*yi fi mu*) from the royal line. In confirmation of this Yaw Twereboanna was allegedly scarred on the neck as a sign of his disqualification, and he was sent with his mother into exile at Womaase in Atwoma. There they

---

[14] A detailed account of Akyampon Panin's life is in Manhyia Record Office, Kumase, GSA/5, "Gyasi Clan Affairs: Correspondence concerning the Abdication of Samanghene Ofori Kain II (18 July 1951)."

stayed until they were recalled to Kumase by the *Asantehene* Kofi Kakari. He formally rescinded Kwaku Dua's exclusion order. But this measure proved controversial. The marks said to be on Yaw Twereboanna's neck could not be removed, and so debate continued to surround the legitimacy of his and his mother's "rehabilitation" (*siesie*). This was still the case when Yaa Afere died in 1882.[15]

The contest between Agyeman Prempeh and Yaw Twereboanna began with a propaganda war as both sides fought to gain support. Yaa Kyaa encouraged doubts about Yaw Twereboanna's legitimacy as a candidate, and put it about that his campaign was paid for by state funds stolen by Akyampon Panin. The Saamanhene countered that Agyeman Prempeh was still a child under the sway of his mother, and charged Yaa Kyaa with a ruthless lack of compassion (*mmoborohunu*) that had led her to murder her own brother Kofi Kakari. By early 1887 Asante was polarised. A meeting was convened at Bekwai to discuss the stalemate. It ended in deadlock, but immediately after it Akyampon Panin and his senior associates were arrested by the Edwesohene Kwasi Afrane acting on Yaa Kyaa's orders. The prisoners were tried and executed and orders were issued for the arrest and detention of Yaw Twereboanna in Kumase. The way now seemed clear for Agyeman Prempeh to become Asantehene. But Yaa Kyaa had gained the upper hand through exercising that violent ruthlessness attributed to her by her opponents. This alienated a number of the greater divisional rulers (*amanhene*) of Asante, and Kokofu took the lead in mustering Mampon, Nsuta and Agona to Yaw Twereboanna's cause. In May 1887 Kokofu troops defeated Agyeman Prempeh's forces and threatened Kumase. But Yaa Kyaa still held Yaw Twereboanna captive. She rallied her supporters and an uneasy truce was arranged between the exhausted antagonists.

At the close of 1887 the conflict entered a critical phase when Yaw Twereboanna escaped from Kumase to Kokofu. This impelled Yaa Kyaa to decisive action. On 5 March 1888 she presided over a meeting in Kumase convened to proceed with the immediate election of an Asantehene. Yaw Twereboanna's supporters absented themselves, but those present formally confirmed Agyeman Prempeh as heir-apparent and announced that he would be enstooled as Asantehene on 26 March. The Kokofuhene sent to ask for a postponement pending the negotiation of an amnesty, but Yaa Kyaa rejected this delaying tactic. Accordingly, in the night of *monodwo* (Monday) 26 March 1888 Agyeman Prempeh was made Asantehene, albeit with certain of the Golden Stool rites unperformed because of the absence of so many non-Kumase office holders. With her son enstooled, Yaa Kyaa now made

---

[15] Old Manhyia Palace, Kumase, "Emblems of Rank of the Asantehene", prepared by A.A.Y. Kyerematen, n.d. (but in the 1950s), Notes of conversations with Fredua Agyeman. This informant was the penultimate child born to Yaa Kyaa's sister Akua Afriyie. He died in the 1970s.

conciliatory overtures to her opponents. Unsurprisingly, these were rebuffed and Yaw Twereboanna's supporters resumed military action. In June, Kumase forces under the Edwesohene Kwasi Afrane won a crushing victory in south Asante; Yaw Twereboanna, the Kokofuhene and thousands of their followers fled south over the Pra river to seek refuge in the British Gold Coast Colony. By the end of 1888 north Asante had also been cleared of Agyeman Prempeh's opponents and the civil war was over. It was formally concluded on 27 January 1890 when surviving office holders from both sides assembled in Kumase to swear oaths of allegiance before the Asantehene Agyeman Prempeh.

Whatever the national issues of governmentality, authority and power involved, the civil war unfolded as a conflict between Kumase dynasts. Violence deepened existing cleavages among the royal Oyoko and left an unforgiving legacy. After victory, Yaa Kyaa insisted that Agyeman Prempeh formally reimpose the exclusion of Yaw Twereboanna and his kin from the royal line. But now the ban was extended to make sexual intercourse with any of Yaa Twereboanna's five uterine sisters a capital offence. These women were divorced from their husbands and kept in seclusion. Then in 1891 Agyeman Prempeh's old *kuo* associate Yaw Daani accused Kwasi Agyei, the head of the royal hammock carriers, of conducting a sexual liaison with Yaw Twereboanna's sister Akosua Berenya. At trial guilt was proved and both accused suffered the death penalty. In royal tradition this episode is termed "silence" (*kommyɛ*), for Agyeman Prempeh was so troubled by the circumstances of the case that he forbade discussion of it. The reason was that he inclined to clemency, but Yaa Kyaa demanded the full penalty of the law and insisted he impose it. By report, this matter led to heated exchanges between the two of them before Yaa Kyaa got her way. This was a revealing passage in Agyeman Prempeh's emergence into adult life. As Asantehene his say was final, but the history of his relationship with his mother led him to listen to and give in to her. This affirmed that Yaa Kyaa's guiding influence over the boy would continue with the man, and goes some way towards explaining Agyeman Prempeh's palpable sense of disoriented loss when she died. It is said that after the events of 1891 Agyeman Prempeh never again executed anyone. Whatever considerations of policy led to this decision, it is symbolic of the tensions and ambiguities that eddied beneath the surface of the interdependent relationship between mother and son.[16]

---

[16] Basel Mission Archives, Basel, D-20.4,5, N.V. Asare, "Asante Abasɛm (Twi Kasamu)", 1915 and National Archives of Ghana, Kumase, ARG 1/2/25/9, "Candidates for the Kumase Stool", Kwame Tua to Chief Commissioner (Ashanti), dd. Kumase, 30 May 1931.

AGYEMAN PREMPEH, ASANTE, AND THE BRITISH

The Asantehene Agyeman Prempeh inherited a disunited polity and weakened government. Within Asante itself the authority of Kumase was much eroded. In the closing stage of the civil war Agyeman Prempeh and Yaa Kyaa were constrained to offer concessions—subjects, lands, titles and regalia—to secure the support of the Edwesohene Kwasi Afrane and others. The people and villages given up to ensure victory were removed from Kumase office holders and awarded to non-Kumase generals.[17] Furthermore, large numbers of Asante were living as unreconciled refugees in the Gold Coast Colony. Beyond Asante too the debilitation and then implosion of central government led to an ever-escalating defection of tributaries and allies alike from the 1870s onwards. The history of the ways in which the government of the Asantehene Agyeman Prempeh sought to remedy these problems is well known.[18] But Kumase initiatives throughout were shadowed, subverted and in the end terminated by the British. This was the predominant theme of Agyeman Prempeh's reign. It also shaped the course of the rest of his life.

Agyeman Prempeh's extensive correspondence shows that his attitude towards the British was moulded by history and family. After all, the British had been a fact of Asante reality since the eighteenth century, and so Kumase had long established protocols and precedents upon which to draw in dealing with them. These may be summarised as follows. During the nineteenth century the British became the dominant and then the only European power on the Gold Coast. The Kumase government treated the British as a sovereign foreign power in terms of diplomacy and trade and expected reciprocal consideration. That a series of wars (1807–74) had cast Asante and the British as enemies was regarded by the former as the fault of the Fante and other southern peoples. These defied Kumase by interrupting Asante commerce with the Gold Coast and then involving the British in protecting them from retribution. The view from Kumase—and as with all governments it is vital to emphasise the power of perception—was that the norm in relations with the British was, in a common Asante usage, "peace and open roads." Even those who argued for a military resolution in the Gold Coast wanted to discipline its recalcitrant inhabitants so as to restore harmonies of interaction and commerce with the British. Agyeman Prempeh subscribed to these normative views and for him they were reinforced by family history. The Asantehene Kwaku Dua was renowned for his policy of maintaining peaceful and productive relations with the British, and Agyeman Prempeh often cited his grandfather's example as a

---

[17] T.C. McCaskie, "*Ahyiamu*—"A place of meeting": an essay on process and event in the history of the Asante state", in *Journal of African History*, 25, 2 (1984), 169–88.
[18] The fullest narrative account is in Wilks (1975).

guide to his own conduct. However, the problem with continuity in perception was that it was ill equipped to take account of and keep up with rapid change in the thing perceived. To put it simply, British attitudes towards Asante shifted in the last decades of the nineteenth century. This transformation needs no explanation here, for it was a part of the global growth of European territorial empires.[19]

The gap that was opening up between Asante perception and British attitudes was apparent during the civil war. On several occasions Yaa Kyaa and her councillors requested British mediation to help end the fighting and install an Asantehene. But the observations of British emissaries, from Barrow in 1883 to Barnett in 1888, showed a sharp rise in criticism of Asante and in interventionist rhetoric. Increasingly too in the 1880s the Gold Coast government meddled in Asante affairs by proxy, drawing its agents and informants from the ranks of highly politicised refugees who had fled from the reach of Kumase's authority. As Gold Coast officials looked at post-civil war Kumase, and beyond to its slackening grip on an interior now open to French or German predation, they began to hold the view that Asante was no longer a power to be reckoned with but rather a problem to be solved. In April 1891 the Gold Coast government invited the Asantehene Agyeman Prempeh and his councillors to "place their country under British protection" because it was in danger of "gradually falling into decay." Agyeman Prempeh repudiated the idea of a disintegrating Asante, and rejected the British offer of protection in the following measured terms.

> I am happy to say we have arrived at this conclusion, that my kingdom of Ashanti will never commit itself to any such policy; Ashanti must remain independent as of old, at the same time to be friendly with all white men. I do not write this with a boastful spirit, but in the clear sense of its meaning. Ashanti is an independent kingdom and is always friendly with the white men; for the sake of trade we are to bind to each other, so it is our Ashanti proverb, that what the old men eat and left, it is what the children enjoyed.[20]

This restatement of the established Asante perception of relations with the British would have been familiar to Agyeman Prempeh's grandfather Kwaku Dua and indeed to that ruler's predecessors in office. But by the 1890s it was null and void, for it made appeal to principles of sovereignty and equality

---

[19] T.C. McCaskie, "Cultural Encounters: Britain and Africa in the Nineteenth Century," in A. Porter ed., *The Oxford History of the British Empire, Volume III. The Nineteenth Century* (Oxford, 1999), 665–89.

[20] British Parliamentary Papers, *Further Correspondence relating to Affairs in Ashanti*, C.7917, 1896, Asantehene to Governor of the Gold Coast, dd. Kumase, 7 May 1891. See further W. Tordoff, "Brandford Griffith's Offer of British Protection to Ashanti (1891)", in *Transactions of the Historical Society of Ghana*, 6 (1962), 31–49.

once held in common but now unilaterally abandoned by the Gold Coast government.

The British persisted. In 1894, following Asante attempts to reassert control over Atebubu and Nkoransa in its northern hinterland, the Gold Coast government proposed that Kumase permit a British resident and the Asantehene and his senior advisers accept British stipends. On 11 June, at the formal meeting of the assembly of the nation (*Asantemanhyiamu*) summoned to discuss this proposal, Agyeman Prempeh was formally enstooled on the Golden Stool when the rites that could not be performed in 1888 were at last completed. Unsurprisingly, he took the stool name Kwaku Dua, becoming the third ruler to adopt it after his paternal grandfather and uterine brother Agyeman Kofi. This was a significant occasion. Asante once again had a ruler, a government and a national assembly. On 28 June a letter to the British reasserting Asante sovereignty enclosed a confident declaration about the nation's future. Agyeman Prempeh wrote that he planned to advance Asante

> to a prosperous, substantial, and steady position as a great farming and trading community such as it has never occupied hitherto, and that the trade between your Protectorate (of the Gold Coast) and my Kingdom of Ashanti may increase daily to the benefit of all interested in it.[21]

Agyeman Prempeh's plans for his country included a development programme. This was a logical step. First, Asante was rich in gold and other natural resources. Second, Asante people had first hand knowledge of infrastructural and other economic improvements in the Gold Coast Colony. Third, Agyeman Prempeh could call on the advice of two western educated Asante with coastal and European business connections. These were the brothers John and Albert Owusu Ansa, patrilineal grandsons of the Asantehene Osei Tutu Kwame (1804–23). Their father Owusu Ansa was handed over to the British to be educated in England by the terms of the Anglo-Asante treaty of 1831. He returned to Kumase in 1841 and thereafter pursued a varied career as catechist, teacher, diplomat and trader in both Asante and the Gold Coast. When he died in 1884 both of his sons were launched on civil service and business careers, and both then became involved in the affairs of Asante. It was John Owusu Ansa who raised with Agyeman Prempeh the idea of sending an Asante embassy to London to negotiate with the British government over the heads of Gold Coast Colony officials and to secure private investment capital to fund an Asante development programme. In June 1894 this proposal was approved by the *Asantemanhyiamu*, following which Agyeman Prempeh appointed the English speaking John Owusu Ansa "Ambassador Extraordinary and Minister

---

[21] *Ibid.*, C.7917, 1896, Asantehene to Governor of the Gold Coast, dd. Kumase, 28 June 1894.

Plenipotentiary" as head of a mission that comprised his brother Albert and six Asante officials headed by the Kyidomhene Kwame Boaten.

It is clear that Gold Coast Colony officials did everything in their power to obstruct and discredit the Asante mission to London. The embassy was held up on the coast for four months by a mix of threat, avoidance and prevarication until Governor Griffith reluctantly gave it permission to sail in April 1895. In the interim, British emissaries hurriedly dispatched to Kumase in January held tense meetings with the Asante government. Agyeman Prempeh—but not the British—recorded that the Gold Coast representatives once more raised the matter of protectorate status but this time in a directly threatening manner. In May the embassy reached London via Liverpool. Despite support from sympathetic MPs and newspapers, the British government refused to recognise its credentials or receive its members. Instead, the Colonial Office drafted an ultimatum demanding that Asante accept a British resident and pay outstanding indemnities imposed by the treaty that ended the Anglo-Asante war of 1873–74. On 10 October this was presented to the government in Kumase. But on 21 October in London the Asante embassy signed an agreement with the businessman George Reckless that empowered him to raise capital to form a chartered company to develop Asante.[22] This greatly alarmed both the British and Gold Coast administrations and armies of speculators who hoped to invest in and profit from Asante when (rather than if) it was annexed.

The British moved quickly to retake the initiative. They now agreed to receive the embassy's submissions, but opened communication only to convey barely veiled threats. On 16 November the ambassadors finally agreed to a British resident in Kumase under the impression that the alternative was war. They were right, for on 22 November Colonial Secretary Chamberlain drafted the first of a succession of plans to overthrow the Asante government. He proposed that Asante be broken up, and that the Asantehene Agyeman Prempeh be replaced by a puppet ruler in Kumase itself; the man suggested for this role was the penniless refugee Yaw Twereboanna, who combined legitimate royal status with complete dependence on the British. In the meantime, Governor Maxwell of the Gold Coast set about organising a military expedition to Kumase.

In Asante Agyeman Prempeh had intelligence of all these proceedings. Through its lawyers, the embassy in London communicated regularly with Kumase (via Cape Coast) by cable and letter. In September 1895 two of the ambassadors arrived back in Kumase to report. On 16 December four more disembarked in the Gold Coast. Three days later they were in Kumase with dismaying news of British military preparations at the coast. Finally, the Ansa brothers arrived back on the Gold Coast on 27 December. Throughout their

[22] The text of the embassy's agreement with Reckless is reproduced in Wilks (1975), 651–52.

absence they had cautioned the Asante government—in Agyeman Prempeh's words—"not to accept any term or arrangement" until their return.[23] But now they were told by Maxwell that the British expeditionary force would definitely go to Kumase; and on their way up to Asante they passed through the British military camp on the Gold Coast-Asante frontier at Praso. On 4 January 1896 they reached Kumase to find the Asante government engaged in emergency discussions of the crisis. In the debates that ensued the Ansa brothers took a legalist position, urging that their agreement with Reckless was valid in British law and arguing on that basis that a political solution was still possible. They were supported by most of the *amanhene* present and by a minority of Kumase councillors. Those who disagreed—including Yaa Kyaa, Kwasi Gyambibi and other senior sons of the Asantehene Kwaku Dua, and a majority of Kumase office holders—argued that the only option left to Asante was armed resistance.

The Asantehene Agyeman Prempeh's role in government was to listen to both sides of this debate and then deliver his verdict. Whatever his personal views, his primary responsibility was to the welfare of his people and country. With this uppermost in his mind he ordered that no military resistance be offered to the British. In this defining moment of his life he now made a speech to his office holders. He outlined the historical and political bases of his reasoning and made it clear that he understood the personal price he might be called upon to pay for his decision. Eyewitnesses recalled his words which were set down on paper by his successor the Asantehene Osei Agyeman Prempeh II (1931–70).

> Since the time of my accession to the Stool of my ancestors, it has been my chief aim to gather together all my people who had been scattered abroad through civil wars since the reign of my uncle ex-King Karikari up to this time, in order that Ashanti might once more become a powerful nation as before; and in doing this if the English Government had taken it as an offence, because I have asked for the return of the peoples of Adanse, Kokofu, Dadease, Manso-Nkwanta and Dwaben, who had sought refuge in the Colony, and because of this if they wish to take me away as a prisoner without any justification, despite all my efforts to maintain the cordial relations between the Asantehene and the British Government from the reign of my grand Uncle King Osei Bonsu I, and as hard as I have tried, they have refused to bring about a peaceful settlement, I am entirely prepared to sacrifice myself to save the lives of my people, and to avert the destruction of my country, rather than by allowing them to fight.[24]

---

[23] National Archives of Ghana, Accra, ADM 11/1/1905, Report by Lt. Col. A.C. Duncan-Johnstone on the Repatriation of ex-King Prempeh, including "History relating to the capture of Ex King Prempeh" (reproduced in full as MEM/1924 in Chapter 8 below).

[24] Manhyia Record Office, Kumase, "The History of Ashanti", ms (with letters and accompanying notes) prepared by a Committee of Traditional Authorities under the Chairmanship of Asantehene Osei Agyeman Prempeh II, n.d. (but in the 1940s), 35.32–33.

On 17 January 1896 British troops entered Kumase. The following day Governor Maxwell arrived. He announced that he would meet with Agyeman Prempeh, his mother and councillors on 20 January. At that meeting Maxwell, surrounded by British troops, required both the Asantehene and Asantehemaa to make a public submission by embracing his feet. The Governor then demanded the payment of a war indemnity of 50,000 ounces of gold. After this stunning announcement he drew from his pocket a document with a list of names. He read these out, declaring that everyone mentioned was under arrest and would be immediately deported from Asante to the Gold Coast. The list was headed by Agyeman Prempeh and his mother Yaa Kyaa. It went on to name Agyeman Prempeh's father Kwasi Gyambibi, his younger brother Agyeman Badu, five senior Kumase office holders and three *amanhene*. Shock and horror greeted this announcement, but as the Asantehene had ordered there was no resistance. Thereafter, Agyeman Prempeh and his fellow prisoners were conveyed under armed guard to Cape Coast to begin an exile that, for the survivors, was to last for twenty-eight years.

A word of epilogue is in order. Yaw Twereboanna was deemed surplus to Maxwell's plans and returned to the Gold Coast where he lived in straitened circumstances until his death in 1908. Instead, Maxwell launched upon improvising a new government for Asante. This went beyond his remit from London and caused alarm among the British government's legal advisers. In essence the Gold Coast administration, supported by mining and other commercial interests, had carried out a coup in Asante. Nothing symbolised the new order better than the Ashanti Goldfields Corporation that was set up in the late 1890s. This was an analogue of Agyeman Prempeh's development plans, but one that was controlled from outside an Asante that was now part of the British Empire.

CHAPTER TWO

Agyeman Prempeh in the Seychelles, 1900–1924

A. Adu Boahen

INTRODUCTION

On 11 September 1900 Agyeman Prempeh landed on the Seychelles Islands as a political prisoner of the British Government. He would not be repatriated to Asante until November 1924, and, even then, only as a private citizen. The circumstances that precipitated his deposition, exile and deportation from Kumase first to Elmina, then to Freetown in 1896, and thence to the Seychelles in 1900 have already been dealt with in other works, and in the preceding essay.[1] We are concerned here with examining what happened to him and his followers during their exile in the Seychelles. Why were they repatriated in, or rather why were they not repatriated until, 1924, and what impact did their long stay have on them?

Agyeman Prempeh was accompanied to the Seychelles by a captive group of fourteen chiefs, 13 women, 13 children and 12 attendants. In June 1901, another group of 15 chiefs, 2 women and 4 attendants who were all captives from the Asante War of Independence (1900–1901), were sent to join Agyeman Prempeh.[2] Thus by the end of June 1901, there was a total of 73 Asante political prisoners and their attendants and dependants in the Seychelles. Though 34 of them were repatriated to Kumase in 1907, the number had risen to 84 by 1915, 32 of whom had been born there.[3]

Agyeman Prempeh and his followers were settled on Mahé, the largest of the Seychelles group on which the capital town, Victoria, is also situated. It was on Mahé that the British government leased for the Asante prisoners an estate of about 27 acres two and half miles from Victoria, known as Le Rocher. At

---

[1] F. Fuller, *A Vanished Dynasty, Ashanti* (London, 1921); and W. Tordoff, *Ashanti under the Prempehs, 1888–1935* (Oxford, 1965).
[2] See Chapter 9.
[3] A. A. Boahen, "Prempeh in Exile," in *Research Review*, 8:3 (1972), 3–20; and *idem*, "A Nation in Exile: the Asante on the Seychelles, 1900–1924," in E. Schildkrout, ed., *The Golden Stool: Studies of the Asante Center and Periphery* (Washington DC, 1987), 146–60.

first only Agyeman Prempeh, his mother, father, brother and Asibe, the Kokofuhene, were accommodated at Le Rocher. The rest were settled at what was called the African or Plaisance Camp closer to Victoria, where the prisoners from the 1900 war were also accommodated. Later, probably in December 1901, the rest were transferred to Le Rocher.[4] All the Asante lived on this estate, which came to be known as the Asante Camp, till their repatriation in 1924.

The Seychelles Government, which was assigned the responsibility for looking after Agyeman Prempeh, and his followers, did everything possible to make life in the Camp as normal and comfortable as possible. The houses were constantly repaired and occasionally renovated and refurnished.[5] Agyeman Prempeh's house was completely renovated in 1912 by Charles Morgan, a contractor of Victoria.[6] The Camp was eventually supplied with water and electricity.[7] Each of the chiefs was also paid a monthly allowance according to his rank. It is not yet known how much each received from the beginning but by 1918, Agyeman Prempeh was being paid Rs 244.12 a month, his mother Rs 109.69, Yaa Asantewaa Rs 106.19, Asibe Rs 73.24 and each of the surviving ten chiefs—Kwadwo Appia, Asafu Boakye, Henry Boaten, Kofi Kofia, Kwabena Nkwantabisa, Kwame Dwansa, Adu Kofi, Kwame Akroma and Kofi Afrane— Rs 60.87 each.[8] They were also allowed to share the proceeds from the coconut and other trees on the estate in the proportion of one-half for the Asantehene and Asantehemaa and the other half for the rest of the chiefs.[9]

Though the Seychelles authorities officially described Agyeman Prempeh as ex-king throughout, in practice they regarded him as king and the leader of all the political prisoners and treated him with every respect and dignity. He was acknowledged as the main medium of communication between the inmates of the Camp and the Government. Complaints made to the officer-in-charge of the Camp were often redirected to Agyeman Prempeh for settlement. He was invited to official receptions by the Governor and was treated on such occasions with every respect. He was supplied with stationery free of charge every six months, and he was allowed to communicate with members of his family back home and with the Kumase Oyoko Clan in particular.[10] He was allowed to attend church in Victoria every Sunday, and he could on prior application visit some of the neighbouring estates and places of interest. In the Camp itself, he was recognized by all as the Asantehene. Thus, whenever

---

[4] SNA, the Administrator to the Secretary of State (SOS), 4 Dec. 1901.
[5] NAG, Accra, ADM 11/1499. Administrator of the Seychelles to Governor of the Gold Coast, 7 March 1904.
[6] MA, Correspondence Book of King Prempeh I whilst in the Seychelles, 1912–21, 26–29, 114–5.
[7] *Ibid.*, 114–5.
[8] SNA, 1905–28. Enclosure in Prempeh to Governor of Seychelles, 29 Dec. 1920.
[9] MA, Correspondence Book, 1912–21, 92–3; and Correspondence Book, 1916–21, 24–5.
[10] *Ibid.*, 1912–21, 95; and 1916–21, 8–21. Correspondence Book, 1913–17 is also full of letters from Prempeh to his sisters, wives, close relatives and some of the Kumase chiefs.

anybody died and left behind assets and or liabilities, these were shared among the chiefs in the ratio of 1/3 for Agyeman Prempeh and 2/3 for the rest of the chiefs.[11] Moreover, the chiefs went to offer him customary greetings every morning.

DAILY LIFE AT LE ROCHER: ASANTE IN MICROCOSM

How did Agyeman Prempeh use his time, and what were his main concerns and preoccupations? His first major preoccupation was to see to the survival of himself and his people by ensuring the maintenance of peace, law and order in the Camp. Here he worked in close cooperation with the Senior Police Officer who was put in charge of the Asante political prisoners. For a considerable length of time, the officer was L. A. Tonnet. He would send a police constable round the Camp to see that peace and discipline were maintained. For the administration of the Camp, what was referred to in the records as the Committee was established. This, however, was obviously the King's Council, which was composed of the leading chiefs and presided over by Agyeman Prempeh. This Committee met quite often to make bye-laws and regulations for the Camp and to settle disputes that arose with the assistance of Tonnet. A great deal of the time of the Committee was taken up with settling quarrels between man and wife, between chiefs and among families and in settling problems arising from the death of inmates of the Camp and the raising and repayment of loans and debts.

Agyeman Prempeh's second preoccupation was to ensure the welfare of the inmates in conducting their daily lives. He insisted that they made farms on which they cultivated plantain, cocoyam, cassava, potatoes, vegetables and sugarcane. They also reared hens, pigs, sheep, goats, and poultry for sale and to feed themselves. Agyeman Prempeh himself had a farm. In 1912, he wrote to the keeper of the Botanical Station as follows:

> As the palm seed is a favourite food to us Ashantis, I have the honour to ask you if you would kindly sell to me some ripe seeds and also lease to me all the palm seeds which will get ripe at Botanical Station. If your men do not know how to cultivate the palm tree in order to bear and ripen quickly, I will send my men to instruct your men to cultivate the same.[12]

In 1914 he asked for 2,000 vanilla and rubber seedlings to be planted "on our property".[13] Asante Camp food consisted of the staples listed above. It would appear that as time went on, rice became the main food, and the letters

---

[11] *Ibid.*, 1912–21, 2–9 & 15.
[12] *Ibid.*, 1916–21, 142–3.
[13] *Ibid.*, 1916–21, 142–3.

of Agyeman Prempeh to the Administration are full of complaints about its rising cost and the consequent need for increases in the monthly allowances.

The health and physical wellbeing of the inmates were also of concern to Agyeman Prempeh. He reported the sickness of every inmate of the Camp to the Medical Officer of Health and saw to it that free treatment was given. In 1908, however, it was decided that a consolidated amount of Rs 1000 a year each should be spent on medical care and education.[14] In many letters to the Seychelles authorities, Agyeman Prempeh drew attention to repairs that had to be done to the houses or to the water supply and saw that these were carried out. In May 1912, he asked the Governor to send him the Magic Lantern with views of the British Isles for he wished to show these to his people.[15] In January 1921, he asked for a football park and cricket pitch to be made in the Camp "for games and amusement". This was granted and Rs 600 was voted for these projects.[16]

Agyeman Prempeh ensured that his followers obtained employment. Some worked as labourers and servants soon after their arrival in the Seychelles. They proved such efficient workers that an enquiry was made as to whether it would be possible to obtain labourers from the Gold Coast Colony for work there.[17] He also saw to it that his educated followers and their children gained employment and he consistently wrote to the Seychelles Administration enquiring after jobs for them. Thus Frederick Prempeh was employed as a typist in the Police Department and later as a storekeeper at Victoria Prison. James Prempeh was employed as chief clerk by Victoria Town Board, Alfred Prempeh as gatekeeper in Victoria Prison, Richard Kuffour as messenger by the Eastern Telegraph Company, and Paul Boatin as a cook-steward and later as a clerk in the Public Works Department (PWD). Yaw Dabila and James Kweku Fin also became owners and drivers of rickshaws. Josephine Kuffour became a seamstress and some of the younger women were employed as maids and cleaners.[18] Above all, he constantly drew the attention of the administration to the inadequacy of their allowance and his correspondence books are full of letters on this matter. At an interview with the newly appointed Governor Sir Eustace Fiennes on 22 October 1918, after raising the issue of repatriation, Agyeman Prempeh complained that their allowances were "too small for us to live on".[19] Despite Agyeman Prempeh's efforts, it is clear from the recurrent complaints

---

[14] SNA, Crew to Davidson, 4 Aug. 1908.
[15] MA, Correspondence Book, 1912–21, 24.
[16] NAG, Kumase, Prempeh to Fiennes, 1 Jan. 1921.
[17] SNA, Governor of Seychelles to SOS, 16 Feb. 1901.
[18] NAG, Accra, ADM 12/5/117. Nominal Roll of Asante being Repatriated, enclosed in Governor of Seychelles to SOS, 12 Sept. 1924.
[19] MA, Correspondence Book, 1916–21, 139.

about allowances and the rising cost of living that life was far from being comfortable.

Daily life went on normally in the Camp. Indeed, the population grew at a rate that would have alarmed a modern demographer. Though about 34 persons were sent back home in 1907 leaving 40 people, this number had increased to 84 by 1915. In other words, the population more than doubled in a matter of 8 years. Indeed, 32 of these 84 were born in the Camp.[20] As one would expect, death also occurred and this became one of Agyeman Prempeh's main concerns. When anybody died, it was he who informed the Administrator and made the necessary funeral arrangements. Thus, when Osei Kwadwo Krome died on 28 September 1913, Agyeman Prempeh "announced it with regret" to the officer-in-charge.[21] When his mother Yaa Kyaa died, he wrote to the Governor of the Seychelles asking that the Governor of the Gold Coast inform the royal family in Kumase and Asante chiefs that she had passed away on 2 September 1917.[22] Agyeman Prempeh then saw to it that the deceased was given proper burial in the public cemetery and he bore the initial expenses, which were later refunded by the Administration. Again, when Nana Yaa Asantewaa died on 17 October 1921, Agyeman Prempeh sent the following letter to the Officer-in-Charge of the political prisoners:

> With my regret to inform you of the death of the old sub-queen mother Ya Asuntiwor who passed away yesterday the 17th at 3:30 p.m. I shall make necessary as usual and submit my account. As for the coffin I would like you to ask Superintendent of Works to have one made of Takama wood.[23]

It was the rule in the Camp that whenever any political prisoner died, his wife, children and attendants were repatriated and his assets and liabilities shared among the chiefs under the supervision of Agyeman Prempeh. In all 49 people died on the island, 24 of whom were chiefs.[24] In 1920, Agyeman Prempeh built a special vault with the permission of the government in which the remains of the chiefs buried in the public cemetery were deposited in boxes.[25] These remains were packed into two cases and shipped from the Seychelles in October 1929. These cases arrived in Kumase in January 1930, and the remains were distributed to the appropriate stool families for burial.[26]

---

[20] *Ibid.*, 1912–21, 166–8.
[21] *Ibid.*, 73.
[22] *Ibid.*, 1916–21, 34.
[23] SNA, 1905–28. Prempeh to the Officer-in-Charge, 18 Oct. 1921.
[24] MA, "History of Nana Prempeh's Adventure".
[25] MA, Correspondence Book, 1916–21, 113–18.
[26] NAG, Accra, ADM 12/5/117. Commissioner of Eastern Province (CEP) to Chief Commissioner of Ashanti (CCA), 8 & 12 Sept. 1928 and 27 Jan. 1930; CCA to Acting Colonial Secretary, 20 Sept. 1928; Superintendent of Public Works, Seychelles, to CCA, 9 Oct. 1929; and CEP to Prempeh and other chiefs, 18 Jan. 1930.

Finally, Agyeman Prempeh saw to it that friendly relations existed between the inmates of the Camp and the people of Seychelles. From the accounts given by those who were born and grew up in the Seychelles during my interviews with them in February 1984, it appears that he was enormously successful in this area.[27] The fact that seven of the inmates of the Camp married Seychelles women, namely Paul Akroma, Kwame Dwansa, Alfred Prempeh, Frederick Prempeh, James Prempeh, Richard Kuffour, and J.K. Fin, is further evidence of the congenial relations that prevailed. This author was also surprised to find a family that was still calling itself Prempeh when he visited Seychelles in 1972; these people were descendants of James Prempeh.

EDUCATION, CHRISTIANITY, AND MODERNITY

Agyeman Prempeh's major means of coming to terms with modernisation was education, which became his other major preoccupation for himself and other inmates of the Camp, notably the children. For this purpose, the first teacher appointed was Timothy Korsah, a Fante from Saltpond, who was employed in Freetown by the British Government as interpreter to the political prisoners. Agyeman Prempeh continued his studies after Korsah returned to the Gold Coast in 1904. It is interesting to note that he did not want to be literate in the English language only, for in August 1907 he asked for a person to teach him how to read and write in his own language. The government turned down this request on the unconvincing grounds that he could "always communicate with his friends in Ashanti in the English language".[28] Agyeman Prempeh continued with his education throughout his stay and by the time of his repatriation he had become well educated and could speak English with some fluency.

Even more important was the education of the children in the Camp. Upon arrival, Agyeman Prempeh sent some of his own children and other Asante children in the Camp to school. They were given free education but in 1908 it was decided that the amount spent on education should be limited to Rs 1000 annually for ten years,[29] after which the "Government of the Seychelles should assume the responsibility of providing for the adequate education of the children in the Ashanti camp".[30] In 1909, an infant school was established in the Camp as a preparatory school for the children of the political prisoners.

Agyeman Prempeh followed the progress of this school with great interest. In March 1912, for instance, he wrote to inform the authorities that the floor of

---

[27] Interviews with Tom Boatin, Paul Boatin, Harold Boatin, Josephine Kuffour, Francis Gyamfi, William Prempeh, Ruth Prempeh, and Jeanette Prempeh, Feb. 1984.
[28] SNA. Acting Governor to Administrator, Seychelles, 9 Dec. 1903.
[29] SNA, SOS to Davidson, 4 Aug. 1908.
[30] SNA, Administrator to SOS, 27 Sept. 1918.

the infant school was very bad and needed urgent repairs and he also asked for an extra chair for visitors.[31] In April 1912, Agyeman Prempeh protested to the Principal of King's College and to Inspector Tonnet about the increase of fees.[32] In February 1919 the Government of the Seychelles expanded the Camp School by converting the empty houses in the Camp caused by the death and repatriation of some of the Asante inmates into "a Government School in the Asante Camp which would be open not only to Ashanti children, as at present, but to all children living in the neighbourhood".[33]

Besides promoting and encouraging education, Agyeman Prempeh, in his pursuit of modernisation, also insisted on the boys being introduced to technology. Thus, as Harold Boatin told me:

> Those who finished the Middle School Leaving Certificate were apprenticed to a tradesman. An example was that Prempeh was apprenticed to a surveyor, somebody else was apprenticed to a draughtsman and my own brother was apprenticed to a tinsmith. The girls too had home-science. Some of the ladies stayed at these homes and came back at the weekend.

As a result of Agyeman Prempeh's interest and efforts, many of the elderly people and the children returned to Ghana well-educated and speaking the local Seychelles language which was a form of pidgin French.

But Agyeman Prempeh did not only promote the education of the Asante in the Seychelles. In his letters to his relatives and others in Asante, he urged them not only to embrace Christianity but also to send his cousins, nephews and nieces to school and he followed their progress there with interest. As he wrote to his sister Nana Akua Afriyie in Kumase: "I am also very pleased and proud to see Kwame Chirchuae [Kyeretwie] being educated. I should like to know from you the school progress of my nephew Kobina Tannosuoh and others".[34]

Probably second to Agyeman Prempeh's concern for education was his wish to become a Christian and to win as many of his followers as possible over to Christianity. This preoccupation was obviously not only to demonstrate publicly his acceptance of new ideas but also to show his coming to terms with his traditional belief and religion. It is recounted that upon his arrival in the Seychelles, Anglican and Roman Catholic priests rushed to convert him and he is said to have asked them:

> "What religion is the King of England?" Immediately the Anglican clergyman replied he belongs to my Church. "Oh", said Prempeh, "I am of opinion that all

---

[31] MA, Correspondence Book, 1912–21, 16.
[32] *Ibid.*, 18–19.
[33] NAG, Kumase, Governor of Seychelles to Governor of the Gold Coast, 27 Sept. 1918; and Governor of the Gold Coast to Governor of Seychelles, 18 Feb. 1919.
[34] MA, Correspondence Book, 1913–17, 4–6.

kings should have the same religion, therefore I accept the Church of England and am willing to attend same".[35]

He and some of his followers therefore immediately began to attend the Anglican Church in town. As the government of Seychelles reported to London in November 1901:

> Ex-king Prempeh and the Queen Mother have been for some time regular attendants at the Anglican Church, and the spectacle of Prempeh, the Queen-Mother and the two ex-kings of Uganda, Mwanga and Kabrega, sitting side by side in church is not devoid of interest.[36]

Agyeman Prempeh also began to receive religious instruction from chaplains of the Church Missionary Society. In February 1902, he in fact requested that the civil chaplain of Seychelles be employed to give religious instruction to the political prisoners on a salary of Rs. 500 per annum.[37] Though this request was rejected by government, it would appear that instruction continued, for on 9 May 1904 Agyeman Prempeh and his mother were baptized and given the Christian names of Edward and Victoria, presumably after the British monarchs of those names.[38]

Agyeman Prempeh wanted to be confirmed and so in 1908 he asked that two of his wives, Akua Morbi and Amma Kwahan, should be sent back home "to conform to the principles of the Christian religion, [by not] having three wives". He undertook to give them "a present of one hundred and twenty rupees each on the day of their departure and ten rupees a month as pension".[39] This request was granted and the two wives were repatriated. However, Agyeman Prempeh was still not confirmed by December 1920 because he was still not married to only one woman. Through the intervention of the Governor, he was finally confirmed on 28 December 1920.[40]

Agyeman Prempeh also saw to it that any member of the Camp who wanted baptism received it. As he wrote to the Bishop of Mauritius on 28 December 1920: "I reverently beg to inform you that an Ashanti woman by name Afuah Abensah, wife of Ex-Chief Kojo Appia wishes to be baptised. I reverently beg to ask my Lordship to be so kind as to grant an authority to the Civil Chaplain in order to baptise any Ashanti man or woman who intends to become Christian".[41] Many of the inmates including his mother, his brother,

---

[35] J. Bradley, *A History of Seychelles*, 2 vols.
[36] SNA, Administrator to SOS, 5 Nov. 1901.
[37] SNA, Governor of the Gold Coast to Administrator of Seychelles, 21 May 1902.
[38] Tordoff, *Ashanti under the Prempehs*, 168.
[39] SNA, Prempeh to Governor of Seychelles, 3 Feb. 1908; Roger to SOS, 11 June 1908; SOS to Davidson, 4 Aug. 1908; and Governor of Seychelles to SOS, 27 Sept. 1908.
[40] MA, Correspondence Book, 1916–21, 141.
[41] *Ibid.*

Yaa Asantewaa and numbers of the chiefs and their wives did become converts. Through his exhortations, advice and prompting some of his relatives in Asante also became Christians. Furthermore, Agyeman Prempeh persuaded his son John to embark on a religious career, and he sent him to train in Mauritius as a chaplain in 1921. John successfully completed his training and returned home to Asante in 1930 or 1931, where he worked as a chaplain till his death.[42] If today the Oyoko family of Kumase and its descendants are predominantly Anglican, and if the Anglican Church in Kumase is more or less their official church, this is because of the conversion and religious activities of Agyeman Prempeh.

AGYEMAN PREMPEH, ASANTE, AND REPATRIATION

Some historians are of the view that during his exile Agyeman Prempeh "must soon have lost touch with events at home".[43] But the evidence shows that he never lost contact but rather kept in close touch not only with events in Asante but also with its traditions and history throughout the long period of his exile. Indeed, for reasons discussed above this became one of his major preoccupations. It must have been his determination to preserve the traditions and history of Asante for posterity and above all to legitimize his Oyoko lineage and perpetuate its rule that he embarked on the preparation of the history presented in this volume.

While producing his history, Agyeman Prempeh monitored events going on at home. Thus he kept up regular correspondence with his wives Akua Morbi and Amma Kwahan, with his sisters Adwoa Dwantua and Amma Dusa, and with such chiefs of Kumase as Kwaku Brenya, Kwaku Fin and Akwasi Ampon of Asokwa, and, finally with G. W. Morrison, the Anglican Chaplain of Kumase. Agyeman Prempeh also asked for copies of the annual reports on Asante produced by the Gold Coast Government.[44] In 1912 and again in 1916, he also asked for "monthly newspapers of Ashanti" to be paid on his account via the Governor of Seychelles, and he added:

> Through the kind permission of both the Governor of the Gold Coast and of Seychelles, I am allowed to receive news of the colony. It is such a long time since I left home and so I should be pleased to know the new changes which had and which are still taking place for I hope that all the old fashions had been changed.[45]

The reply was that there were no newspapers in Asante.

[42] NAG, Accra, ADM 12/5/117. Prempeh to Duncan-Johnstone, 20 March 1928.
[43] W. Tordoff, "The exile and repatriation of Nana Prempeh I of Ashanti, 1896–1924", in *Transactions of the Historical Society of Ghana*, 4:2 (1960), 33–55.
[44] MA, Correspondence Book, 1912–21, 51–52.
[45] NAG, Kumase, File No. 1480. Prempeh to Governor of the Gold Coast, 29 Aug. 1916.

Probably no question occupied the attention of Agyeman Prempeh more than that of the repatriation of himself and his followers to Kumase. He submitted his first petition for repatriation only a month after his arrival in the Seychelles and another followed on 31 October 1901. The reply from the Secretary of State to the latter could not have been more forthright: "I regret that it is not possible to hold out any hope that they will be allowed to return to Ashanti at an early date".[46] A third followed in November 1902 and the Administrator forwarded it to the Secretary of State with the comment that "the behaviour of the political prisoners has been excellent". But the reply was no less forthright:

> You (Administrator of Seychelles) will inform the signatories that their petition has been received and the Government of the Gold Coast has been consulted in regard to it, but that I am still unable to hold out any hope of political prisoners being allowed to return to Ashanti at early date.[47]

Another was sent in July 1904. Probably because of the negative reactions of the British Government, it was not until 1907 that Agyeman Prempeh followed this up with another petition. Similar letters and petitions ensued, at times signed by himself alone but often with the other chiefs and his close family, in 1910, 1911, 1912, 1913, 1915, 1916, 1917, 1918, 1920, 1921 and 1922, at times twice a year. The last petition that Agyeman Prempeh sent that is known to this writer is the desperate one dated 10 February 1924, addressed to the Bishop of Ashanti, M. S. O'Rourke. In this, he pleaded desperately "with both my knees bent to most humbly beseech your Lordship to intercede on my behalf to the Almighty God to beg for forgiveness of my sins and to ask God to be pleased in the name of his dear son Jesus our Saviour to take away his eyes from my sins and to allow me to return to my native land safe and sound to see the face of my family once more and always to remain God's true worshipper".[48] Particularly long was the petition that Agyeman Prempeh and his chiefs sent on 16 October 1913. In this he reviewed the history of Asante from the time of Asantehene Kofi Kakari (1867–1874) until his own arrest, accepted the blame for all the mistakes that the Asante had committed and passionately pleaded for forgiveness and repatriation.[49]

Of all the petitions, the most moving was the one that Agyeman Prempeh sent on 21 January 1918.

> I beg your Excellency grace to convey to His Right Honourable the Secretary of State and from him to His Majesty the King to ask his Majesty to pardon us for our

---

[46] SNA, Administrator of Seychelles to SOS, 5 Nov. 1901; and J. Chamberlain to Administrator, 23 Dec. 1901.
[47] SNA, Administrator to SOS, 29 Nov. 1902; and J. Chamberlain to Administrator, 27 May, 1903.
[48] NAG, Accra, ADM 11/1342. Prempeh to Bishop of Ashanti, 10 Feb. 1924.
[49] MA, Correspondence book, 1912–21, 78–84; and SNA, Prempeh to Col. O'Brien, Governor of Seychelles, 16 Oct. 1913.

serious offences which our ancestors have committed to our knowledge or beyond our knowledge against the sovereign of Great Britain; and most reverently to ask His Majesty to look no more over our offences but with pity and mercy to cast a glance over his captives and by His Majesty's great mercy send us word to release us to our native land. Praying His Majesty to consider how wretched I am, for I was being taken prisoner together with father; mother; brother and chiefs for now 22 years; and now how miserable to see that father, mother, brother and nearly ¾ of the chiefs are all dead. The remainder ¼, some are blind; some are worned out with old ages-and the rest being attacked of diverse diseases. And now I do not find where to glance and where to comfort myself. And my sole hope and comfort is by giving myself wholly to God by whom all things are comforted and to His Majesty by whose mercy and Love I would be released from sorrow and captivity. I end by earnestly beseeching His Majesty to take my humble petition into consideration- and to submit for release to my native land where I swear by whole strength and truth to remain a true and ready servant of our King and Empire.[50]

That Agyeman Prempeh should sound so desolate and downcast is not at all surprising because in September 1917, he lost not only his mother Nana Yaa Kyaa, but what shocked him even more, his brother Agyeman Badu. The former passed away on the 3rd and the latter on the 29th. It should be pointed out that on 6 August 1916 Agyeman Prempeh had petitioned not for repatriation but rather for a transfer "from Seychelles to any of the British colonies in Africa either to Sierra Leone or to any other Colony in West Africa". The plea he advanced for this transfer was that he was "actually in deep sorrow to find that the only brother who is near by me has fallen ill".[51] Such was the petition he submitted a year before the death of his brother. Is it surprising then that the petition he submitted after Agyeman Badu's death should have been so melancholy and so heart rending? However, all these petitions were turned down.

The question, then, is why did the colonial government turn down all these petitions until 1924? It was obvious, from the circumstances leading to Agyeman Prempeh's deposition and exile—from almost a hundred years of resistance and wars culminating in the Yaa Asantewaa war of 1900—and from the fact that the property for the Asante political prisoners in the Seychelles was leased for 15 years, that the British had no intention of granting an early release to the prisoners. Hence, the peremptory rejection of all the applications over these many years. Indeed Hodgson, the then Governor of the Gold Coast, informed the Asante chiefs in March 1900 that "Prempeh would never come back to rule over Ashanti". Then in January 1910, his successor in office informed the Kumase chiefs who had petitioned for repatriation that he could not "at present entertain the return of ex-king Prempeh to Ashanti and that it depended altogether on their behaviour and on the general

---

[50] MA, Correspondence Book, 1916–21, 51–52.
[51] *Ibid.*, 30–32.

progress and development of the country if the request could be considered in the future".[52]

However, the then Chief Commissioner of Ashanti (henceforth, CCA), Francis Fuller, in a confidential letter of 12 June 1911 to the Colonial Secretary recommended in reply to another petition sent by the Kumase chiefs for repatriation that "the time has now arrived when the return of Prempeh although unsettling at first, would prove beneficial to the Administration." The Asante were now

> imbued with true Feelings toward the crown. It mainly depended on Prempeh himself whether his return would act as a stimulus to Anti-Government intrigue and conspiracy. If he totally lacks a sense of proportion and still holds absurd ideas in regard to the military powers of his people, to the respective values of the European and Ashanti civilisation, and to the utter hopelessness of renewed resistance, he should on no account be allowed to return. But I cannot believe this to be possible. I cannot believe that an exile of 15 years in British Colonies has not had a marked effect on the man and not completely revolutionized all his ideas and mode of thought.[53]

But even Fuller insisted on "one condition of absolute obedience and complete devotion to His Majesty's person and Government" from Agyeman Prempeh and his followers. But the Governor turned down Fuller's recommendation on the grounds that he was "not in favour of Prempeh's return nor do I think that the Secretary of State would favour it."[54]

The second reason for delayed repatriation was the First World War of 1914–1918. Political decisions of this sort were suspended for the duration. As Acting CCA Philbrick advised, "nothing should be done until after the war," in reply to the petition for Agyeman Prempeh to be sent somewhere in West Africa.[55] Indeed, it was not until 1918 that Agyeman Prempeh's repatriation was raised in official circles in the Gold Coast.

It was from February 1918 that the issue of repatriation became increasingly salient. Its resolution could no longer be ignored. This change was caused by a number of developments, which occurred in the Gold Coast between 1918 and 1924. These events were the growth of mutual respect, confidence and loyalty between the Asante and the British caused by the First World War itself and the Golden Stool episode of 1921; the improvement of Asante and of Agyeman Prempeh himself by 1920; the intensification of the pressure for repatriation; the administrative needs of the colonial government; and, finally,

---

[52] NAG, Accra, ADM 12/5/117. Petition of the Oyoko Clan and 18 chiefs of Kumase to CCA, 20 Jan. 1910, and Governor's minute, 20 Jan. 1910.
[53] NAG, Accra, ADM 11/1342. Fuller to Colonial Secretary, 12 June 1911.
[54] *Ibid.* Minute by the Governor, 7 July 1911.
[55] *Ibid.* P. Arthur to Governor, 5 Feb. 1918.

the growing convergence between the British and the Asante on the question of repatriation.

If the outbreak of the First World War ruled out the issue of repatriation until 1918, the role that the Asante played during the War was a contributory factor to its eventual resolution. Instead of taking advantage of the British preoccupation with the War to embark on further protests or resistance as occurred in other parts of Africa, the Asante instead demonstrated support for the British and contributed materially to the war effort. In 1918, the Governor of the Gold Coast reported that: "the record of the chiefs and people of the Dependency during the past four years has been one of unswerving and often enthusiastic loyalty. The call for recruits in the early months of 1917 was well responded to and had from the first time, the keen support of the chiefs". He added:

> The Chiefs and people of Ashanti have been an active part in subscribing to the Patriotic Fund, to the Red Cross and to the other war Charities. The gift of three (3) Aeroplanes to His Majesty's Government by the chiefs and people of this dependency has always been noted: and the support and assistances, which have always been afforded to the Government by the natives of the Dependency during all these years of stress and trial deserve, as they have received, the fullest measure of recognition and publicity.[56]

It is not surprising then that the Asante petitioners pleaded for "due and early favourable consideration, if for no other reason, in appreciation on the part of His Majesty's Government of the loyalty displayed by the people of Ashanti during the great war and since"; nor is it surprising that the then Governor Guggisberg commended this request to the British government only three months after its receipt. It is interesting and significant that the Governor of the Seychelles, Eustace Fiennes, also suggested to the Governor of the Gold Coast in 1919 that the signature of the peace treaty might be made the occasion "for pardoning ex-kings Kabarega of Uganda and Agyeman Prempeh of Ashanti and their followers and to repatriate them to their country"[57] Finally, in June 1918, Fuller, the CCA, suggested that as a reward for their excellent attitude since the outbreak of the War, the Ashanti should be favoured by a special act of royal clemency, and that this act should take the form of a pardon to Agyeman Prempeh and withdrawal of restrictions on the liberty of his movements. This was qualified by the following conditions: (a) the yielding up of the Golden Stool as an essential preliminary to the pardon; (b) that he agrees to return as a private individual; (c) that he consents to remain a government pensioner; and (d) that he enters into a Bond not to interfere in political matters and will not seek, or exercise any administrative powers.[58]

---

[56] *Ibid.*
[57] NAG, Accra, ADM 11/1342. Fiennes to Governor of the Gold Coast, 11 Sept. 1919.
[58] *Ibid.* Fuller to Acting Colonial Secretary, 1 June 1918.

Chapter Two

Thus the role of the Asante during the War cleared all doubts about their loyalty and their acceptance of the colonial order of things. Most probably, Agyeman Prempeh would have been repatriated soon after the War but for what the CCA described as "derangement of the normal atmosphere in Ashanti consequent on the War and the complete failure of the cocoa market in all but the commercial centre, which has made the young men very restless and discontented".[59]

But if the First World War rehabilitated the Asante people in the eyes of the British as to their devotion, loyalty and cooperative attitude, the Golden Stool episode of 1921 also dispelled any lingering distrust that the Asante entertained about the British. It is important to note that as late as June 1918, even a pro-Asante and sympathetic CCA like Fuller minuted as one of the conditions for Agyeman Prempeh's repatriation "the yielding up of the Golden Stool as an essential preliminary to the pardon". For Fuller surrendering the Golden Stool would be the supreme evidence of Asante loyalty and a guarantee of Asante cooperation over Agyeman Prempeh's return.[60] Again, at meetings with the Kumase chiefs on 30 October 1919 and on 27 April 1920, even the progressive Governor Guggisberg repeated the same conditions. At the latter meeting, he told the chiefs:

> I would like to see Prempeh come back under certain conditions. This is now a very prosperous and happy country. It is a very different country from the time when Prempeh lived here and I am not going to run any risk of having this country upset. There are certain conditions which, if, you are willing to accept, then I will recommend (I am going home next month and I will talk to the Secretary of State) Prempeh's return. The first condition is that the Golden Stool must be given up to the Government. That is absolutely fixed. The second condition is that Prempeh returns as a private individual and does not interfere in any way in political matters.[61]

The answers that the chiefs gave are interesting. One stated that they were willing to sign any bond for good behaviour, but lacked information as to the whereabouts of the Golden Stool. Another also pleaded that the stool was not the private property of Agyeman Prempeh, but belonged to Asante. He begged that the stool question should not be entwined with Agyeman Prempeh's repatriation. Guggisberg's response was to shelve the issue.[62]

However, on 15 September 1921, the CCA told the same Kumase chiefs for the first time that he was "not going to call for the Golden Stool nor any of its

---

[59] *Ibid.* CCA to Governor, 5 Feb. 1918.
[60] *Ibid.* CCA to Acting Colonial Secretary, 1 June 1918.
[61] *Ibid.* Meetings of the Governor with the Kumase Council, 30 Oct. 1919 and 27 April 1920.
[62] *Ibid.*

insignia". He repeated this on the 21st of September.[63] Furthermore, on 16 February and 31 March 1922, at meetings with the Kumase chiefs, the Governor himself also repeated the same assurance. On the latter occasion, he said:

> This has been a great year. The case of the Golden Stool was a big event. I congratulate the chiefs on the wise manner in which they dealt with this business. The Government fully recognised what the Golden Stool is to you and as far as government is concerned they make no claim to the stool. The Government, on the other hand, will help you in the preservation of the stool, and will help you preserve the reverence and respect for that stool which belongs to your nation. So the government will only interfere if the stool becomes degraded by a bad fetish, or if it is used for seditious purpose.[64]

There was therefore, quite clearly, a radical change in the attitude of the colonial administration towards the Golden Stool between 1921 and 1922. The question then is why this radical change? There is absolutely no doubt that the reason for this complete *volte face* by the Government was the Golden Stool crisis referred to in the quotation above.

The crisis was precipitated in September 1921 when the Golden Stool was stripped of its gold and all its precious ornaments of gold trinkets and bells and beads.[65] The news of this desecration spread like wildfire throughout Asante after 12 September. The whole nation was plunged into a state of shocked mourning. In every town and village people put on *kuntunkuni* or mourning cloth and besmeared their faces and arms with *ntwuma* (red clay). They poured into Kumase in their thousands daily to witness the trial of the 14 people who were accused of the desecration. The trial lasted from 23–27 September 1921. It was precisely this spontaneous national reaction, which caused the colonial administration through its newly appointed anthropologist, R.S Rattray, to find out about "the history of the Sika Agua Kofi (the Golden Stool) and anything in connection with the subject . . ."[66] The results of this investigation and the recommendations made were submitted in a memorandum to the colonial government. In this memorandum, subsequently published in an abridged and revised form in his book *Ashanti* in 1923, Rattray traced the history of the Asante nation and of the Golden Stool. He pointed out how ignorant and wrong the administration had been about the nature and significance of the

---

[63] Rhodes House Library (RH), Oxford University, Papers and Diary of Sir Charles Harper. CCA to Kumase Chiefs, 22 Sept. 1921, enclosed in CCA to Governor, 3 Oct. 1921.
[64] *Ibid.* Meeting on 31 March 1922.
[65] The full story of the desecration of the Golden Stool has still not yet been told. However, see E. W. Smith, *The Golden Stool* (London, 1926), 1–17; and K. A. Busia, *The Position of the Chief in the Modern Political System of Ashanti* (London, 1951), 113–17.
[66] NAG, Kumase, File No. 154/57. Amanhene to CCA, 30 Sept. 1921, enclosed in CCA to Colonial Secretary, 3 Oct. 1921.

Golden Stool, revealed early on in Governor Sir Frederick Hodgson's ill-fated and misguided demand for "it to sit upon" in 1900, which precipitated the Yaa Asantewaa War.[67] Rattray submitted this memorandum to CCA Harper a few days after the desecration of the stool became known. It is evident from Harper's diary that this report and his conversations with Rattray about Asante had a profound impact on the CCA's perceptions. In forwarding his detailed report on the Golden Stool crisis to the governor, Harper recommended that the government should retract its claim to the Golden Stool.[68] The conclusion, then, is that it was Rattray's memorandum, which brought about the turnaround in the official position on the Golden Stool.

This welcome and most opportune change of policy impacted on the question at issue in two ways. First, it saved both the British and Asante a second Yaa Asantewaa rebellion and its consequent political instability, animosity, destruction and bitterness. With the avoidance of armed conflict, the chances for Agyeman Prempeh's repatriation were further enhanced. Second, this change of policy facilitated the government's decision to allow the Asante to handle the investigation and trial of the culprits themselves. These two moves on the part of the colonial government not only eliminated the deep suspicion the Asante had against it, but they also strengthened the trust and confidence that the Asante had in the administration. Both factors thus enhanced the chances of an early consideration of the return of Agyeman Prempeh and his followers. Thus by 1921, the only remaining impediment in the way of repatriation was the hostile or lukewarm attitude of the Asante amanhene or principal chiefs, and this impediment was not removed until 1923–24.

The changing social context in Asante in the first two decades of the twentieth century, and the reformed character of Agyeman Prempeh encouraged the British to accede to petitions for his repatriation. The establishment of missionary and government schools in Asante, the construction of motorable roads and railway links between Kumase and Sekondi, the erection of European-style solid brick buildings in a well-planned Kumase, and the flourishing of the new cocoa industry all convinced the British that not even Agyeman Prempeh's return could turn back the clock of "progress". From being described by the British as a barbaric, pagan and blood-thirsty tyrant, Agyeman Prempeh had by the time of his return become civilized, educated and a sincere Christian, "as much at home in European dress at a meeting of the town Council, as an hour before perhaps in crown ornaments and Ashanti robes presiding over a tribunal or at some national pageant".[69] Or as CCA Harper described him in a letter of 23 November 1921 to the Colonial

---

[67] *Ibid.* A Memorandum on the Golden Stool, Rattray to CCA, enclosed in CCA to Colonial Secretary, 3 Oct. 1921.
[68] RH, Harper's Papers, Rattray to Governor, 30 Oct. 1921.
[69] Boahen "Nation in Exile", 151.

Secretary, "Agyeman Prempeh is educated, a Christian, has seen something of the world and is disciplined".[70]

Another factor that worked in favour of repatriation was the increasingly depressed and lonely state of Agyeman Prempeh as the exile wore on. This won him widespread sympathy and support. His mood was palpably revealed in his petition for repatriation of 21 January 1918, which was given wide publicity in the Gold Coast press in the early 1920s. In their petition of 21 March 1923, the Kumase chiefs also referred to the "pain of anguish that he (Prempeh) has been undergoing during his exile by the losses sustained by him in the deaths of his mother, father, brother and several of his chiefs, remaining at present PREMPEH himself and two only of his chiefs," and appealed for his immediate repatriation "in order to avert the possibility of his ever dying in exile".[71] Thus, by 1922, favourable political, social and economic conditions now prevailing in Asante, coupled with the civilised demeanour of Agyeman Prempeh on the one hand and his sad personal state on the other, combined to make his repatriation only a question of time.

But it still needed two more factors to push the colonial administration into approving repatriation. The first of these was the increasing pressure for repatriation, which assumed national and international dimensions after the First World War. Until then, the demand for repatriation had been confined to Agyeman Prempeh himself and his followers in the Seychelles on the one hand, and on the other to the Kumase chiefs and members of the Asante Kotoko Society, formed in 1916 by educated Asante young men with the principal purpose of campaigning for repatriation. But from 1917 onwards this pressure became not only countrywide but also international. The first group outside Asante to join the campaign for repatriation was the unofficial African members of the Legislative Council of the Gold Coast. This issue was raised for the first time in 1917. During the discussion of the subject of the maintenance of Agyeman Prempeh, these members asked whether he might not now be allowed to return to the Gold Coast. They contended that: "the loyalty of the chiefs and people of Ashanti is now so assured that, no danger need be apprehended from his return".[72] Nana Ofori Atta raised the same question during a debate in 1919 and pleaded that Agyeman Prempeh should be allowed to return and that if his presence in Ashanti was undesirable he should be allowed to live in the Colony. But Guggisberg minuted that "on no account whatever should Prempeh return".[73] But the African members of the Legislative Council persisted. At its meeting on 22 September 1922, Casely Hayford moved that "it is undesirable that there should be any further delay in the repatriation of the

---

[70] NAG, Accra, ADM 11/1342. CCA to Colonial Secretary, 23 Nov. 1921.
[71] *Ibid.* Kumase Chiefs' meeting with the Governor, 21 March 1923.
[72] *Ibid.* Extract from the Report of the Select Committee on the Estimates for 1918.
[73] *Ibid.* Report on the Estimates for 1919.

ex-king Prempeh in view of his advancing years". This motion was seconded by Dr. Quartey-Papafio and supported by Nana Ofori Atta and Nana Essandoh III.[74] However, the Governor rejected the motion on the grounds that whatever "the majority or I would say rather the whole of the chiefs are not quite sure that they want Prempeh back". He, however, gave them the undertaking that "sometime before the tenure of my own appointment—if it runs its normal course—is completed, King Prempeh will be back in Africa (Applause from African members)".[75] On the strength of this assurance, the African members did not ask for a division on this motion. Indeed in a minute of 6 December 1922, Guggisberg stated that Agyeman Prempeh could be brought home in 1924.[76]

Besides the Asante Kotoko Society, other societies such as the Gold Coast Aborigines Rights Protection Society (ARPS), and the National Congress of British West Africa (NCBWA) joined the campaign for the Asantehene's release. On 25 September 1923, the ARPS requested that a telegram should be sent to the Secretary of State for the Colonies to ask for Agyeman Prempeh's repatriation.[77] In the same year, the NCBWA meeting in Freetown also passed a resolution demanding repatriation.[78] Local newspapers, especially the *Gold Coast Independent* and the *Gold Coast Leader*, also took up the cause and few issues between 1921 and 1924 appeared without mentioning the repatriation question and asking the British administration to heed the call not only by the Asante but also by others. In February 1924, M. S. O'Rourke, the Anglican Bishop of Ashanti, also forwarded a moving appeal for his release from Agyeman Prempeh to the Governor with the request that he should express, "some words of comfort that I could transmit to the ex-king".[79] Finally, the question of repatriation was taken up by the Secretary of State for the Colonies as well as the British Parliament. On the basis of a request from Casely Hayford via Mr McCallum Scoll, M.P., Secretary of State Milner wrote to the Governor of the Gold Coast to find out whether the special objections which he had expressed in his letter of 31 October 1919 to Agyeman Prempeh's return "have now been removed".[80] In his reply, the Governor referred to the conditions that he had already laid down for Agyeman Prempeh's repatriation in his statement to the Kumase chiefs on 30th October and his speech to the Legislative Council in November 1919. He added that he would supply a definite recommendation upon the return of CCA Harper from leave.[81]

[74] Gold Coast, *Legislative Council Debates*, 22 Sept. 1922.
[75] *Ibid.*
[76] Gold Coast, *Legislative Council Debates*, 6 Dec. 1922.
[77] NAG, Accra, ADM 12/5/117.
[78] D. Kimble, *A Political History of Ghana, 1850–1928* (Oxford, 1963), 484.
[79] NAG, Accra, ADM 11/1342. O'Rourke to Governor, 10 Feb. 1924.
[80] *Ibid.* Milner to Governor of the Gold Coast, 20 Dec. 1920.
[81] *Ibid.* Guggisberg to SOS, 15 Feb. 1921.

In spite of all the pressure and positive signals, had the administrative needs of the colonial administration not been served, then repatriation would not have materialised in 1924. The first such was for a new Native Jurisdiction Ordinance to regulate and guarantee the permanent break-up of the Asante Kingdom into independent states since Prempeh's exile, and to prevent the immediate revival of the Confederacy on his return, while at the same time strengthening the administration of the Kumase Division itself by providing it with a headship. Effective local government in the Kumase Division required that an omanhene be in place there, but Kumase chiefs had declined to appoint to such an office after the deportation of Agyeman Prempeh. The result was the chaotic nature of administration in the most important division in Asante. Repatriating Agyeman Prempeh, and even installing him as Kumasihene, had become a distinct administrative possibility by the early 1920s.

The last and most important move in repatriation was undoubtedly the almost total consensus among the Kumase chiefs and all the amanhene over the question by the beginning of 1924. Up to the end of 1922, all the petitions for Agyeman Prempeh's repatriation had been sent by the Kumase Chiefs and very close Oyoko relatives of Agyeman Prempeh, namely, the amanhene of Kokofu and Nsuta. Worse still the British administration believed that "while many of the signatories (to these petitions) outwardly agree to Prempeh's return and openly 'touch the pen', they are really strongly opposed to his return fearing that they will lose the position and wealth they have acquired under the new regime".[82] It was not until 26 February 1923 that all the Asante amanhene and the Kumase chiefs sent a joint petition asking for Agyeman Prempeh's repatriation.[83] Any doubt about this consensus among the Asante was dispelled by a second petition of 18 December 1923 and a third of 12 January 1924 addressed and signed by all eleven amanhene and 17 other chiefs.[84] It is not surprising therefore that only two months after the receipt of the petition of 12 January 1924, CCA Maxwell informed the Governor of the concurrence of "the political officers without exception" in "recommending that the ex-king and all the other chiefs and their dependents who are now in the Seychelles be repatriated and respectfully ask that I be given at least 6 months notice to prepare for Prempeh's return".[85]

Governor Guggisberg accepted these recommendations and passed them on to the Secretary of State for the Colonies, J. M. Thomas. As Guggisberg put it in his letter of 15 March 1924, when forwarding Maxwell's recommendation:

---

[82] *Ibid*. Fuller to Acting Colonial Secretary, 1 June 1918.
[83] *Ibid*. Petition by some Ashanti Chiefs, 26 Feb. 1923.
[84] NAG, Accra, ADM 12/5/117. Petition by Ashanti Chiefs, 18 Dec. 1923 and 12 Jan. 1924.
[85] *Ibid*. Enclosed in Governor to J. M. Thomas, 15 March 1924.

Up to the present I have not been certain in my own mind if the desire for the return of ex-king Prempeh was universal throughout Ashanti. It appeared to me in my various conferences with the chiefs of Coomassie that the desire was chiefly confined to them and did not extend to the most important chiefs outside Coomassie. I have now, however, received a petition, (of 12 Jan. 1924) a copy of which is enclosed, signed by all the important chiefs in Ashanti. I commend the Petition generally to your notice.[86]

Guggisberg, however, submitted the following condition for approval:

(1) That ex-king Prempeh should be permitted to return to Ashanti after the new Native Jurisdiction has become law. (2) That he should return as a private individual. (3) That he should reside in or in the vicinity of Coomassie and that his movements should be confined to the Coomassie Political District.[87]

With this unanimity in Asante and colonial official opinion in the Gold Coast, it is not surprising that in his telegram of 8 April 1924, the Secretary of State accepted Guggisberg's recommendations and approved "the return of Prempeh and his dependents on conditions proposed".[88] The final conditions for Agyeman Prempeh's repatriation, marked by a bond in the sum of £500 signed by 17 Kumase chiefs on 12 July 1924, were as follows:

(i)   Prempeh remains a private individual holding no official status in Ashanti.
(ii) That he takes no part nor interferes in political matters.
(iii) That he does not call for or accept any of the Ashanti stool properties, insignia or Treasure.
(iv) That he will reside in or near Coomassie.
(v)   That he does not leave his place of residence in or near Coomassie.

In addition, the Kumase chiefs agreed to contribute an amount of £3,000, while all other chiefs who signed the final petition for repatriation were to contribute another £3,000 for Agyeman Prempeh's maintenance on his return and for the building of a house for him.[89]

HOMECOMING

In his telegram of 8 April 1924, the Secretary of State for the Colonies did not only order the release of Agyeman Prempeh and his followers but also advised that an officer of the Gold Coast administration be detailed to escort them back home. This advice was accepted and A. C. Duncan-Johnstone, Deputy

---

[86] *Ibid*. Maxwell to Governor, 11 March 1924; and Governor Guggisberg to J. M. Thomas, 15 March 1924.
[87] *Ibid*. Guggisberg to SOS, 15 March 1924.
[88] *Ibid*. Confidential Telegram from SOS to Governor, 8 April 1924.
[89] NAG, Accra, ADM 12/5/117. CCA to Colonial Secretary, 3 Dec. 1924.

Provincial Commissioner of the Eastern Province of Ashanti, was selected by the Secretary of State in consultation with Guggisberg for this assignment. Duncan-Johnstone was informed that the party would leave the Seychelles on 13 September 1924.[90] The Governor of Seychelles was asked to make the necessary travel arrangements and to ask Agyeman Prempeh to sign an agreement to the conditions for his repatriation. This was done on 27 May 1924, and a departure date was fixed for 13 September. Duncan-Johnstone left the Gold Coast in July 1924 and arrived at Mahé via England and Bombay on 26 August 1924 to take charge of the repatriation.

It had been arranged that the party was to depart on 13 September but the ship arrived thirty hours ahead of time and scheduled an early departure. The Governor of Seychelles managed to get the sailing postponed until 3 p.m. on 13 September, but even this meant a hurried embarkation for the Asante party, their Camp being two miles distant from Port Victoria.[91] On boarding however, Duncan-Johnstone found that the captain knew nothing about the Asante party and so no accommodation had been provided. However this problem was sorted out and at the scheduled time on 13 September, Agyeman Prempeh and his entourage numbering 50 boarded the ship. The party included only one of the ex-chiefs, James Asafo Boakye, then 95 years of age. Nine of Agyeman Prempeh's children (Frederick, Alfred, Joseph, Henry, William, Ruth, Alice, Elizabeth, and Mary) and nine grandchildren were among the party. Of the total number, 33 had been born on the island. Agyeman Prempeh and his entourage arrived at Bombay on 19 September and departed on the 22nd, arriving at Liverpool on 27 October. They left Liverpool on 27 October and docked at Sekondi on 11 November 1924. Agyeman Prempeh was met by Deputy Provincial Commissioner Jones of the Western Province, and Major Gosling, District Commissioner of Kumasi. The Asante party landed at 5 p.m. and at once boarded a special train, which was in readiness on the jetty. At Sekondi Agyeman Prempeh was welcomed by representatives of the ARPS, as well as by a large and excited crowd. Finally, the train arrived in Kumase at 6 a.m. on November 12 and halted at the Agricultural Station, from where Agyeman Prempeh and his party were conveyed by motor car to the Asafohene's new house at Asafo. There vast crowds were assembled to greet him.[92] After 28 years in exile, the Asantehene had returned home.

---

[90] *Ibid.* SOS to Governor, 24 June 1924; and Reade to Duncan-Johnstone, 20 June 1924.
[91] *Ibid.* Duncan-Johnstone's Report.
[92] *Ibid.*

CHAPTER THREE

Agyeman Prempeh's Return from Exile, 1924–1931

Emmanuel Akyeampong

INTRODUCTION

After twenty-eight years of exile (1896–1924), Britain endorsed the repatriation of the former Asantehene Agyeman Prempeh. Two conditions were stipulated: first, that the former king would return in the capacity of a 'private' citizen, and second, that he would reside exclusively within the political district of Kumase. The Asante chiefs and Agyeman Prempeh agreed to these terms, and an overjoyed Asantehene landed at Sekondi on 11 November 1924. In the twenty-eight years of his absence, the Asante had refused to consider their ruler deposed, and had not replaced him. This left a conspicuous gap in the Asante constitution and political administration, as Agyeman Prempeh was both the Asantehene and the paramount chief of Kumase. According to custom, then, Agyeman Prempeh remained the Asantehene, despite the British deposition. On Agyeman Prempeh's return to Asante, three major parties would be involved in renegotiating the nature of 'kingship' in Asante: the British colonial government, the Asante (with their varied interests), and Agyeman Prempeh himself.

The colonial government was concerned with the successful implementation of indirect rule in Asante, and the presence of a paramount chief in Kumase would be conducive to that process.[1] But the government was not prepared to entertain the restoration of the old Asante confederacy with Agyeman Prempeh as king. The Asante generally regarded the ex-king as still

---

[1] Indirect rule was the British colonial policy of ruling through indigenous political structures and authorities. It was systematized by Governor F. Lugard of Northern Nigeria, and introduced in a formal sense to the rest of British West Africa in the late 1920s and 1930s. The British endeavour to introduce native treasuries based on local levies necessitated the consolidation of chiefly authority, and the absence of a paramount chief in Kumase militated against the success of indirect rule in the Asante capital of Kumase. On indirect rule in British West Africa, see the essays in M. Crowder and O. Ikime (eds.), *West African Chiefs: Their Changing Status under Colonial Rule and Independence*, Ile-Ife and New York, 1970; and A. Adu Boahen, *African Perspectives on Colonialism*, Baltimore, 1987, ch. 3.

the Asantehene, but had contending notions of his kingship. Agyeman Prempeh was very conscious of his place in Asante history, and anxious—in the light of the momentous events of his reign—to bequeath kingship in a form recognisable to that which he had inherited.[2] As all parties worked on their agendas, kingship in Asante gained two faces: a public one and a private one. And as all parties realized that their objectives were not necessarily incompatible, the colonial government recognised Agyeman Prempeh as "Kumasihene" in 1926. This restored the office of the Asantehene to its original status in the late seventeenth century before the concentration of political power in Kumase.[3] In 1935, four years after the death of Agyeman Prempeh, the colonial government restored the Asante confederacy and recognised the office of Asantehene, signalling the perfect overlap in the interests of the parties negotiating kingship in colonial Asante. Colonial rule remained, but Asante existed once again in territory and political structure.

OUR KING IS BACK! BUT WHAT KIND OF KING?

That the Agyeman Prempeh who returned to colonial Asante in November 1924 was a transformed person is not in doubt. The ex-king had converted to Christianity while in the Seychelles, even becoming monogamous in his endeavour to receive confirmation and communion in the Anglican Church. Agyeman Prempeh and the Asante exiles in the Seychelles had also received English lessons, and Agyeman Prempeh was capable of keeping up his own written correspondence. Conscious of changing times, he embraced the spirit of innovation, experimenting with new knowledge or technology that would strengthen Asante on the return of the exiles.[4] As early as 1921, the colonial government speculated about the administrative role the transformed Agyeman Prempeh could play in the colonial regime in Asante on his return. The Chief Commissioner of Asante, C. H. Harper, highlighted the obvious

---

[2] Agyeman Prempeh's reign (1888–1931) had witnessed the British annexation of Asante in 1896, the exile of several prominent Asante chiefs, and the desecration of the Golden Stool—the symbol of Asante nationhood—in 1921. For some discussion of the implications of the end of Asante autonomy, see Emmanuel Akyeampong, "Christianity, Modernity, and the Weight of Tradition in the Life of Asantehene Agyeman Prempeh I, c.1888–1931," in *Africa*, 69, 2, 1999: 279–311.

[3] See Ivor Wilks, "Aspects of Bureaucratisation in Ashanti in the Nineteenth Century," in *Journal of African History*, 7,2, 1966: 215–33; and George P. Hagan, "Ashanti Bureaucracy: A Study of the Growth of Centralised Administration in Ashanti from the Time of Osei Tutu to the time of Osei Tutu Kwamina Esibe Bonsu," in *Transactions of the Historical Society of Ghana*, 12, 1971: 43–62.

[4] A. Adu Boahen, "A Nation in Exile: the Asante on the Seychelles Islands, 1900–24," in Enid Schildkrout (ed.,), *The Golden Stool: Studies of the Asante Center and Periphery*, Washington, D. C., 1987: 146–60; Joseph K. Adjaye, "*Asantehene* Agyeman Prempe I, Asante History, and the Historian," in *History in Africa*, 17, 1990: 1–29; and Akyeampong, 1999a.

need for an ɔmanhene (paramount chief) in Kumase. "Prempeh," he wrote, "if he is the unanimous choice of the Coomassie would not be I think objectionable. He is educated, a Christian has seen something of the world and is disciplined."[5]

In a detailed report dated 8 May 1926, R. S. Rattray, a deputy provincial commissioner and a government anthropologist, would strongly recommend the appointment of an ɔmanhene for Kumase for the efficient administration of colonial rule in the Kumase division.[6] Although traditionally the occupant of the Kumase stool was the same as the Asantehene, the colonial government separated the two positions and granted the Kumase division a paramount chief in 1926.

The Asante themselves were divided into two constituencies. One group, led by the Kumase chiefs, perceived Agyeman Prempeh's return as tantamount to the restoration of the old order, albeit within the colonial dispensation. A second group of largely educated Asante viewed the return of the educated and Christian Agyeman Prempeh as ushering in a new order with them in the forefront. For both groups there was no question that Agyeman Prempeh remained the Asantehene. The ɔmanhene of Kumawu, the host of Agyeman Prempeh's first officially sanctioned visit outside Kumase in 1925, was in the first camp. The visit to Kumawuhene Kwame Afram was a disaster and Agyeman Prempeh's liaison officer with the colonial government, A. C. Duncan-Johnstone, later pieced together what transpired:

> When Prempeh arrived at Kumawu he was met at the door of the palace by Kwami Afram, the paramount chief, who conducted Prempeh to the inner courtyard of his house and there, tied to a stake, was the Grunshi slave with the executioner's knives (*sepow*) driven through his cheeks to skewer his tongue down so that he could not swear the 'Great Oath'. Kwami Afram told Prempeh that he proposed to sacrifice the slave at a funeral custom to those of Prempeh's followers who had died in exile. Apparently Prempeh took one look at the victim and fled back to Kumasi. He was then in a predicament for he was actually an accessory before the fact and yet if he informed on Kwami Afram he would set the chiefs against him, so he decided to say nothing.[7]

It was as if the past had caught up with Agyeman Prempeh. Here was a loyal chief, demonstrating sympathy and spiritual solidarity in the Asante fashion. But Agyeman Prempeh saw human sacrifice as one of the reasons for his deportation. His Christian experience may have deepened his ambivalence

---

[5] Rhodes House, Oxford, Mss Brit. Emp. S.344, C. H. Harper papers, Harper to Colonial Secretary (Accra), dd. Kumase, 23 November 1921.
[6] National Archives of Ghana (NAG), Accra, ADM 11/1/1906.
[7] Rhodes House, Oxford, Mss Afr. S.593, A. C. Duncan-Johnstone papers, "Notes on King Prempeh's return to the Gold Coast in 1924."

about this old Asante practice. And the colonial government could deport him for complicity, even if he had no foreknowledge of Kwame Afram's intentions. Agyeman Prempeh was rescued from this quandary when the colonial government dismissed the case against Kwame Afram.

Kingship took on a private face, especially for those who worked behind the scenes to restore the old order. As the official history of Asante compiled in the 1940s states: "Though all the Divisional chiefs had already signed a Bond that Nana [Agyeman Prempeh] should come back as a private man, yet all his subjects recognised him as their king."[8] The force of tradition was an important instrument. Even before the colonial government recognised Agyeman Prempeh as "Kumasihene" at the end of 1926, his loyal sub-chiefs activated his traditional perquisites. Chief Kwabena Kokofu of the Gyaase division (royal household) reminded the people of Derma of their past obligation as hunters for the Asantehene. He requested that they resume their duty of providing the repatriated Agyeman Prempeh with game meat. The ɔmanhene of Berekum, elevated to that rank by the colonial government, objected to Derma hunters killing two buffaloes on his land. He accused Kwabena Kokofu of trespassing and fined him £50, but quickly dropped the charges when Kwabena Kokofu peremptorily reminded him "that he perfectly knows that his ancestors are hunters to Asantehene from ancient time . . ."[9]

Educated Asante and enterprising traders interested in social change sometimes found out that their vision of the new Asante clashed with Agyeman Prempeh's agenda. One of Agyeman Prempeh's acts, when recognised as Kumasihene, was to abolish the Kumasi Gentlemen's Club, a group of wealthy commoner-traders who had usurped the sumptuary privileges of chiefs in their lifestyle.[10] Some educated members of the Asante Kotoko Society, a group that had worked tirelessly for Agyeman Prempeh's repatriation, were disappointed that the educated and Christian Agyeman Prempeh seemed more interested in restoring the old Asante. In 1926 the acting Chief Commissioner, Ashanti, F. W. F. Jackson, shared his thoughts on this faction:

> The chief point is that J. O. Agyeman and his followers originally thought that the return of Prempeh, as an enlightened man, would mean the creation of a semi-independent Ashanti kingdom, with the power of the chiefs considerably lessened,

---

[8] Nana Osei Agyeman Prempeh II, "The History of Ashanti," Kumase, n.d.: 430–1. This work was compiled in the 1940s by a committee working under the chairmanship of the Asantehene.

[9] NAG, Kumase, ARG 6/2/5: Headchief Kwabena Kokofu (Kumase) to the District Commissioner, Kumase, February 1926.

[10] James Wilson Brown, "Kumasi, 1896–1923: urban Africa during the early colonial period," Ph.D. Dissertation, University of Wisconsin at Madison, 1972: 198. On these rich traders (akonkɔfo), see Kwame Arhin, "A note on the Asante Akonkofo: a non-literate sub-elite, 1900–30," in *Africa*, 56:1, 1986: 25–31.

and many lucrative offices to be held by himself and the members of the Kotoko Society.[11]

Some educated Asante found galling certain acts by Agyeman Prempeh, such as the restoration of the Asantehene's harem. Agyeman Prempeh became polygamous and ceased to be a communicant of the Anglican Church in Kumase. But what was Agyeman Prempeh's agenda on his repatriation to Asante? A. Adu Boahen informs us that it is clear from oral and documentary sources that Agyeman Prempeh set himself four goals on his return. These were, he writes,

> "the revival, unity and peace of the Asante nation; the economic and social development of Kumase in particular and Asante in general; the encouragement of education; and the promotion of Christianity.[12]

Historical events in Asante are remembered by the reigns of Asantehenes. It weighed heavily on Agyeman Prempeh that his reign had witnessed such disruption to the state he had inherited—among others, foreign annexation, the exile of several royals, and the desecration of the Golden Stool. A prediction by Okomfo Anokye, the spiritual architect of the Asante nation, that the state would collapse if a fair-skinned person was installed Asantehene, disturbed the light-skinned Agyeman Prempeh. He yearned to bequeath to his successor an Asante recognisable to the one he had inherited. At the same time he was very aware of changing times, having, while in exile, confronted and embraced 'modernity.' He knew Asante could not remain wedded to the past, and that innovation was crucial to a strong and prosperous Asante in the future. Agyeman Prempeh effectively guided Asante through a critical period in its history, earning the description of Asante's last traditional king and its first modern one.[13] Let us turn our attention to the colonial regime for the context of Agyeman Prempeh's last years in Asante, 1924–31.

BRITISH COLONIAL RULE IN ASANTE

Though British colonial rule in Asante was only formalized from 1901, the annexation of Asante was effective from 1896 with the deportation of Asantehene Agyeman Prempeh, for this left a glaring gap in the Asante political system as William Tordoff underscores:

---

[11] NAG, Accra, ADM 11/1906, "Ex-King Prempeh, 1926–7", Acting CCA Jackson to Acting Governor, 1 September 1926.
[12] Boahen, 1987: 153–54.
[13] Akyeampong, 1999b: 308.

He was the centre of the Ashanti constitutional circle and therefore the one man who could reforge the links in the chain which had held together Kumasi and the other member-states of the Ashanti confederacy until it was broken by the British in 1896.[14]

Early British colonial policy in Asante was one of balkanization, and the links between the six important nuclear states of the Asante confederacy—Kumase, Bekwae, Dwaben, Mampon, Kokofu, and Nsuta—were broken. Each was viewed as a separate native state headed by its *ɔmanhene*. With the exile of Agyeman Prempeh, Kumase had lost not only the Asantehene, but also its *ɔmanhene*. A council of chiefs comprised of those loyal to Britain was constituted in 1905, to advise the Chief Commissioner, Ashanti, on Kumase affairs.[15] The colonial government discouraged these Kumase chiefs from extending their influence outside the Kumase Division, and their claims over land and subjects outside Kumase and its environs were dissolved. The colonial government raised new *amanhene* to fill the gaps in the Asante political system. The result was the disintegration of the Asante confederacy, which lacked an effective head, and chaos in the affairs of the Kumase Division.

Colonial knowledge of Asante increased substantially in the 1920s through the ethnographic studies of the anthropologist and political official, R. S. Rattray.[16] With this knowledge came a strong awareness of the superficiality of the colonial political structure created in the Kumase Division. With the formal implementation of indirect rule in the 1920s, it became apparent to the colonial government that Kumase needed its traditional political head if indirect rule was to work in the most important political division in Asante. In 1926, Rattray, then also a deputy Provincial Commissioner in Asante, wrote a special report to the Chief Commissioner, Ashanti, in which he strongly recommended the enstoolment of an *ɔmanhene* in Kumase to redress the chaos in its administration.[17] Indirect rule with its concomitant features of tribunals, stool treasuries, and direct taxation, would only work in Kumase with the presence of a recognised *ɔmanhene*.[18]

It is at this juncture that the administrative objectives of the British converged with the fervent desire of several Kumase chiefs to see Agyeman Prempeh appointed to a position of "Kumasihene" and also restored to the office of Asantehene. With the explicit British commitment to prevent a revival of Asante power, the Kumase chiefs astutely concluded that the reinstatement

---

[14] William Tordoff, *Ashanti under the Prempehs 1888–1935*, Oxford, 1965: vii.
[15] Francis Fuller, *A Vanished Dynasty: Ashanti*, London, 1921: 216.
[16] R. S. Rattray, *Ashanti*, Oxford, 1923; *Religion and Art in Ashanti*, Oxford, 1927; and *Ashanti Law and Constitution*, Oxford, 1929.
[17] National Archives of Ghana (NAG), Accra, ADM 11/1906, "Reports on King Prempeh's Life in Kumasi," Rattray to CCA, 8 May 1926.
[18] Tordoff, 1965: 214.

of Agyeman Prempeh as Asantehene was improbable in the short term. So they decided to explore the possibility of the colonial government recognizing Agyeman Prempeh as Kumasihene with the inner consolation that, customarily a Kumasihene would also de facto be the Asantehene. In March 1926, the Kumase chiefs petitioned the colonial government that Agyeman Prempeh be appointed Kumasihene, and the government acceded in October 1926. Though Rattray anticipated potential difficulties in the particular nomination of Agyeman Prempeh, as he had held both positions of Kumasihene and Asantehene and it would be natural for his subjects to associate both offices with his person, he also observed that the colonial government by its special treatment of Agyeman Prempeh since his repatriation in 1924 had cultivated Asante hopes that he would be reinstated.[19] Agyeman Prempeh also had strong points in his favor: his literacy, his dignified composure, his influence over the chiefs and people, and his significant contributions as a member of the newly formed Kumasi Public Health Board.[20] With his recognition as Kumasihene, Agyeman Prempeh now overtly embarked on his agenda of restoring Asante's past greatness through the fusion of the old and the new.

RENEGOTIATING 'KINGSHIP' IN COLONIAL ASANTE: AGYEMAN PREMPEH, 1924–31

The colonial context constrained Agyeman Prempeh's endeavour to restore Asante's past greatness, as this conflicted with the expressed position of the colonial government. Symbolism gained great centrality in Agyeman Prempeh's manoeuvres as he strove to revive past symbols of Asante sovereignty. Thus kingship continued to have both a private and a public face as the Asante and colonial definitions of it differed. Agyeman Prempeh drew satisfaction from the perception that the British would not understand the cultural significance of these symbols, and hence his actions would not draw the colonial government's ire. But his chiefs and people would understand the cultural discourse, and draw inspiration and strength from the gradual resuscitation of Asante sovereign power. The rehabilitation of the Golden Stool, restoring the royal harem, rebuilding the royal mausoleum, and seeking the return of the *Aya Kɛsee* (the well-known Bantama Brass Pan) were central to Agyeman Prempeh's manipulation of the symbols of Asante sovereignty.

---

[19] NAG, Accra, ADM 11/1906.
[20] Tordoff, 1965: 215.

Rehabilitating the Golden Stool

On Agyeman Prempeh's arrival in Asante in 1924, the custodians of the Golden Stool handed this venerated object to him in spite of his official status as a "private citizen." Some *amanhene* privately took the oath of allegiance to Agyeman Prempeh in acknowledgment of the fact that the possessor of the Golden Stool was the Asantehene.[21] Agyeman Prempeh quietly began its rehabilitation, replacing the attached ornaments that had been pilfered in the desecration of the stool in 1921. But the stool had to be displayed to assure Asante that all was well again with the nation. During the 1921 upheaval over the stool's desecration, the British finally renounced any intentions of acquiring the stool, an objective that had partly sparked the Yaa Asantewaa war of 1900. Agyeman Prempeh knew the stool could not be hidden indefinitely, and desirous to be recognised as Asantehene before his death, he took the gamble of confiding to his liaison officer in the colonial government, A. C. Duncan-Johnstone, that he had custody and had rehabilitated the stool.

Shortly after being made Kumasihene, Agyeman Prempeh displayed the Golden Stool to Duncan-Johnstone in a context that captured the Asantehene's agenda of blending the traditional with the modern in a new Asante. The colonial government had assisted Agyeman Prempeh in building a large house in Manhyia, which he occupied in 1926. One night, well after midnight, Duncan-Johnstone received a message from Agyeman Prempeh inviting him to the palace at Manhyia. He drove over, and they spent a couple of hours drinking what Duncan-Johnstone described as "indifferent whiskey until after two o'clock in the morning."[22] Then Agyeman Prempeh led Duncan-Johnstone a few hundred yards from the residence built for him by the government, to a new palace he had built in the old Asante style. At a small postern gate, their path was barred by the Sanaahene (chief of the treasury), who was obviously displeased at Duncan-Johnstone's presence in the inner sanctum of the palace and whatever Agyeman Prempeh intended to show him at that late hour. The drama and the images in this confrontation deserve quotation.

> However Prempeh standing there in his blue blazer with the crest of the Golden Stool on the pocket and a pair of old grey flannel trousers suddenly lost his patience and barked out a command whereupon two executioners, with their half shaven heads and bandoliers of knives, appeared silently from behind us, and threw the Sanahene face downwards to the ground. Prempeh then stepped on his head and went on through the gate into the courtyard and across it to a small stone building with a red tin roof, rather like a powder magazine.[23]

---

[21] *Ibid.*, 205–6.
[22] Rhodes House, Oxford, Mss. Afr. S.593, A. C. Duncan-Johnstone papers, "Notes on King Prempeh's Return to the Gold Coast in 1924.".
[23] *Ibid.*

This was royal majesty displayed in very Asante terms by a king, dressed in the comfortable attire of the English elite, who had built a traditional palace with modern conveniences such as electricity. The Sanaahene grudgingly unlocked the door, turned on the electric light, and there on the table lay a bulky object covered in an Asante cloth. It was the Golden Stool. Agyeman Prempeh asked Duncan-Johnstone to inform the colonial government that he possessed the stool and had the support of the Asante chiefs. Would the government recognize him as Asantehene?

By 1929, two years before his death, Agyeman Prempeh had probably concluded that his most fervent wishes, to have the Asante Confederacy and the office of Asantehene restored, would not occur in his lifetime. At a thanksgiving service at the Anglican Church of St. Cyprian's in 1929, Agyeman Prempeh took the Golden Stool to the church to celebrate God's goodness in repatriating him from exile. Since the colonial government had not acted to deprive him of the Golden Stool after his disclosure to Duncan-Johnstone, Agyeman Prempeh was fairly confident that he could exhibit it. By choosing the context of a thanksgiving service in the Anglican Church, the established church of the British monarchy and the colonial government, he rid his action of any potential allegation of subversion. It was an event reminiscent of the old Odwira festival, which celebrated state and kingship in Asante.[24]

Restoring the Royal Harem

Restoring the royal harem was a more controversial endeavour that alienated even some Asante and the Anglican Church. On his return from exile, Agyeman Prempeh once again became polygamous, raising interesting questions as to the sincerity of his Christian commitment.[25] Agyeman Prempeh had reportedly restored the harem in late 1926, and Martha Appiah, one of the Seychelloise returnees, had been made head wife. The educated Asante Kotoko Society expressed concern about the "revival of many of the old pagan customs." Agyeman Prempeh also revived the title of Hiahene, the officer in charge of royal wives. The colonial government decided that the harem was Agyeman Prempeh's private affair and chose not to intervene.[26]

Abrogating the harem was impossible for Agyeman Prempeh, considering his desire to repair tradition and bequeath to his successor an Asante state quite similar to the one he had inherited. Asante kings had specific families in their areas of political jurisdiction that provided the king with stool wives (*ayetɛ*) from generation to generation. These are important political families, and

---

[24] See T. C. McCaskie, *State and Society in Precolonial Asante*, Cambridge, 1995: 144–242.
[25] See Akyeampong, 1999b.
[26] NAG, Accra, ADM 11/1906. "Monthly Report on Edward Prempeh for August 1926."

Asante administration is based on alliances serviced by marriage exchanges. To abolish the harem would have meant tearing down the Asante administrative structure, as Agyeman Prempeh knew it. Thomas Boatin, an Asante elder born in the Seychelles, explained the centrality of *ayetɛ*:

> Asantehenes marry from specific families in the realm. This arrangement exists for good reason. These are the social alliances that underpin the state. To abrogate it would be to reject your national duty and obligations. If you leave these wives, their families would withdraw. Practices like *ayetɛ* forged an elaborate social network with *mma mma dwa* [patrilineal service stools] to constitute a sort of administrative machinery. These families provided certain services to the Golden Stool.[27]

Tradition and the determination to leave a "good name" (*din pa*) tied Agyeman Prempeh's hands and constrained his ability to innovate. He built a "modern" house to contain a traditional institution like the harem.

The Royal Mausoleum and the Aya Kɛseɛ

Less controversial than the matter of the harem was Agyeman Prempeh's determination to rebuild the royal mausoleum at Bantama. In this endeavour he even had the colonial government's support and assistance. Having secured a new palace, it was necessary that Agyeman Prempeh rebuild the royal mausoleum at Bantama that had been destroyed by British troops in 1896. This was the final place of rest for all Asantehenes, and the mausoleum was divided into various compartments housing the skeleton of each Asantehene, his blackened stool, and his favourite personal possessions. After Agyeman Prempeh was installed as Kumasihene, he started the construction of the new mausoleum at Bantama, but this was incomplete without the large brass pan (*Aya Kɛseɛ*) that stood outside it. The brass pan had been removed from Bantama during the British expedition of 1896,[28] and in the 1920s was housed at the Royal United Service Museum in Whitehall.[29] As the mausoleum neared completion, Agyeman Prempeh approached the colonial government for the return of the *Aya Kɛseɛ*.

The colonial government desired to know the significance of the brass pan, aware that in 1817 T. E. Bowdich, the first British emissary to Asante, had associated it with human sacrifice.[30] This led Agyeman Prempeh to produce a document in which he set the mythical account of the origins of the *Aya Kɛseɛ*. The text is reproduced in Chapter Nine below. The pan supposedly descended from

---

[27] Interview with Thomas Boatin, 28 August 1997.
[28] Prempeh II, "History of Ashanti," n.d.: 400.
[29] NAG, Accra, ADM 11/1/1370. Chief Commissioner, Ashanti, to Colonial Secretary, Kumase, 14 November 1930.
[30] T. E. Bowdich, *Mission from Cape Coast Castle to Ashantee*, London, 1819: 279.

heaven on a gold chain during a thunderstorm and alighted first at Akim-Asiakwa by mistake and then reappeared at Asumennya-Asantemanso, the site claimed in oral traditions for the beginnings of Asante. On the same gold chain came Ankyewa Nyame, ancestress of the royal Oyoko family. The brass pan accompanied the Oyoko family in its sojourns and ended up in Kumase with the purchase of Kwaman, later to be renamed Kumase. Asantehene Osei Tutu (died 1717) directed that the brass pan be placed at Bantama. This document was dated August 1930, but apparently did not explain to the satisfaction of the colonial government why Agyeman Prempeh so earnestly desired its return. In a letter of October 1930, Agyeman Prempeh declared that the brass pan "was not used for anything in particular—but it is a very important thing for Ashanti—and all the souls of the Ashanti are within it."[31]

Interviews conducted by this author in Kumase elicited a different account of the origins of the Bantama brass pan. The clans that federated to form Asante at the turn of the eighteenth century were under the suzerainty of Denkyira. Kumase's expansionism began under Osei Tutu's predecessor, Obiri Yeboa, and the latter was killed in his campaigns against the Domaa of Suntreso. Osei Tutu completed the rout of Domaa, and the Denkyirahene sent a delegation with a large brass pan to claim his share of Osei Tutu's spoils taken from the defeated Domaa Kusi. But Osei Tutu and Okomfo Anokye were by then planning the overthrow of Denkyira rule. The brass ban was retained in Kumase, and Denkyira was eventually defeated at the battle of Feyiase in 1701. Okomfo Anokye placed the pan at Bantama, or to be more precise at Sibrikete, the crossroads at Bantama.[32]

It is intriguing that Agyeman Prempeh's "The History of Ashanti Kings and the Whole Country Itself," dictated in the Seychelles, contains both accounts. According to this work, which we refer to as *HAK*, the gold chain that appeared at Akim-Asiakwa bore "an immense copper dish ornamented by statues of beasts," which is clearly the Bantama brass pan referred to by Bowdich and removed to Britain in 1896.[33] But the first explicit reference to the *Aya Kɛseɛ* in *HAK* is in the context of the war against Domaa and not in the "creation" of Asante at Asantemanso.[34] A huge copper dish sent by the king of Denkyira, Ntim Gyakari, to be filled by gold dust by the chiefs of Asante, is also mentioned in *HAK* as a prelude to the revolt against Denkyira.[35] That the *Aya Kɛseɛ* was taken from Denkyira emissaries rather than descended on a golden chain whether in Akim-Asiakwa or Asumennya-Asantemanso seems

---

[31] NAG, Kumase, Agyeman Prempeh to Provincial Commissioner, Kumasi, 16 October 1930.
[32] Interview with Okyeame Owusu Banahene, spokesperson to the Asantehene, Kumase, 17 August 1997.
[33] See Chapter Five below.
[34] *HAK*, 61, see Chapter Five below.
[35] *HAK*, 66–68, see Chapter Five below.

altogether more likely. Precisely because the *Aya Kɛseɛ* was taken from Asante's overlord, Denkyira, it became entwined with notions of Asante freedom and independence. It became an important symbol of Asante sovereignty, and royal funeral dirges described the Asantehene as hailing from Bantama *Aya Kɛseɛ*. Indeed, the brass pan symbolized the founding of the state and kingship in Asante.[36] Agyeman Prempeh could not reveal this to the colonial government. Hence his written account, "History of the Bantama Brass Pan," skipped any mention of Denkyira and the military union that established Asante. But even his partial account contained two important truths, first that the brass pan was connected to the founding of Asante, and second, that it was placed at Bantama under the direction—or during the reign—of Osei Tutu.

The Chief Commissioner, Ashanti, formally opened the new mausoleum at Bantama on 30 March 1931. This must have been a very fulfilling event for Agyeman Prempeh. The skeletons of the various Asantehenes and their personal possessions were removed from Bantama before the invasion of British troops in 1896. With the new mausoleum completed, the royal skeletons could have been returned to their proper place of rest, a matter fully documented in Chapter Nine. Agyeman Prempeh himself would join these royal ancestors in his rebuilt mausoleum. Even though he had been seriously ill since November 1930, he certainly must have been satisfied as he took stock of his reign. Kumase had been transformed into a bustling, cosmopolitan, commercial centre with a modern imprint. The Golden Stool had been rehabilitated and displayed in a style reminiscent of the old days of Asante power and glory. The royal harem recaptured the ethos of the old palace of the Asantehene, and reasserted the importance of women to the definition of royal power. Even the *nsumanfieso*, the royal college of physicians, in charge of the spiritual and physical wellbeing of the Asantehene and the Asante nation itself, had been resurrected.[37] In March 1931 the Asantehene celebrated the "Great Funeral Custom" for all Asante royals who had died both in Asante and the Seychelles during his period of exile. He thus honoured the memory of those who had suffered exile or deprivation on his behalf. Agyeman Prempeh passed away on 12 May 1931, and was buried with full rites as befitted one whose position as Asantehene had been acknowledged by all Asante during his lifetime.[38] In 1935, the colonial government finally restored the Asante Confederacy, and Agyeman Prempeh's successor, Osei Agyeman Prempeh II, was formally recognised as Asantehene.

---

[36] Interview with Albert Mawere Poku, Accra, 21 August 1997.
[37] Rhodes House, Mss. Afr. S.593, Duncan-Johnstone papers, "Edward Prempeh's Affairs: Report by A.C. Duncan-Johnstone in August 1926.".
[38] Tordoff, 1965: 284.

CONCLUSION

By the time of the demise of Agyeman Prempeh in 1931, some consonance had been established between the competing definitions of kingship in Asante. In spite of Asante feelings of nationhood, British colonialism had become an accepted fact. Agyeman Prempeh, in his exile at Elmina, Sierra Leone and the Seychelles between 1896 and 1924, became strongly aware of a changing world and of the need for Asante to change with it. In the Seychelles, and in his letters to his family in Kumase during the exile, he continuously emphasized the value of western education and the need to learn from western technology. Exposure brought new knowledge, and this knowledge could strengthen Asante in the future. This spirit of innovation shaped kingship in Asante and strengthened it through its adaptability to change. The Asantehene could be a Christian and also remain loyal to his traditions. He was comfortable in cloth or in a suit, at a garden tea party or at a durbar of chiefs and people. Various constituencies in Asante related to different facets of the new kingship. Agyeman Prempeh's adaptability even disarmed the colonial government. He could thus rightly be described as the last 'traditional' king of Asante and its first 'modern' one.

CHAPTER FOUR

Agyeman Prempeh as Author: Textual History

Ivor Wilks

LITERACY IN ASANTE BEFORE THE EXILE

T. E. Bowdich, who was in Kumase in 1817, remarked on "the anxiety of the Ashantee government for daily records, immediately on the establishment of the Moors, who were only visitors until the present reign . . .." Noting that the archives at the English and Danish headquarters on the Gold Coast extended back no more than fifty years, Bowdich added that, in consequence, chronology has to be founded "on that of the Moors."[1] The implication is that the Kumase Muslims ("Moors") had involved themselves in historical inquiries. Joseph Dupuis, who visited the capital in 1820, in fact puts this beyond doubt. Able to read Arabic, he made numerous references to what he described as "the Moslem records" that included a history of the Asante kings from the reign of Osei Tutu to that of the contemporary Osei Tutu Kwame (known also as Osei Bonsu).[2] Indeed, it is most likely that the latter commissioned these for, as Bowdich made quite clear, unauthorised reports about earlier kings were severely discouraged.[3] It has been argued that the writer of the Asante annals was in fact one of Osei Tutu Kwame's close advisers. This was Muhammad Kamaghatay, commonly known as Kramo Togma, whose father, al-Mustafa, and grandfather, 'Umar Kunandi, had been imams of Gonja. Moreover, the last—'Umar Kunandi—is known to have been a contributor to the 1764 redaction of the *Kitab Ghanja*, a work that chronicled the reigns of the rulers of Gonja.[4] Much to the point, at least one section of the *Kitab Ghanja* was present in Osei Tutu Kwame's archive in the early nineteenth century.[5]

---

[1] T. E. Bowdich, *Mission from Cape Coast Castle to Ashantee*, London, 1819: 232.
[2] J. Dupuis, *Journal of a Residence in Ashantee*, London, 1824: 224–250.
[3] Bowdich, 1819: 228.
[4] I. Wilks, *Asante in the nineteenth century*, Cambridge, 1975: 344–52. I. Wilks, N. Levtzion and B. Haight, *Chronicles from Gonja*, Cambridge, 1986: 20–21, 66–71, 204–05.
[5] Wilks, Levtzion and Haight, 1986: 52–53.

It may be assumed that Kramo Togma brought a copy of the *Kitab Ghanja*, or part of it, to the attention of Osei Tutu Kwame, and that the Asantehene expressed a desire to have the deeds of his forebears set down—albeit retrospectively—in a similar form. The innovation was to have committed to writing that which had previously been transmitted only orally by the official custodians of the past, and perhaps most importantly through the *apaee* poems of the *abrafo* or executioners, of Adum, and the *kwadwom* songs of the *kwadwomfo*, or minstrels, of Pankrono.[6] I cite extracts culled by Dupuis from "the Moslem Records," and translated by him in his "Historical Memoirs." These describe the reign of Osei Tutu, who was "dignified by his subjects with the epithet of Great":

> This monarch it was, who first raised Coomassy from an inconsiderable town to the rank it now enjoys as the metropolis of the empire.... He ravaged Assin with fire and sword.... He entirely subdued Quahou, and induced the government of Akim to a limited obedience. He subdued, besides Dinkira and Tofal, a great extent of country beyond the Tano river. He invaded Gaman...."[7]

Despite the translations of the passage from Twi through Arabic into English, something of the style of the original may still be recognisable. Comparison might be made with, for example, extracts from the *apaee*:

> Behold the Great One! / Who dares go to provoke him? / Whoever provokes Osei Tutu / invites war. / He is the creator of a new nation . . . /Behold the Great One! / The Great Invader! / The Great Invader! / Osei Tutu, you sacked Denkyira / and besieged Wasa . . . .[8]

Kramo Togma (if indeed he was compiler of the annals) attempted to work out for the first time an absolute chronology for the reigns of the Asantehenes. The results were inaccurate but by no means bizarre. Dupuis converted the Muslim dates to Christian ones, and the chronology was adopted, and sometimes slightly modified, by a succession of writers over the next century and a half and more.[9] It is, indeed, the chronology that Nana Agyeman Prempeh incorporated into *The History of Ashanti Kings and the whole country itself*.

---

[6] J. H. K. Nketia, *Apaee (poems recited by the Abrafo of the Asantehene on state occasions)*, Institute of African Studies, University of Ghana, 1966. Kwame Arhin, "The Asante Praise Poems," in *Paideuma*, 32, 1986: 163–197. The earliest of such recitals from Asante to be systematically recorded—by phonogram—was that of a Mampon drummer. The recital named, and praised, former Mamponhenes; see R. S. Rattray, *Ashanti,* Oxford, 1923: 242–86.

[7] Dupuis, 1824: 229–30.

[8] Translation from Arhin, 1986: 184, 192.

[9] For the first attempt to rectify the situation, see M. Priestley and I. Wilks, "The Ashanti Kings in the eighteenth century: a revised chronology," *Journal of African History*, I, I, 1960: 83–96. The essay is marred by the interesting though flawed suggestion that an Asantehene had been dropped from the lists; see A. Adu Boahen, "When did Osei Tutu die?", *Transactions of the Historical Society of Ghana*, 16, 1, 1975: 87–92.

Osei Tutu Kwame's early nineteenth century annals have long been lost, but when and in what circumstances is not known. They are not among the large number of manuscripts in Arabic, and of Kumase provenance, which came into the hands of the Danes after the battle of Katamanso in 1826.[10] Literacy, however, continued to be a major concern in the court throughout the century. It was extensively used in the correspondence of the Asantehenes. Among the earliest surviving items are several letters in Arabic exchanged between Osei Tutu Kwame's court and the northern province of Gonja.[11] Thereafter every opportunity was taken to use the services of visitors to Kumase, envoys, consuls, missionaries, captives—and as the century wore on, of literate Asante—to conduct the court's correspondence. Numerous such letters survive in the archives of Europe, written in Danish, Dutch and, most commonly, English.[12]

The Asante exiles deported by the British to Sierra Leone and thence the Seychelles were, then, familiar with literacy since the written word had been used in court and government in metropolitan Asante for about a century. If there is anything to suggest that it had once been regarded as in some sense "magical," by the time of the exile it had long been recognised for just what it was: an extremely useful technology.[13]

LITERACY AND THE EXILES

Agyeman Prempeh enjoyed an amount of leisure in the Seychelles that he had never known as ruler of the complex polity that was the Asanteman. It is not particularly surprising, then, that he almost immediately involved himself in learning to speak, read, and write English. His tutor was Timothy E. Korsah, a Fante who had spent some five years in Britain and was officially employed as Interpreter to the exiles. In 1904 Korsah decided to return home. In July he reported to the Colonial Secretary, Accra, that "Ex King Prempeh now read and write fair well, and sign his own voucher of payment," adding that some of

---

[10] Wilks, Levtzion and Haight, 1986: 52. D. Owusu-Ansah, *Islamic Talismanic tradition in Nineteenth-century Asante*, Lewiston MD, 1991: 18–22. Attention may be drawn to the document entitled *'Asma' muluk Asanti*, "Names of the Kings of Asante," which lists the rulers from Osei Tutu to Osei Agyeman Prempeh, and mentions their wars. The list is said to have been preserved by the *shuyukh al-hafazin* ("custodians of the past"); see B. G. Martin, "Arabic materials for Ghanaian history," *Research Review*, Institute of African Studies, University of Ghana, II, 1, 1965: 74–83.
[11] Wilks, Levtzion and Haight, 1986: 217–21.
[12] See Joseph K. Adjaye, *Diplomacy and Diplomats in Nineteenth Century Asante*, Lanham, 1984: 152–218.
[13] On this matter, see T. C. McCaskie, "Innovational Eclecticism: the Asante Empire and Europe in the Nineteenth Century," in *Comparative Studies in Society and History*, 14, 1, 1972: 30–45.

the chiefs were able to do likewise. Six weeks later Korsah wrote to the Gold Coast Secretary for Native Affairs, expressing his pleasure that he had been able to teach "Ex King Prempeh and his people in English Lessons etc, which now, they can do without Interpreter." In an attached *nota bene* he added that "Ex King Prempeh, was not only taught to talk and read English. But he also learn to be christian . . ."[14] Such was Agyeman Prempeh's progress that in August 1907 he made a request to the Seychelles Administrator, that "a person should be appointed to teach him to read and write in his own language." His petition was sent to the Governor of the Gold Coast, who would be responsible for paying a tutor. It was turned down on the grounds that the former king "can always communicate with his friends in Ashanti in the English language."[15] We may feel reasonably sure that neither the Administrator in Seychelles nor the Governor in Accra had any idea of the reason why Agyeman Prempeh—or Edward Prempeh as he was becoming known—wished to be able to write in Twi.

In the first decade of the exile in the Seychelles, Edward Prempeh had been given singularly little grounds for hoping that he would one day be repatriated. The Asante monarchy had been systematically dismantled, and he did not think that the Asanteman could, at least in its historic form, survive the catastrophe. Remembrance of things past would become irrelevant in an Imperial present. In these circumstances it seems that his mother, Yaa Kyaa, was instrumental in goading him into action, for she is said to have been fearful that as her "family" died in the Seychelles, "all their names would be lost."[16] In such a context of gloom, Edward Prempeh conceived a mission for himself and his compatriots in exile: specifically, to make use of the written word to record for posterity something of the ways of Asante before its loss of independence. He engaged himself in collecting various kinds of information from a number of the exiles, and by 1907 was beginning the synoptic work that was to be named, *The History of Ashanti Kings and the whole country itself*—henceforth *HAK*.

The problem that confronted Edward Prempeh was not so much that of a lack of information, but rather that most of those on whom he relied for information spoke no English. To record their testimony, therefore, involved two quite distinct but challenging operations, the one of translation from Twi and the other of writing in English. The wonder is, that Edward Prempeh was

---

[14] National Archives of Ghana, Accra, ADM.11/1499, Korsah to Col. Sec., Accra, 4 July 1904; Korsah to Governor, 10 August 1904; Korsah to Secretary of State for Native Affairs, 18 August, 1904.

[15] Seychelles National Archives, C/SS/2, Vol. II, Governor, Gold Coast, to Administrator, Seychelles, 9 December 1907.

[16] Conversations, March-April 1983, T. C. McCaskie and I. K. Agyeman (who drew upon the recollections of the aged Yaw Mensa, a grandson of Asantehene Mensa Bonsu).

able to arrange this. That he was depended in no small measure upon the capabilities of his son, Frederick A. Prempeh.

Frederick A. Prempeh was born in Asante in 1894.[17] In 1896 mother and child joined Agyeman Prempeh in captivity in Elmina, and thereafter accompanied him into exile first to Sierra Leone in 1897, and then to Mahé, largest of the Seychelles Islands, in 1900. Frederick was immediately sent to Victoria School. "E. Prempeh" attended the prize distribution there at Christmas, 1900, and doubtless felt very much the proud parent when Frederick, who had at that time only been learning English for five weeks, "very creditably" recited a short piece of English poetry.[18] Two months later the Administrator could make reference to, "Prempeh's son and heir, a smart little boy, of whose progress at the Victoria School I have received good accounts from the Head Master."[19] It was, then, to Frederick Prempeh that his father turned in 1907. The title page of *HAK* has the notation, "Written by me F. A. Prempeh and was dictated by E. Prempeh. Commence on 6th August 1907."

Frederick's handwriting was by no means illegible, and, being written on paper with ruled lines, was far superior to his spindly and wandering penmanship of 1906.[20] The thirteen-year-old took his Preliminary Cambridge Certificate in December 1907, and entered the Junior Cambridge class. It comes as something of a surprise, therefore, to find that in March 1908 G. Mackay, Headmaster of Victoria School, put in an adverse report to Seychelles Governor W. E. Davidson. His comments on Frederick Prempeh included the following: "incorrigibly lazy," "shows no desire to improve," "not of clean habits," "homework consistently bad," "playing truant, bringing fictitious notes explanatory of absence," and "lying." Though not intended as such, the nearest approach to praise was the comment that "caning seems to affect him little." Mackay's recommendation was, that "any attempt to educate the boy beyond the stage he has reached, of being able to read and write English, is useless . . ."[21] It is difficult to believe that Mackay's hopeless student, and Edward Prempeh's persevering amanuensis, are one and the same person. We may perhaps allow ourselves to wonder whether anything written by G. Mackay is being pored over by scholars, a century later!

The material compiled in *HAK* falls into three categories, broadly identifiable as history, ethnography, and genealogy. The material in the history section

---

[17] Seychelles National Archives, C/SS/2, Vol. IV, "List of Ashanti Political Prisoners and Followers," n.d. but 1924. This gives Frederick Prempeh's age in that year as 30.

[18] Seychelles National Archives, C/SS/2, Vol. I, Despatch to Secretary of State, 31 December 1900.

[19] Seychelles National Archives, C/SS,2, Vol. I, Despatch to Secretary of State, 16 February 1901. It is rather odd that the Administrator still apparently did not understand that Asante succession was matrilineal.

[20] Seychelles National Archives, C/SS/2, Vol. II, E. Prempeh to Inspector of Police, 9 October 1906.

[21] Seychelles National Archives, C/SS/2, Vol. II, Mackay to Governor, 5 March 1908.

(Chapter Five) is in part mythic, presenting ancient stories that provide the genealogies (Chapter Seven) with a setting for the appearance of the apical royal ancestress, Ankyewa Nyame.[22] By far the larger part takes, however, the more tangible form of chronicle, the deeds of the early rulers being recounted reign by reign. The second category, that of the ethnographic material (Chapter Six), comprises several items interpolated, and usually rather clumsily so, into the basic text of *HAK*. The topics chosen cover a broad range of matters, from a relatively mundane listing of the days of the week to a highly esoteric description of the mortuary customs for Asantehenes. The third category, that of genealogy (Chapter Seven), must be accounted in many respects the most impressive section of *HAK*. The material is presented in eighteen pages, virtually without intercalation, and the many branches of the royal family are dealt with in a technically adroit manner.

There were other fields of inquiry the results of which found no place in *HAK*. Asante medical knowledge—for the most part herbal, one assumes—was recorded in a book that seems never to have been brought back to Asante. It is well remembered in Seychelles, though its present whereabouts are uncertain.[23]

HISTORY OF THE TEXT OF *HAK*

The existence of *HAK—The History of Ashanti Kings and the whole country itself*—became known to me in the late 1950s when, in the course of conversations about Asante history, Nana Osei Agyeman Prempeh II from time to time made reference to it. It was common knowledge that Nana, with the assistance of a committee, had been compiling what he intended to be the definitive history of Asante. Confident that it would supersede *HAK*, Nana did not wish me to use the older work but rather to wait for the appearance of his forthcoming magnum opus.[24] A.A.Y. Kyerematen was more fortunate. In his 1966 Oxford D. Phil. dissertation he referred to his sources:

> The bulk of my information ... has been given me by the reigning King himself, Otumfuo Sir Osei Agyeman Prempeh II, K.B.E., Asantehene, assisted by his cousin, Barima H. Owusu Ansah. He has placed at my disposal notes on a history of Ashanti prepared by him, assisted by a small committee, with the late Mr. Obeng as recorder, as well as notes on the same subject prepared by his predecessor while in

---

[22] I here use "wrapped" to translate the Twi concept, *nnuraho*, for which see I. Wilks, *Forests of Gold. Essays on the Akan and the Kingdom of Asante*, Athens, OH, 1993: 146.

[23] I. Wilks, "An Asante Pharmacopeia?," and E. Akyeampong, "Asante Medicine in the Seychelles," in *Ghana Studies Council Newsletter*, 11, 1998: 4–5, and 12, 1999: 5–6.

[24] I. Wilks, *Conversations*, FN/77, interview with Nana Osei Agyeman Prempeh II, 5 November 1963.

exile, that is, by King Agyeman Prempeh I, with the late Mr. Frederick Prempeh as scribe.[25]

The fact of the matter was that Nana Osei Agyeman Prempeh II had intellectual difficulties with important parts of *HAK*, and he explained the problems to Meyer Fortes in 1945. With reference to the story of the emergence of clans (*mmusua*) from the ground at Asantemanso, Nana remarked, "We now know that this story is not true though my uncle [Agyeman Prempeh I] thought so—it is the way the old people thought . . . ." The Asante must, Nana postulated, have come "from a distant country, perhaps Egypt or Arabia."[26] In 1983 McCaskie talked with I. K. Agyeman, who said frankly that Nana Osei Agyeman Prempeh II did not regard Agyeman Prempeh I as an educated man; that Agyeman Prempeh's mother, Yaa Kyaa, told him what to put in his book; and that it was not a "true history" of Asante but only of his own family.[27]

Be this as it may, it was in mid-1968 that I was first able to obtain direct access to *HAK*. In July and August of that year I was directing a joint University of Ghana and Northwestern University field project in Yendi. I spent a few days in Kumase in September, and it was in the course of a conversation with Joseph Agyeman-Duah, an old friend and then Secretary and Financial Secretary of the Kumase Traditional Council, that I was told that I might have access to *HAK* on an "overnight loan."[28] That evening the document was brought to me at the Kumase Rest House. It was, to the best of my knowledge, a unique text, and I decided to copy as much of it as possible. I was fortunate in being able to call upon Phyllis Ferguson, one of the Northwestern participants in the Yendi project, for help. We had no access to any copying device, so the Rest House became a *scriptorium* for the next eleven or so hours. We agreed that, in the circumstances, dinner was an indulgence to be denied. The temperature refused to drop below 90° or so, and the ceiling fan did not work. Ferguson, who was left-handed, copied the verso pages, and I,

---

[25] A. A. Y. Kyerematen, "Ashanti Royal Regalia: Their History and Functions," D. Phil. thesis, Oxford, 1966: 2. The late Alex Kyerematen belonged to the Abanase group in the palace, custodians of the royal wardrobe, and was a grandson of Kyidomhene Kwame Boaten who died in exile in the Seychelles in 1918.

[26] Notes by Meyer Fortes on a conversation with Nana Osei Agyeman Prempeh II, n.d. but March 1945, from papers of the Ashanti Social Survey in possession of T. C. McCaskie. For a recent vindication of "the way the old people thought," see I. Wilks, *One Nation, Many Histories. Ghana Past and Present*, Ghana Universities Press, Accra, 1996: 13–26.

[27] T. C. McCaskie, conversations with I. K. Agyeman, March-April 1983. In this context it is important to realise that Nana Agyeman Prempeh I and Nana Sir Osei Agyeman Prempeh II belonged to different "houses" within the royal family, for which see Wilks, 1975: 356–70.

[28] I note here that in 1963 Asantehene Osei Agyeman Prempeh II had expressed his willingness to cooperate fully with the work of the Ashanti Research Project; see J. H. Kwabena Nketia, A. S. Y. Andoh, and Ivor G. Wilks, *Ashanti Research Project. First Conference May 17–May 20, 1963*, Institute of African Studies, Legon, 1964: ii.

right-handed, took the recto. The handwriting was very difficult to read, and only some familiarity with the Twi language enabled many of the place and personal names to be deciphered. The problem was compounded by the deterioration of the paper, such that the contrast between foreground (the writing) and background (the paper) was greatly reduced. Nevertheless, when dawn broke, some 50 of the 87 pages of the text had been copied, specifically, pages 4–35 and 54–71. *HAK* was duly returned to the palace soon after first light.

Had I known the subsequent history of *HAK*, more detailed notes on its condition would have been made. The text was written on 46 leaves of a side-sewn ledger that was an item of standard Crown Agents supply. Each leaf measured 5½ × 12 inches, had 32 ruled lines very lightly printed in green, and five vertical columns in red. There was considerable flaking on a few of the outer edges. The title page was unnumbered, and its verso was blank. The text of *HAK* was contained on the next 87 pages, written on both recto and verso of 44 leaves. Pages 1 and 2 were unnumbered. Pages 3 to 87 were numbered by hand. The verso of page 87 was blank. The recto of the next leaf had been used to commence a table of contents, but only the first five pages of *HAK* were covered. The remainder of the ledger was blank.

The importance of the document was quite apparent. I was, however, about to take up a position at Cambridge, and saw no possibility of completing the transcription of *HAK* in the near future. I did not see it again until the autumn of 1973. In the meantime the manuscript was moved from the palace proper to the nearby Manhyia Record Office. This repository had been established by an agreement between Nana Sir Osei Agyeman Prempeh II and A. S. Y. Andoh, Secretary of the Institute of African Studies, Legon, in order to make available to researchers the voluminous records of the Asante courts. It was presumably after the death of Nana in 1970 that Andoh, by then a personal secretary to Nana Opoku Ware II, was authorised to deposit *HAK* in the Manhyia Record Office. For protection it was provided with plain cardboard covers into which it was, it seems, glued.

In mid-1971 A. Adu Boahen examined the copy of *HAK*, and was perturbed by the brittle state of the paper. He obtained permission to take it for restoration and copying at what was then the Padmore Library in Accra. He also took for copying six volumes of correspondence that he had located in the palace, covering the period 1912 to 1931.[29]

---

[29] Adu Boahen remembers that, in one of the palace offices, he noticed a typist seated on a column of documents, thereby to attain sufficient height to use the keyboard comfortably. Curious, he examined the support system, and found that it contained six volumes of correspondence. Copies of these were accessioned 10687–10692 in the George Padmore Library collection; see Adu Boahen to Wilks, Kumase, 19 September 2000. An extensive search of what is now known as the George Padmore Research Library on African Affairs was carried out by McCaskie in mid-2000. He was unable to locate any copy of *HAK*.

In order to begin work on the preservation of *HAK*, it was necessary to disbind the ledger in which it was written. The loose leaves would then be photocopied—in fact, xeroxed—and finally laminated before being rebound. The theory was sound, but problems arose in practice. The following comments are based on an examination of the photocopied pages. The technician who carried out the disbinding first attempted, so it seems, to tear out the leaves from the binding. This resulted in considerable damage not only along the tear lines, but also on the outer edges where it was necessary to grip the sheets. He realised the problem immediately, and decided that cutting rather than tearing the sheets was the answer. This largely eliminated further damage to the outer edges. There were, however, points at which the cutting tool in use failed to slice cleanly through the leaves, so causing further and sometimes extensive damage (exemplified at its worst by pages 37–38). In general, however, the technician was able to sever the leaves about half an inch from the bound-in edges; in other words, the disbound leaves were typically 5 inches in width. A leaf cut in this manner was usually wide enough to include the ends of the lines on both recto and verso, but not infrequently a few letters and sometimes words were lost.

At this stage the technician had before him the disbound ledger, now comprising 46 leaves and a scatter of detached flakes. The next procedure was to make a xerox copy of each page, verso and recto. The disbinding process had, it seems, reversed the order of the leaves, that is, the title page was now at the bottom, and the table of contents at the top. Accordingly the verso pages were xeroxed, turned over, and then the recto pages xeroxed. Further damage occurred as a result of this procedure, so that some recto pages show more flaking than their versos, especially on the fragile inner edges. Occasionally, before xeroxing, the technician tried to restore larger flakes to their proper positions. The most bizarre result of this is to be seen on the xeroxed pages 3 and 5, where part of the missing left side of page 3 is to be found neatly relocated on the left side of page 5!

From this point the history of the text of *HAK* followed two different courses. The disbound leaves were laminated at the Padmore Library, and reassembled in their correct order in a hard red binding. The volume was returned to the Manhyia Record Office where it was available to researchers for consultation. In 1973 I was able briefly to make use of it. I particularly needed to check, for research purposes, a number of readings between pp. 29 and 39. I had some time to spare, however, and typed a few more of the pages of *HAK* that I had been unable to copy from the ledger in September 1968. Unfortunately I did not have my 1968 draft with me, and I was unable to recollect the page numbers of the missing sections. I made a stab at it, and in the limited time available typed pages 40–63. This, in fact, turned out to be more of a miss than a hit: only pages 40–53 were new additions to my transcript. In 1974, however, having by then had access to my 1968 draft, I was fortunate to obtain the assistance of Eva Thorpe, a Northwestern student then staying in Kumase. She made a new (typewritten) copy of pages 1–39 and 63–87 of the text. I was thus finally able to put together as complete a text of *HAK* as possible, and also to obtain a second reading of the handwriting of many pages. Sometime thereafter, but it is uncertain exactly when, the bound volume of *HAK* was returned to the palace, and placed in the private library of Nana Opoku Ware II.[30] Since his death in 1999, the precise whereabouts of the work is unknown.

We return, then, to the copies of *HAK* that were made at the Padmore Library from the disbound ledger. These consisted of 89 xeroxed pages: title page, table of contents, and 87 pages of text. An attempt was made to produce something approximating to a facsimile of the original text. To this end the pages were re-xeroxed back-to-back. Unfortunately, however, the machine operator appears to have been puzzled by the two unnumbered pages, the recto and verso of the first leaf. He set them aside, only coming back to them when all else had been done. There was one blank page on the reverse of the title page, and one of the unnumbered pages—page 2 in fact—was copied on to it. This left the second unnumbered page—page 1—to be dealt with. In some desperation, perhaps, the operator, having placed the table of contents on the reverse of page 87, decided simply, and apparently arbitrarily, to insert the single leaf between pages 86 and 87. The xeroxed pages, now double sided, were finally stapled into a new heavy paper cover, carrying the printed title, "The History of Ashanti. Narrated by Edward Prempeh King of Ashanti. 1907." We cannot be sure how many copies were produced, but probably no more than six. The only ones presently known to us are those in the possession of Adu Boahen, A.S.Y. Andoh, and P. L. Shinnie.[31]

GENESIS OF THE NEW EDITION

Having been instrumental in bringing *HAK* into the public domain, Adu Boahen subsequently became interested in preparing an edited text of it for publication. He and I talked this matter over when he visited Northwestern University in 1976, and I showed him the various transcripts I had made. On his return to Ghana, Adu Boahen wrote to confirm his interest in publishing the text, and asked if I would be willing to make the transcripts available.[32] I readily agreed to do so, and used the occasion to produce the best text I could, using my 1968 transcripts from the original ledger to restore readings at points where text had been lost by flaking. I sent this provisional transcript of *HAK* to Adu

---

[30] Boahen to Wilks, Accra, 19 September 2000, citing A. S. Y. Andoh.
[31] We are particularly grateful to Peter Shinnie for making his copy of the text readily available to us.
[32] Boahen to Wilks, Los Angeles, 18 June 1976.

Boahen. A long silence ensued, and it was not until 17 June 1980 that I wrote to him, inquiring about its status. Adu Boahen had not received the document. "I am sure it must be with the Special Branch!" he wrote; "I am still planning to publish the manuscript but since the last three years, for obvious political reasons, I have not been able to do any original work."[33] Adu Boahen was, of course, referring to the harassment he had suffered as leader of Ghana's major opposition party. It was at this time that Adu Boahen told me that he was hoping to take a sabbatical leave from the University of Ghana in 1981-82, and that he would like to spend it at Northwestern University. We might, he wrote, make the editing of *HAK* "a joint effort of ours."[34]

The signs looked auspicious, but the reality proved otherwise. Adu Boahen's visit to Northwestern did not materialise for his involvement in Ghana politics became, if that was possible, even deeper. I was also at the time in the throes of researching and writing *South Wales and the Rising of 1839*. Neither of us regarded the publication of *HAK* as having, in the circumstances, an overwhelming priority, but the provisional draft of the text was made available to several scholars to whose work it was relevant.

In the event it was not until the Spring of 1991, when Adu Boahen was Visiting Professor at the State University of New York at Binghamton, that he wrote to express his continuing enthusiasm for the project. As a result, I made further revisions to the draft text, and put the new version on disk. Nevertheless, other commitments continued to take priority, and it was not until the Autumn of 1994 that work got finally underway. Adu Boahen and I were agreed that the projected book should comprise several introductory essays by one or other of us, the best text of *HAK* that we could produce, and a series of notes identifying people and places, and glossing difficult passages. We also considered producing a shorter and popular version of *HAK*, to be published in Ghana, and a start was made on this.[35] Then, in mid-1997, Emmanuel Akyeampong and T.C. McCaskie made known their interest in the editing of *HAK*. By this time Adu Boahen and I had become only too aware of the complexities of the project, and were happy to proceed in collaboration with them. On 16 April 1999 Otumfuo Nana Osei Tutu II reaffirmed the support that his predecessor, Nana Opoku Ware II, had given to the project, and McCaskie was able to secure the British Academy's interest in the publication of Agyeman Prempeh's writings.

---

[33] Boahen to Wilks, Legon, 4 July 1980.
[34] Boahen to Wilks, Legon, 2 February 1981.
[35] Wilks to Boahen, Evanston, 25 September 1994; Boahen to Wilks, Accra, 29 September and 24 November 1994. Boahen wrote a general introduction, "Backdrop to the writing of Agyeman Prempe's History of Asante." I began work on a "plain speech" version of the text.

ESTABLISHING A TEXT OF *HAK*

The text of *HAK* presented in Chapters Five to Seven is for the most part taken from the copy made at the Padmore Library in 1971 and subsequently returned to Kumase where it was deposited in the Manhyia Record Office. The pages were digitally scanned by Nancy Lawler, who was able to restore something of the original contrast between background and foreground that had been lost as a result of the heavy browning of the paper, and these may be consulted at the British Academy website, www.britac.ac.uk/pubs/src/fha/ashanti. Nevertheless, the text we use necessarily falls short of being definitive, for the original ledger was irreparably damaged when it was disbound in 1971. This situation is only partly alleviated by the existence of the manual copy made in 1968 for this, as we have noted above, unfortunately covered only about two-thirds of the work.

Frederick Prempeh's handwriting is, we have said, by no means illegible, but its quality is certainly not such as to facilitate a reading of the text (see Plates 1–6). It must be said, however, that his command of English was, for a learner, impressive. A modest proportion of words are misspelled, and errors of grammar are common but seldom such as to obscure meaning. The confusing and confused use of the prepositions "he" and "she," and related gender words ("his" and "her," etc.), is a familiar enough problem in translating from Twi, and has to be guarded against. A major problem with Frederick's text, however, is his rendering of Asante place and personal names into English.

In order to overcome the difficulty in representing certain Asante sounds in English, in the earlier parts of *HAK* Frederick Prempeh made use of a range of diacritical marks, including French *grave* and *acute* accents. A bar was used to indicate the long "a" in what is, in present day orthography, a double "aa," as in "Yaa" [*HAK* 8:22, 18.16]. A bar over a "u," as in "Manu" for example, has the same purpose [*HAK* 5:22]. Frederick, however, did not achieve consistency in his use of these marks, and at some early point in time discarded them. Most of his renderings are readily recognisable with or without them. "Cha Cha" [*HAK* 9:22], for example, is obviously the modern Kyakya; "Anchui" [*HAK* 3:6] the modern Antwi; and so forth. The occasional use of English "l" for Asante "r" creates no problems for the reader, but Frederick's difficulty in dealing with the palatal consonant "ny" does. Thus the personal name Nyaako is rendered "Guarcun," using what looks like a labio-velar "gu" [*HAK* 6:9, 12], but the place name Anyinase appears as "Ignarsi" [*HAK* 26:1] although one might expect "Iguarsi." Asante "w" is frequently transcribed with a "y," so that Owusu usually appears as "Oyusu" [*HAK* 7:20, 8:4]. More bizarre is the regular transcription of Awere as "Ayulis" [*HAK* 55:27 (with bars on both "A" and "u"), 57:30, 62:24]. There is an interesting study to be made of all of this, with reference to the Anglo-French patois current in the Seychelles. Such, however, is beyond the scope of the present work. We have chosen to enter all names, as spelled by Frederick Prempeh, within inverted commas in the Concordance, cross referencing them to what we believe is an acceptable equivalent in present-day orthography.

One of the difficulties in presenting *HAK* is that Frederick Prempeh's text was copy edited (as it were) probably not long after it was written. The spelling of names was sometimes corrected. Thus, for example, Yafilé was regularly amended to Ya Efirae [*HAK* 11:6, 31; 12:1, 7,8]. Sometimes the changes are in the nature of substantive, rather than spelling, corrections. *HAK* 1:21 has the change from "man sitting on" (a stool) to "woman carrying," for example, and *HAK* 26:12 from "into Ignarsi" to "at Ajusoo." *HAK* 31:14 has "citizens of Ashanti" substituted for "families." Here and there additions of several lines were made to the original text, specifically, on *HAK* 3, 65, 78, and 82. From the handwriting of the postulated copy editor, we feel confident that it was Agyeman Prempeh himself who made most if not all of the changes. Frederick Prempeh also made numerous corrections as he was writing, mostly to do with spelling or the choice of words. The concerned reader may consult these at the British Academy website, but we have ignored them in our transcript other than in places where the alterations are of significance to an understanding of the text. For ease of reference, the conventions we have used are set out at the beginning of Part II (p. 83).

HAK, A RELATED TEXT, AND OTHER PIECES

It is not entirely clear just how *HAK* was compiled. There can be no doubt that the genealogies were written directly into the ledger, presumably in English from dictation in Twi. Had they been copies of older texts, then the presence of crossed-out sections, as in *HAK* 6:19–26, is inexplicable, for it may be assumed that it is the rare copyist who piously reproduces effaced sections from his (or her) exemplar. It seems, however, that other parts of *HAK* were copied from shorter pieces, written before so ambitious an undertaking as a synoptic history of Asante had been conceived. The existence of some of these is signalled, perhaps, by formulaic phrases in the text, for example, "here endeth the history of King Otti Akenten" [*HAK* 53:3–4], and "here endeth the story of King Obi Yaeboa" [57:32]. At one point in *HAK* Frederick Prempeh notes, "vide the blank paper" [*HAK* 31:17], and copied from it a regnal list obviously extracted from a written source (and one, as we have noted above, derived ultimately from the Muslim chronology transmitted by Dupuis).[36]

---

[36] By "blank page" Frederick Prempeh probably meant an unlined sheet of paper, unlike the ledger book he was using.

It may be assumed that the earlier pieces were discarded once their content had been woven into *HAK*. The reason for thinking this is at least one such piece, displaying the use of French accents characteristic of the early parts of *HAK*, has survived, and has probably done so for the very reason that it was *not* incorporated into *HAK*. The document in question comprises four pages in the hand of Frederick Prempeh. Pages 1:1 to 3:22 are entitled, *King Otti Akenten. Bodies of men or Regiments—organised by King Oti Akenten,* and pages 3:23 to 4:31, *King Obi Yaeboa. Bodies of men or regiments organised by King Obi Yaeboa*. This item, reproduced in Plates III–VII, will be referred to as *OA/OY*. In 1984 J. K. Adjaye gave me an incomplete but carefully typed version of it, which he had obtained from the Padmore Library of African Affairs, Accra. In 2000, McCaskie located the hand-written exemplar in the Asantehene's palace.[37] The transcriptions of the text have been inserted at relevant places in Chapter Five with the exception of the account of royal funerary practices [*OA/OY* 1:25–3:1]. This seems to be an insertion into the historical narrative, and will be found in Chapter Six.

It will be readily apparent that the two parts of *OA/OY*, the one relating to Oti Akenten and the other to Obiri Yeboa, are structurally similar. Each has a title of the same form, and each ends with a formal summary, the one headed "Summary" and the other "Decorations." We can be confident that these originally formed part of a trilogy, for a parallel piece that does appear in *HAK* was composed for Osei Tutu, that is, *HAK* 61:11–65:18 lists the offices created by Osei Tutu, and it too ends with a "Summary." Again, as with the ethnographic pieces clumsily inserted into the historical narratives, the evidence points clearly to *HAK* having been, in part, compiled from earlier written fragments. It was with this consideration in mind that it was felt that, in this new edition, a full understanding of *HAK*, and of the intellectual interests of Edward Prempeh and his collaborators, would best be served by attempting to deconstruct the text, separating out distinct topics of inquiry the one from the others. In general *HAK* lends itself to this exercise, its "seams" being for the most part quite manifest. However, one relatively lengthy piece, "The Origins of Atɔperɛ, and the Adanse Denkyira Conflict," is in need of particular comment. It has to do with a period before the emergence of the unified Asante monarchy, and lacks the Kumase focus that is characteristic of virtually all other parts of *HAK*. We suggest that Frederick Prempeh may have taken it down from the dictation of Kwabena Nkwantabisa, the Adanse-Odumasehene who was

---

[37] The typewritten copy has the diacritics of the exemplar carefully added by hand. Comparison with the hand-written copy leaves no doubt that the latter was indeed the exemplar, which must therefore have been among the papers taken by Adu Boahen to the Padmore Library for copying, in 1971. It remains unexplained why a typed rather than a photographic copy was, at some point in time, made.

among the exiles, and accordingly have—with some trepidation—set it in Chapter Six rather than Five.

For the convenience of the reader Figure 1 correlates the text of *HAK*, by page and line, with the corresponding pages in this new edition.

HAK MS: BY PAGE AND LINE	THIS EDITION: BELOW, BY PAGE	*HAK* MS: BY PAGE AND LINE	THIS EDITION: BELOW, BY PAGE
1:1 – 2:31	85 – 6	45:14 – 45:23	122
3:1 – 3:13	131	45:23 – 53:4	93 – 6
3:16 – 3:32	87	53:5 – 54:5	97 – 8
4:1 – 4:15	131	54:7 – 55:13	126
4:16 – 5:20	90	55:14 – 55:30	98
5:21 – 23:30	133 – 46	56:1 – 56:18	117
23:31 – 28:26	87 – 9	56:19 – 68:29	98 – 105
28:28 – 30:16	116	68:30 – 76:3	107 – 10
30:17 – 32:26	127 – 8	76:4 – 76:17	119
32:26 – 35:9	122 – 3	76:18 – 81:9	110 – 13
35:9 – 38:17	90 – 2	81:10 – 83:8	105 – 6
38:18 – 39:31	117 – 18	83:9 – 84:20	125
40:1 – 40:18	93	84:21 – 86:13	106 – 7
40:18 – 45:6	120 – 1	86:14 – 87:30	113 – 14
45:7 – 45:13	115		

Figure 1: Textual Correlations, *HAK* exemplar and present edition

The materials in Chapters Eight and Nine are neither part of *HAK* nor are they closely related to it. The former belongs to the genre of memoirs, and in this case memoirs put together by Agyeman Prempeh to validate his role in the events that preceded, first, the British occupation of Kumase on 17 January 1896, and second, the coup d'état carried out by Governor W. Maxwell of the Gold Coast Colony three days later. Chapter Nine treats of Agyeman Prempeh's report to the Asanteman after his return from exile in 1924, *inter alia* listing those who died and those who were born during the exile.

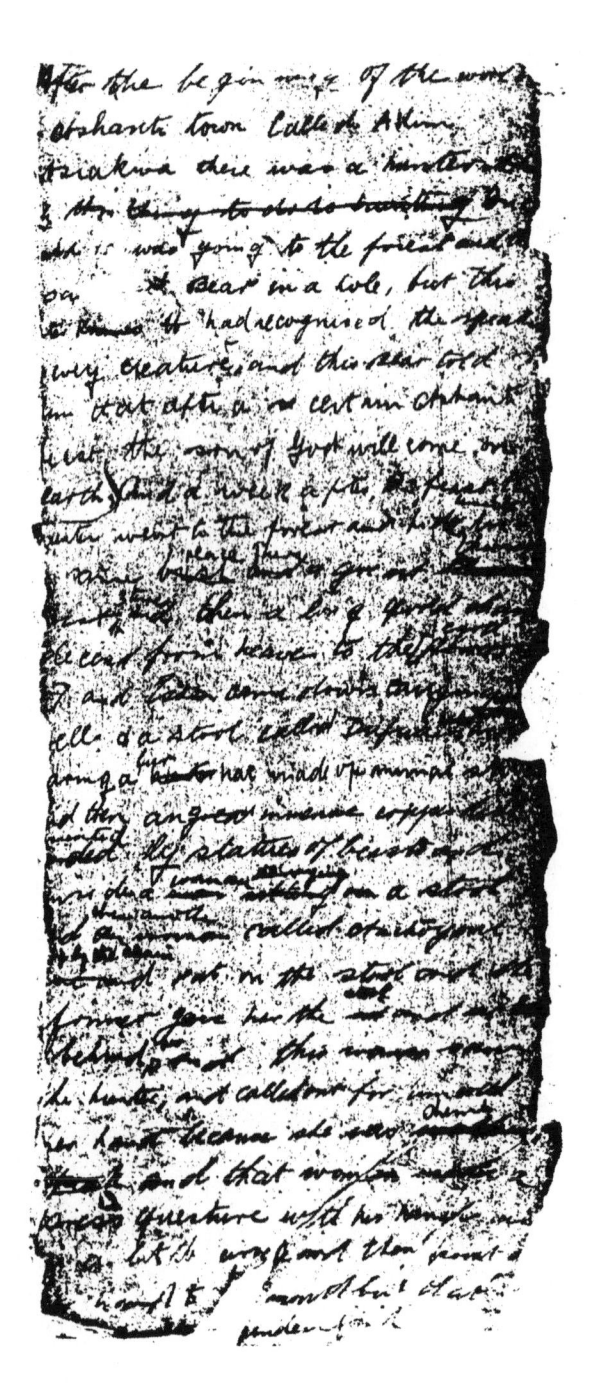

Plate 1: *HAK* 1

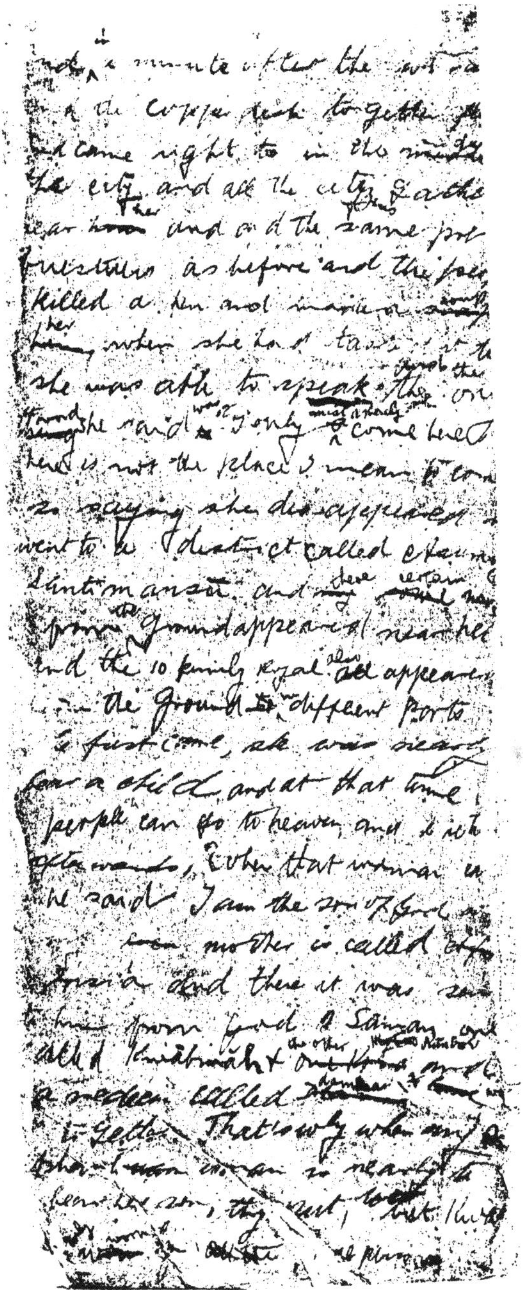

Plate 2: *HAK* 2

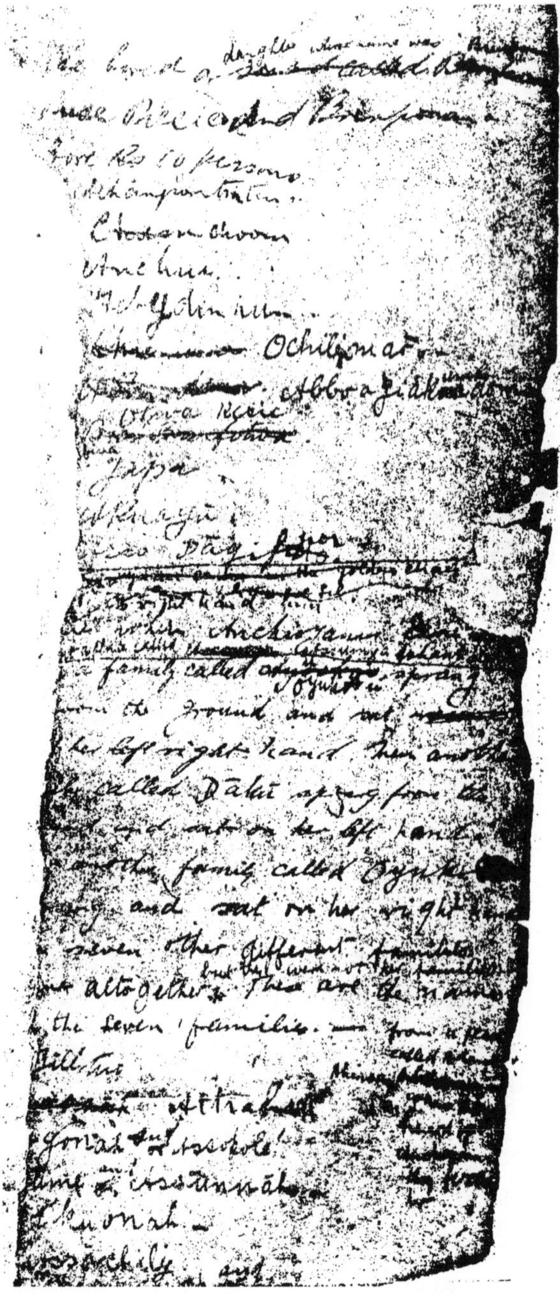

Plate 3: *HAK* 3

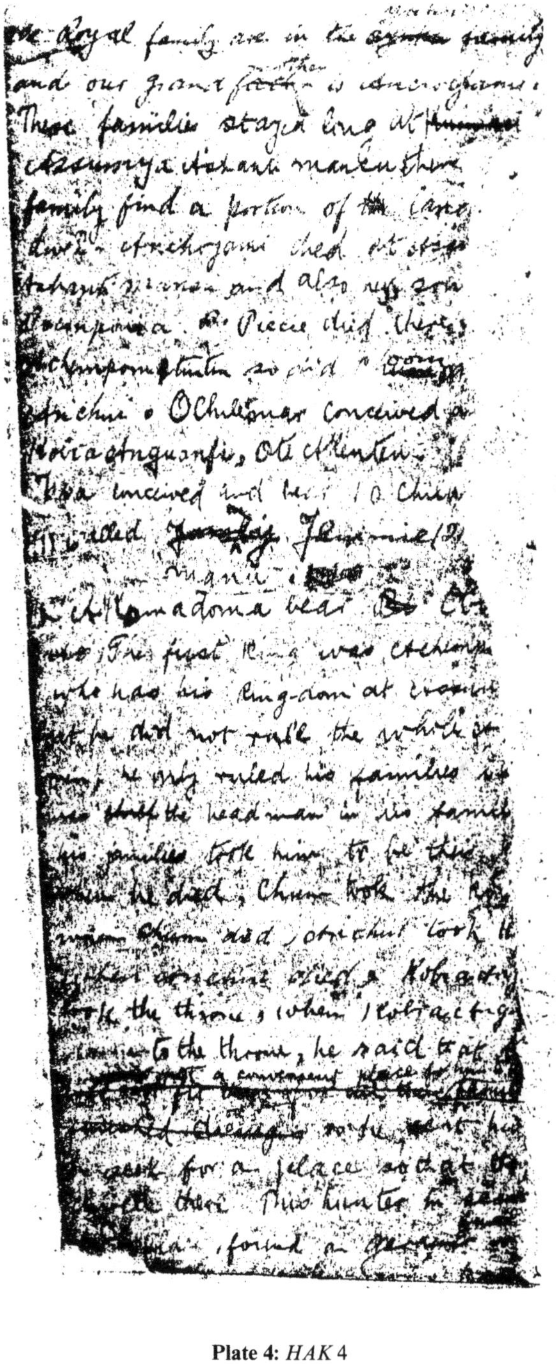

the Royal family are in the ~~[illegible]~~ family
and our grand~~father~~ mother is [illegible].
These families stayed long at ~~[illegible]~~
[illegible] make there
family find a portion of the land.
[illegible] died at [illegible]
[illegible] and also my son
[illegible]. [illegible] died there.
[illegible] so did [illegible]
[illegible]. [illegible] conceived a
[illegible], [illegible].
She conceived and bore 10 children
called ~~[illegible]~~ [illegible]
[illegible]
[illegible]
who. The first King was [illegible]
who has his kingdom at [illegible]
but he did not rule the whole [illegible]
[illegible] he only ruled his families [illegible]
was ~~[illegible]~~ the head man in his family
his families took him to be this [illegible]
when he died, [illegible] took the [illegible]
[illegible] died, [illegible] took the
[illegible] died, [illegible]
took the throne, when [illegible]
came to the throne, he said that
~~[illegible] not a convenient place [illegible]~~
~~[illegible]~~
~~[illegible]~~ [illegible]
[illegible] for a place so that [illegible]
[illegible] there. This hunter [illegible]
[illegible] found a [illegible]

Plate 4: *HAK* 4

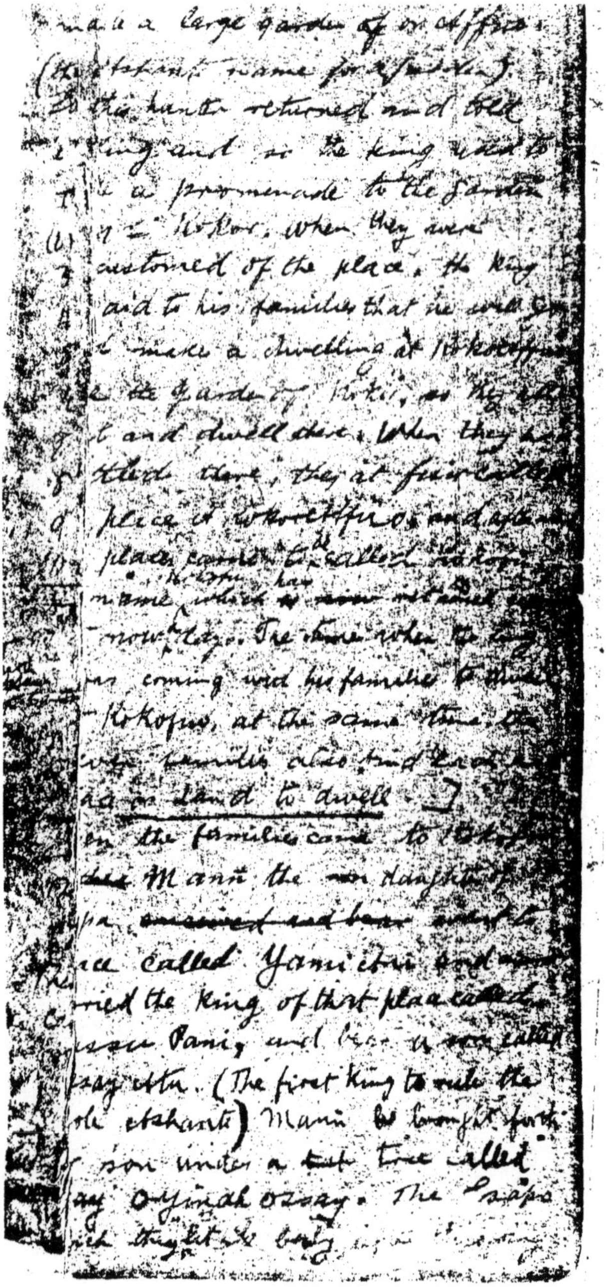
make a large garden of oo Koffiro.
(the Ashanti name for Garden).
So the hunter returned and told
king and so the king used to
[illegible] a promenade to the Garden
[illegible] Kokor. When they were
accustomed of the place. the king
said to his families that he would
[illegible] make a dwelling at Kokofu
[illegible] the garden of Kokor, so they [illegible]
and dwell there. When they
settled there, they at first called
place it Kokoffu and after
place ~~cannot~~ be called Kokofu
name which [illegible]
now Kagyo. The time when the king
was coming with his families to dwell
Kokofu, at the same time the
other families also find [illegible]
[illegible] land to dwell.
When the families came to Kokofu
Manu the daughter of
[illegible] went to
place called Yamieso and
married the King of that place called
Asare Pani, and bore a son called
Asayeiba. (The first King to rule the
whole Ashanti) Manu brought forth
son under a [illegible] tree called
[illegible] Oyinah Osay. The [illegible]
[illegible]

Plate 5: *HAK* 5

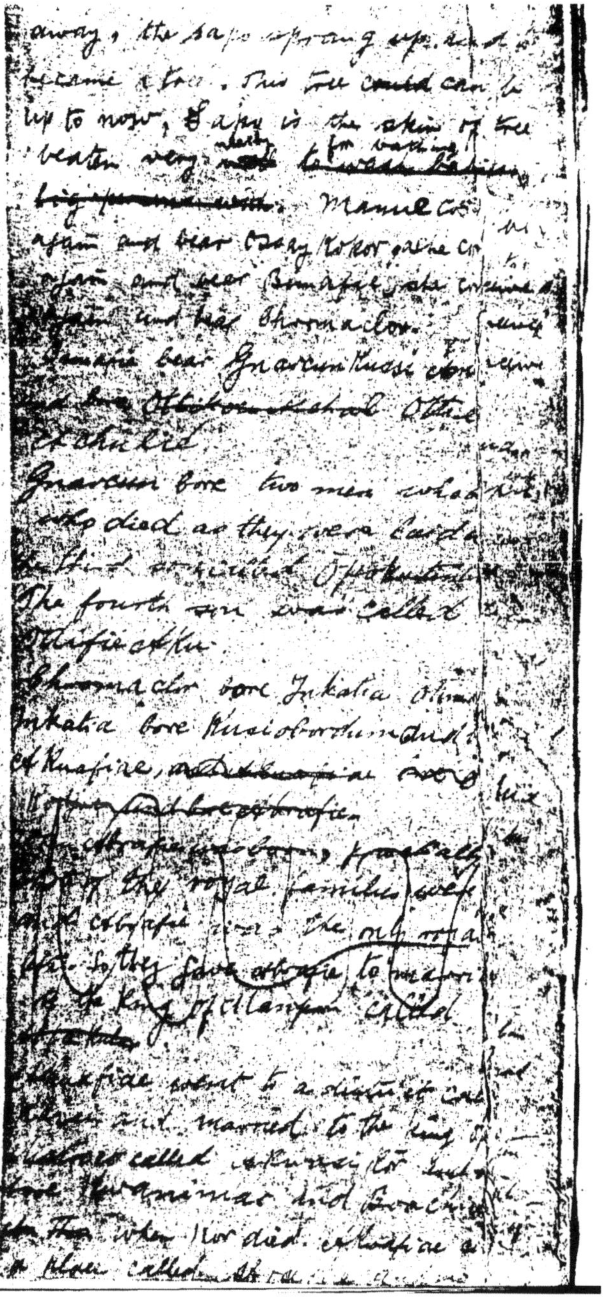

away, the sapo sprang up and
became a tree. This tree could can be
up to now, Sapo is the skin of tree
beaten very neatly for washing
[illegible] Manue co[illegible]
again and bear Osey Kokor, she co[illegible]
again and bear Bonafie, she [illegible]
again and bear Ohomaclor.
[illegible] bear Gnarcum Kussi [illegible]
[illegible] Otti[illegible]
[illegible]
Gnarcum bore two men who [illegible]
[illegible] died as they were [illegible]
the third [illegible] called Ofokutu[illegible]
The fourth son was called
[illegible]fie Akku.
Ohomaclor bore Inkatia [illegible]
Inkatia bore Kusi Obodum and
Akuafine, [illegible]
[illegible]
[illegible] Abrafie was born, [illegible]
[illegible] the royal families [illegible]
[illegible] Abrafie [illegible] the only royal
[illegible] So they gave Abrafie to marry
to the King of Mankessim called
[illegible]
[illegible]fie went to a district called
[illegible] and married to the King of
[illegible] called Akuassi [illegible]
[illegible] and [illegible]
[illegible] when Kor died. Akuafie [illegible]
a place called [illegible]

Plate 6: *HAK* 6

King Otti-Akenten

Bodies of *[illegible]* or Regiments organised by King Ottu Akenten

The only departments organised by King Otti Akenten from Nkofu to Kumasi which now remains is the chief of Akwaboa*[illegible]* and the chief of Abusai — and the chief of Akra-fuo — *[illegible]*.

These two bodies of men take no orders from any one at Kumasi; but they are joined to the *[illegible]*. In time of *[illegible]* they are to take their orders from the *[illegible]* of the *[illegible]* — if it be either a share of gain or paying. — In times of great assembly the Akra-fuo *[illegible]* sits just in front of the King and the Akwaboa *[illegible]* sits a little back between the *[illegible]* and Akwaboa *[illegible]*.

In time of war the society Akra-fuo take their march in front of the *[illegible]* and Akwaboa in the rear of the *[illegible]*.

When Otti Akenten came to Kumasi and became king, he made the following societies

1st First of all he may his third society — The *[illegible]*; this society only blows or whistles the King's doom — and they are under the control of *[illegible]*

Fourthly, the "*Akoom-fuo*" (more *[illegible]* at *[illegible]*) under the control of *[illegible]*

Fifthly, the "*[illegible]*" that is hammock bearers residing at *[illegible]*. These hammock bearers residing at *[illegible]* were ordered not to carry any living king; but their duties are to carry a dead king to cemetery. — If any one of this society was mistakenly caught hold of the king *[illegible]* to help to carry a living king, he is at once executed. —

The second duty of this society is as follows: — When an Ashanti king is dead, he could not be buried *[illegible]* all the *[illegible]* and chief in the Ashanti Empire meet to swear — before the dead king. —

A year after an anniversary of the dead king is celebrated which is known as *[illegible]* — Eight days after this, there is another celebration known as *[illegible]*. — This is carried out as follows: —

On the day of *[illegible]*, the *[illegible]* and the Akwaboa *[illegible]* a general mobilisation of their armies and proceed to *[illegible]* the gold stool and bring with them to the forest cult *[illegible]*.

* The word had before the name of any body of men means the *[illegible]* of that *[illegible]* of men.

Plate 7: *OA/OY* 1

forest with their [illegible] and the chiefs will enter the stool: —

Then there is something which is known as [illegible] (clearing the path)
There is a certain place called Dar-boary and at that place is found the statues or busts of Ashanti Kings. The princes of [illegible], [illegible] [illegible] on that day under the leadership of [illegible] proceed on that day with necessary tools to prepare or clean the road leading to Darboary and when they are doing this, the proclaimed king and the ten [illegible] of [illegible] plus the [illegible] of the [illegible] around all come to assemble at a place call [illegible]. When the clearing of the road is finished, the princes returned with their tools and placed them in heap before the King and the King at once gives them £ [illegible] & [illegible] drink [illegible] every [illegible] give what they wish. — Then with the woods they had cut in the clearing, an arch is made just facing the King's palace. —

There in the arch the bust of the dead King (which was sculptured by a society of women [illegible] at [illegible]) is being brought by the women in an earthen pot and placed the bust in the pot on a special stool in the arch and all the decorations and jewelleries of the Ashanti King is placed around the bust according to its proper [illegible] — —

Then the [illegible] and [illegible] bring back the gold stool and hand it over to the King and the King pays £ 24 & [illegible] sheep and drinks and on that day the King take the throne to his house in the palace. —

In the afternoon, a woman of the royal family is given to carry the pot with the bust to Darboary and there the [illegible] perform their sacred duty by giving a hold to the pot which is on the lady's head lest it falls. — and there a great procession of princes, princesses, royal families & chiefs follow with all the decorations of the King behind and before, in order just as when a living King is in full uniform.

From the arch to Darboary, a man is taken from each [illegible] department of the royal house servants and placed right and left along the road with an executioner behind each man. — And when the procession has reached Darboary, three big stones are chosen and are placed in triangular form as a cooking tripod and three chosen servants are killed and legs broken and the broken legs are placed on the three sides of the tripod just as [illegible] are placed between tripods for cooking and the pot with the statue is placed on the top.

On the next day, the Queen and the royal ladies go there [illegible]

Plate 8: *OA/OY* 2

[illegible] to prove that the ceremony of the deceased sovereign is completely ended.

Sixth. At Kumasi; there is a very nice polish stone called DRA [illegible]

The Diabone was got by King Osei when he fought with and defeated the King of [illegible] out of Kumasi and took Kumasi. In taking possession of Kumasi, he found that stone (lying) in the upper part of the defeated King's bed. and King Osei took the stone and placed it at the upper part of his bed.

Up to 1896, where the stone was found was the very place where the bedroom of King Osei [illegible] situated.

Seventh. In the reign of King Osei [illegible], umbrella was not known and great assembly of the King and his chiefs were under a large shed which was especially built and covered with leaves.

When chief [illegible] of the district of [illegible] came to Kumasi, he was clad in [illegible] and King Osei ordered his men to [illegible] the same sort of cloth for him and it with a piece of the [illegible] to cover only part of the shed where he sat.

Eight. At the reign of King Osei [illegible], gold dust was not known for money; but [illegible] a sort of brass was used.

Summary

Society or Body of men organised by King Osei [illegible]

Decorations [illegible] (gold) Dra-[illegible] 3

Money used is a sort of brass called [illegible]

Remarks: —— . ——

King OBi Yaeboa

Bodies of men or regiments organised by King Obi Yaeboa.

The first body of men was the [illegible] – a man called [illegible] was the leader

Second [illegible] leader of which was called [illegible] but the latter takes his command from [illegible]

Third [illegible] leader of which was called [illegible] the latter takes his command from [illegible]

Fourth [illegible] chief of which was called [illegible], under command [illegible] (Obi Yaeboa was the first to introduce [illegible] soldiers)

Fifth [illegible] (infantry) Chief of which was called [illegible] commander. The latter was also chief of [illegible] (cooks for the King's palace) under [illegible]

Plate 9: *OA/OY* 3

Sixth – [illegible] [illegible] chief of which was called [illegible] under Command of [illegible] – (finished with [illegible])

To his son Sabin :–

seventh – Donkah-[illegible] leader of which was his son [illegible] – –

Eight: King [illegible] Osei [illegible] made Oti Kotia a petty chief of [illegible] under command of Sabin – from Oti Kotia came that [illegible] known as [illegible] for he was the first [illegible] in Ashanti – –

ninth – He made [illegible] to be the chief at [illegible] and command of Sabin. When [illegible] died, [illegible] succeeded him and the latter married to the royal girl call Marnoo and begat Osei Tutu who became the first King of Ashanti and gained great Kingdom for Ashanti. –

Tenth (A) He made [illegible] to be chief of [illegible] and [illegible] him to be under Sabin. –

eleventh (B) He appointed the district of Oh-[illegible] to be under Sabin

Twelth (C) He appointed [illegible] to be [illegible] of [illegible] and [illegible]. –

Thirteen (D) He appointed a chief to command the district of [illegible] under Sabin

Fourteen (E) He appointed [illegible] to be under Sabin. –

Fifteen (F) He appointed [illegible] to be chief of [illegible] under Sabin. –

Sixteen – He appointed a chief in the district of [illegible] & [illegible] to be under Sabin

Seventeen – He appointed [illegible] to be under Sabin. – (Sabin [illegible])

To Gharsi (Royal House guards)

First – Bari chief of Gharsi

Second – He appointed [illegible] – chief of [illegible] (under no body)

Third – He appointed [illegible] a chief under no body –

Decorations –

First – He [illegible] umbrella (which was known as [illegible]) and covered it with [illegible] ([illegible])

Second – He organized a body of men to be [illegible] and these people were under [illegible]. –

Plate 10: *OA/OY* 4

PART II

THE SEYCHELLES WRITINGS

Transcribed and presented by
Nancy Lawler, T. C. McCaskie and Ivor Wilks

CONVENTIONS

A number of conventions have been introduced to facilitate use of the texts of *HAK* and *OA/OY* in Chapters Five to Seven. All references to *HAK* and *OA/OY*—for example, *HAK* 53:5 or *OA/OY* 1:10—are to pages and lines of the original manuscript texts. A reader wishing to consult these may do so at the British Academy website, www.britac.ac.uk/pubs/src/fha/ashanti/

The Concordance (Part IV) serves, inter alia, to index *HAK* and *OA/OY*, so enabling references to individuals and places to be found by page numbers of this volume (and thereby located by pages and lines in the original texts). Otherwise, the following procedures have been adopted:

(1) Section headings in the texts of *HAK* and *OA/OY* in this volume are not in the original manuscripts, but have been added (in square brackets) as an aid to readability.

(2) Frederick Prempeh's use of paragraphs was quite unsystematic so, again in the interests of readability, editorial discretion has been exercised in the matter.

(3) [........] indicates significant words and phrases that have been crossed out and corrected by F. A. Prempeh in the course of writing. These are not always legible.

(4) [*........*] shows words and phrases that have been crossed out by, it is thought, Edward Prempeh himself. In such cases the corrections have been incorporated into the text, as the preferred reading.

(5) (?) indicates that a reading is uncertain.

CHAPTER FIVE

Historical Pieces

[THE ARRIVAL OF ANKYEWA NYAME AT ASANTEMANSO]

We know of no account of the origins of the ruling dynasty of Asante that is earlier than that in *The History of Ashanti Kings and the whole country itself (HAK)*. The apical ancestress of the royal Oyoko is Ankyewa Nyame. The story tells of her arrival from the sky and of the emergence of her people from holes in the ground, thus in effect registering the claim that the Asante are an autochthonous people, that is, none of them is an immigrant from north, south, east or west. Immigrant origins are described in "flatland," but indigenous ones utilise a different dimension extending from "up" (from the ground) to "down" (from the sky).[1] The antiquity of such stories is well attested, for three hundred years ago the Dutch trader Willem Bosman, when on the Gold Coast, had heard about "first Men," that is, ancestors, who "came out of Holes and Pits."[2]

The setting of the story in *HAK* is Asantemanso, some fourteen miles south of Kumase and near Asumenya. In 1923 R. S. Rattray gave a splendid description of the site in his first report as Head of the Anthropological Department in Asante.[3] P. L. Shinnie and B. C. Vivian carried out excavations there over three seasons, in 1986, 1987, and 1989–91, and their full report is eagerly awaited.[4] Carbon dates from the site show evidence of human activity extending from the first millennium A.D. to recent times. Wilks has argued elsewhere that the transformation of the forest Akan economy, from one based on the exploitation of the wild resources of the land to one based on the cultivation of food crops, occurred in the course of the sixteenth and seventeenth centuries. Asantemanso, long a major seasonal camp of hunting bands, became a centre from which farming peoples dispersed.[5] Shinnie argues that the chronological setting Wilks gives these developments is too late, but McCann has recently adduced further arguments that support Wilks's views.[6]

HAK 1:1 – *HAK* 2:31

After the beginning of the world at an Ashanti town called Akim Asiakwa there was a hunter. [Then the thing to do is hunting.] Once he said he was going to the forest and then he saw a Bear in a hole, but this hunter [knows all] had recognised the speaking of every creature, and this Bear told him that after a

---

[1] See I.Wilks, *One Nation, Many Histories. Ghana Past and Present*, Accra, 1996: 13–26.
[2] W. Bosman, *A New and Accurate Description of the Coast of Guinea*, London, 1705: 147.
[3] Published in *Ashanti*, Oxford, 1923: 121–32.
[4] B. C. Vivian, "Origins of the Asante Research Project: 1989–90. Excavations at Asantemanso," *Nyame Akuma*, 34, 1990: 19–22. Peter Shinnie, "Early Asante: Is Wilks Right?", in J. Hunwick and N. Lawler (eds.), *The Cloth of Many Colored Silks*, Northwestern University Press, 1996: 195–203. Peter and Ama Shinnie, *Early Asante*, Dept. of Archaeology, University of Calgary, 1995, and Pregee Printing Press, Kumasi, 1998.
[5] Ivor Wilks, *Forests of Gold. Essays on the Akan and the Kingdom of Asante*, Athens, OH, 1993: 41–90.
[6] James C. McCann, *Green Land, Brown Land, Black Land. An Environmental History of Africa, 1800–1990*, Portsmouth NJ and Oxford, 1999: 111–28.

certain Ashanti feast, the son of God will come on earth. And a week after the feast the hunter went to the forest and hid himself in some [bush and] place. Then a great thunder bust 3 times and then a long gold chain descend from heaven to the earth and Essen came down carrying a bell & a stool called Dufua[7] and wearing a fur [hunter] hat made of animal skin and then an immense copper dish ornamented by statues of beasts and inside a [*man sitting on*] woman carrying a stool and then another woman called Anchōyami [*came*] by the chain and sat on the stool and the former gave her the stool and sit behind her and this woman saw the hunter and called out for him with her hand because she was [*something . . .*] Ohemah and that woman made a press gesture with his hands and sat(?) in a little circle and then pointed his hand to his mouth but that man(?) was unable to understand it. And in a minute after the woman and the copper dish together flew and came right to in the [middle] midst of the city and all the citizens gather near [him] her and did the same press gestures as before and the people killed a hen and made a soup for [him] her when she had tasted it then she was able to speak. The only [thing] word she said was "I only mistakenly come here. Here is not the place I mean to come."

So saying she disappeared and went to a district called Asumyia Santimansū. And there certain [people?] from the ground appeared near her and the 10 family Royal [all] also appeared from the ground in different parts. The first came, and she was nearly bear a child and at that time people can go to heaven, and return afterwards. When that woman enter(?) he said: I am the son of God and my mother is called [Afua(?)] Insua and there it was sent to him from God 2 Sūman[8] one called Kwābināh & the other [one Kotuo(?)] Kūntror and a medicine called damtua [came] with(?) together. That's why when any Ashanti [man] woman is nearly to bear her son, they put (cloth?), but Kwabinah is only [won] worn by all the royal persons.

[ANKYEWA NYAME AND THE GATHERING OF THE CLANS (*MMUSUA*)]

The story continues, chronologically, with an account of the origins of the various Oyoko and other *mmusua* (or, loosely, "clans") that came to be associated with Ankyewa Nyame. However, a list of the ten children of Birempomaa Piesie, the only offspring of Ankyewa Nyame mentioned in *HAK*, was inserted at the top of page 3 of the ledger [*HAK* 3:1–3:13]. It belongs, logically, to the beginning of the genealogies, and will be found in that position in Chapter Seven below. The motive in situating it in the story of origins was presumably to draw attention to the fact that there were families descended from Ankyewa Nyame herself, apart from those who came to be adopted (in some sense or other of that word) by her. As a result of relocating this list, however, the compiler

---

[7] Twi *dufua*, an early form of stool consisting of a solid block of wood with a handle.

[8] Twi *suman*, which, following Christaller, can mean either "charm, amulet, talisman," or "any protecting power, including the abosom [spirits]." The second sense seems to be intended here.

appears temporarily to have lost his train of thought. The next two lines [*HAK* 3:14–3:15] are crossed out, and only the words "the golden chain" can be read with any confidence. The main story of the gathering of the *mmusua* is resumed briefly in *HAK* 3:16 to *HAK* 3:32 and, conclusively, in *HAK* 23:31 to *HAK* 28:26.

HAK 3:16 – *HAK* 3:32

When Anchioyami came upon a place called [Accomassi] Asumyia Ashantimansu a family called [Ayoukos] Oyuku sprang from the ground and sat at her [left] right hand. Then another family called Dākū sprang from the ground and sat on her left hand. Then another family called Oyuku sprang and sat on her right hand. Then seven other different families came altogether but they were not her families.—(Marginalia: from a place called Adansi Ahinsan [Adansimansu]. When they heard of Anchoyami they flocked to her).[9]

Biletuo
Atnah (?)
Agonah [or] and Assokole
Jume [or] and Assunnāh
Ekuonah
Assachily
Adduanah [or] and Achua.

HAK 23:31 – *HAK* 28:26

But there are some more Ayuku which are not families of Anchiayami. At that time when Anchiayami came to Assumi Asantimanso but it has been further explained that Yuku were the first people to come to her. There are three kinds of Oyuku. When these Yukun came near to her she asked one "Who are you?" and they said we are [part] member of your Yukun: and she told them "if you are Yukus, then I am Yuku-Kor-Kor-Kon, i.e. I am more Yuku than you." She also asked them what was the name of their Yukus and they said "we are Oyuku Abohen." To the second Yukun she asked them what was the name of their Yuku, they said "we are Yuku Atutuō. " To the third she asked the name of their Yuku and they said [that] "we are Yuku [Blémän] Blaémarn."

There are three kinds of Oyukun Abohen
1st are called Asarman (The [*chief*] head of all Yuku)
2nd are called Kenassie.
3rd are called Manpontin.
There are three kinds of Atutuo
1st are called Adenchimansu.
2nd are called [*Papasu*] Panpasoo.
3rd are called Ayuomu.

---

[9] This marginal note is, we think, in the hand of Agyeman Prempeh.

4th are called Ahinkulo but the Ahinkulos did not come the same day as the first three. The Ahin Kulo came from a district called Achim, and they came to Kumasi at the time of King Osai Tutu. When they came they said to the King that they wish to join his Yukus because when they were at their country, they were Yukuos and their Yuku was called Atutuo and they beg the King to add them to Yuku Atutuo. That is the reason why these are four. The King agreed to it.

At first Adenchimansu was the chief of all the Atutuo. At the time of King Ossai Kodjoe the chief man of Adenchimansu came to Ahin Kulo and settle there,—and so made Ahin Kulo became the chief of all Tutuo. It will be explained the reason why he went to Ahinkulo.

There are two kinds of Blaemarn: Fa-Ba-Wa-li was the chief and Silésu came second.

[At Ignarsi there is another Yuku; they came from {Achim} Assumi Santimansu and when they came, they were added to the Yukus but they were not Blaemarn, neither Abuhen nor Atutuo. If Blaemarn, Abuhen and Atutuo have a share, only a small portion is given to them and the rest is divided equally among them. Blaemern Atutu and Abohen, put together, the chief is {called} Asaman.]

At Ignarsi there is another Yuku, they came from Asantimansu together with other Yukus, but they are not Abuhen neither Atutuo nor Blaemarn; they were not the real Yuku, but they were as a nurse to the real Yukus. They live at a district called [*Ajujua(?)*] Ajusoú and when [*they*] all the Yuku come to Kumasi but they live at Ignarsi, they are very close to the real Yukus. When Manu the mother of great King Ossai Tutu died, [*she*] the body was put [*into Ignarsi*] at Ajusou so that those people will have a look on the body.

From the reign of King Ossai Tutu to the reign of King Kwakudua, when the real Yukus has a share, they never give them. From the reign of King Kwakudua, Poku the chief of the Ignarsi Yuku asked [. . . (?)] the king that they should now join the share of the real Yukus, when there are any because they are also Yukus. So King Kwakudua told to the three real Yukus to give a portion of their share when they have any. From that time when the three Yukus has a share, they only give a little portion of the share to them, and the rest they divided into three equal parts. So Ignarsi join the other Yukus to make ten in number. All the Yukus put together, the Chief is called Assaman. [Then the great woman]

Then the great woman Anchioyami turned to her left and ask those who were sitting on her left "who are you" and they said we are Ōdācor. they are also Yukus and they [are] live at Insūtar and at Ajuarsi. The great woman also asked Contenasy and Akōkofae "who are you" and they said we are Oyukōr, their chief is Contenasy. And the head of Odacor and Oyukor is Insutar.

Historical Pieces

There are some Yukus who do not come from Assumya Ashanti-Mansu. These Yukus is called Juabin and they came from a district in Akim called [Gwansu(?)] Guansah. This Yuku is equal to the other Yukus. At the time when everyone was at Assumya Ashantimansu with Anchoyami then Juabin came and [*join*] accompanied their Yukus with the other Yukus of Anchoyami also Dadiesi was a province of Juabin at that time but now a province of Kokofu and also Bekwa was a province of Dadiesi at that time.

So they all came together to Anchoyami and his Yukus. Manpon came from a district called Adansi Ahinsan. Once at Adansi Ahinsan the earth opened, and seven families came out and arrange in seven group according to each family. Then the queen of them all sprang up, then an executioner sprang up. Immediately the King himself sprang. But as the King sent his head forth first, all his men praised him for he was very beautiful; but as soon as they began shouting, the King sank again and his executioner, which came before jump into the hole again and as his [jump] sank, a round iron wire which was hanging from his neck stayed [*(?) the mud*] by the hole and this iron wire can now be found [seen] at Ahensan.—

A great silence was made and all the people asked the queen—"where is the King." The queen said "It was the King who was coming last [but he] and who sank back on account of your shouting. Therefore this place came to be called Adansi Ahensan.[10] Then the queen gave names to the different kinds of the families.

(1) She called Blaetuo
(2) She called Agunār
(3) She called Attinār
(4) She called Assokoli.

The queen was called blabu Ashanti.

Having given names to the families, she brought them all to Anchoyami. Therefore every [*one from*] nation who hears her name flock to her at Anchoyami because she was the greatest of all.

[THE REIGNS OF AKYAMPON TENTEN, TWUM, ANTWI, AND KWABIA ANWANFI]

C. C. Reindorf made no mention of Akyampon Tenten, Twum, and Antwi in his *History of the Gold Coast and Asante*, but refers to Kwabia Anwanfi of Asantemanso as the "first king" of the district of Amanse. "All that we know of him," Reindorf wrote, is "that in his days gold was not known, the currency was pieces of iron."[11] *HAK* is perhaps the earliest written source for the first

---

[10] See the Twi ɔhene, "king, ruler, etc," and *san*, "return, go back."
[11] C. C. Reindorf, *History of the Gold Coast and Asante*, Basel, 1895: 47.

three of these rulers, but records no information about them other than that their status was that of *abusua-panin,* "head of a clan," rather than *omanhene,* "ruler of a nation." Kwabia Anwanfi is, however, treated at much greater length, for his time was that of the dispersion from Asantemanso, and he himself is said to have left there to settle at Kokofu, while his peers founded Dwaben, Mampon, Nsuta, and Nkoransa.

HAK 4:16 – *HAK* 5:20

The first King was Achempontintin who has his King-dom at Assumya but he did not rule the whole Ashanti men, he only ruled his families i.e., he was [chief] the head man in his families and his families took him to be their king. When he died, Chum took the kingdom, when Chum died, Anchui took the throne. When Anchui died, Kobia Anguanfi took the throne.

When Kobia Anguanfi came to the throne, he said that Assumya [was not fit . . . (?) for all their families finished dieing in] was not a convenient place for him to dwell with his families so he sent his hunter to seek for a place so that they may dwell there. This hunter in searching for a place, found a gardiner by name Kokor who had made a large garden or Affuo (the Ashanti name for a garden). So this hunter returned and told the King and so the king used to make a promenade to the garden of Mr. Kokor. When they were accustomed of the place, the king said to his families that he will go and make a dwelling at Kokor Affuo, i.e. the garden of Kokor, so they all went and dwell there. When they had settled there, they at first called the place A Kokor Affuo, and afterwards the place came to be called Kokofu. The name Kokofu which has retained up to nowadays.

The time when the King was coming with his families to dwell at Kokofuo, at the same time, the seven families also find each a place or land to dwell.

[——————————————————————]¹²

HAK 35:9 – *HAK* 36:30

When Kobia Gwanfi transferred from Assumya Ashantimansu to Kokofu and at the same time the other nations of families also found their land. When Kobia came to Kokofu, King of Juabin came to Aguanpon, then he transferred his Kingdom to [Aguanpon. Families(?)] Juabin and at that time Bekwi and Dadiasi were under him [so he(?)] with them he came to Juabin. Manpon from Santimansu came to Accrofunsu then the King [referred] transferred his Kingdom to Manpon. Insuta from Santimansu came to [*Ajuabunma(?)*] Ajuabumoar and the King transferred his Kingdom to Insuta. Inkransan from Asantimansu came to Antoa and from there they transferred to Inkransan.

---

[12] The line and square bracket at this point are obviously intended to indicate some sort of a break. In fact the major genealogical material commences with *HAK* 5:21, and will be found in Chapter Seven.

These are the [big] largest families, the other families went to each an island (?) and then from thence they transferred to another. Affiguarsy and Jamarsi both are under King Manpon. IIIII[13]

While Kobia wanphie was still at Asanti his sister [*Febre*] O'guebrydinhun and the King of Garmarsi was called Adu [Guanfi] Janfi, and Adu Janfi took Febredinhun as wife. While everyone was leaving [from] at Asantimansu, Adu Janfi told Febredinhun that [*they*] he is going to look for a land and when he gets[14] were no leaving but he wish Febredinhun should come and visit him. Janfi before going to Jamasi, he lived at [Owon ... (?)] Oun ... (?).

When Febredinhun was at Kokofu, she told to one of her servant O'Yam Pani [that, her husband has] the following word "O'Yam, my husband told me that I should come to him but I don't know the way to his country. So go and [fetch] find me a way." On coming nigh to a town which is now called Kumasi, he saw smoke in air and when came to Kumasi, there he found that the climate was good and he continued strait course to Ownano where [*the King*] Janfi lived. When he saw the King, Yam [saw] returned to his [Mother] mistress that he had found the way and then Febredinhun took the same course and went to his husband at Owoano. Before Febredinhun went to see her husband, her eldest brother Kobia Kwanfi died.

[THE REIGN OF OTI AKENTEN]

The only earlier reference to Oti Akenten known to us is the brief notice in Reindorf's *History of the Gold Coast and Asante*. After the death of Kwabia Anwanfi, Oti Akenten succeeded. "He made war," Reindorf writes,

> with the king of Kwadane at the place where Kumase was afterwards built, and captured Dareboo. At that time the Amanse people had the opportunity of seeing that place, and desired to remove there; but they were told that it belonged to Kwaku Dompo, the king of Tafo. Oti Akenteng was intending to remove there, when he was overtaken by death ... ..[15]

A much fuller, and largely incompatible, account is to be found in *HAK*. It begins with the words, "Otti Akenten her brother was crowned king ... .." The "her" refers to Ofebiri Odeneho, that is, the "Febredinhun" of the preceding passages [*HAK* 36:1–30]. It ends on *HAK* 53:4 with the words, "Here endeth the history of King Otti Akenten." The narrative is not, however, continuous. Clumsily inserted into it are various other pieces. The lengthiest of these is an account of Osei Tutu's mission to Denkyira. It was presumably written into this section of *HAK* because the compiler believed—probably correctly—that it occurred during the reign of Oti Akenten. It has been left in position.

---

[13] "IIIII" is inserted at the very end of *HAK* 35. It is presumably intended to indicate the change of topic at this point.
[14] The words, "he is going to look for a land and when he gets," are an insertion by Agyeman Prempeh, but do not slot well into the text.
[15] Reindorf, 1895: 47.

To the account in *HAK* we add the part of *OA/OY* headed "King Otti Akenten." We have, however, restored this to something approximating its original form—with the focus on Oti Akenten's departure from Kokofu and settlement in Kumase—by transferring the piece on the funeral customs for an Asantehene to Chapter Six.

Interestingly, Reindorf observes that Oti Akenten, like Kwabia Anwanfi before him and Obiri Yeboa after him, belonged to the Ekuono clan.[16] Certainly no support for any such claim is to be found in *HAK*, which firmly locates the three early rulers among the descendants of Ankyewa Nyame and therefore in the Oyoko clan. The matter cannot be dismissed out of hand, however, for as K. Y. Daaku remarked in 1966, "the foundation of what became Ashanti appears to have been the joint work of both the Oyoko and Ekoona [Ekuono] clans..... It is traditionally known that the early rulers, before Obiri Yeboa, were all related on the paternal side to the Ekoona clan..... It may be said that there was a change of dynasty."[17] During the process that led to the selection of Nana Osei Tutu II as Asantehene in 1999, a claim that the Golden Stool could be held by an Ekuono was made, but swiftly dismissed.

A piece on the Asante reckoning of time [*HAK* 38:18–39:31] appears in Chapter Six.

HAK 37:1 – *HAK* 38:17

Otti Akenten her brother was crowned king. After Akenten had [... (?)] Febredinhun came to her husband at Onnano. While Febredinhun crossed through Kumasi to her husband's country, she found that the climate of Kumasi was good; then she send to her brother Otti Akenten the king telling him that the climate of Kumasi was better than the climate of Kokofu so he had better come and live there. Otti Akenten agreed to her word and [transported] arranged(?) his kingdom to Kumasi. There they found a tree called <u>Kuma</u>, and the person with her families who lived under that tree was called Adoa Inkra Youli. When the King Otti saw that woman, he saluted her and he asked what family does she belong? And she asked the King what family does he belong? The King answered her and said that he was pure Yuku [... (?)]. She answered back saying "We want to join your Yuku so that we shall be the same family."

The King agreed to take her to his family. The King answered "But I do not want to live on other people's property so give me this to buy and I will take you near me and be one family. The woman agreed and sold to Otti the whole of Kumasi for 30 preguans.[18]

The King agreed and paid the sum. Kumasi is called after tree Kuma. (anyone from this(?) part who are [going] coming to there(?) says "we are going to Kumasi." Kuma is the name of the tree, and "si," Under Kuma (i.e. under) so Kumasi. The King who firstly reigned is called Otti Akenten. Kumasi was still there when [they(?)] took the Country and made prisoner the King. Up to then real family of Adoa Inkra Youli were three, one woman and boy and one man called Nunu. These people live at Asaman(?).

---

[16] Reindorf, 1895: 112n., and see also 47.
[17] K. Y. Daaku, "Pre-Ashanti States," in *Ghana Notes and Queries*, 9, 1966: 12.
[18] Twi *peredwan* (pl. *mperedwan*), key piece in the Asante system for weighing gold, equivalent to 2¼ troy ounces, and conventionally reckoned at £8 sterling in the 19th century.

HAK 40:1 – *HAK* 40:18

When King Otti Akenten had bought Kumasi, all the other [families] Ashantis who had scattered abroad came to [live] see him at Kumasi. At that time there was no master or King. There was continual civil fighting between [each] two country. So all the people [agreed] took council to abolish cheating and fighting and to do that they appointed a King who will rule them all. (At that time Otti Akenten was not a king of all the nation but he [was a King on] rule his families only). When the resolution was formed, Otti was appointed King of all the whole nation. But before he became king the people made him paid 30 preguans or £106 10s. This sum was paid by him in order to keep the agreement which was made to him and also for the purpose of ruling them. The money was divided among the nations.

[OSEI TUTU AT DENKYIRA]

HAK 45:23 – *HAK* 52:18

At the end of every year, Adansi and Asim pay a tribute of liquor to the King of Denkira to celebrate the year and the Ashantis pay a tribute of palm-oil.

Denkira gave orders to all the principal countries which are under him that they should send each a royal family to live at Denkira. After the great battle which King Annicocobro won, did not stay long on the throne and his brother in law called Bua Punsem succeeded him. When such [new?] order as has been already pointed out was passed The Ashanti King at that time was called Otti Akenten. Otti Akenten sent his [brother in law] uncle Ossai Tutu to represent him at Denkira, and all the principal countries sent each as may be called a consul.

While Ossai Tutu was going to Denkira, he brought 7 servants with him and these are the name of his servants in chiefs according to rank. The mother of Ossai Tutu is called Manū and the chair-bearer of lady Manu is called Docu.

Amanquatchia was the son of Docu. So while Ossai Tutu [*crossed out*: is coming] was going to Denkira, Manu gave Amanquatchia as a chair bearer to her son Ossai Tutu.

Names of the chiefs according to rank:
1) Amanquatchia
2) Ossafu Passuanpah
3) Jaedukumanin
4) Achampon Kofi (given to him by the King) (the King's son).
5) Brofuapayou
6) Tufuor (gun bearer)
7) Awucolonilly

These are the 7 chiefs or servant which he brought with him.

When Ossai arrived at Denkira, the King of Denkira gave him a man as a present to be his bed bearer. When Ossai got that man, he gave him another name which was called Occra Punsem.

Ossai Tutu was given a gun called Hūmū and with this gun, he has to present himself to the King every day.

While king of Denkira was going to fight with King Broomaankama the King of Sahŵi. The battle was fought near a large [lake] river, each army on each bank of the river. The Sahŵi were defeated, but no one was able to cross the river and see if they had fled. Ossai Tutu joined the fight.

Ossai Tutu with his 8 men endeavoured to cross the river, and they succeeded in crossing the river. when they reached on the other side of the river where the enemy was, they found that they had fled and going to plunder. They found the King's house and it may be said that everything was in gold, even the cieling of the house was made of gold. So Ossai loaded his 8 men with as much gold as they can carry and he himself took a gold bell, a gold doll, the [*glass*] jugs of the King which was made with lead and some other things which he himself can carry. Then he caught one of the enemy and cut his head, and coming near the river, he held the head of the man up, and told the army of Denkira that the enemy had fled.

At these words, the Denkira also tried to swim and they succeeded and they plundered the country. Then the King of Denkira told to Ossai to give him all that he has got, but he refused to give it. But it did not please the people and they did not say anything concerning it again.

One day 2 men came to the King and informed him that they had seen something strange:—

Early in the morning we saw [two] a man in the midst of the road, with two drums beating and when we approached near, he vanished.

The King sent two of his huntsmen and they ordered them that to ascertain it and to shoot the man. The two hunters watched and early in the morning, they found him beating, they fired and the man hastily flew up to heaven with one drum and he went straight to heaven and sit down on the moon and laid the drum before him. (Those who want to know the truth, may watch the moon and they will see a man with a drum sitting down). The man left the other drum and the hunters took it to the King. The man who is now sitting on the moon is called Ochrémayanor.

The King's drummers could not imitate the sound as [the] Ochrémayanor do. So the King ordered the drum to be beaten in imitating his name Boapunsem. So he made 1000 others just as he had received, and the one he received, he wrapped it with carpet and put it in a brass pan, and it was never beaten. The 1000 others are beaten while the other is carried on the head of a man. The name of the drum is called Ammonpon.

When Ossai Tutu went to Denkira, he married a girl at Denkira and one day the King sent a present to the wife of Ossai Tutu and as his wife went to thank the King, the King missed respect of her and took her. When the woman came, he told the tale to his husband.

Ossai Tutu had a false prophet called Akumasoa with him. (This false prophet consists of a little earthen ball.) One day Ossai took this prophet and put it in a bag which was hanging in his shoulder and he took 2 long knives with him and he went straight to the room where the King was sleeping. As soon as he enter, he shut the door.

Ossai Tutu [said] put the two knives before the King's bed and said "Why did you took my wife?" The King denied with a great fear. Then Ossai said There is an oath, take. If you don't, I will kill you on the spot. The King took the oath with a great fear. As soon as the King took the oath, Ossai took his knives and his prophet and came home straight.

As soon as Ossai arrived home, he went to Kumasi with his men and told his two wives to come afterwards. When Ossai was going, the King summoned his chiefs and related to them all what has happened in the morning. Then the chiefs approved to order Ossai to return to Denkira and to discuss with him. But when he heard that he is persuaded, he walked faster and at last he saw a man with palm-wine, he took it and drink and put some on [the] red ground and made mud with it and with his left hand he took some mud and made with the mud a mark from his neck across his shoulder and down to his tetee. Then he stood still and said "This mark meant that "no one can be able to cut my neck off." When he arrived to Kumasi, his families hid him at a place called Takiman, and he went there with one servant called Adoom Aoawina. At last the pursuers arrived at Kumasi and related the matter to the King and asked the King to send him with them. But the King denied that he has not seen him at all and he gave the pursuers order to look for him, but they returned to Denkira without finding him.) When Ossai went to Takiman, he married the queen of that place called queen Kwakru. She was a queen who has [very large] plenty of money. One day as Ossai and the queen was sleeping, Ossai killed the queen. And [at the same night] he took as much money as he and his servant can carry and set on their journey at the same night without the knowledge of any one. Early in the morning the queen's servant came to the [King] queen to welcome her, and they stayed behind the door till 11 a.m. and when they broke the door, they found that the queen was dead and they sought for Ossai Tutu. They did not see him and the whole city pursued him. When Ossai saw that he will be nearly overtaken, he and his servant entered into a big hole which was made by an animal called opprah.[19] When the pursuers arrived near the hole, it was the

---

[19] Twi *apra*, armadillo.

just time when the animal was coming to enter into his hole, and the pursuers caught the animal. After pursuing him for a great distance, they returned because they were afraid to bring war at Kumasi.

When the people had all returned, he set on with his journey again to Kumasi.

[THE FIRST DOMAA WAR]

HAK 52:19 – 53:4

At that time Kumasi was divided with the King of Doma. And the boundary was made by a garden. Once Kumase King and the King of Doma quarrelled in the said garden and this quarrelled led to a great war. The King of Doma was defeated. There was a huge stone called Drabuo at the bed side of King Doma and then Otti Akenten (Kumasi King) took the stone and placed it at his bed side. The kingdom of Doma was transfereed to a place called Suntresoo. Otti Akenten took the whole of Kumasi and then he died. Here endeth the history of King Otti Akenten.

OA/OY 1:2 – 3:21

Bodies of men or Regiments—organised by King Otti Akenten.—

The only remaining Departments organised by King Otti Akenten from Kokofu to Kumasi which now remains is the chief of Abontemu Akwasi-Kor chief of Kharsi—and the chief of Abra-fuor—Yam Panir.—

These two bodies of men take no order from any one at Kumasi, but they are joined to the contilé.—In time of sharing they used to take their share from the share of the contileheni if it be either a share of gain or paying.—In time of great assembly the Abrafuorheni sits just in front of the king and the Abontemuheni sits a little back between the contileheni and Akomheni thus:—
    contileheni   V   Akomheni

  Abontemuheni

In time of war the society Abrafuor take their rank in front of the contilé and Abontemu in the rear of the contilé.

When Otti Akenten came to Kumasi and became king, he made the following societies

1st First or better say his third society – the "Incanphékesier": this society only blows or whistles the King's horn.—and they are under the control of Fantiheni.

Fourthly – the "Ahoom-fuor" (now residing at In-nua-soo) under the control of Gharsiwah Primcor

Fifthly – the "Asoam-fuor" that is hammock bearer residing at Parkosoo. These hammock bearers residing at Parkosoo were ordered not to carry any living king; but their duties are to carry a dead king to cemetery.—If any one of this society ever mistakenly caught hold of the king or come to help to carry a living king, he is at once executed.—

Sixth. At Kumasi, there is a very nice polish stone called **DRABUOR**. This Drabuor was got by King Otti when he fought with and defeated the King of Dommar out of Kumasi and took Kumasi.—In taking possession of Kumasi, he found that stone lying on the upper part of the defeated King's bed, and King Otti took the stone and placed it on the upper part of his bed.—

Up to 1896, where the stone was found was the very place where the bedroom of King Otti Akenten situated.—

Seventh. In the reign of King Otti Akenten, umbrella was not known and great assembly of the King and his chiefs were under a large shed which was especially built and covered with leaves.

When chief Ka-n of the district of Bon-you-ler came to Kumasi, he was clad in Youkoumar and King Otti ordered his men to manufacture the same sort of cloth for him and with a piece of the Youkoumar he used to cover only part of the shed where he sat.—[20]

Eight – At the reign of King Otti Akenten, gold dust was not known for money; but nah-boo a sort of brass was used.—

Summary

Society or Body of men organised by King Otti = 2 from Kokofu and 2 at Kumasi [5] 4

Decorations are Youkoumar cloth and Dra-Buor and Abrafuor 3

Money used is a sort of brass called Nah-boo.

[THE REIGN OF OBIRI YEBOA]

The account of the reign of Obiri Yeboa begins in *HAK* 53:5, after a three line gap in the text, with the words, "When Akenten died his brother Obi Yaeboa succeeded him." The text follows on, seamlessly, from the treatment of Oti Akenten, and continues the saga of the development of Kumase. It ends in *HAK* 57:32 with the words "Here endeth the story of King Obi Yeboa." The fragment "King Obi Yaeboa," *OA/OY* 3–4, clearly belongs here. The narrative in *HAK* refers to Osei Tutu, under advice from Okomfo Anokye, seeking refuge in Akwamu at the time of the second Domaa war. An insertion at this point [*HAK* 54:6 – *HAK* 55:13] deals with traditional relations between Asante and Akwamu, and will be found in Chapter Six.

HAK 53:5 – *HAK* 54:5

When Akenten died his brother Obi Yaeboa succeeded him. When he came to the throne, he was eager to fight King of Doma and to drive him away from

---

[20] For three cloths known as *Oyokoman ogya da mu*, *Oyokoman Asonawo*, and *Oyokoman Amponhema*, see Rattray, 1927: 238, 240.

the little portion of land in which he lived so that he will have the whole land for himself.

When they were preparing for the war, there was a town called Agona and the King was called Agona Yamua and that king was a worshipper of a prophet called Buabodro. Yamua [told to Yaeboa] was warned by his prophet to tell Yaeboa that [he must before he asks is chiefs] he must give a sum of 60 preguans or (£480) to his chiefs in order to buy amuniations. But Yaeboa only gave 30 preguans instead of 60.

Annochi was the brother of Agona Yamua. So Annochi went and told Ossai Tutu saying, "The order which my brother the prophet gave to Obi Yaeboa concerning the war was not executed. So this war will not be good, they will be defeated. Therefore I will take you with me to Akom." So Ossai and Annochi went.

HAK 55:14 – *HAK* 55:30

When Obi Yaeboa had given the 30 preguans, and when everything for battle was ready, they set on their journey.

He had to summon the other petty Kings to help him. The mother of Yaeboa was called [*Akim*] Akomadoma and the maidservant of Akimadoma was called Amuamochaichai. (Her only work she do was to fill the pipe of Akumadoma). The son of Amuamochaichai was called Ayulis. And Akumadoma gave Ayulis to his son Yaeboa as a present. Yaeboa made Ayulis a chief and gave her a class of men called Soadro.

HAK 56:19 – *HAK* 57:32

Kragualier was given at the head of a man called Kofi Amanfun. But Amanfun was under Ayulis. Then he made a chief called Kodjoe [*Krob(?)*] Kroom and gave him in comander [of] by Ayulis. He further erect [the following] some chiefs under command by Ayulis. Ohiem Dicko was also under Ayulis. All these chiefs and their men who are under Ayulis put together are named by a class of man called Soadre.

So Ayulis became the [first] leading man in the country. The [royal . . . (?)] soldiers in the royal household were given in command of the King of Worna. In time of war Ayulis and his men and the royal soldiers, occupied the front, and in his back, he erected soldiers and gave under the command of Sabin his son.

In the war other petty Kings helped him and his own soldiers were those under command of Ayulis, Worna and Sabin.

At that time they fought with arrows and spears. When the battle began, the Ashantis were much surpressed and in fighting Obi Yaeboa was pierced and died. He died because his own soldiers did not take much care on him. When

Sabin saw that his father had fell, in haste he took his father and carried him to Kumasi and buried him with out the knowledge of anyone. When he had buried him, he then returned to battle again. The Ashantis were defeated. When the battle [had been] was ended, Ayulis was pursued and he got into a big hole which had been made in the ground by an animal [called Abidier[21]] The enemy returned and Ayulis came to Kumasi. Here endeth the story of King Obi Yaeboa.

OA/OY 3:24 – 4:31

Bodies of men or regiments organised by king Obi Yaeboa.—

The First body of men was the *Soaduro*—a man called Awelli was the leader

Second *Kojo kroemdiclo* leader of which was called Abrèfa Panir but the latter takes his command from Awelli.—

Third, *Eh-Hwim-diclo* leader of which was called Achrer-kūn Kojan, the latter takes his command from Kojokroemdiclo.—

Fourth *Acra-fuor* chief of which was called wrer-Dan-fuor, under command Eh-Hwim-diclo. – (Obi Yaeboa was the first to introduce Acrafordier)

Fifth *Chwa-fuor* (infantry) Chief of which was called Awor-soum-marn

The latter was also chief of *Soedoe* (cooks) in the King's palace) under Awelli.

Sixth – *Akwasiasy* diclo[22] chief of which was called Chwafuor Taby under Command of Chwafuor. – (finish with society under Awelli).

To his son Sabin:—

Seventh – *Domāh-Kwaïr* leader of which was his son Sabin.—

Eight King [Os(?)..] Obi Yaeboh made Oti Kotia a petty chief of *Amoakùn* under command of Sabin—from Oti Kotia came that intror known as *Aboa-Dier* for he was the first aboadier in Ashanti.

Ninth – He made Ah Poon Sem to be the chief at *Yamir Annir* under command of Sabin. When Ah Poon Sem died, Owusu Panin succeeded him and the latter married to the royal girl call Marnoo and begat Osei Tutu who became first King of Ashanti and gained great Kingdom for Ashanti.—

Tenth (a) He made Boagy Assaillir to be chief of (?)*Bisay arsy diclo* and ordered him to be under Sabin.—

Eleventh (b) He appointed the district of *Oh-kùn-ah-diclo* to be under Sabin.

---

[21] Marginal note, in the hand of Agyeman Prempeh. Twi *abedeɛ*, a duiker.
[22] Twi *odekuro*, the head of a village, responsible for the management of its affairs.

Twelth (c) He appointed okaïň to be diclo of *Banjahi* and *offoonassy*.—

Thirteen (d) He appointed a chief to command the district of *Phiarsy* under Sabin.

Fourteen (e) He appointed Kokofu ajummah moo to be under Sabin.—

Fifteen (f) He appointed Akoulah mi Yaw to be chief of adoùn-Coo-diclo under Sabin.—

Sixteen – He appointed as chief in the district of Seper-diclo and Dorlit-diclo to be under Sabin

Seventeen – He appointed Séoūah-diclo to be under Sabin. – (Sabin endeth)

To Gharci (Royal House guards)

First – Barū chief of Gharci.

Second – He appointed Boachie – chief of Inkwanta Boachie (under no body)

Third – He appointed Aboagar – chief under no body—

—Decorations—

First – He invented real umbrella (which was known as Ban Chiny-Yer) and covered it with Youkoumar. – (First man to introduce umbrella ... sah(?).).

Second – He organised a body of men to be goldsmiths at [(?) asarmarn], and these people were under Youkou-heni.

[OSEI TUTU SUCCEEDS OBIRI YEBOA]

HAK 58:1 – *HAK* 60:31

A great Committee was passed in order to find someone to succeed the King. And messenger was sent to the family of late King Obi Yaeboa at Asaman to [send] find one to take the throne. But an answer was sent by the family stating that they cannot send someone to take a mortifying crown.

A messenger was again sent to Kokofu to summon Gamby to come and take the crown. He refused to come and wants to continue in his blacksmith.—

[Then they sent ...] The chief said "[We have come] "No one wants to take the crown" [therefore any crown ... will do] So they sent to call Fredua, the king of Kenassy to take the throne. Fredua answered them, "If you want me, I will come, but I am in debt and before I will come you must send me the sum of 100 preguans i.e. £800 to pay the debts." The chiefs refused to give. [At Antoi] The King of Antoi was called Sakudie Dater and he proposed that Ossai Tutu, the son of Manu at Akom to take the crown. And it was carried out.

The King of Ahensan sent men from the families at Kumasi were sent to Akom to announce to Ossai Tutu to take the crown of his late uncle. Ossai agreed to take the crown. Ossai told this to his husband King of Akom who agreed to it. When Ossai was coming the King of Akom gave him men and a bead called Abodom and money.

When Ossai was coming he brought Adum Asamua to accompany him. Another name was given to that bead called Chumasadier. On his way to Kumasi, he received small pox. And Annochi ordered a hut to be build for Ossai till he is well. And Annochi ordered that powdered corn should be given to him which was called Esam in the Ashanti. When he has recovered, Annochi striked the head of a man and called his name Dossam (after Esam) and told him that he will find him men and he will be their head. He gave the name Ah-Same to the village. And the only work they do is to make Esam (powdered corn). When Ossai came to Kumasi he had to mourn for the death of his uncle then to succeed his place. Ossai had no man to kill to celebrate the death so he took his servant Amanquatchia (the man who was presented to him by his mother Manu) and washed him with red mud and promised him that he is going to be killed to celebrate the [day] feast. Amanquatchia said "I alone is not sufficient and if you want give me soldiers and I will go and fight some one and I will get you about a hundred or sixty men and you will kill them to celebrate the [day] feast."

Ossai agreed to it and sent him with some soldiers.

I. He fought with the 7 Saepaes and defeated them and took some prisoners.

II. He fought at [with the Chuar . . .] Chundroassi and defeated them and took some prisoners.

III. He fought with the [Panclo . . .] Panclon annu. He defeated them and took some prisoners. And altogether he got 100 prisoners and gave them to Ossai which he received with very thanks.

So Amanquatchia in order to escape his life, went to fight to get this 100 men.

When Ossai had come to Kumasi, he took the throne.

[OSEI TUTU DEFEATS THE DOMAA]

HAK 61:1 – 61:10

When he first ascended the throne, he swored that he would do as his uncle he will go and fight the King of Doma on behalf of his uncle death. At the length of 3 years everything for battle was ready.—

The King Doma Adom Kussi was defeated and killed and the others fled to Absim, but he gave his name Doma to the town instead of Absim.

[REORGANISATION OF THE KUMASE ARMY]

HAK 61:11 – 65:18

When Ossai returned to Kumasi, he was warned by Annochi to make Amanquatchia a general and to name him by the name of e'Kunti (because it is Amanquatchia who had won the 1st battle). [Ekunti ....[23]]

When he had created Amanquatchia a great general, he further created the other men with whom he went to Denkira subgeneral under command of Amanquatchia (for the names of the other men see p. 46). These six generals with Amanquatchia are called Contile (Atuo Insun[24]) (That is to say Contile consists of 7 great generals).

He further established a large town called Bantama and give it to those generals to dwell. Ossai Tutu at that time lived at Aya Kesihun. Annochi gave to Ossai Tutu a huge stone to carry on his head, and told him "You will walk with this stone on your head and where you will be tired, [put] lay it down, and the place which you will lay them will show the length or boundary of your country."

He journey very far and [where he arrived at] was tired; he laid the stone down and called that place [Jay] Gia buor Suor and he ordered the 3rd general Yae du Kumanni to watch the stone. Annochi told him, "You must erect a class of men and call them by the name of the town in which you were before you were made King."

Then he changed Soadro the name of the class of men under Ayulis and called it by the name Akom. He did not make any [clear] great difference between Contile and Akom, but in time of war or meeting, Akom was ordered to occupy in front and Contile behind.

Akom was [higher] greater than Contile, but Contile gain Akom by fighting bravely. The power of Akom was reduced because when King Obi Yaeboa went to fight at Doma, Akom did not take a good care on Yaeboa and let him be [prisoned] killed. But when Contile went to fight at Doma the Contile took great care of King Ossai Tutu and won the battle. So Contile [got] became [the first general stool] higher than Akom [. . . surrendered(?)].

Sabin the son of Obi Yaeboa was made a great general by Ossai. Ossai further made Efriyae (his son) a general under command of Sabin, and told Sabin, "it is good to have a son, for if not you, your father's body would have been taken by the enemy. So here I give you my son and in case I die in a battle, he will take me home.

When Sabin died, Efriyae took the place of Sabin. And his men which he commands are named by the name Achimpim.

---

[23] Two lines deleted, and illegible.
[24] Twi *atuo nson*, literally, "seven gunners."

He further made Krapunsem (the man whom he got from the King of Denkira when he was there) a general and gave him a class of man called Kidom to be the head. He further had under him Kwasem. But Krapunsem and his men were under command of Efriyae.

Annochi prophecied to him saying, "If thou go to battle and the general which you kill, take out one of his teeth and hang it on the neck of one of your son whom you will chose to give. And the name of the child will be O'Kraodomsin."

To O'Kradomsin Ossai gave a class of man called Hinar to be command. One of Ossai's servants was called [Tortoduawoo (?)] Toto Jassae (lived at Saepae) and to him he gave a class of men called Akumantraé, but Akumantre was under command of [Efriyae] Hinar and Hinar was command of Efriyae.

Summary
Kidom, under command of Hinar,
[Kontilé] Akumantré under command of Hinar,
Hinar under command of Efriyae,
[Efriyae] Chief of Achempem.

In those days [the Ayuku were under the] Akompondiawuo [was] the chief of [the Ayuku] Yukus was also the crown prosecutor. After Akompondiawuo [Ayuman(?)] Ahinsan took the place of crown prosecutor. There was a man called Saffier who lived at Adansi and Ossai took good admiration on that man to be a judge and asked the King of Adansi to give the said man to him. The King was pleased to give him.

Then Saffier was made the crown prosecutor [after the death of Ayuman(?)] and Ahinsan suceeeded. All those who succeeded Ahinsan are to give oath to the King of Ashanti when he is crowned.—He also gave Saffier a class of men called Doma Kwayir. The latter also was under Efriyae. Achimpim held the head and Saffié the foot.

Sabbim became so great on account of the brave deed he performed.

To Adoom Asamua he gave him the command of the Adooms but the real head man was Ayulis.

[THE DEFEAT OF ASIEDU PAPAA KESE]

HAK 65:18 – *HAK* 66:20

[Ossai Tutu went to the King of Akyim called Assié dū Papā Kesié]

[Ossay] Assié dū pāpā Kesié the King of Akim came to Juarsi to mourn for the death of his mother-in-law and while coming the King brought 40,000 soldiers. There was a man called Intobby Awinsin and that man lived at Juarsi. When that man saw that Assié dū pāpā Kesié had come to Juarsi, sent a message to inform the King Ossai Tutu, and the latter on hearing the news, [sent a] resolved to take the King by storm in the same night. Ossai Tutu set on at the same night with the few [regular soldiers] soldiers in the capital, and early in the morning reached Juarsi. The other King was not expecting their coming, and when he heard Ossai had come, asked for what purpose he has come to attack him. Then Assié took his carpet from in his hammock and tored a small piece and tied his waist saying, "I must die today:" and he went and sat under a tree and when his men saw their enemy coming, they all fled and the King was taken prisoner.

When Tutu returned to Kumasi, his other great generals asked him why he has gone to fight without their knowledge. But he satisfied them by giving them 30 preguans or £240.

[THE DISPUTE WITH DENKYIRA]

HAK 66:21 – 68:29

As had been already read, that the country of Assin had to pay a yearly tribute of a barrel of liquor to the King of Denkira. When this barrel of liquor was given to Boapunsem the King of Denkira ordered that it should be open immediately to be drunk by all. The servants opened the barrel and as the King was presenting his glass to be filled, a big fly came out and flew away. His servants said "Do not drink this liquor master", but the King disobeyed and drank some. When the King drunk, he got fever, which he afterwards died. The leading men of the country ordered that Odruo Apinsemuo (the man who brought the barrel of drink) should be [find] found and put to death.

Odruo escaped and came to Kumasi. At that time the people of Denkira [called] gave the name Kwaman to Kumasi. Intimi Jakali took the throne of Denkira. The latter sent one of his Esen[25] and one of his sword bearer with a huge copper dish to inform Ossai Tutu for what cause he had kept Odruo in his country [and] a man who has poisoned their King and therefore they must send Odruo back without delay (at that time Ashanti was under the rule of Dinkira) and to punish Ossai and the inhabitants of Kumasi, [they must] the King and each of the leading men of Kumasi must send one of their wives whom they love most and one of their children whom they love most and to fill the copper dish with money and to send a bangle of bead called Chi Chili Konnah (the most precious bead). Ossai Tutu summoned all the people that are under him and conveyed the said news to them.

Adar Kwar Yia Dom the King of Juabin stood up (first) and said "This [man] King wants to fool us, and so we will never give him what he has [asking]

---

[25] Twi *esɛn*, "herald, messenger."

demand." And he took a stone and made a prayer to the Gods saying that they [will] shall never never give anything and he threw the stone in the copper dish and all the chiefs did the same thing till the dish was full of stones.

The sword bearer was killed and his sword was [took from Killed and he] taken and placed among the stones in the dish. And the Esen was sent to inform the King of Denkira that they will never give what he demands and if he do not satisfy, come and fight them. And Annochi the great prophet stood up and said "I will help you." When this was informed to the King of Denkira, he sent [them] the Ashantis a word that he is ready to fight them.

But Annochi said "All the soldiers of the Ashanti Kingdom cannot be compared to the smallest wing of the Denkira King. So I will change the mind of half of their armies in such a way that during the fight, half of them will come to help you (Ashantis) and the other half I will discouraged them so that you will be able to fight them and defeat them.

[OKOMFO ANOKYE AND THE PREPARATIONS FOR THE DENKYIRA WAR]

This account of Okomfo Anokye's role in organising the alliance of Kumase and other *aman*, put together to overthrow the Denkyirahene, clearly belongs both chronologically and logically at this point in *HAK*. For whatever reason it was apparently overlooked, and only inserted at a later position in the ledger. A piece on the division of the spoils of war [*HAK* 83:9 – *HAK* 84:20], here located in the context of the preparations for the Denkyira War, will be found in Chapter Six.

HAK 81:10 – *HAK* 83:8

Before [King Tutu] the battle of Domar, Annochi prophesied two things to King Tutu saying (i) "While late King Obi Yaeboa was going to fight Domar, my elder brother prophesied that Yaeboa must give £480 to be shared among all the chiefs who were going to the fight he did not obey and only gave £240 instead of £480 and the result was that he was defeated, so I advised you now to give £480 in order to gain the fight."

To this King Tutu agreed and at once gave the £480.

(ii) Obi Yaeboa was defeated because he [occupy the front . . . for yours(?)] [. . . middle wing, as for you(?)]. I will give you a medicine and this medicine will turn the heart of some one will come to ask you to let him [occupy the front for your stool] . . . middle wing.

Annochi ordered all the chiefs to assemble. When they had assembled, he stood before all and exclaimed "Who will be able to buy [the front] [the title of the commander . . .] middle wing for £240." Akorsa Yiadom stood and said "I can [buy] pay for it," and one of his drum servants standing behind him said "Master, take this offer. I will pay this £240 for you;" and a few minutes after the servant brought the £240 and gave it to his master and [his mas] Yiadom offered it. After offering this £240, he said I and the King must take an oath; if during the fight I am oppressed by the enemy, you the King must come and defend me and if your (King) side is oppressed I, will do the same. This oath [between the] has long during the whole generation between the Kingdom of Ashanti and the Kingdom of Adontin.

[*margin*: The Akorsa Yiadom said publicly "My servant the drummer is a slave [......] and as He had bought such a great power for sure, I wish that whenever he shall die he be buried with me.]

When this had been settled, the Ashantis always gain victory when met with black army.

While King Tutu was making preparation to fight the Denkira, Annochi prophesied to King Tutu to give to Boahin Nantuo the first King of Manpon the commander of the whole Ashanti army.

So King Tutu gave "the right wing," "the [front] Adontini," "the left wing" and also Contile Akom [on commander to Nantuo] Jarsi and Kidom in commander to Nantuo.

King Tutu told to Adarkwar Yiadom the King of Juabin to be the head in commander of the Yukus and Dakus. The Yukus are Kokofu, Bekwi, Insutar, Abohin, Atutuo, Bremand, Contanasi, Akokofer and Ajuarsi.

HAK 84:21 – *HAK* 86:13

[While the fig(ht?)]

While preparation to fight Denkira was made, [Annochi told to King Tutu] it was [made] seen that the left wing had more men than the right and the front.

Annochi said "We shall really conquer the King of Denkira but in returning from fight King Tutu will die and so I will turn the death of the King to come on another man." And Annochi exclaimed, "Who wishes to die for the King." Assensoo Pani of Agumakarsi replied "I will, but the King must drink an oath never to kill any of my family when they have done wrong." And Annochi [said you] ordered a copper dish to be placed on the head of Agumakarsi and he will go to the sky and pour heavenly medicine in the dish while it is on the head of the man. Annochi said to the man, "you see that I am pouring heavenly medicine on your head but after the fight you must [not] never clean your teeth except the mouth." But he promised every [one not two] that it would be bad for the one who will say bad thing against him when he is gone. As he had gone the men of the left wing began to say bad words against him saying "he is a liar he can't pour heavenly medicine down." Not long everyone saw something like powder falling. As he came down [. . .] his left eye was shut and said some one had said bad words against me and as my left eye is shut, it is quite sure that the words came from you members of left wing. And to the left wing he said: you members of left wing will always be small and his word became very true [?].

[After the battle, when . . .] When they had come to Asocat on returning from the fight Asenso Pani was sleeping, his wife who was the daughter of King Ossai Tutu was [sleeping] sitting near him, and his wife took a wood and wanted to clean his teeth. As she touched his teeth he awoke and said "You have killed me," and related the story which Annochi said to her and immediately got fever and on reaching his country he died a few days after.

[THE DENKYIRA WAR]

The Asante war of liberation against Denkyira can be accurately dated from the records of the European trading companies on the Gold Coast. In mid-1699 it was known that a war was imminent, and by June 1700 it was clear that the opponents of the Denkyira were those calling themselves the Asante. In May 1701 fighting was in progress, and by November word had reached the coast that the Asante victory over the Denkyira was "very complete."[26]

HAK 68:30 – *HAK* 74:9

Description of the battle.

The King of Denkira made ten classes of men and [are under A.........]. These men and woman are there to offer their bodies as a sacrifice to the King whenever a royal family is dead and these men were called Abon Chuma Fuor[27] and these headmen were called Ajae Bi, Youdyayim, and Kokobin.

And these 3 men decided that they are dissatisfied with the treatment they are receiving and so they will come and help the Ashantis when the battle is declared. So they left their land to come to Kumasi to help the Ashantis. When they were nigh to Kumasi, they sent a word to Ossai Tutu that they are coming to help him in war and they sent their chief Kokobinny to take an oath before the King and to ascertain before him that they are coming to help him with clean spirits. And they asked the King to send them one of his families to take an oath before them and to ascertain that the King will not kill them when they come to help him. The King sent his nephew Otie Cu Achulier to those men and they in return sent one of their men called Kwakwabin to take oath. When oath had been taken on both sides, they came to Kumasi. Ajaebi came 8 days before Youdyayim. When they came, the King gave them a district called Kojokulom to live. It came to pass that the King asked those men to give him [Kwakwabin] Kokobin so that he will name him after his birth day. These people agreed, and gave Kwakwabin to him and they also in return asked Otié Cu Achulier to come and live with them at Kojokulom. This was given.

---

[26] See, for example, Wilks, 1993: 111–12.
[27] Reindorf, 1895: 57 refers to those in Denkyira reserved for slaughter on the death of a royal person. They were, he writes, "called the Bontwumafo, now Atwomafo . . ."

When the Chumas came and found that nothing was done to them, the Dāoū Daoū also came and when the battle was nearly to commence, the [Da] Inkwayulaes and the Sobis came. All came to assist the Ashantis. Ochilé mah Dier Abaetiae came with 1000 men to the assistance of the Ashantis.—(Ochile mar Diae Abaetiae [[was the head man of the tribe of men called under the name of Otimannou(?)] brought with him the drum which was received by shooting the beast. They came to Kumasi and lived at a district called Inkukuah. Akodam & Nuamoah the chief of the musicians also came to assist the Ashantis with 1000 men. The trumpet which Akudan carried himself was made of gold. Many others that cannot be mentioned came. These are the [wonderful things] principal wonders done by prophet Annochi before the battle began.

1st. He said to tell you that I will surely make you defeat the enemy, I will (pointing to a tree) speak to this tree and the root will go up and the trunks and the branches will go down to the bole. And it was so. Then Annochi said to make you sure that you will defeat the enemy, I will go to Denkira and there I will change myself into a woman and the King of Denkira will love me and [after taking] if he takes me, I will be sure that I can change [him into] his courage to be a woman courage and then you will be sure to [get] gain victory over him. Indeed he went and it was done as he spoke.

2nd. When the Denkira king [had] was coming to meet the Ashantis, they came to a district and there they pitched their camp. So Annochi said to Ossai Tutu, "I will take you and your son, [and] Japa and one servant to carry a sheep and we four shall go into the enemy's camp and there I will dig hole and make prayers and then to bury this sheep. The enemy will see us doing so but they will not be able to catch you and I will bring you all safe." And it was so.

[The King of Denkira brought 200 000 men and the Ashantis were only 20 000. But through the . . . of Annochi they were . . .]

The King of [Asha] Denkira sent a messenger to tell the chief of [Aduakwa] Adoonkoo. Ossai says that he is coming to sleep in his town (Aduku possess 30 soldiers). So Adunku sent the messenger to tell the Denkira King that if he comes he will fight him with his 30 men.

The next day the King came and Adunku was able to push one of the wing then he ran back to Ossai and the King took the town of Adunku.

In the way of Ossai to meet the enemy, Ossai said to Annochi "I want some drink but there is none.

3rd So Annochi said to a palm tree, "O father palm, my King asks of thee thy drink" and immediately the palm bent its boughs and pour its drink and the King drank. When they reached a place called Féyiasi, [the] Annochi said "I am going to see the enemy so he and his son Japa climbed a tree and the footsteps of Annochi and his son could still be seen all along the tree where his feet touched.

4th. On his return Annochi said, They are too numerous so you (Ossai) and all your men must come and hid yourself behind this tree and because a single volley of the enemy will crushed you all.

And so the Ashantis hid themselves behind the said tree and it was said that as soon as the enemy fired, the tree enlarged in itself and all the balls stucked to the tree but as soon as the Ashantis fired the tree became small and the balls killed the enemy. The balls of the enemy could still be seen on the tree.

The battle began at 7 p.m. and at 11 oclock the whole army of Denkira was defeated.

[Adunukwa son is] When the army of the King had fled [Adunakwa] Aderkwar Yardum saw the King of Denkira playing with a gold [(?)chain pla] wally[28] and at the same time had tied his feet with gold chains and that meant that the Ashantis can never catch him even if he put himself in chains. When [Adunakwa] Adarkwar saw him he lift up his sword to struck the King and the King protected himself with his hand and the sword struck the gold ring on his arm and broke it, then the men [of Adunakwa] of Afoanpon caught the King and killed him.

5. The blood of the King which fell down had risen into a hill and the cola which the King was eating fell down and it grew up into a big tree. All these can still be seen.

The King of Denkira brought 200 000 men and the Ashantis 20 000.

But through the Genius of Annochi the Ashantis defeated the people and became the leading nation over all the largest countries around it. After this great battle, the Ashantis became the most powerful of all the other countries around it.

[THE ELMINA TRIBUTE]

The Elmina tribute was one that had long been a major issue in Asante politics. Several letters dictated by Asantehene Kofi Kakari (1867–1874) had to do with the matter, and are extant. The topic has been treated in several recent works.[29]

HAK 74:10 – *HAK* 75:16

The people of Lamina gave as a tribute to the King of Denkira the sum of £96 (but cannot tell why the tribute was paid).

When the King of Denkira was coming to fight the Ashantis, he sent a word to the Laminas to lend him guns, powders, balls up to the sum of £8 000. And

---

[28] Twi *ware*, the board game.

[29] Ivor Wilks, *Asante in the Nineteenth Century: the structure and evolution of a political order*, Cambridge, 1975: 231–35; René Baesjou (ed.), *An Asante Embassy on the Gold Coast. The mission of Akyempon Yaw to Elmina 1869–1872*, Leiden and Cambridge, 1979: 7–52; Larry W. Yarak, *Asante and the Dutch 1744–1873*, Oxford, 1990: 133–69.

the Ashanti King sent a word to the Laminas to lend him guns, powder, and balls up to the sum of £2400. When the Ashantis had [defeated] conquered Denkira, they sent the sum of £2400 to the Laminas to pay for the ammunitions which they had taken. The King of Lamina sent a word to the Ashantis, stating that they have received the sum of £2400 with thanks but since [they] the Ashantis had [defeated] conquered Denkira so they expect the Ashantis to pay back the £8 000 for them. The Ashantis refused to pay the £8 000 because that does not concern them. Ossai Tutu agreed with his chiefs. But he said that he would pay the money since the throne of Denkira is now attached to the Ashanti throne. So the money was paid to them. The people of Lamina appreciated [*margin*: Ossai] very much for paying the £8 000, and they promised Ossai that the sum of £32 which was paid yearly to the King of Denkira will now be paid to him yearly.

[From] This tribute was paid yearly from the time of Ossai Tutu up to the time of King Karkari.

[THE WAR WITH ADANSE]

HAK 75:17 – 76:3

[When] While King Obi Yaeboa went [going] to the Domar war, the King of Adansi made an evadation[30] and came to Kumasi and slew some of the royalists and many others and took some prisoner. [D .... of the Adansi troops] The head Royalist who were taken prisoner was called Inkatiar Ottim.

After King Tutu had defeated the [Adansi] the Denkira and taken their power, he went to Adansi to war, with their King called Apiani Cramo for the reason of having taken and killed some Royalists while Obi Yaeboa was with war with the [Domar] Adar Kussi, the King of Domar, to take back their royalists but they did not get back the royals, the Adansis were defeated and retreated from the interior.

But before Ossai went to Adansi, Inkatiar Otim (the head of the royalist) died and left 2 children, Kussi Obodum, and Ekua Efriyae.

[THE DENKYIRA REBELLION]

HAK 76:18 – *HAK* 78.6

After the war with Denkira, Annochi warned Ossai Tutu that "if ever the people of Denkira [repel] rebel, you King Ossai must never go yourself to fight them but send someone to fight them in your stead."

---

[30] That is, invasion.

At last Intim the King of Denkira died and Bodu Acafun took the crown and the latter raised an army of 40,000 men and began to rebel but at that time Annochi was still alive. When the news stating that Bodu had rebelled again was informed to Annochi, he said that it is impossible for a nation to rebel after being defeated; and there must be someone here in Kumasi who is [making a] working bad medicine to bring hostile army to Kumasi here again.

So Annochi said I will stand in the midst of this city and shout [for] calling the one who is [working bad medicine] doing that work.

So he stood and cried three times and a man called Odro Agin Samuo (it was through the very man which led the first war between Kumasi and Denkira) shouted It is I! It is I! who is doing bad work to bring hostile army to Kumasi because it was through me that that you got war with Denkira; and in the war you defeated the people and got a rich treasure for in the town and out of this treasure I got nothing; so it is through that that I am now doing this work. And Annochi replied "You are right so this war which is now going to be fought, the King himself will not go but will send Boansy Kuffu the chief of Adan Chimansu in his stead and you must go too and when you return from the war you will be rewarded. The war was gained and got some more treasure and men and to reward him he got 300 men.

[THE ATTACK ON KAASE]

HAK 78:7 – *HAK* 78:28

The [4th] 5th war King Tutu fought was at Karsy.

When King of Karsy died, such news was informed to King Tutu. Once before Tutu became King he had a quarrel with one royal family of Kasi [*inserted in margin*: about who is to take the throne after the death of the present King] but [*crossed out*: Ossai] Tutu did not take any step to fight him and when such news was informed that the King of Karsi was dead, Tutu ordered that the one of the royal member who quarrelled with him once must be brought dead before he will come to assist the funeral. But the Karsian refused to kill their master and when it was informed to Tutu, Tutu ordered his soldiers to shoot the Karsians. The Karsians were defeated and their royal was killed, and few others; when the King had killed this royal, then he buried the King who was dead.

[THE ATTACK ON TAFO]

HAK 78:29 – *HAK* 79:13

The 6th war was at Taffoo.

At that time [the] each king tries to get some elephant teeth about 16 or 20

112   *Chapter Five*

to make whistle [*margin*: called Intahila³¹]. Tutu and King of Taffoo had succeeded in getting the horn [and]. Tutu sent a word to Osafu Acontun the King of Taffoo to send him as present one of his sweetest horns. Acontun sent a reply "I shall not send you; you are too jealous." Tutu answered I will fight you for telling me that I am jealous. King Osafoo Acontun broke the gun. Acontu was defeated and killed and everything was taken. And the fragments of the horn was taken to Kumasi and repaired and is now exist.

[THE ATTACK ON AMAKOM]

***HAK* 79:14 – *HAK* 81:9**

The 7ᵗʰ war as at Ama Come.

The King of Amah Come was called Akorsan Yiadom.

[King] To the latter King Tutu gave his niece Guarcum Kussi Amua in marriage to him.

[This marriage rendered both Kings to be of good terms]

There was a man called Asie Bragnare who was one day challenging with his friends and said I can make these two Kings fight each other; the other said "no" and he said let us bid for £8; if I succeed you will give me £8; if I fail I'll give you £8.

One day Asie Bragnare went to Amah Come and said to the King "Arise for King Tutu is coming with an army to fight you." Akorsan Yiadom at once ordered the drum to be beat which is a sign to call the men to take up arms. Asié bragnar seeing the diffusion and there on rushing to battle, at once came to Kumasi and told Tutu that Akorsa Yiadom is nigh to Kumasi with an army to fight you. Both King before meeting sent spies to watch whether the army is coming: and the spies of each King met together and return to inform their Kings. So they believed the story of Bragnare. In few hours the army of both King met face to face. During the fight the wife of Yiadom sent men to his nephew King Tutu to ask the reason why he [raised an army to fig] had given her in marriage and then to raise an army to fight her husband. So King Tutu replied, I know nothing, but I heard that you and your husband had raised an army to fight me and I made ready for you. So we are fighting without cause and both King ordered their men to stop the fight. The two Kings met together and asked questions and found that Asie bragnar who had caused the fight. And Asie bragnar and his friends were summoned and said "I was challenging with this my friend and I said that I can make you both fight each other and he said that I can and we bid for £8, and to prove that I can, I came and told each

---

³¹ Twi *ntahera*, the horn of that name.

of you that you are preparing to meet each other." When they asked the other man, he asserted the same thing. Therefore Tutu gave £8 to Asie bragnar for having done this and immediately ordered both to be killed.

[OSEI TUTU AND THE SUCCESSION]

This is the final section of *HAK* as that work is currently known to us. It is not impossible that further parts will, in time, come to light, but there is little reason to be optimistic about this. Our instinct, and it is no more than that, is to think that the writing of a synoptic history of Asante was, for whatever reason, discontinued at this point. Perhaps the services of F. A. Prempeh were no longer available. Whatever the case, the last section offers no account of the circumstances of Osei Tutu's death in 1717, but does – rather skilfully – introduce the figures of Opoku Ware and Boa Akwatia who were both to claim the succession, with the former gaining it.[32]

HAK 86:14 – *HAK* 87:30

[Akua An . . .] Amani [Apon] Anpon King of Manpon got a dispute which led to a war with the people of Chen Chen [Roulou] Roo. So Ampon asked King Tutu to assist him with men to fight the Chen Chen Rulu. Boa Katia the nephew of Obi Yaeboa was to succeed King Tutu when he is dead. King Tutu on hearing the petition of Anpon told to Katia to be the commander of the army with whom he will assist Anpon.

Together with Katia there was Poku Tintin the grandson of King Tutu, and then soldier. When Katia was going King Tutu asked him to condemn to death those who will [..........] break the law either to kill or to take money. To Poku Tintin he said "Here is a box full of gold, reserve this case to [help] lend to those men who when being condemned to pay money will ask you, moreover those who will come to tell you to ask pardon for him when he is condemned to death by Katia, you must try your very best to let him escape his death." When Anpon received help, he was able to defeat the Chen Chen Rulu. The order of King Tutu was executed by both men. In the fight the people of Manpon got a silver dish and the valuable beads of Inchiukro Kuna[33] and gave them to their King Anpon. But Katia asked them to give him the dish and the bead to give to King Tutu. Anpon said I came and asked King Tutu for men so if I have got something I will send some for King Tutu when I reached my country. This led to a quarrel and Katia gave Anpon a [slap to] blow. And at once Anpon "I will give you these two things." When this was informed to King Tutu, he said "It is not lawful to give a blow to King Manpon so return these things to Anpon King of Manpon. At that time the royal families on the side of King Tutu were less than

---

[32] Wilks, 1975: 327, 329–30; Wilks, 1993: 254–55; McCaskie, 1995a: 47, 370 n. 10.
[33] Twi *nkyekyerekona*, the beads of that name.

the part of Boa Katia, so when Poku Tintin was borned, King Tutu ordered the child to be brought into a cottage to a woman called [Amma(?)] Wanni, at Pampaso.

Annochi said to King Tutu "I will show thee two signs, and you will see whether the chair will still remain in your family [or] go to the part of Boa Katia.

CHAPTER SIX

Ethnographic Pieces

INTRODUCTION

The pieces that comprise this chapter may be described as broadly "ethnographic" in character. Scattered throughout the pages of *HAK* and *OA/OY*, they attest to the quite extraordinary interest that the Akan have in *atetesem*, "tradition," and especially in the origins of cultural phenomena.

It was undoubtedly this characteristic of the Asante that led C. H. Harper, Chief Commissioner, Ashanti, 1920–1923, himself no mean ethnographer, to create an Anthropological Department. In July 1921 he appointed as its head R. S. Rattray, whose major work, *Ashanti*, was in fact the Department's first annual report. Rattray benefited greatly from the readiness of Asante informants to explain their understanding of "custom" to him, and he wrote warmly of his "many good friends among the chiefs and people of Ashanti," acknowledging his "heartfelt thanks for all their generous help, their affection, and their encouragement."[1] He was, however, unaware of Agyeman Prempeh's writings.

[THE AKAN "CITIES"]

Correctly, these are the *Akanman piesie nnum*, "the five firstborn Akan centres." Following the order in *HAK*, these are Asenmanso, Adansemanso, Abankeseso, Asantemanso, and Abuakwa Atwumamanso. All are located in the forest country in the Pra and Ofin basins, and each is regarded as a "cradle" of one or other of the forest Akan peoples.[2]

HAK 45:7 – *HAK* 45:13
Asante Akan noom
The mean Ashanti divided into five cities
1) Asin
2) Adansi
3) Denkira
4) [Ashan] Asanti or Ashanti
5) Akim

---

[1] R.S. Rattray, *Ashanti*, Oxford, 1923: ix.
[2] Ivor Wilks, *Forests of Gold. Essays on the Akan and the Kingdom of Asante*, Athens, OH, 1993: 71, 91–92.

[THE *NTƆRƆ* AND SOUL-WASHING]

The *ntɔrɔ* are cultic organisations concerned with "washing," that is, purifying, the *kra* or soul. Membership is determined by reference to patrifilial ties, and an *ntɔrɔ* possesses a set of distinct names, which are taken by those belonging to it. Thus, for example, the names Osei and Owusu alternate in the Adufudeɛ, and Opoku and Adu in the Asafodeɛ, branches of the Bosommuru *ntɔrɔ*. There is a considerable literature on the institution.[3]

HAK 28:28 – *HAK* 30:16

. . . now we are explaining that which is called Intor.[4]

According to the several families, your mother's part is your real family and your father's part is your Intro. i.e. one cannot marry anyone who is in same family as your mother whether it be any one but provided it bear the same title. In the same way one cannot marry the Intro of his father. But there are two families which bear nearly the same name but this they can marry one another but provided it is not the same family.

Here is an example:—

There is a kind of Intro called Ashanti *Abuadie* and another Intro called Akim *Abuadie*. These two families signed *Abuadie* [but] and are also Intro. But they can marry one another. There is another one which is a bit complicated to understand and the law against it is for everyone at [Kumas] Ashanti. If a man and a woman have a boy and a daughter, this two are forbidden to marry, but the daughter [& boy of] and son of a sister and brother can be allowed to marry together. The son of a girl calleth the brother of his mother *wofa* and the daughter of a boy calleth the sister of his father *missiwa*.

The most distinguished of the Intro are (1) Abuadie (2nd) Achim Abuadie 3rdly Adufodier 4thly Acrudie 5thly Assafodie 6thly [A?i..made] Achundie 7thly Assabidie 8thly Assani..... 9thly Annifidier [10thly] they are two kinds of Annifidier 10thly Ammaddie 11thly Appipladydie 12thly Abrādie 13thly Abranie 14thly Adumakundie 15thly Akom another name is Busukony 16thly Busumchui another name is Agimadie 17thly Inkatia 18thly Afuardie 19thly Ankamady

many others more—[5]

---

[3] See, for example, Rattray, 1923: 45–54; A. C. Denteh, "Ntorɔ and Ntɔn," in *University of Ghana Institute of African Studies Research Review*, III, 3: 91–96; Ivor Wilks, *Asante in the Nineteenth Century: the structure and evolution of a poltical order*, Cambridge, 1975: Ch. 9 passim, 730; T. C. McCaskie, *State and Society in Precolonial Asante*, Cambridge, 1995: 166–72.

[4] Three lines are crossed out at this point: "All ..... from the relatives of your mother is called your families and the relatives of your father is your Intro."

[5] A space of about five lines occurs in the text here. Presumably the original intention was to add further names at this point. The list may be compared with those in Rattray, 1923: 47–48 and McCaskie, 1995a: 170–72.

HAK 56:1 – *HAK* 56:18

It was Obi Yaeboa who brought what is known as Accra Jua Dier[6] which means to worship your soul and your father's family which you belong on the day in which you were borned. For an example.

If your father's intro or family is called Abuadiae and you were borned on [Wednesday] Thursday, [.....] Wednesday is chosen [to worship] for all those who [worship] belongs to that intro which is called Abuadiae to worship it. So on Wednesday you must celebrate that day and on Thursday again you must celebrate it because you were borned on that day. This is called Akraguădie.

[THE CALENDAR]

The Akan calendar in general, and the Asante in particular, have been the subject of many studies. One of the most detailed of these, that by J. B. Danquah, unfortunately remains unpublished.[7] Most recently, McCaskie has published a critical study of the Asante Odwira in its calendrical setting.[8] It may be noted that the names of the seasons and of the days of the week, as listed in *HAK*, are little changed in contemporary Twi, but the names of the months show radical differences.

HAK 38:18 – 39:31

When Kumasi was first founded there were three seasons—

	Native		English
(1)	Assusobilé	=	Summer
(2)	Oppébilé	=	Spring
(3)	Offupé	=	Winter[9]

The natives takes the year to be 360 days. 360 days arrived, they make feast called Ojūla[10] (Christmas of the natives). [The reason why they take the year to be 360 days is . . . take]. A year is called Affi in the native.[11] For their weeks, they take [.....] every Monday week to be a [......] i.e. from Monday 1st–Monday 8th [.....] So the day comes exactly 360.

The natives called the week as Naryuchi.[12]

The name of the weeks are[13]

---

[6] "Accra Jua Dier," "Akraguădie," see the Twi *odwareɛ nɔ kra*, "washing the *kra*."
[7] J. B. Danquah, "Adaduanan. A Gold Coast Calendar of 'Forty Days'," ca. 1963, typescript in Wilks Papers, Africana Library, Northwestern University, and copy in Institute of African Studies, University of Ghana, Legon.
[8] McCaskie, 1995a: 144–58.
[9] Twi *asusɔberɛ, ɔpɛberɛ, ofupɛ*, respectively the great rainy season, the dry season, and the period between the dry season and the great rains.
[10] Twi *odwira*.
[11] Twi *afe*, "year." The Akan year is basically one of nine months, each of 42 days, but regular corrections have to be made by an adjustment in the number of months in a year.
[12] Twi *nnawotwe*, "week," literally, eight days.
[13] In current usage, the days of the week are: *Dwoada, Beneada, Wukuada, Yawoada, Efiada, Memenada*, and *Kwasiada*.

118   *Chapter Six*

Native	English
Juoda	Monday
Binada	Tuesday
Wukuda	Wednesday
Yawada	Thursday
Fira	Friday
Miminada	Saturday
Kwasiada	Sunday

Children are called after the day in which they were born, then you receive another name which your father will give you.—
Ex: when a person is borned on Sunday he is called Akwasi and a girl is called Akosua.

These are the names of the months

Native	English
Jojuan (Juanjuan)[14]	January
Oflesuo Ajin Kwa[15]	February
Ohuan Kotonima[16]	March
Ayer hūn mu mo (Aiye whū mu mu)[17]	April
Kokosukogua[18]	May
(Bompondia,)[19]	June
Sandakesie[20]	July
Ahinir Moōr (Kran . . . .)[21]	August
Bubuo[22]	September
Openima[23]	October
Opoponoo[24]	November
Odiefu[25]	December.

[THE ORIGINS OF APAFRAM]

The Apafram is the most sacred national *suman* or charm in Asante, and plays a central but shrouded role in the Odwira. The tradition reported in *HAK*, to the effect that the Apafram came

---

[14] Twi *odwannuane*. The current word for January is ɔpɛpɔn.
[15] Twi *oforisuo*. Currently used for April.
[16] Twi *kɔtɔnima*. Currently used for May. The current word for March is ɔbenem.
[17] Twi *ayɛwohomunɔ*. Currently used for June.
[18] Twi *kɔsukwaia*. Not in current use.
[19] Not in current use.
[20] Twi *ɔsannaa*. Currently used for August. The current word for July is *kitawonsa*.
[21] Twi *ahinime*. Currently used for October.
[22] Twi *obubuo*. Currently used for November. The current word for September is ɛbɔ.
[23] Twi *ɔpɛnimmaa*. Currently used for December.
[24] Twi *ɔpɛpɔn*. Currently used for January.
[25] Twi *ogyefuo*. Currently used for February.

to Asante from "Akim," is anachronistic. It seems that it was brought from Akwamu, and was part of the Apafram that is still at the core of that state's Odwira. It should be noted, however, that at the time in question, the late seventeenth or early eighteenth century, Akwamu controlled much of the territory that was to become Akyem Abuakwa and Akyem Kotoku.[26]

HAK 76:4 – 76:17

[*marginalia:* Bré Kuran] The son of the chief [Ayulis] in the rank of Akom went to a district called Akim and found a Suman (native name) called Apafram. When Ossai tutu got the suman, he [informed] published it, all through his districts and countries and told them that [they will] a day once in a year will be appointed for [all] every one under Ashanti Kingdom to celebrate the suman. When the feast is near everyone is informed and they all meet on the eve; called Apafram Mimida. [because] As usual the feast is always celebrated on Sunday.

[THE ORIGINS OF *ATƆPERƐ*, AND THE ADANSE-DENKYIRA CONFLICT]

This section is strikingly different in character from the surrounding pieces—having to do with Kumase and the reign of Oti Akenten—into which it has been inserted. It seems likely that the principal informant at this point was the Adanse-Odumasehene Kwabena Nkwantabisa, who had been exiled for his part in the 1900 war. Indeed, in this part of *HAK*, Frederick Prempeh may have been writing at his, rather than Edward Prempeh's, dictation. The narrative begins with an extraordinary tale that has to do with the origins, in the animal world, of the mode of execution for particularly heinous crimes known as *atɔperɛ* ("Toppler").[27] A Denkyirahene made a case for this form of execution when a son of Adansehene appropriated one of his wives. The Denkyirahene pointed out to Adansehene that *atɔperɛ* was the recognized punishment for such an offense. The Adansehene ignored the message. It was believed that this led to the outbreak of hostilities between the two Akan polities. Clearly Kwabena Nkwantabisa, if indeed it was he, was attempting to explain this.

The story is an obscure one, having to do with the period preceding the emergence of the unified Asante kingdom. The Adanse and Denkyira struggles occurred in the mid-seventeenth century, and are documented in contemporary European archives. In 1659, for example, the Director-General of the Dutch trading establishments on the Gold Coast complained of the disruption of trade resulting from the conflicts.[28]

---

[26] R.S. Rattray, *Religion and Art in Ashanti*, Oxford, 1927: 127n., 135; Wilks, 1993: 115–18; McCaskie, 1995a: 222, 303.

[27] See, for example, T. E. Bowdich, *Mission from Cape Coast Castle to Ashantee*, London, 1819: 33–34; Rattray, 1927: 87–89; T. C. McCaskie, *State and Society in Precolonial Asante*, Cambridge, 1995: 254–57.

[28] K. Y. Daaku, *Trade and Politics on the Gold Coast 1600 to 1720*, Oxford, 1970: 27, 156–57. See also R. A. Kea, "Trade, State Formation and Warfare on the Gold Coast, 1600–1826," Ph.D. Dissertation, University of London, 1974: 150–51.

HAK 40:18 – HAK 43:6

In the year 1620 Kingdom of Ashanti was overspread. At that time the most powerful country was a country called Adansi. At that time, Ashanti, Dankira and Assin were under the influence of Adansi. The King of Adansi at that time was called Apiani Clamo.—

One day 2 of Adansi hunters went into the forest to hunt. There they saw a number of beast which is called Contronfi (or baboon).[29] Those two men noticed the following things. These Contronfis had caught one Contronfi and had tied its back behind it and then they had taken knaughted cord and had tied in his nose, then each of the Contronfi had a knife and one of them had a drum. When the drum is beaten, they all dance with the [knife] knives in their hands and when they had danced awhile each one come and cut a part of the flesh of the poor Contronfi. These two hunters watched them and then returned and related their news to the King. Then the next day the King sent some more hunters with the two to watch them and to try their best to get the drum. When they went they saw the same thing as it was related by the other two; with a shot, all of them ran away and left the drum, and, so the hunters took the drum.

Dansi king sent his son whose name is Blé Blé to bring the drum to show King of Dankira and he ordered his son to tell him that this drum is beaten for two occasions.

1st when one [is to be beat to death] has committed a murder.

(2) when one has taken the wife of a [great man] King's, and to imitate as the Contronfis were doing.

When King of Dankira saw it, in order to please the King of Adansi, made 3 gold men heads and attached them to the drum. Then to please the young prince Blaeblae he gave him £106.10s, 30 preguans and some other things. The gun was called Toppler. When the young prince was returning from Dankira to Adansi. (At that time Dankira King was called Anni Kokobu).

A misfortune happened that when Blaeblae was at Dankira, he took the wife of Dankira King as a wife. And the day when Blaeblae was leaving Dankira for Adansi, he told to the wife of Dankira King to accompany him in carrying his wages. The people refused to give him the wife of King Dankira, and King of Dankira sent men to Adansi to the King. Saying, "You have sent this drum to show me, with your order that those who commit murder, this drum shall be beaten in order to tell people that the murderer is going to suffer death. 2ndly. This drum shall be beaten when anyone has taken a king's wife in order to let others know that the one is going to suffer death. And to please you I have taken 3 gold man's head and attached to the drum and besides I have given 30 preguans and some other things and given to your son. But while your

---

[29] Twi *kontromfi*, "baboon."

son was at my house he took one of my wives, but nothing was said about it. On the day he was leaving Dankira, he told to my wife to carry his baggages so that on arriving at Adansi he will marry her. But this was not agreed to him so here is what your son has done. For your information. The King of Adansi did not even answered the messengers nor he did not neither tell anything to his son. When the messengers announced the behaviour of Adansi King, they did not do anything again.

HAK 43:6 – *HAK* 45:6

There is one of the King Dankira's island called Ajuan Pon [Awar] Awukuo and this place was the chief trading centre of Dankira and Adansi.—

Once Bléblé said, "I am going to Ajuan Pon Awukuo." There was a man from Dankira called Abo-oh who lived at Dankira. When prince Bléblé came to the market place, he quarreled with that man whose name is Abo-ōh and the inhabitants of the town begged the prince to leave the town and go to his house. And they brought Abo-oh home. When Bléblé reached mid way, he took a knife and cut half of his long beard and when he reached to his father he said, "Father when I went to the market, a man quarreled with me and the whole inhabitants fell on me and they cut half of my beard." When Adansi King heard such thing, he did not send any message to ask the Dankira King why his men had beaten his son. He immediately he sent some soldiers to capture the inhabitants on the town of Ajuan Pon Awukuo. When the soldiers came they took all the men at Adjuan Pon Awukuo as prisoners. Whenever the soldier caught a woman, she said, "Abo-o", if not through Abo-o we would not have now been caught. And so it come to have the shout Abo-ō. When King of Dankira heard that King of Adansi had taken one of his towns prisoner, he did not say nothing. A committee was passed at Dankira. The people claimed "It happened once that his son took the King's wife and nothing was said concerning the matters. 2ndly "he has sent his soldiers to take our town, without cause. During the calamity of Dankira, they were making preparation. One day King Dankira sent a message to King of Adansi declaring that he wished to pay him a visit. The King of Adansi did not imagine whether Dankira can do him any harm. When King Dankira was going, he collected a powerful army and as soon as they had arrived nigh the city, the soldiers made a circle round the city and unspectedly took the King and all the inhabitants of the country as prisoners. Whenever a soldier caught a man, he cried out, "If Blaeblae did not go to Dankira and bring fault, there will be no fault here." And this proverb [is still . . .] has been used for century. (Brebre amba inke ama di amba).

[From that time] Before Adansi was taken by Dankira, the power [of] on Western Africa was at Adansi. When King of Dankira took Adansi, her power was transported to Dankira.

HAK 45:14 – *HAK* 45:23

When the powers were removed from Adansi by the powerful army of Dinkira and at the time, Asin and Denkira was under the Kingdom of Adansi. And the same when Denkira conquered Adansi, both Adansi, Asim and Ashanti turned and serve the Kingdom of [Adansi] Denkira. The King of Denkira at that time was called King Anni Cocobro.

[THE "RESERVE" ASANTEHENES]

HAK 32:26 – *HAK* 35:9

When a King is crowned someone is always kept in reserve to take the King's place when he is dead. This system was at first began at Achimadie. This system was commenced at the reign of Ossai Kwami and the first of the Achimadie King was called Opoku Kwami the [daughter] son of Kwandu. That is, this King was kept in reserve to take the place of Kumasi King if he die. But Opoku Kwami died before the real King and so Poku Offiae the son of Kwandu was replaced. As soon as Poku Offiae came to Achimadie, the Kumasi King died and so Poku Offiae got the throne. After this the Achimadie's Kingdom was brought to Adoom, and the first man to take the throne at Adoom was called Ossai Kofi the son of Kwardu [and] but he died at Adoom. [And the man called Bonsu] The throne at Adoom was offered to Bonsu the son of Kwandu but he refused to take it. When Poku Offiae died all the chief men at Kumasi agreed in putting Bonsu to the Kumasi throne before going to Adoom on account of his goodness and good conduct. And Adoom was offered to Ossai Du the son of Kwandu. Ossai Du was [killed] died while accompanying [...........war between] his brother Bonsu in the war between the Ashanti and the Fanti. The sister of Bonsu called Akua Krukru was also [killed] died in that war for she also accompanied her brother.

Kwandu had 11 children and half of her sons were real Kings and the other half were reserve Kings. All her daughters were queens [but] except Akua Krukru who did not become Queen. After the death Ossai Du, Ossai Yaw took the throne [Kwandu's son] of Kumasi. Then Kwakudua son of Ambah Sewah [had became the King after] took the stool of Adoom. [.....] When Yaw died Kwakudua became King. [Then] and Ossai Kodjo came to Adoom the son of Afua Sapon. Kodjo was dethroned. Then Kobinah Annii the son of Afua Kobbi came to Adoom. Annii died at Adoom.

[Then Kakari came to Adoom, he became King afterwards]

Then Karkari the son of Afua Kobbi came to Adoom, he became King afterwards.

Then Mansah the son of Afua Kobbi came to Adoom, he became King afterwards.

Then Kwankua II son of Yachia came to Adoom, he became King afterwards. Then Prempeh son of Yachia came to Adoom, he became King afterwards. Then Adjiman Badoo came to Adoom. But Prempeh and Queen Yachia and Badoo was taken prisoner by English. Then it came to be said that all the royal families are in care of Adoom [King] chief. If there is any dispute between any two royal families, the chief [.....] of Adoom will settle the case before the knowledge of the King. In case if the king of Adoom is absent, the case cannot be judged, it must wait for his return.

[THE FUNERAL OF AN ASANTEHENE]

This item is extracted from *OA/OY*, the document headed, *Bodies of men or Regiments ... organised by King Otti Akenten*, where it is inserted into the section dealing with the Asoamfo, or hammock-bearers. We know of no comparable account of funerary practices for an Asantehene. Rattray describes certain rites, but made no reference to the sculpting of a bust of a dead king by the women of Abuakwa.[30] He does, however, refer to the *sora* ("S-oulah") ceremonies which formally close the funeral: *nne na ye sora ye wie wa 'yi yo*, "today with the *sora* rite we finish your funeral."[31] Excavations in the Twifo Heman area show that the Akan tradition of funerary portraiture—*nsɔdea*—extends back at least to the seventeenth century.[32]

Wilks has argued that European accounts of indiscriminate slaughter at the funerals of Asantehenes, Asantehemaas, and other notables, were grossly exaggerated, though he accepts that many might be killed, some quite willingly, in order to accompany a dead person to the Asaman, the land of the ancestors.[33] The account in *HAK* indicates that a number of servants from the royal household were slain as part of the ritualistic deposition of the pottery busts at Daaboase. The last occasion when such full funeral rites might possibly have been performed was after the death of Nana Kwaku Dua in 1867. His successors, Kofi Kakari (1867–74) and Mensa Bonsu (1874–83), were both obliged to abdicate, and Kwaku Dua Kumaa (1884) died of smallpox before installation procedures were complete. As Agyeman Prempeh himself often reiterated, any kinds of mortuary slayings had been discontinued long before his reign.

OA/OY 1:25–3:18

The second duty of this society [*"Asoam-fuor"*] is as follows.—

When an Ashanti king is dead, he could not be buried unless all the amanheni and chiefs in the Ashanti Empire meet to swear before the dead king.—

A year after an anniversary of the dead king is celebrated which is known as Yer-tua ayier – Eight days after this, there is another celebration known as S-oulah. This is carried out as follows:—

On the day of Soulah, the contileheni and the Akomheni order a general mobilisation of their armies and proceed to take the gold stool and bring with them to the forest call Pha-fra-hamoo.—and encircle the whole forest with their armies and the chiefs sit near the stool.—

---

[30] Rattray, 1927: 104–121.
[31] *Ibid.*, 1927: 164–65.
[32] James O. Bellis, "Archeology and the Culture History of the Akan of Ghana, a case study," Ph.D. Dissertation, Indiana University, 1972: 89–100, 138–53.
[33] Wilks, 1993: 215–240.

124 *Chapter Six*

Then there is something which is known as Er-kwan-bor (clearing the path). There is a certain place called Dar-boasy and at that place is found the statues or earthen busts of Ashanti Kings. The princes of Kumasi, Kokofu, Bekwi etc etc on that day under the leadership of Achinpimheni proceed on that day with necessary tools to prepare or clean the road leading to Darboasy and when they are doing this, the proclaimed king and the ten Youkous of Kumasi plus the Youkous of the country around all come to assemble at a place call Saguarsy. When the clearing of the road is finished, the princes return with their tools and placed them in a heap before the king and the king at once give them £24. Plus drink then every Youkou give what they wish.—Then with the woods and branches of trees they had cut in the clearing, an arc is made just facing the King's palace.—

Then in the arc the bust of the dead King (which was sculptured by a society of women residing at Abooakwah) is being brought by the women in an earthen pot and placed the bust in the pot on a special stool in the arc and all the decorations and Jewelleries of the Ashanti King is placed around the bust according to its proper situations.—

Then the contile and Akom bring back the gold stool and hand it over to the King and the King pays £24. Plus sheep and drinks and on that day the King take the throne to his house in the palace.

In the afternoon, a woman of the royal family is given to carry the pot with the bust to Darboasy and there the Asoamfuor perform their *second duty* by giving a hold to the pot which is on the lady's head lest it falls.—and there a great procession of princes, princesses, royal families and chiefs follow with all the decorations of the King behind and before, in order just as when a living King is in full uniform.—

From the arc to Darboasy, a man servant is taken from each Department of the royal house servants and placed right and left along the road with an executioner behind each man.—and when the procession has reached Darboasy, three big stones are chosen and are placed in triangular form as a cooking tripod and these chosen servants are killed and legs broken and the broken legs are placed on the three sides of the tripod just as fire woods are placed between tripods for cooking and the pot with the statue is placed on the tripod.

On the next day, the Queen and the royal ladies go to act as..........[34]

This is to prove that the ceremony of the deceased sovereign is completely ended.—

---

[34] The narrative ends abruptly at this point, on the last line of the page. It seems that the story was broken off after the fifth item on the *asomfuo* [*OA/OY* 1:24] in order to introduce the material on funeral practices; that a blank page 2 was set aside for this purpose; that the main narrative was immediately resumed on page 3 with the sixth item, the story of Drabuo; and that when the account of the funeral practices came to be written, it could not all be accommodated on page 2.

[THE DIVISION OF REVENUES]

HAK 83:9 – 84:20

To the Ashanti chiefs and petty Kings he [Osei Tutu] said "I don't know how things are to be shared between the King and the chiefs."

The sharing are of two kinds:—

Things obtained when a victory is gained is shared differently between the King and chiefs than when there is no fight.

Things gained in war,

The things are divided into three, and the King received 1/3 of them.

The remainder 2/3 are mixed and is again divided into 3 and the Commander of the whole army received 1/3 of it again.

Then a portion of the remainder 2/3, is taken and shared among the judges. The rest is divided into [four] three. 1/4 belongs to Juabinhin and the Yukus and Dakus. 1/4 belongs to those, [.....] chiefs who occupied the right, left and front wings. 1/4 belongs to Contilé and Akom and Jarsi and Kidom. [The remainder belongs to Kidom and Jarsi]

In Kumasi the King receives more than in the time of war because all the expenses in war are made by the King alone.—

In Kumasi money got by those who are condemned are divided into two and the King receives 1/2 (half).

The remainder half, a portion is given to the Queen. The remainder is divided into two and the Judges receive half (1/2). The remainder 1/2 is again divided into four.

1/4 belongs to Juabinhin and Yuku & Daku.

1/4 belongs to right, left and front wings.

1/4 belongs to Contile & Akom.

The remainder 1/4 to Kidom & Jarsi.

Thus are the manner the King and chiefs shared the things.

[THE AKWAMU FACTOR IN THE RISE OF ASANTE]

An important role in the emergence of the unified Asante monarchy was taken by Akwamu, a state the capital of which was then located under Nyanaw Bepow, some twenty miles inland from the busy European ports of call at Accra. The Akwamu origin of the Apafram *suman* has been referred to above. In 1895 C. C. Reindorf gave an account of early Akwamu and Asante relations, not dissimilar to that in *HAK*. He describes the Akwamuhene as taking Osei Tutu as his "male-consort," whereas HAK uses the phrase "as a manly wife."[35] Inevitably, in this day and age, there have been those eager to see in this evidence of homosexual relationships in Akan courts. This suggestion has been questioned by Wilks, who points out that in an account of the matter given him by

---

[35] C. C. Reindorf, *History of the Gold Coast and Asante*, Basel, 1895: 48–50, 55.

the Banmuhene of Akwamu in 1957, Osei Tutu was said to have become the Akwamuhene's *ɔkra*, a word having, in this context, somewhat the sense of the English "soul-mate."[36]

HAK 54:7 – 55:13

The sword which is called Manyile came at the time when Ossai Tutu and Annochi went to [Kumasi] Akom. The King of Akom was called Akom Akoto.

When Akoto saw Ossai Tutu he said to him "I love you dearly, my soul has come to you and I love you dearly as I love my wife so I take you as a manly wife." [(The native word for manly wife is Akoto.)] Then Ossai said "If you love me dearly and take me [for your dea] as a manly wife, I will be your faithful [.....] wife." When Ossai was at Akom, he [.....] gave him his best care. [.....] When Ossai was to crown King, messengers were sent to call him from Akom. When Ossai came to Kumasi to be King, he always remained as a manly wife to Akoto. This had been kept through generations and whenever a King succeeded Ossai and another King succeeded Akoto, the two new King carry on the same law. It is the custom of the Ashanti women to put leaves in their hair when their husbands die.

So if Kumasi King is dead, the King of Akom come and stick leaves in his hair and whenever a King at Akom is dead, the King of Kumasi sends a man to replace him and that man sticks [le in his ear] in his hair.

---

[36] Ivor Wilks, *Akwamu 1640–1750. A Study of the Rise and Fall of a West African Empire*, Trondheim, 2001: xl – xli.

CHAPTER SEVEN
Office Lists and Genealogies

OFFICE LISTS: INTRODUCTION

A few dated lists of Asantehenes appeared in print in the course of the nineteenth century. As noted in Chapter Four, the chronology from Asantehene Osei Tutu to that of Asantehene Osei Tutu Kwame is that established by Muslim savants at the court of the latter in the early nineteenth century, and transmitted through the writing of the British consul in Kumase, Joseph Dupuis.[1] For whatever reason, Edward Prempeh decided to use one such list in *HAK*. It had obviously been earlier copied out on a separate sheet, referred to as the "blank paper." It has not proved possible to identify the precise source used, but the dates from the succession of Opoku Ware to that of Osei Tutu Kwame are precisely those given by Dupuis.[2]

The text of *HAK* at this point clearly shows the ambivalence that Agyeman – or Edward – Prempeh felt towards those remembered as having ruled in the Kumase area before the emergence of the unified kingdom under Osei Tutu. His fluctuating thinking on this issue is interestingly captured on paper. His compromise was to add Oti Akenten and Obiri Yeboa – without dates – to the king list, but to exclude Akyampon Tenten, Twum, Antwi, and Kwabia Anwanfi on the grounds that they died before the founding of Kumase. The list of Asantehenes in *HAK*, from Osei Tutu to Agyeman Prempeh himself, is accurate with respect to the order of succession but unreliable for the chronology. More correct dates have now been established, and these will be found in the Concordance.

The list of Asantehemaas presented in *HAK* appears to have been compiled in Seychelles, drawing heavily, one may guess, upon the knowledge of the Asantehemaa in exile, Yaa Kyaa.

HAK 30:17 – *HAK* 32:26

Here illustrates all the Kings and queens who have been crowned on Ashanti throne. It the time when all the inhabitants of Ashanti were at Assumya Ashanti Mansu, there were no [family] King for all the citizens but each separate family [has] appointed a king or a chief for themselves. In the family of great woman Anchoyami, Achempōntintin was the first King. [The second King was called Chum]

According to the order of the Kings at Assumya Ashanti Mansu
1   Achempontintin
2   Chum
3) Anchui
4) Kobia [.....] Amanphie

---

[1] J. Dupuis, *Journal of a Residence in Ashantee*, London, 1824: 239–247.
[2] Dupuis obtained his A.D. dates by fairly accurate conversions from the A.H. dates of his Muslim source.

[5 Oti Akenten]
[6 Obiyaeboa (he was killed at battle)]
These four kings were only for families.

After the death of these four kings, All the [families] citizens of Ashanti united and said that they will appoint one King and called him Ashanti King (vide the blank paper.)-

The Ashanti Kings according to their order.
1) Oti Akenten
2) Obi Yaeboa (he was killed at battle.)
[3) Ossay Tutu (——ed about .... 1700 died 17...)]
[4) Ossay Opoku]
3) Osai Tutu reign about 1700–1731 died [*killed]
4) Opokutintin reign about 1731–1742 died
5) Kussie reign about 1742–1752 dethroned [died]
6) Ossai Kodjoe reign about 1752–81 died
7) Ossai Kwami reign about 1781–1797 dethroned
8) Poku Fofie reign about 1797–1799 died
9) Ossai Bonsu I reign about 1799–1824 died
10 Ossai Akoto reign about 1824–1838 died
11 Ossai Kwakudua I reign about 1838–1867 died
12) Kofi Karkari reign about 1867–1874 dethroned
13) Ossai Bonsu reign about 1874–1885 dethroned
14) Kwakudua II reign about 1885–1888 [taken prisoner] died
15) Kwakudua III Asaman Prempeh reign about 1888–1896 taken prisoner.

The Ashantis began to have queens in the reign of Ossai Tutu.

The Queens of Ashanti

1) Guarku Kussi Amua mother of Pokutintin
2) Inkatiar Otim Abamu mother of Kussi Obodum
3) [Kofiae] Akuafriae mother of Ossai Kudjoe
4) Kwandu Yardom (4 of her children are Kings)
   {The four King's names are (1) Ossai Kwami (2) Opoku Fofiae (3) Ossai Bonsu (4) Ossai Yaw}
5) Aduma Akosua (dethroned
6) Ambah Sewah daughter of Kwandu and the mother of King Fredua Adjiman
7) Yà Difiae daughter of Kwandu
8) Afua Sapon daughter of Ambah Sewah (deposed)
9) Afua Cobbi daughter of Afua Sapon (deposed) and the mother of Karkari and Mensah
10) Yachia daughter of Afua Cobbi (taken prisoner). Yachia was the mother of Kwakudua II and Kwakudua III (Prempeh).

THE GENEALOGIES

There are several nineteenth century sources that have to do with the genealogy of the ruling dynasty of Asante. Of considerable interest is that compiled by Captain Knapp Barrow who, in April 1883, visited the court of Asantehene Mensa Bonsu on behalf of Governor of the Gold Coast Sir Samuel Rowe.[3] To the best of our knowledge Barrow was the first to realize the importance of male descent (that is, *ntɔrɔ*) as well as female (*abusua*) in the determination of that which he called "true royal blood." C. C. Reindorf's fuller chart, "Kings and the Royal Family of Asante," in which he showed the parentage of all the Asantehenes and depicted the relationship between them, appeared in 1895.[4] The existence of such sources shows that a body of genealogical information existed in Asante in the later nineteenth century. Neither Barrow nor Reindorf, however, was able to access it on anything like the scale that Agyeman Prempeh did in the early twentieth century.

The overriding imperative in *HAK* was to chart the families matrilineally descended from the apical ancestress, Ankyewa Nyame, whose arrival at Asantemanso from the sky is recounted in the opening parts of the work (see Chapter Five). This served to identify the "royal families" from which an Asantehene or Asantehemaa had to be chosen. In fact, all such families are treated as deriving matrilineally from Ankyewa Nyame through her first daughter, Birempomaa Piesie (Twi *birempɔmaa*, "great person, female," and *opiesie*, "first-born"). Husbands, however, are usually named and sometimes identified by office, thus testifying to the importance attached not only to the transmission of *mogya*, (roughly, 'blood') through the mother – determining *abusua* – but also of *ɔkra* (roughly, 'personality') through the father – determining *ntɔrɔ*.[5]

Although the thrust of the genealogical material compiled in *HAK* has clearly to do with establishing who is an *ɔdehyeɛ* or "royal" of the Golden Stool, three different approaches to the matter are made. The first, *HAK* 3:1 – 3:13 and *HAK* 4:1 – 4:15, treats relationships between the pre-Asante rulers; the second, *HAK* 5:21 – 14.26, lists the descendants of Manu, mother of the first ruler of the unified kingdom; and the third, *HAK* 14:27 – 23:30, is a census of "royals" alive in 1896, at the time of Agyeman Prempeh's abduction.

THE PRE-ASANTE RULERS

The purpose of this section is to bring early rulers, associated in tradition with Asantemanso, into the category of the descendants of Ankyewa Nyame. To achieve this the list of the ten children of Ankyewa Nyame's daughter, Birempomaa Piesie (*HAK* 3:1 – 3:13), was inserted into the story of the foundation of Asantemanso, thereby making a clear distinction between those Oyoko adopted by Ankyewa Nyame and those descended from her. However, the capricious nature of the data on the pre-Asante period is revealed in the multiple alterations made to the list of the children of Birempomaa Piesie, and in incompatibilities between this list and other material in *HAK*.

Appearing among the names of the children of Birempomaa Piesie is, for example, Ofebiri Odeneho ("Febydinhun"), but in one of the historical pieces (*HAK* 36:1 – 37:24) she is described as

---

[3] Knapp Barrow "Ashantee Report" 5 July 1883, para. 35, in British Parliamentary Papers, Accounts and Papers LVI, 1884, "Further Correspondence regarding the Affairs of the Gold Coast," enclosure 2 in Rowe to Derby, Accra, 21 August 1883. Rowe had G. E. Ferguson compile the information in the form of a delightful pictorial family tree.

[4] C. C. Reindorf, *History of the Gold Coast and Asante*, Basel, 1895: 346b, and for his sources see T. C. McCaskie, "Asante and Ga. The History of a Relationship," in Paul Jenkins (ed.), *The Recovery of the West African Past. African Pastors and African History in the Nineteenth Century*, Basel, 1998: 139–44.

[5] For this topic see Wilks, 1975: 327–73; McCaskie, 1995b: passim.

130   *Chapter Seven*

a sister of Kwabia Anwanfi and Oti Akenten and therefore, by implication, as a granddaughter rather than daughter of Birempomaa Piesie. Another of Birempomaa Piesie's children is listed as Aboagye Akomadoma. Elsewhere Akomadoma is treated as daughter of Abena Gyapa, and therefore again as granddaughter rather than daughter of Birempomaa Piesie. The matter was of particular importance, since Akomadoma is also treated in *HAK* as mother of Obiri Yeboa. Was he, then, grandson or great-grandson of Birempomaa Piesie? If the latter, then he would be first cousin of (and genealogically junior to) Osei Tutu. This is quite incompatible with what is virtually received wisdom in Asante, that Obiri Yeboa ruled before Osei Tutu, and that he was in some sense an "uncle" to him.[6] It seems, then, that in incorporating the pre-Asante rulers into the nexus of the descendants of Birempomaa Piesie, Akomadoma was entered twice, as both her daughter ("Abboagi akumadoma") and her granddaughter ("Akumadoma"), the effect of which was to drop Obiri Yeboa by one generation. Finally, it will be noted that the entry for Birempomaa Piesie's daughter, Abena Gyapa, attributes ten children to her but lists only four [*HAK* 4:12 – 4:15], and these, moreover, cannot be reconciled with the line of descent from Abena Gyapa recorded in *HAK* 22:18 – 23:15.

The most plausible readings of *HAK* 3:1 – 3:13 and *HAK* 4:1 – 4:15, suggest that the links between the pre-Asante rulers are as shown in Figure 2.

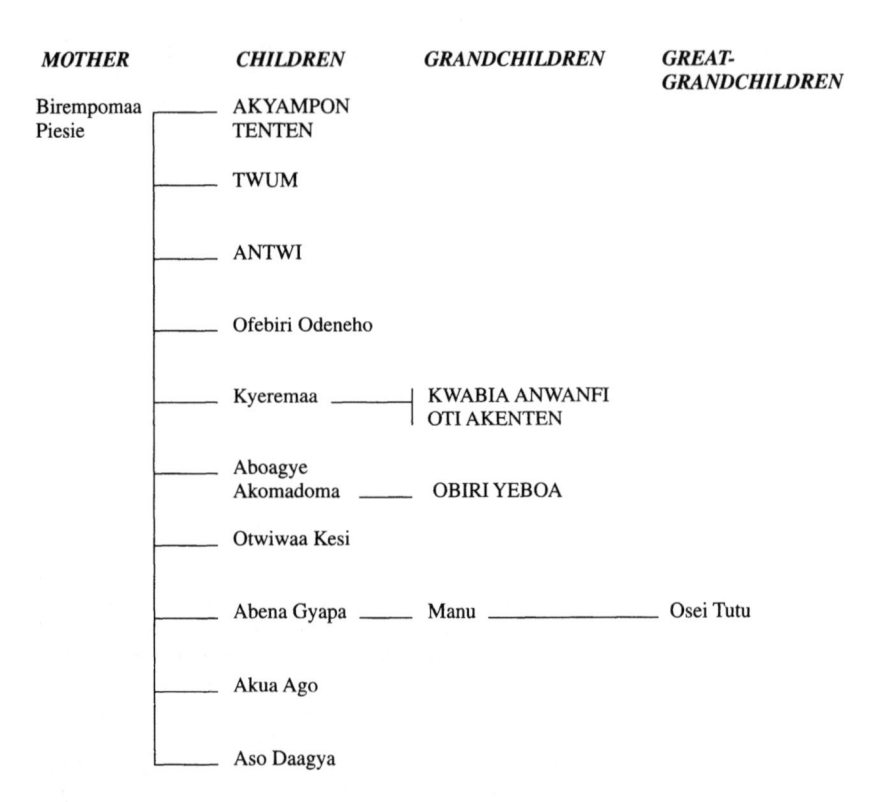

MOTHER	CHILDREN	GRANDCHILDREN	GREAT-GRANDCHILDREN
Birempomaa Piesie	AKYAMPON TENTEN		
	TWUM		
	ANTWI		
	Ofebiri Odeneho		
	Kyeremaa	KWABIA ANWANFI OTI AKENTEN	
	Aboagye Akomadoma	OBIRI YEBOA	
	Otwiwaa Kesi		
	Abena Gyapa	Manu	Osei Tutu
	Akua Ago		
	Aso Daagya		

Figure 2. Relationships of the Pre-Asante Rulers (shown in capital letters), based on *HAK* 3:1 – 3:13, and *HAK* 4:1 – 4:15.

---

[6] See, for example, Reindorf, 1895: 49, 50, 346b.

HAK 3:1–3:13

She [Ankyaa Nyame] bored a [son that called] daughter whose name was Brinpoma Piecie. And Brinpoma bore this 10 persons—

1 Achampontintin
2 [Cham] Choom
3 Anchui
4 Febydinhun
5 [Chirema(?)] Ochilemār
6 [...(?)] Abboagi akumadoma
7 [B...(?) Bomfotwa(?)] Otiwa Kesie
8 Obina Japa
9 Akuagū
10 Arso Dāgifuor.

HAK 4:1 – 4:10

We Royal family are in the [Oyuku] Yuku family and our grand [father] mother is Anchoyami. These families stayed long at [Kumassi] Assumya Ashantimansu then each family find a portion of land to dwell. Anchoyami died at Assumya Ashantimansu and also her son Birempoma Piecie died there, so did Achempomtintin so did Choom and Anchui.

HAK 4:10 – 4:11

Ochilermar conceived and bear Kobia Anguanfi, Oti Akenten.

HAK 4:12 – 4:15

Japa conceived and bear 10 children. (1) called Jemmie. (2) Brayiae. Third Manu. Fourth Akumadoma bear Obi Yaeboa.

THE DESCENDANTS OF MANU

With the entry for Manu [*HAK* 5:21], daughter of Abena Gyapa and mother-to-be of the first Asantehene, Osei Tutu, the data become firmer. Thereafter the various lines of descent from Manu are systematically followed, from generation to generation. Remarkably, the births listed include some, but presumably not all, cases of those stillborn or dying in infancy. In *HAK* 5:21 to *HAK* 14:26 a genealogical nexus is established which shows, inter alia, the descent from Manu of the Asantehenes from Osei Tutu to Agyeman Prempeh, and the Asantehemaas from Nyaako Kusi Amoa to Yaa Kyaa. The section ends with the notation, "This book was written at Seychelles."

There is a very substantial corpus of written material pertaining to Asante in the eighteenth and nineteenth centuries. The bulk of it is contained in the records of Danish, Dutch, and English trading establishments on the Gold Coast, but much is also to be found in the writings of those who visited Kumase itself. This corpus provides independent verification for the succession of Asantehenes presented in *HAK*. It also occasionally confirms other information in a somewhat dramatic way. For example, in the list of Asantehemaas the fifth, Adoma Akosua, is annotated "dethroned" (*HAK* 32:17). Joseph Dupuis, British consul in Kumase in 1820, learned the story behind this. Adoma Akosua had been removed from office a year or so previously, and executed for plotting against Asantehene Osei Tutu Kwame at a time when he was at the war front in Gyaman. Dupuis also reported that Adoma Akosua was succeeded as Asantehemaa by a sister of Asantehene Osei Tutu Kwame, which is in agreement with *HAK*.[7]

It is reasonable to assume that the genealogical information in *HAK* was taken down principally if not entirely from the narration of Agyeman Prempeh's mother, the Asantehemaa Yaa Kyaa, who was to die in exile in 1917. For ease of reference, the pedigree of the Asantehenes and Asantehemaas as presented in *HAK* is shown in Figure 3.

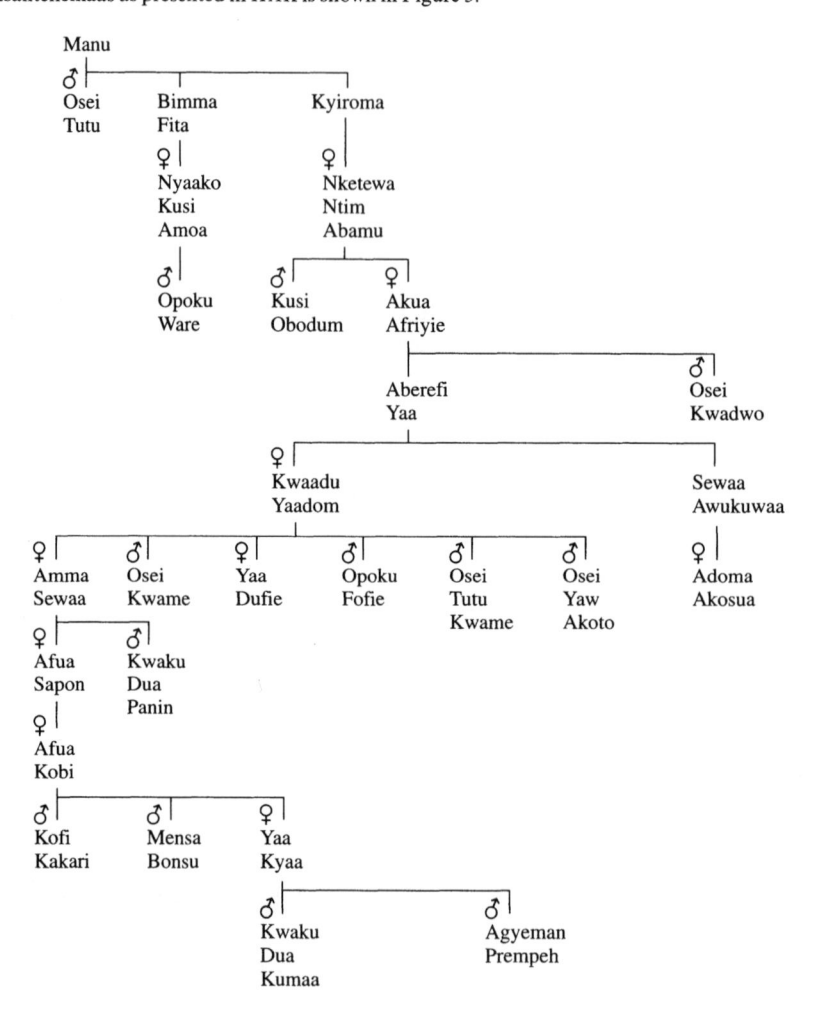

Figure 3. Pedigree of the 18th and 19th Century Asantehenes and Asantehemaas, based on *HAK* 5:21–14:26, and *HAK* 30:17–32:26, showing descendants of Manu. KEY: ♂ Asantehene ♀ Asantehemaa

[7] Dupuis, 1824: 115–16. For this event, see further, Wilks, 1975: 355–356, and T.C. McCaskie, "Anti-witchcraft Cults in Asante: An Essay in the Social History of an African People," *History in Africa*, 8, 1981: 125–54.

The systematic mode of presentation of the material commands respect, as does the overall accuracy of the data in so far as this can be checked against independent documentary sources. However, at one particular point, having to do with Asantehemaa Kwaadu Yaadom, there are severe problems that have been shown to involve substantial issues of dynastic politics. Briefly, it is likely that Asantehemaa Amma Sewaa was a daughter not of Asantehemaa Kwadu Yaadom, but of an expurgated Asantehemaa Akyaama (who does not, of course, appear in Figure 2).[8]

Descent of Kwaadu Yaadom and Sewaa Awukuwaa from Manu

HAK 5:21 – 6:8
When the families came to Kokofu, Manū the daughter of Abina Japa [conceived and bear] went to a place called Yami Ani and married the King of that place called Oyussu Pani, and bear a son called Ossay Atu. (The first King to rule the whole Ashanti). Manū brought forth her son under a tree called Oyinah Ossay.[9] The sapo which they gave the little baby, after throwing it away, the sapo sprang up and it became a tree.[10] This tree [could] can be [seen(?)] up to now, Sapu is the skin of tree beaten very [well to wash babies big ... .(?)] neatly for bathing. Manue conceived again and bear Ossay Kokor. She conceived again and bear Bimafie, she conceived again and bear Chromaclor.[11]

HAK 6:9 – 6:11
Bimafie bear Guarcun Kussi Amua and bore [Ottokou Achal] Ottieku Achulie.

HAK 6:12 – 6:16
Guarcun bore two men who [...(?)] who died as they were laid down. The third son called Opokutintin. The fourth son was called Odifie Aku.

HAK 6:17
Chromaclor bore Inkatia Otimabamu.

HAK 6:18 – 6:26
Inkatia bore Kusiobordum and bore Akuafiae, [and Akuafiae bore Ossay Kodjoe and bore Abrafie. When Abrafie was born, practically the whole of the

---

[8] Wilks, 1975: 327–73 and especially 337–38; Wilks, "A Note on Career Sheet ACBP/28: Kwaadu Yaadom," *Asantesem*, 11, 1979: 54–56; T. C. McCaskie, "*Konnurokusɛm*: Kinship and Family in the History of the *Oyoko Kɔkɔɔ* Dynasty of Kumase," *Journal of African History*, 36, 1995: 357–89; T. C. McCaskie, *State and Society in Precolonial Asante*, Cambridge, 1995: 180–85, 412 n.110.
[9] Twi *onyina*, the silk cotton tree.
[10] Twi *sapɔ*, a large forest climber, *Momordica augustisepala Harms*.
[11] The reading in both *HAK* 6:8 and 6:17 is clearly "Chromaclor." We interpret the first element in the name as Kyiroma, but offer a tentative reading for the second, "Korɔ."

royal families were finished and Abrafie was the only royal left. So they gave Abrafie to married to the King of Manpon called Atta Kular].[12]

HAK 6:27 – 7:8

Akuafiae went to a district called Karsi and married to the king of that district called Akwasi Kōr and Akuafiae bore Kwanimar and Boachiwar. When Kor died, Akuafiae came to a place called Abradie and married to the king of that district called Opoku Atia, and bore Abrafie. Then Opoku Atia died.

Then Akuafiae married to Achempem Afriae, but their children did not live long, then they bore Ossay Kodjoe. Ossay Kodjoe was the eight son of Akuafiae.

HAK 7:8 – 8:5

At that time the royal families were nearly finished and the only one Royal family left was Abrafie. So they brought Abrafie to the King of Manpon called Atta Kular to marry her but Atta Kular was too old to make any son so he gave Abrafie to his uncle Assūmgimmah instead of him. So Assūmgimmah married to Abrafie and bore Kwadu Ya-dom. Assūmgimmah gave Kwadu Yadom to Oyusu the King of Apar. When Assūmgimmah died and Ossafu Kantanka took his place and married to Abrafie again and bore Sewah Okuwar. And Ossafu Kwantankan told to Apar Oyusu that Kwadu Ya Dom the daughter of my wife Abrafie whose father Assumgimmah gave her to you to be married [and], but now I (Ossafu) am the King and greater than you so send your wife to me and I will marry her together with her mother, and I will replace you another wife by giving you my daughter Sewah Okuwa. Apar Oyusu agreed to the word of his King.

HAK 8:5 – 9:12

When Ossafu married Kwadu together with her mother and Kwadu bore Achia Kesie, & Achia Kesie was dead in the way to Kumasi at a place called Nitibansu, at the time when the child was going to be shown to his families. Kwadu conceived again and bore [Amuor] Ambah Sewah. She conceived again and bore Ossai Kwami. After the birth of Ossai Kwami, Ossafu Kantankan her husband died. Kwadu camed to Kumasi from Manpon after the death of her husband and there married a prince called Adu Chum and Kwadu conceived and bore Opoku Kwami; then she bore Yā Odifiae, she conceived again and bore Akua Akrūkrū. She conceived for the 4th time and bore Opoku Ofiae. After the [death] birth of Opoku Ofiae her husband Adu Chum died. Kwadu

---

[12] Close examination of the text at this point makes it clear that the piece in square brackets was not the result of a copying error. It can, then, only be an error in recording, showing that the genealogies in *HAK* are original transcripts of the spoken word.

went to [Assokoli] a district called Assokoli Manpon and married a prince called Yusu An Sa the son of King Osai Kudjoe.

Kwadu conceived and bore Ossay Kofi and she bore Ossai Asibi for the second time. She bore Ossai Doo for the third time. After the birth of Ossai Doo her husband Yusu An Sa died. Kwadu went to a district called Annowuo and married [again?] Yusu Yaw. [and] She conceived and bore Ossai Yaw, she conceived again and bore one more and died as the child was laid down.

HAK 9:13 – 9:31

Sewah Awukooār, the younger sister of Kwadu whom Ossafuor gave to Apar Oyusu in place of Kwadu conceived and bore Adoma Akosua. Adoma married to Oyusu and bore Akua Sewah. She conceived again and bore Ossai Akwasi, and bore Ossai Kodjoe Kuma.

Akua Sewah married and bore Opokua, Kodjoe Tufor, Konfuōr Briwah, 4 Poku Cha Cha and lastly Adu [Opokua] [Sewah] married and bore [Adu] Atah.

Pokua married and bore, Ossai, after Ossai she bore two more but they died then she bore Ossay Glusso [*illegible*]. Up to this boy Glusuo is the families of Sewah Okua, and they all dwell at a place called Bronkome in Kwantannan at Kumasi.

Descendants of Asantehemaa Amma Sewaa

HAK 10:1 – 10:29

The second son of Kwadu whose name is Amah Sewah married to Apāou Pani at the district of Api Buosu. Apāou [Apayu] Pani is the son of King Kussi Obordum. Amah Sewah conceived and bore Chen Chen Heni. She conceived for the second time and bore Kwami Kussi then she bore 3 sons but they died. She conceived for the sixth time and bore Afua Sapon. After she bore Afua Sapon, Apaoū Pani died. Amah Sewah went to a district called [Inkwantannan] In-Kwa-Ta-Nan and married to Boachie Yam Kuma. Amah conceived and bore Oti Akenten. She conceived for the second time and bore Achempon Akwasi. She conceived for the third time and bore Kwakudua Asamu but his surname to signify greatness is Fre'dua Ajiman. After the [death] birth of Asamu, Boachie Yam Kumaa died. Amah Sewah went to Juabin and married to Prince Ochily Kotokū the son of King Juabin whose name is Akuamua Pani. Amah [conceived fo] lost her first born son. She conceived again for the second time and bore Kwami Boatin. After the birth of Kwami Boatin, Amah Sewah died.

HAK 10:29 – 11:12

Afua Sapon the sixth son of Amah Sewah went to a district called Apaga and married to Prince Afriae the son of [King] Ossay Kojo the king of Kumasi.

Sapon conceived and bore Ossay Kojo. She conceived again but the child died. She conceived again for the third time and bore Afua Kobi. She conceived for the third time and bore [Yafriae/Yafilé] Ya Efriae. The fourth time she bore Akua Friae. The sixth son died. The seventh was called Odae. The eighth was called Affua Sewah. The nineth was called Abraefi. Then Sapon stop making son.

HAK 11:13 – 11:25

Afua Kobi the 3rd son of Sapon went to a district called Asukwa and married to the Chief Justice of Kumasi called Kofi In-Tea; Afua bore Kobinah Anni. The second time she bore Karkari. Third son was called Boensu. The fourth child was a daughter called Ya Chi-a the present queen of Kumasi. The 5th child was daughter called Akua Friae. After the birth of Akua Friae, Kofi In-Tea died. Afua Kobi married to the new Chief Justice whose name is Boachie Tin-Tin. But they made no son.

HAK 11:26 – 12:19

Ya Efriae [Yafilé] the fourth son of Sapon went to Yami Anni and married to king Kām Kām. Their first son was called Abinah, the second was called Kwadu, the third was called Akua Ader. The fourth was called Nanchui. Ya Efriae [Yafilé] without the knowledge of her husband took another man by name Boadje who was an Essen. Ya Efriae [Yafilé] bore Akosua Braegua with Boadie but the public came to know and when her real husband Kamkam heard of it, he was wrath and sent her away. King Kwakudua was very angry and forced Ya Efriae [Yafilé] to pay the sum of £48. Then Ya Efriae [Yafilé] married to Asabie Boachie and bore Achule Boanah the latter was the 6th son of Yafilé. The seventh son was called Boatin. The eighth was called Adjuah. The ninth was called Inkrunba. The tenth child died the same day of its birth. Then Asabie Boachie took the wife of chief Bantuo, the chief [....] of Kumasi. Then Asabie Boachie was expelled from Kumasi and sent to a district called Amanchia.

HAK 12:20 – 12:26

Akua Fraie the fifth [daugh/chol] child of Afua Sapon married to Boachie Dankua the eldest son of King Kwadua. They bore two children which, died immediately the third child was a boy called Kofi Mansa, after this he bore many sons but they died the same day of their birth.

HAK 12:27 – 13:2

Oday the seventh son of Sapon went to Apy Buosu and married to Apaoú but they made no child. When Apaou died, Abu took the place of Apaou and married to Oday and they bore Akwasi Ajim, their second child was a boy who did not live longer.

HAK 13:4 – 13:10
.. eight daughter son was called] Afua Sewah the eight son of Sapon was given in marriage to [Adontin] Boatin the King of Adontin, but [but they made no child and] Afua Sewah died leaving no child because her husband did not care much for her and when she died, Boatin [was] did not [angry] felt sorry.

HAK 13:11 – 13:12
Abraefie the ninth son of Sapon died when still young.

HAK 13:13 – 13:16
Of the children of King Kwakudua there were three of them whom he liked most, namely:—Akwasi [Abayae] Gembili, Akwasi Abayae, Kwami Silibuo.[13]

HAK 13:17 – 14:7
Yachia the fourth son of Afua Cobi married to Akwasi Abayae and bore Kwakudua, secondly a daughter called Akua Fokuo, thirdly a man called Kobina Chrechuae, fourthly a daughter called Akua Bakumma, fifthly Akuafriae. Then Abayae died.

Yachia married again to Akwasi Gembibi and bore Amah Mansah; secondly a daughter called Yachia thirdly a daughter called Brayae fourthly a boy called Kwakudua Asamu whose surname is Prempeh. This surname Prempeh was a nickname given to him by the Chief Justice called Kodjoe Fofie. The fifth son was called Adjiman Badoo. The sixth was a daughter called Kwadu. The seventh was called Ajua [Antuo] Jantu-O. The eighth was called Amah [Adussan] Aduesan. All the children of Yachia put together were equal to 13 persons. Both Yachia and Gembibi stop making children for they were old.—(-) IIII[14]

HAK 14:8 – 14:25
Akua Friae the fifth [daugh] son of Afua Kobbi went to a town called Dominasie and married to Krāpah the petit King of Dominasie and they bore two twins and secondly they bore Ohenafré Ya or thirdly they bore Akwasi Berkun, fourthly [Akwa] Akosua Insia, fifthly [Akosua] two twins who died early, sixthly Akosua Manhya, seventhly Akua Badoo. After the birth of Badoo, Prince Krapah [died] the son of King Kwakudua. And Akua went to a

---

[13] This comment seems intrusive at this point, though the birth of Kwaku Dua Panin is recorded in the next section.

[14] The significance of the lines and bars is, as elsewhere, unclear, since they do not always mark any break in the text.

town called Asafu and married to Asafu Boachie and bore Ambah Akom secondly they bore two twins thirdly they bore Ambah Adjiman. Fourthly they bore two twins, fifthly they bore Ya bah, sixthly they bore Kwakudua, seventhly Fredua Adjiman, eightly they bore one more but she died early. (Akua had 20 children all told.)

HAK 14:26

This book was written at Seychellis.

THE CENSUS OF "ROYALS"

This section of the genealogical materials commences under a new rubric: "These are the following children borned to our families before we were taken prisoner in the year 1896" [*HAK* 14:27 – *HAK* 14:29]. This marks a subtle but important shift in purpose.

The genealogies presented in *HAK* 5:21 to *HAK* 14:26 served to locate Asantehenes and Asantehemaas within the network of the *Manu adehyeɛ*, that is, the royal descendants of Manu. This section, *HAK* 14:27 – *HAK* 23:25, identifies by family and sometimes address, the Asante royals who were alive at the time of Governor of the Gold Coast W. E. Maxwell's coup d'état in 1896. In this respect it has many of the characteristics of a census, specifically, one intended to serve as a directory of all those alive in 1896 who could have claims on the offices of Asantehene or Asantehemaa. It invites comparison with the counts of war dead that were carried out in the aftermath of nineteenth century campaigns,[15] and foreshadows the careful census of the Seychelles exiles presented to the nation by Agyeman Prempeh on his return to Kumase (see Chapter Nine).

The section commences by listing the descendants first, of seven daughters of Asantehemaa Yaa Kyaa (*HAK* 14:30 – 17.5), and second, of five daughters of her full sister, Akua Afriyie (*HAK* 17.7 – 18.20). The survey regresses, that is, sweeps backwards in time to pick up living descendants of Yaa Afere, daughter of Asantehemaa Afua Sapon; of Asantehemaa Yaa Dufie, daughter of Asantehemaa Kwadu Yaadom, and of her full sister, Akua Akrukruwaa; then of Bimma Fita, daughter of Abena Gyapa; and finally of Otwiwaa Keseɛ and Akua Ago, daughters of Birempomaa Piese. Granted the mass of data, there are remarkably few contradictions between that in the main genealogies and that in the census. But there are a few. Were "Akua Ader" and "Akosua Begran" (*HAK* 11.26 – 12.19 and *HAK* 18.27 – 19.17), for example, daughters or granddaughters of Afua Sapon?

At this point, *HAK* 23:28, the presentation of the pedigree of the Asante royal family, and of the census of royals alive in 1895/6, ends – "Up to this 23rd pages showing the sons and grandsons of Anchuanyami," the writer comments.

HAK 14:27 – 14:29

These are the following children borned to our families before we were taken prisoner in the year 1896—

---

[15] Wilks, 1975: 81.

Descendants of Asantehemaa Yaa Kyaa

HAK 14:30 – 15:22

Akua Fokuo the second child of Yachia was given in marriage to Mamponhene[16] Koobina Jummor,[17] the King of Manpon, he was a very good King. The King took a good care of Fokuo and not only his wife but moreover the families of Fokuo. But he died leaving no child with Fokuo. Fokuo came to Kumasi and married a judge called Jubin. Fokuo bore a boy called Akwasi who died very early. Jubin was a very [cruel] wicked judge but at first he showed some kindness to Fokuo and after the death of their only begotten son he began to show his cruelty to the girl and then he became the enemy of her families. At last the girl was taken way and from her and then he was put to death. And that girl Fokuo was given to a very [big] great man called Ossai Tutu and they bore Oyusu Kwantabisa secondly [Achan] Achar Kesie thirdly Oyusu Ansa. Fourthly a boy whom died early & that child was born on the third day before [we] King Prempeh was taken prisoner.

HAK 15:23 – 15:30

Akua Bakuma the fourth child of Yachia [went to] married to the inferior judge called Kwaku Ysu and they bore Akua Pim Pim & then she bore two twins who died very early thirdly Akua Friae fourthly Kwami fifthly Ossai Kwami sixthly Sewah. When Sewah was borne [we were] Prempeh was taken prisoner.

HAK 15:31 – 16:5

Akua Friae the fifth child of Yachia married to Boatin the [son] uncle of King Adontini. They bore Akua who died while yet still young secondly [Kodjoe] Kwaku, thirdly she was in her family when I was taken prisoner.

HAK 16:6 – 16:17

Ambah Mansah the sixth child of Yachia married to Kwaku Asukwa the king of [Assuchui Assushui] Assonchui, they bore Kofi, [secondly] after the birth of Kofi, the king was dethroned. Then Mansah married to Kobina [Safu] Asafu the king of [Santiaru?] Santah, they bore Akosua Abruāh. Abruah was borned at the same day as Prince Akwasi, who was born in the morning and Abruah was born at 3 pm. Secondly they bore Kodjoe then I was taken prisoner.

---

[16] "Mamponhene" in the text is struck out, but the word inserted above it is illegible.
[17] The original, struck out, reads "Gamaur" or the like. It is corrected to "Juben," also crossed out, and finally to "Jummor."

HAK 16:18 – 16:25

Achar the seventh child of Yachia married to a chief at Boemtamah called Kwami Jansah. Achar died at the very day when she was giving birth to her son and her son died together with her. At this sorrow the whole people of Kumasi was in grief and felt their best sympathy for her families.

HAK 16:26 – 16:29

Brajoe the eighth child of Yachia married to [Kwa....] Kwabiah the king of Himan and they bore one 1 son called Kobinah whose birthday I was taken prisoner.

HAK 16:30 – 17:2

Kwadu the eleventh child of Yachia married to Gimmah the king of Asskoli and they bore a son called Yaw—then I was taken prisoner.

HAK 17:3 – 17:5

The two other girls of Yachia were not given in marriage and I was taken prisoner.

HAK 17:6

Here endeth the sons of Yachia.

Descendants of Akua Afriyie

HAK 17:7 – 17:22

The [first son] second [son] daughter of Akua Friae who is the fifth child of Afua Gobbi. That child was called Ohen Afrae Yow was brought to a place called Jamassi and given to the king of that district called [Brobay] Bro Bay. They bore a girl called Kra Korhuer, after the birth of that girl, Manponhen invaded Jamassi then that girl [.....] Ohen Afraewuo came to Kumasi and married Kofi Chem and they bore Ambah [Brobo.....] Abror, then she lost her first born child Kra Kohue. Another King was crowned at Jamassi Yaw Séchilé told Kofi Chem to give him [Aqua Friae] Ohin Afrwo, (because she was the wife of his elder brother Brobay [Bro Bay....) and [Aku] Ohinafrwo & Sechile bore Yachia (a girl) and they bore another one called Akwasi and then King Prempeh was taken prisoner.

HAK 17:23 – 17:28

Akosua Insia the 5th child of Akua Friae married to the king of [Annolan] Annoyu called Atta. And they bore [Yok] Akua [Yaku?] Guarkun but the latter died very early, they bore a boy called Akwasi and they bore another girl called Akua. Then they took the King Prempeh prisoner.

HAK 17:29 – 18:3

Akosua Manhyia the ninth child of Akua Friae married to Yaw Danie (the King's bearer) and they bore Yaw Sanheni and they bore another called Kobinah then King Prempeh was taken prisoner.

HAK 18:4 – 18:9

Akua Badoo the tenth child of Akua Friae married to Atta Akwasi (King's sword bearer) and they bore Akwasi Ader. Secondly Akua Badoo died as [they we....] she was giving birth to her child (both the mother and the child died). Then during two weeks her first child Ader died.

HAK 18:10 – 18:14

Ambah Kom the eleventh child of Akua Friae married to Akwasi Prah at the district of [hiaw] Hiau, their first borned child died, the second child Ambah, then Prempeh was taken prisoner.

HAK 18:15 – 18:17

The twelveth child called Ambah Adjimān and the thirteenth Yā Abah, these two were not given to married.

HAK 18:18 – 18:20

Here endeth the sons of Akua Friae and here endeth all the families of Afuah Gobbi and they live at Assukwa.—

Descendants of Asantehemaa Afua Sapon

HAK 18:21 – 18:27

Yā [*crossed out*: Friae] Frae the fourth child of Afua Sapon. Kwandu the first child of Ya Fraie [*Frae*] [begot] married to Subri and begot Adjua [married to Subri] who died lately and beget another one called Ambah Sewah, then they beget a boy called Kussi then they beget a [child] girl [called] who died immediately.

HAK 18:27 – 18:28

Akua Der was the fifth child of Sapon, but she did not bear any child.

HAK 18:29 – 19:17

Akosua Begran was the sixth child of Sapon who [beget] married to the queen's manservant by name Intim and they beget Afua Inpla Chilé, then they made a divorce and that girl married to a man called Oyusu and they beget Ambah Sewah, then a divorce was made. That girl married to Kwami Boachie and beget Afua Sapon, then they beget Boatin, Kwakudua (I) and Kwakudua II. Other of his children died.

Afua Inpla Chilé married to Yaw Berkun and beget Yachia, and secondly beget Kobinā Annae, then they made a divorce. Then she married to a man belonging to Andansie. They beget a girl then [.....] Inpla died. Ambah Sewah beget a child but no one knew with whom it was.

HAK 19:18 – 19:21

Here endeth the [families of Afua Sapon] children and grandsons of Yā Friae, and they All stayed at [Aefua?] Ajoar.

Here endeth the generations of Afua Sapon.

Descendants of Asantehemaa Yaa Dufie

HAK 19:22 – 19:26

Yā Dufiae the fifth child of Kwandu married to Abu and they begot Kwaku Pipim, they divorced and that girl married to Oyusu and they begot Adjua Sewah [..... ....] Ya died.

HAK 19:27 – 19:29

Adjua Sewah married to Adu, they begot Akua Nansiwar, and Pokua, then Sewah died.

HAK 19:30 – 20:6

Akua Nansiwar went to Api Buosu and married to Appau and they begot Abina Sapon. They made a divorce and she came to Kotorku and married to [Afua Kwa] Affoi Kwah the chief man of the district and they begot Akwasi Chiu (?), then [Akua? Kwa] Affoi Kwa was put out of his position. From this that woman married no more.

HAK 20:7 – 20:19

Pokua the second child of Adjua Sewah went to Ankobia and married the chief man of that state called Kwaku Taeyua and they begot six children.

Ajae Kum the first borned.

Ya Intia was the sixth Child. They divorced and she married to Apia Kor [Korkor], they begot Pipim, the [third] second child was called Adjua Sewah died, the [fourth] third was called Ambah [Intobor] Intoboo, then they begot Badoo, Takiau and Kodjoe [Brōbi] Broenir. Then [Sewah died] Pokua died.

HAK 20:20 – 20:23

Ya Intia the sixth child of Pokua married to Akwasi Gembibi, they begot Kwaku Dua, Kwandu, Pipim. Then that girl Ya Intia died.

HAK 20:24 – 20:27

[.....] Adjua Sewah the eighth child of Pokua, and she married to Kodjoe Ader and bore only one child who died lately. Then Adjua Sewah also died.

HAK 20:28 – 20:31

Ambah Intubu married to Akwasi Tobo the son of a judge and bore Poku. Then Akwasi [Tob......] Tobo died. Then Intubou married to the servant of his uncle, but they made no child.

HAK 21:1 – 21:4

Badoo the tenth child of Pokoa married to Afriae, the ex-King of Otikrom and bore Ossai Kodjoe, then she bore Sewah. Then Badoo died.

HAK 21:5 – 21:7

Takiau the eleventh child of Pokua got a child called Poku but no one knew with whom she got the child.

HAK 21:8 – 21:10

Here endeth the generation of Ya Dufiae and they all live at [Akarasi] Akanasi. IIIII

Descendants of Akua Akrukruwaa

HAK 21:12 – 21:14

[Here endeth] Akua Kru Kru the sixth child of Kwandu married to Oyusu and bore Atar Sewah.

HAK 21:15 – 21:20

Atar married to Adou and bore Poku. Then they bore Adjua Kutu, then they bore Yaw Afriae, then Adjua Chilé, then Sor-Asū-Dā, then Pokua, then Poku [Tipor] Tikor, then Badoo. Then she stop bearing children.

HAK 21:21 – 21:22

Adjua Kutu married to Oyusu and bore Ossai, then Sewah. After this Kutu died.

HAK 21:23 – 21:25

Adjua Chile married to Yusu. [And St.] Her first three children died, then she bore Yā Nany, then Ossai Akwasi, then Manu.

HAK 21:25 – 21:27

Then Pokua married to Adou and bore Yamua, then Saebae. Then she stop bearing children.

HAK 21:27 – 21:28

Badoo borned two children but no one knew with whom.

HAK 21:29 – 22:1

[Sewah then] Ya Dufiae the child of Kutu married to a man called Kwajum, they bore a child who died in its infantry.

HAK 22:2 – 22:3.

Sewah the child of Kutu borned Akua In (* Yen*) timi but no one knew with whom. Then Sewah died.

HAK 22:4 – 22:5.

Ya Annany bore 1 girl and 1 boy, also no one knew with whom.

HAK 22:5 – 22:7

Akua Intim married Kodjoe Konson Kwar and bore Sewah.

HAK 22:7 – 22:9

[Here end] There will be explanations given further on for the cause that some of these women did not married.—

HAK 22:10 – 22:17

Here endeth the sons and grandson of Akua Krukru and they all live at [Anuaminakun] Anamarkun. But that district got another name on account of the sons and grandsons of Akua who dwelled there. This district [was] is called Assum Milamu and the people who dwell there is called Assum Milamufuo.

Descendants of Bimma Fita

HAK 22:18 – 22:20

[Binna] Obeny Fītār the first borned child of Abinah Japa and Fitar bored Bimma Dihie.

HAK 22:21 – 22:26

[(Anchiu was the first borned child of Bimma Dihier)] Bimma Dihie married to Intim and her first borned child was called Anchui, secondly Ya Mānfui, thirdly Yā Pany, fourthly Abina Achempoma.

HAK 22:27 – 22:30

Ya Manfu the second child of [Dihie] Bimma, she married to Adu and she bore Poku, secondly Ambah Adéder thirdly Ossai Kofi.

HAK 22:31 – 23:3

Yā Panīj the third child of [Dihie] Bimma [.....] married to Sabin, the servant of King of Insuasie and she bore a girl called Koatimar secondly Kwami Ajim, then Sabin died.

HAK 23:4 – 23:10

Abinah Achempoma the fifth child of Bimma married Oyusu Ansa Pani the [King] chief of Annamil-ankum [*insertion*: Annamarkun] and she bore Ossai, then they separated, after this the women married no more and she died and the [King] chief also died.

HAK 23:11 – 23:13

Ambah Adider the third child of Ya Manfu bore a girl called Adébilayua.

HAK 23:13 – 23:15

These are the sons and grandsons of Bimma Fitar and they all live at Wāwāsiē. –

Descendants of Otwiwaa Keseε and Akua Ago

HAK 23:16 – 23:17

Ottīwar Kesie bore Oboa Kwatiar.

HAK **23:17 – 23:22**

Akua Gu the brother of Ottiwar Kesie and Akua Gu was brought to Achuma at Takiman and [they] she was given in marriage to [Agabie] [Gamasie] Ajaeby the King of that district and she bore Dār Kun Dārkun.

HAK **23:23 – 23:25**

The sons of Ottiwar Kesie and Akua Gu live at Asaman Kwadan in district of Kumasi. [Here endeth the group or families.of.royal.]

HAK **23:26 – 23:30**

[These following passages relates the] Up to this 23rd pages [relates] showing the sons [Here endeth the sons and] and grandsons of Anchuanyami.....

CHAPTER EIGHT

Memoirs

INTRODUCTION

The documents in this chapter comprise three accounts by Agyeman Prempeh of the events leading up to his abduction and exile in 1896. The first of these, written in 1913, will be referred to as MEM/1913, the second, commenced in 1922, as MEM/1922, and the third, seemingly written in 1924, as MEM/1924. In both MEM/1913 and MEM/1922, Agyeman Prempeh began the narrative with the invasion of the British Protected Territory of the Gold Coast in 1873, at which time he was no more than a year old. The genre is more that of memoir than of autobiography. History, however, was interpreted and put to work.

MEM/1913 is a petition to the British colonial authorities to sanction the return of the exiles to Asante. A copy of it, in 10 foolscap pages, is preserved in the Seychelles National Archives.[1] MEM/1922 is more in the nature of a report to be made to the Asante Nation after repatriation had become a fact. It is highly critical of Britain's Asante policy in the late nineteenth century, and was presumably not intended to be made public, at least until the Asantehene's repatriation was assured. It was among the papers that Agyeman (or Edward) Prempeh brought back to Kumase from the Seychelles Islands in 1924. In 1971, Adu Boahen located the original text of MEM/1922 among papers in the Asantehene's palace in Kumase. It consisted of 13 foolscap pages. A photocopy of it was made, and accessioned, at what was then the Padmore Library in Accra.

A shorter version of MEM/1922 is also extant, and is entitled "History relating to the capture of Ex King Prempeh." In the event, Agyeman Prempeh gave a copy of this to A. C. Duncan-Johnstone, Deputy Provincial Commissioner of Asante's Eastern Province, who had been chosen to escort him from the Seychelles to Kumase. Duncan-Johnstone reported that it had been dictated by Agyeman Prempeh to his son Frederick. It is preserved in the National Archives of Ghana, Accra.[2] The last dated reference in the document is to December 1923. It could not have been written later than September 1924, when Agyeman Prempeh left the Seychelles. We shall describe it as MEM/1924.

THE PETITION OF 1913

In MEM/1913 Agyeman Prempeh construes the events leading up to 1896 with the firm conviction that the best way to the British heart was by contrition. ". . .[W]e now take the opportunity in submitting this petition," he wrote, "to confess our sin and fault which has led us to this fate, and to

---

[1] Seychelles National Archives (henceforth SNA), C/SS/2, vol. II: Edward Prempeh *et al.* to Governor C. R. M. O'Brien, 16 October 1913.
[2] National Archives of Ghana, Accra, ADM11/1/1905: Report by Duncan-Johnstone on the repatriation of ex-King Prempeh, including "History relating to the capture of Ex King Prempeh." Duncan-Johnstone comments: "From his conversation I gather that he considered himself somewhat unfairly treated by the Administration which deposed him and his account of it as dictated to his son Frederick whilst in the Seychelles seems to bear this out."

humble ourselves lowly and reverently for your Excellency's kind consideration." The petition was addressed to the Governor of the Seychelles Islands, C. R. M. O'Brien. It was dated 16 October 1913, and was signed by Agyeman Prempeh ("Edward Prempeh Ex King of Ashantis") and the marks of twelve others of the senior exiles. The petition was summarily dismissed, Governor of the Gold Coast Hugh Clifford having recently communicated his opposition to repatriation.[3]

MEM/1913

Our ancient King Kofi Karkari in his time raised up a large army against the Fantis who were close to the Coast without any cause or reason of attacking them. A great battle was fought in which the Fantis were defeated and driven as far as to a district known as Afoutou Manpon. Where Amanquatchia, the commander-in-chief of the Ashanti received a message from the English Governor on the coast that His Excellency congratulates the Ashantis for their bravery in expelling the Fantis to such an extent and requested the Ashanti troops to retire from Afoutou Manpon where they had reached and to give up the fight and fail to do so, the English Government will interfere in the fight and take up the part of the Fantis for the said place where they had reached is a British town.

The Ashanti's army neglected the advice given to them by the Governor and continued to fight and persued the enemy as far as to a district known as Bankranpan where the Ashanti army met with the English army under the command of Lord Wolseley; the Ashanti army was defeated and Lord Wolseley entered the capital Kumasi.

But Lord Wolseley remained three days at Kumasi and was so good towards us that he did not devastate our town but only laid a fine on us which we were allowed to pay by instalments to the English Government to recover the cost of Lord Wolseley's expenses in the war; and before Lord Wolseley set off from Kumasi, he gave the following orders to the Ashantis that:

1st. Not to kill people.

2nd. Not to block the route of traders to prevent communication from the coast to the main-land.

3rd. To have a new route be made from Kumasi to a district known as Fominah.

4th The Ashantis from the date have not to go to war without the permission of the English who are from the date bind themselves to protect them.

Only a minimum part of the fine laid upon them was paid; the King and the chiefs did not carry out the orders given to them; and the result was that King Karkari was dethroned and his Younger brother Bonsu was crowned; the latter also did not carry out the orders and raised up an army against the King of Juabin without the knowledge of the Governor. After the war the Governor sent ambassadors to Kumasi to claim for the fine laid upon them by Lord

---

[3] SNA, C/SS/2, vol. II: Officer in Charge of Political Prisoners to Governor, Seychelles Islands, 17 Oct. 1913.

Wolseley. The reason for having gone against the 4th rule of Lord Wolseley; but King Bonsu only paid £2400. –. –. out of the rest of the fine.

The Governor sent another ambassador to King Bonsu asking him to accept the institutions of school buildings for training at Kumasi; The King and the chiefs refused to accept same; and the end was that King Bonsu was dethroned by his own people.

After the dethroning of King Bonsu, there was a great rebellion in the country which lasted about ten years and all the time the chiefs in the town were trying to put a King on the throne to obtain peace, but their trials were in vain. Then the chiefs sent ambassadors on the Coast to the Governor to ask for assistance; the Governor acted very kindly and sent two English officers to Kumasi to help the chiefs and about four months the officers had completed the task which had lasted the Ashantis ten years and even had not been able to find an end of it.—and I Prempeh was proclaimed the King of Ashanti under an age of about 16 years.

A couple of months after I was proclaimed, the Governor sent another officer to Kumasi to announce that as his Excellency himself has set a King on the throne, he will make the King as a planted tree which is being watered and had grown up favorably; and to be able to do so, there must be Education Buildings for training;—and if we do accept this term, the officer to remain 40 days at Kumasi to put everything in proper order. But I the King and all the inhabitants not knowing that it was for our own good, refused to accept same.—

In the last rebellion most of the Ashantis went and served under the Government on the coast and when through the help of the English I was made a King, I sent ambassadors to the Governor and begged to send back my men who were under him. The Governor in reply sent an English officer named Captain Stewart and an interpreter Froem and announced that if education is accepted in Kumasi, all my men under the Government shall be sent back to me.—

2nd. The Government will not interfere in the exercising of my power against my people.—

3rd. The Government will also pay to me, the Queen and each regiment each a certain amount per year.

4th. The Government will also hold responsible to protect Ashanti against her foes.

These were the 4 messages sent to us by the Governor and to this excellent bargain, we allowed ourselves to be deceived by our own mischieviousness and refused to accept same.—

Besides these few instances we have procured, there are many other faults which we had done to Government and which we confess they are too numerous to procure; we always under the persuasions that ours were the best.—

After refusing several advices, the Government at last set on to exercise its power over us by taking us prisoners; and when the time that we should be captured was nigh, I reflected over the past good deeds of the English Government towards me by putting me on the throne and moreover promised to make the best of me which we refused, we made up our minds to surrender than to resist to make matters worst.—

About 4 or 5 years after I and some of my chiefs were captured, the few remaining chiefs at Kumasi instead of submitting themselves loyally and reverently under the supervision of the English Government and followed my step of not to resist, they misbehaved and after resisting against the Government, they were also captured and sent to meet me. And since we are here, we sympathise greatly for our misdeeds; but we blessed our Sovereign King George V for the kind treatment and Supervision we still receiving in His Majesty's hands . . .

THE MEMOIR OF 1922–23

In 1922 Agyeman Prempeh commenced writing a longer and much revised account of the events leading to his exile. The project was inspired by a major change that had occurred in his circumstances. On 31 March 1922 Agyeman Prempeh once again petitioned the Seychelles Administration on the matter of the repatriation of the Asante exiles and was, surprisingly perhaps, permitted also to make a direct approach to the Secretary of State in London—none other than Winston Churchill.[4] Churchill consulted C. H. Harper, Chief Commissioner Ashanti, who conveniently was on leave in London at the time. Harper replied to Churchill, copying his letter to F. G. Guggisberg, Governor of the Gold Coast. At this point in time the repatriation of the Asante exiles was impossible, so Harper argued, but they should be told to reapply in two years hence, when there would be the necessary Native Jurisdiction Ordinance in place.[5] This, Harper thought, "will not close the door to a renewal of the ancient confederation should the trend of political affairs render its renewal desirable and acceptable."[6] Churchill approved, and so did Guggisberg who made it known in Kumase that Agyeman Prempeh might be repatriated in 1924.[7] Even more to the point, the Governor of Seychelles Islands officially informed Agyeman Prempeh that his application for repatriation should be renewed in two years.[8]

It was in this context that Agyeman Prempeh began the drastic revision, and expansion, of his account of the events leading to the coup of 1896. Convinced that his repatriation was assured, he began putting together an account of his abduction that would, at one and the same time, resound to the credit of the Asante Nation generally, and of its king—himself—specifically. MEM/1922 is transcribed fully below.

---

[4] SNA, C/SS/2, vol. II: Administrator to Governor, 4 April 1922.
[5] For a recent review of the policies of the Chief Commissioners in Asante, see I. Wilks, "Asante Nationhood and Colonial Administrators, 1896–1935," in C. Lentz and P. Nugent (eds.), *Ethnicity in Ghana. The Limits of Invention*, Macmillan, 2000: 68–96.
[6] SNA, C/SS/2, vol. II: Harper to Secretary of State, 9 July 1922.
[7] SNA, C/SS/2, vol. II: Guggisberg to Churchill, 12 August 1922; Churchill to Administrator, Seychelles, 11 October 1922.
[8] SNA, C/SS/2, vol. II: Clerk to Governor to ex-King Prempeh, 7 December 1922.

MEM/1922
7/8/22
REIGN OF KOFI KARKARI, KING OF ASHANTI

(a) Karkari invade the Fantis (a tribe nearer to the Coast)

(b) General Amanquatchia was sent in command of the Ashanti army to fight the Fantis.—

(c) The Fantis were defeated of and driven to a place call Afoutou Mampon.—

(d) On arriving at Afoutou Mampon, the English Governor sent a message to general Amanquatchia advising him to stop fighting and not to try to advance further then Afoutou Mampon or else if fighting continues, the English troops will have to act in favour of the Fantis against the Ashantis.—

(e) General Amanquatchia neglected the advice and proceeded to the town of Bakrampah where they meet with the English troops and there the English and the Ashantis fought and the Ashantis were defeated and driven back as far as Dasoo where King Karkari left Kumasi and met the English troop under the Command of Lord Wolseley.—

(f) King Karkari was defeated and driven from Dasoo to the capital Kumasi and entered Kumasi.—

(g) Lord Wolseley did not attempt to make the King a prisoner but ordered 4 rules to be executed by the Ashantis.—

The 4 rules were:—

1st To pay a damnity of £375,000 and the amount is to be paid by instalments

2nd Not to kill anybody.—

3rd To trace a new road from Kumasi to the town of Fominah.—

4th Not to make any fight or invade any country without the permission of the English Governor from the Coast.—

Ref: to No. 1, a first instalment was paid by King Karkari

Ref: to No. 2—King Karkari ordered no one to be Killed

Ref: to No. 3—The road to Fominah was not traced.—

Ref: to No. 4—King Karkari made no fight.—

King Karkari was dethroned by his own people and sent to a far village.—

REIGN OF KING BONSU (YOUNGER BROTHER TO KING KARKARI)

Nana Asafu Egay the leader of Juabin province (a province under Ashanti) rebelled against King Bonsu and the latter sent an army against him and defeated him and did not first inform the English Governor as stated in Rule 4.—

(b) Asafu Egay being defeated fled for safety under the English Governor.—

(c) The English Governor sent a message to King Bonsu reminding him that he has gone against the 4th Rule and so he is requested to pay the remainder of the damnity.—King Bonsu sent a remittance of £2400.—

(d) King Bonsu furtherly dealt against the 2nd Rule and by ordering people to be executed or killed.—

(e) The 3rd Rule (tracing the New Road) was not complied to by King Bonsu.—

(f) A certain young man call Owusu Tassiah Marndier (being the son of one of the royal family at Kumasi) wronged King Bonsu and the latter wanted to inflict a certain punishment on that youngman and the youngman knowing to be punished excaped to the English Governor.—

King Bonsu knowing the young man had escaped sent a messenger Asabia Enchui to the English Governor to ask him to send back to Kumasi that gilty youngman who had escaped to him from Kumasi.—

The Governor refused to order the youngman to return to Kumasi and the messenger said to the Governor "I understand that the English King and the Ashanti King are in good terms and if you (Governor) refuse to order that youngman to go back to Kumasi, I am afraid there would be an emnity between King there 2 Kings.—"

The Governor then got vexed and said to the messenger, "You mean to say then that the Ashantis wanted to fight the English; then I shall not wait for the Ashanti army to come and meet me I will then raise up an Army against King Bonsu"

(g) During that time at the coast, there was a certain chief called Busumulu Julah who also was sent by King Bonsu to the Governor for private affair, and the latter seeing that the Governor was vexed at the word of the messenger, offered an apology to the Governor on behalf of the King—The Governor agreed and accepted the apology and asks for a further damnity of £8000.=.= for having accepted the apology and withdrawn the British troops which were on march to Kumasi.—Busumulu Julah sent a messenger to King Bonsu and the King Bonsu sent the £8000.=.= by Chief Boachi Tin and same was given to the Governor.—

After this the chiefs rebelled against their King to dethrone him.—King Bonsu knowing his fate sent a message to the Governor for urgent help.—

The Governor complied and sent an officer and when the officer reached Kumasi, the King had already been dethroned 8 days before and so nothing was done.—The officer wanted to send for Ex King Bonsu but the chiefs objected.—And Kwakudua II was proclaimed King.—

5 weeks after the proclamation, King Kwakudua II died.—

The rebellion since the time of King Bonsu was still going on and civil war raging and this lasted 10 years.—and during that time no chief was able to restore peace.—

The Queen Ya Echia was still reigning being supported by the minister Asafu Boachie.—

At the commencement of the 11th year of the rebellion, Queen Ya Echia and Asafu Boachie sent a message to the Governor that they are unable to restore peace and so requesting the Governor for help to restore peace and to proclaim a King.—

The Governor sent an officer to help the Queen and Asafu Boachie and peace was restored and myself Prempeh was proclaimed King in the presence of the officer.—

When every peace was restored, the officer returned to the Governor.—

REIGN OF KING PREMPEH.—

[*deleted*: The Governor sent a second officer by name Hall to Kumasi]

A second officer by name Hall was then sent by the Governor to Kumasi to announce to the King Prempeh and chiefs that His Excellency wishes to construct a mission house at Kumasi and His Excellency is sure that when missionary has started his work, peace and tranquility would reign.—

2nd. His Excellency would appoint King Prempeh, to be the King of all the africans.—

3rd His Excellency would not interfere of any law of the country except (murdering people)—

4th His Excellency would hold himself responsible to fight any other nation who would attempt to invade Ashanti.

5th His Excellency is ready to pay to King Prempeh £1000 a year.

6th The Queen and chiefs would each be paid.—

If these conditions are agreed upon, he would remain at Kumasi 40 days to restore everything in order before returning to the Coast.—

No reply was given to the officer the first day; and the case was postponed to hold a counsel.—

King Prempeh ordered two subchiefs to remain with the officer as a [*deleted*: guardian] companion.

Three days after King Prempeh called for a Counsel at night to discuss the above terms.—

When the Counsel was holding, the two subchiefs who were put to accompany the officer, came running and entered the counsel room and said that the officer had arranged his soldiers in battle array—

King Prempeh sent a message to the officer the cause of putting his soldiers in battle array.

The officer replied that he is obliged to put himself in readiness for he does not see how a counsel should be formed at night time.—And so the best thing is to dismiss the counsel and he would withdraw his soldiers.—

King Prempeh dismiss the Counsel and early the next morning King Prempeh sent a messenger to ask the officer to come to receive a reply of his terms.—The officer refused to come and set on his journey to the Coast.—

King Prempeh again sent a 2nd message Ahinkroe Apia to the Governor stating that the officer Mr Hall whom he sent to Kumasi was sent for to take reply of the terms and he refused entirely to come and set off to the Coast.—

The Governor again sent Captain Stewart and Mr. Froem to Kumasi.— When they reached Kumasi, they were welcomed and on the very night, Captain Stewart sent a message to King Prempeh asking him to send the following chiefs for he wants to have an interview with them the very night and the next morning he would come and see the King himself:—viz. Chiefs [*deleted*: Asafu] Amanquatchia; Asafu Boachie; Kofi Subri; Kwaku Fokuo; Nanchui and Akwasi Gembibi.—

King Prempeh ordered the 6 chiefs to go and when they went.—Captain Stewart again said to them "If [*deleted*: Captain] Officer Hall had refused to take the reply of the King as to the terms asked for by the Governor, I am then sent by the Governor to bring you the same terms and to ask for reply. And the Governor further states that a withered tree worth nothing for he possesses every where from sunrise to sunset.—and to practically ¾ of the Ashanti [*deleted*: people] provinces are under his control.—and so if you accept these terms, he would then unite and hand over all the departed Ashanti provinces to King Prempeh."—

The next morning King Prempeh ordered for a general meeting and Captain Stewart came for and repeated these words before the assembly.—

King Prempeh and the chiefs replied that they are now prepared to go and fight the King of Inkransan (one of the big provinces of Ashanti) and when the war is ended, a reply to these terms would be sent to the Governor.—

Captain Stewart returned to the Coast and the chiefs prepared themselves and set off to the war.—

About 4 to 5 months after, Captain Stewart and Mr. Froem came back to Kumasi and said to King Prempeh "The governor orders me to tell you to send for your army and discontinue the war with Inkransan for formerly the people of Inkransan knew not how to fight and had no ammunition but now the people of Inkransan has learnt how to fight well and has plenty of ammunition.— And if your chiefs insist going to fight, it would be bad for them"

King Prempeh agreed to this and sent a message to meet the chiefs at a district called Asercherdomassy to order them to not to proceed and to return to Kumasi.—The chiefs refused and said they are in close quarters with the enemy and it is now impossible for them to return to Kumasi.—

The above reply from the chiefs was given to Captain Stewart, and he returned to the Coast.—

The chiefs defeated the Inkransan and they returned to Kumasi. Victorious.—

Soon after Captain Stewart came to Kumasi, to receive a reply for the terms which the King and chiefs had promised to give to him when the war with Inkransan will be over.—

Captain Stewart on reaching Kumasi to receive the reply was told that a reply will now be given to him (1) after the celebration of the anniversary of the death of late King Kwaku Dua and (2) when the celebration is ended, King Prempeh will be crowned and after the Coronation, then a reply for the terms will be consulted and given to him.—

Captain Stewart returned to the Coast.—

When the anniversary of the death of late King Kwaku Dua was celebrated and King Prempeh crowned, then a reply was being discussed to be given to Captain Stewart and thereupon came a grandson of one of the Ashanti Kings called Ahinsan (this Ahinsan has been educated at the Coast and knows how to read and write) and advised the committee to decide on contribution of a certain sum of money to be given to him to proceed to [*deleted*: England] London to discuss on that question and to plead to have all the Ashanti provinces which are under the control of the English be [*deleted*: returned to under the] restore to King Prempeh as before.

The Committee agreed upon the advice given by Ahinsan and contributed a certain sum of money.

The King and chiefs ordered the following chiefs Kwami Boatin; Kwaku Fokuo; Inkroma; Bonnah; Achempon Daban and Kojo Tufuor to accompany Ahinsan and the latter brought with him his brother [*deleted*: Alberth] Attah— thus forming 8 persons.—

These 8 persons were ordered to inform the Governor before taking ship to go to England that they are sent by the King and chiefs to discuss certain matters in England. But as the nature of the facts they were not order to disclose to the Governor.—

The 8 persons then set off for their voyage to London.—

These persons on reaching London sent back Kojo Tufuor and Achempon Daban to Kumasi to tell to King Prempeh and chiefs that they had reached London and they are arguing the facts and they hope that their wishes will be accomplished; but they learnt from a source that the Governor of the Gold Coast is preparing to send Captain Stewart and Mr. Froem to Kumasi and when they would reach Kumasi, whatever message they would bring from the Governor, not to accept but only to reply that "No reply to any term would be given unless the expedition sent to London to discuss certain matters return to Kumasi."

Six days after the arrival of these 2 persons from London to Kumasi, Captain Stewart and Froem really came to Kumasi and said "The Governor has again sent us to take reply of the terms which were put before you some time ago; and if a satisfactory reply is obtained from you then the chiefs who are now at London to discuss your case [would also receive a satisfactory reply."—

The King and chiefs having received a message from Kojo Tufuor and Achempon Daban, beforehand, replied to Captain Stewart that no reply would now be given to any term unless the chiefs sent to London return to Kumasi.—

Captain Stewart replied that if these terms are not accepted then your chiefs who are at London would not be able to have any interview with even the servant of the Queen Victoria and they would be in London as sheeps without shepherd.—

The people and women who stood outside the Council room listening to the case took the words of Captain Stewart for vain and false because they were persuaded that the message from the chiefs at London was correct and that Captain Stewart was telling lies.—and so the people and women shouted against him and mocked him.—

Captain Stewart and Froem got angry and on the same day set off for the Coast.—

King Prempeh sent 2 chiefs to see the Governor at the Coast telling him that Captain Stewart had returned to the coast with anger and so to excuse; and a satisfactory reply will be sent very soon.—

These 2 chiefs on reaching [*deleted*: the river] at Bansoo were forbidden to cross to proceed to the Coast because Captain Stewart had left soldiers on the bank of the river to forbid any Ashanti to cross.—

The 6 remaining chiefs at London now entered Kumasi and announced that a reply has been given to the Governor at the Coast that the English flag has now been accepted and that we are now coming to see you. King and chiefs to send the prime minister and 2 princes to go and sign the treat of accepting the British flag in Ashanti.—

At last the King and chiefs agreed upon and ordered chief Asafu Boachie and 2 princes to proceed to sign the treaty.—

Asafu Boachie set off with the 2 princes and on reaching at the district of Asoomya he met with Captain Stewart and the British troops.—

He conveyed the news to Captain Stewart that he is sent with the 2 princes to sign the treaty and to received the Flag to be placed at Kumasi.—

Captain Stewart asked chief Asafu Boachie to return to Kumasi with the 2 princes and he is now coming himself to attend to any case.—

Chief Asafu Boachie returned to Kumasi on a Sunday and on Monday a message from Captain Stewart came to Kumasi and said that chief Asafu Boachie did not want to wait for a reply but escaped to Kumasi.—

Asafu Boachie got angry and decided to set off to meet Captain Stewart on the next day Tuesday. On Wednesday Asafu Boachie saw Captain Stewart at a place called Dasoo.—the servants of the chief were plundered and beaten by the soldiers of Captain Stewart.—This was reported to Captain Stewart who forbid it and in spite of this Captain Stewart gave them no reply but told the chief to return to Kumasi and he would be there very soon.—

The same day Wednesday Asafu Boachie and his party returned to Kumasi and on Thursday Captain Stewart sent a messenger to Kumasi to King Prempeh that he has learnt that he is coming to Kumasi to dethrone him which is a very false complaint.—

He is coming to arrange everything and give it in the hands and control of King Prempeh.—And so he requests King Prempeh to send a messenger with the one he had sent to make 2 to proceed and call for the omanheni of Juabin to come and meet you to witness the arrangements.—

And he Captain Stewart would be here tomorrow Friday to prepare a place for the general himself.

On the next day Friday the general and the British troops entered Kumasi.—

The Governor came on Saturday.—and gave 4 orders.—[9] viz:-

(1) King Prempeh and Queen Ya Echia must in come on Monday before him and take off their sacred sandals and kneel down before him and apologise for having gone against all orders given by Lord Wolseley.

(2) To pay the whole of balance of the war damnity imposed by Lord Wolseley since the time of King Karkari.

(3) As there are so many British troops, King Prempeh and chiefs are each requested to show the places where their treasures are hidden or kept; so that [*deleted*: notices] labels be put on the houses that [?] to caution any soldier to take care not to break through any treasure house to steal.—

Same was shown and labels were put on every house of treasure.—

(4) The Governor asked for 1000 buckets of fresh water on Saturday and 1000 buckets on Sunday—And same were given.—

On Sunday night at 7 p.m. all the label put to the house were removed and communications were cut.—

On Monday morning, King Prempeh and the chiefs went to the meeting and they found the British flag being hoisted in the square and King Prempeh and the chiefs caught hold of the mast and said "We now receive the flag"—

When they had all assembled the Governor asked the King and Queen to come and kneel before him and apologise as stated in the 1st order—

The King and Queen complied accordingly by taking off the crown and royal sandals.

When the King and Queen had got up from their knees, they were asked to pay the balance of the war damnity imposed to King Karkari by Lord Wolseley.—

---

[9] The writer was clearly choosing his words carefully here. The first version read: "brought 3" followed by an illegible word; the second version runs: "gave 3 questions."

Chapter Eight

King Prempeh replied that the said amount was never claimed from him before and it was only on Saturday the day before yesterday that he came to know* (**The writer's footnote*: and moreover the amount was allowed to be paid by instalments.) and so for the present, he is ready to give £2720 = as remittance and ask for 7 days to return the remainder of the amount and for surety during the 7 days, the 2 sisters of the King would be given to be surety.

The Governor refused to accept both the remittance of £2720 and the surety of the 2 sisters of the King up to 7 days to return the balance.—

The King then asked to be allowed to return to his house and to take some more remittance.—

The Governor refused to allow the King to go home and said that unless the amount is paid to him in full at the very moment he will be taken prisoner.—

King Prempeh was then made prisoner together with his mother, father, brother and 10 chiefs making together 14 persons.—

As soon as the King and the others were made prisoner orders were given to the soldiers to plunder and they plundered everywhere were tickets were placed and plundered all the properties in the King's palace and in the houses of the chiefs and then ordered King Prempeh to give the £2720 to him.—

The capture took place on Monday and on Wednesday the prisoners were ordered to march.—

When the prisoners had reached Elmina (a town in the Coast) the remaining chiefs at Kumasi sent Kwami Boatin and Kwaku Fokuo (the 2 chiefs who were lately sent to England) to [*deleted*: Gold Coast (Accra)] Oguar to see 2 lawyers to make a petition for the prisoners to have them released.—

The petition was made as follows. (1) King Prempeh offered a remittance of £2720. = and was refused and (2) further asked 7 days [to] and to give his 2 sisters in Surety to return the remaining balance (and same was refused) and was made prisoner and his properties in the palace as well as of the chiefs were [*deleted*: plundered] taken by force and the refused offer of £2720. = was then taken by force.—

Now the whole Ashanti is governed and ruled by the Governor as we do not see why King Prempeh and his Queen and chiefs should be made prisoner, that is be punished 3 or 4 times for same offence.—

This petition was sent to the King and chiefs while in custody through the Commissioner to be signed by them.—

The Ex King and chiefs signed accordingly.—

The petition was then sent to the Governor who upon receipt of the letter ordered the 2 chiefs Kwami Boatin and Kwaku Fokuo who made the petition to be arrested and sent to Accra and the reply of the petition was that the Ex King and his chiefs would be sent to Sierra Leone.—

The prisoners remained one year at Elmina and the day they were leaving Elmina for Sierra Leone the two chiefs Boatin and Kwaku Fokuo were sent to meet the gang.—

After 3 years and 10 months stay at Sierra Leone, the Governor paid a visit to the camp and announced that war has broke out at Ashanti, and Asibi the omanheni of Kokofu has been taken prisoner and will soon be sent to meet you and after 8 days of his arrival, Every one would be set free and liable to go anywhere that pleases you.—

The King and chiefs being ignorant of the neutralisation did not proceed to sign their names and vow that they knew nothing of the war which had broke out and that they are not in favour of it.—

8 days after the arrival of Asibi at Sierra Leone, the prisoners were removed to Seychelles in Sept: 1900.—9 months after the arrival of the Ex King and ors, 15 more chiefs as political prisoners were sent to meet their King.—

During the stay at Seychelles several [*deleted*: application] petitions have been sent but no favourable reply and in Jan: 1923 there will be 27 years in captivity.

HISTORY AND APOLOGIA

MEM/1924 is an eleven-page document. The grammar and the spelling seem rather more correct than those of MEM/1922, and this may be no more than the result of its being, in a certain sense, a fair copy. Its main interest lies in the supplementary material that addresses the highly sensitive matter of whether Asantehene Agyeman Prempeh was right in not opposing the British advance on Kumase in 1896. He argues, quite simply, that he chose to put himself at risk in order to avoid the loss of Asante lives and property that would have resulted from a war that could not be won. This was his apologia, a written defence of his conduct that, on his return to Kumase, he would present to his people together with the accounts of his good stewardship of the exiles in the Seychelles (see Chapter Nine).

MEM/1924

HISTORY RELATING TO THE CAPTURE OF EX KING PREMPEH.

At the reign of King Prempeh, the English Governor at the Coast sent an Officer whose name was known as Mr. Hall to bring the following messages to King Prempeh stating as follows:—

1st. That for the welfare and peace of the King and his country, His Excellency wishes to cause missionary buildings to be constructed at Kumasi and to carry out missionary works.

2nd. His Excellency would appoint King Prempeh to have control over all the Africans.

3rd. The English Government would not interfere itself in the native laws and ruling of the country with the exception of human sacrifice which would be prohibited.

4th. The English Government would enter in treaty with King Prempeh to punish any nation which would attempt to make war or invade Kumasi.

5th. The English Government would pay to King Prempeh an annual sum of £1,000.

6th. The Queen and Chief would likewise receive pay.

Mr. Hall further added that if the above are agreed upon by King Prempeh, he was to remain 40 days at Kumasi to set down these arrangements in proper order before returning to the Coast.

No reply to the above terms was given to Mr. Hall but the King postponed his reply in order to have a Council with his Chiefs.

King Prempeh then ordered 2 chiefs to remain with Mr. Hall as companion or guide.

Three days after these messages was delivered by Mr. Hall the King ordered a meeting of the chiefs to be held at night to discuss the terms.

During the course of the meeting, the 2 guides of Mr. Hall rushed into the Council room and announced that Mr. Hall has arranged his soldiers in lines of battle and ready for attack.

King Prempeh sent to enquire the cause from Mr. Hall and the latter replied that he would withdraw his soldiers from the lines of attack unless King Prempeh also dissolves the meeting for he seeing that King Prempeh has held a meeting by night, he must then put himself in readiness in case of attack.

King Prempeh dissolved the meting and early the next morning sent for Mr. Hall to be given the reply of his messages. Mr. Hall refused to come and left for the Coast.

King Prempeh sent one called Ahinkroe Apia to report to the Governor that Mr. Hall was sent for to take a reply of the messages but refused to come.

The Governor again sent Captain Stewart and a native interpreter called Mr. Froem to Kumasi who were heartily welcomed by the King, and on the very night they reached Kumasi they asked the King to send to them the following Chiefs for a private interview, viz:—Amanquatchia: Asafu Boachie: Kofi Subri, Kwaku Fokuo, Lanchui and Akwasi Gambibi.

To these 6 persons, Captain Steward told them that he was sent forth to receive a reply of the messages already announced to them by Mr. Hall and the Governor further states that if the branches of a tree are fell, the tree would soon die. British Government possesses every where from sunrise to sunset and also about ¾ of the Ashanti provinces. If the terms are then accepted, the government would unite and hand over all the exile provinces to King Prempeh.

The next morning King Prempeh called for a meeting to receive Captain Stewart.

In the meeting King Prempeh and Chiefs replied to Captain Stewart for information of the Governor that they are now prepared to invade the province of "Inkwansan" and after the war a reply to the terms will be given or sent to the Governor.

About 5 months after Captain Stewart and Froem returned to Kumasi with a message from the Governor to convey to King Prempeh that His Excellency advises King Prempeh to discontinue the war with the Inkwansan for the people of Inkwansan have very much improved in fighting and in ammunition supply than they are considered. And if the Ashanti Army does not retire it would turn bad to them. King Prempeh agreed to the advice and sent an immediate order asking the Ashanti Army to retire. The messenger met the Ashanti Army at the district of Aserchordomasy and conveyed the message of retirement to the commander who refused to retire and stated that he had now reached in close quarters with the enemy and it is now too late to retire.

The messenger returned and Captain Stewart after hearing the news returned to the Coast.

The Ashantis fought the Inkwansan and defeated them.

Captain Stewart learning that the Chiefs had returned from the Inkwansan war, came back to Kumasi to have the reply of the terms for the Governor.

Captain Stewart was then told by King Prempeh and his courts that a reply to the 6 terms will be decided after the celebration of the anniversary of the death of late King Kwaku Dua and the Coronation of King Prempeh.

Captain Stewart receiving this reply returned to the Coast.

After the anniversary of the death of late King Kwaku Dua and the Coronation of King Prempeh a meeting was called to discuss a reply in accordance to the terms.

During the course of the discussion, there came one Ahinsan a grandson of one of the Ashanti Kings (being an educated man) and advised the King and his Councillors to put in abeyance their discussions on the terms brought to them and to decide on contribution of a certain sum of money to be given to him to proceed to London for an appeal against the Government, to have all the Ashanti provinces that are under the British Control restored to King Prempeh. The meeting unanimously agreed upon the decision of Ahinsa and a certain sum of money was contributed and given to Ahinsa. The King further ordered chiefs Kwami Boatin, Kwaku Fokuo, Inkroma, Bonnah, Achempon Daban and Kojo Tufuor to accompany Ahinsa to London and the latter brought with him his brother "Attah" thus forming a party of 8 persons.

These 8 persons were informed to report themselves to the Governor at the Coast before leaving but they were not allowed to disclose to the Governor their object of going to England.

Not long after these people had reached England, Ahinsa and others sent back to Kumasi Kojo Tufuor and Achempon Daban to inform King Prempeh that they are still discussing their facts and hope their objects will meet with success.

And as they had learnt from a true source in England that Captain Stewart and Mr. Froem will be sent to Kumasi by the Governor and so they advise the King and his Councils not to accept any term or arrangement which Captain Stewart would propose but to wait till they return from England before giving reply to any proposal.

Two days after King Prempeh had received such advice from his Ambassadors in London, Captain Stewart and Mr. Froem reached Kumasi and announced to King Prempeh that they had been sent to receive reply of the terms and if a satisfactory reply is obtained, then the Ambassadors who are in England would also meet with success.

King Prempeh having before-hand received an advice from his Ambassadors refused to give any reply to Captain Stewart.

Captain Stewart receiving a reply, said to King Prempeh that as the terms of the English Govenment have not been accepted, the Ashanti Ambassadors in England would not even be able to see or have an interview with Queen's servant and they would be in England as sheep without shepherd.

Upon the above words of Captain Stewart the people and women who were outside the Council room mocked at Captain Stewart and they were persuaded that Captain Stewart's words were false and that of their Ambassadors in England were correct.

Captain Stewart and Froem got angry of having been mocked at and returned to the Coast immediately after the meeting.

King Prempeh sent another 2 ambassadors, viz:- chiefs Kwami Boachie of Attipim and Kokra of Mawellis to the English Governor at the Coast to apologise for what was done to Captain Stewart and that a satisfactory reply will be sent very soon.

The 2 Chiefs (Ambassadors) on reaching at Bansoo on their way to the Coast were forbidden to cross by the soldiers which Captain Stewart had placed in guards: forbidding any Ashanti to cross from Kumasi to the Coast. The 6 remaining Ambassadors at London at last entered Kumasi and announced that their discussions had resulted in acceptance on behalf of the King and his Courts the British Flag into Kumasi and that the Gold Coast Government had been informed that the Prime Minister of Ashanti and two princes will be sent from Kumasi to the Coast to sign the treaty.

King Prempeh and his Chiefs accepted the terms and at once ordered Asafu Boachie and 2 princes to proceed to sign the treaty – but on arriving at Asoomya they met with Captain Stewart and the British troops coming to Kumasi.

Asafu Boachie having conveyed the news to Captain Stewart was ordered to return to Kumasi till he (Captain Stewart) will reach Kumasi to attend to any case or matter.

Asafu Boachie returned to Kumasi on a Sunday and on Monday a message from Captain Stewart was received at Kumasi that Asafu Boachie had cowardly returned to Kumasi without waiting for a reply from him re signing of the treaty.

Asafu Boachie was very much vexed for having been treated coward and proposed to set off to meet Captain Stewart on Tuesday the next day. On Wednesday Boachie met with Captain Stewart at a place called Dasoo.

The properties of the attendants or followers of Boachie were plundered by the British soldiers and when same were reported to Captain Stewart, the latter ordered the British soldiers to return all articles that were stolen. Thereupon Captain Stewart told to Boachie to return to Kumasi and he would be coming very soon – and Boachie then returned to Kumasi.

On Thursday Captain Stewart sent a message to King Prempeh telling him that he is coming to Kumasi to put all things in order and hand over all the Ashanti provinces in the hands and control of King Prempeh. And he is not coming to Kumasi to dethrone King Prempeh as rumours had already been spread out. And for that reason he requests King Prempeh to give a messenger to accompany his own to go for the Omanhene of Juabin to summon him to Kumasi to witness the arrangement which he (Captain Stewart) is coming to make. And he (Captain Stewart) would arrive Kumasi Friday to prepare a place for the English General who would be soon coming. On Friday the English General and troops entered Kumasi. The Governor came on Saturday and on his arrival he ordered.

1st. King Prempeh and Queen Ya Echia to take off their sacred sandals and come on Monday to kneel before him and apologise for having neglected to execute the orders given by Lord Wolseley.

2nd. To pay the whole of the war indemnity imposed by Lord Wolseley since the reign of King Karkari.

3rd. All the important houses and places containing treasure must be shown so that labels would be placed on them as warnings to the troops lest they break through and steal.

4th. 1,000 buckets of fresh water to be supplied on Saturday and 1,000 on Sunday.

All these 4 orders were carried out.

On Sunday at 7 p.m. every label placed on the important houses were removed and communications were stopped.

On Monday morning, King Prempeh, Queen and Chiefs went to the great meeting and there they found the British Flag flying and King Prempeh and Chiefs approached to it and caught hold of same as a sign of accepting same.

When the assembly was filled up, King Prempeh and Queen Ya Echia were asked to comply to the 1st order, i.e. to come and kneel and apologise and which they did.

After the kneeling and apology, King Prempeh was asked to pay the whole indemnity to which he replied that it was the first time on Saturday that the indemnity was claimed from him. And further still the indemnity was allowed to be paid by instalments and he is ready to give £2,720 as an instalment and for the balance he is ready to give 2 Royal family in surety for 7 days to pay the whole.

The Governor refused the offer and King Prempeh asked to be allowed to return to the Palace to bring more remittance.

The Governor further refused and said that unless King Prempeh pays the whole at once, he would be made prisoner.

And of course, King Prempeh having no money on him in the meeting was then made prisoner together with the Queen: (his mother) father: brother and 10 chiefs making a total of 14 persons, vide pps. 11 (a).

After the capture, the palace and everywhere were plundered.

The capture took place on Monday and on Wednesday the prisoners were removed from Kumasi and on arriving at Elmina the remaining Chief at Kumasi sent Kwami Boatin and Kwaku Fokuo (being 2 of the Chiefs who went to London) to Ojar[10] to see 2 lawyers to have a petition made to have King Prempeh released.

The petition was made as follows (on the following grounds).

1st. King Prempeh offered £2,720 as remittance and was refused.

2nd. Ashanti Royals to pay the whole balance of the indemnity and was refused.

3rd. Asked to be allowed to return to the palace to take some more remittance and was refused. And having been made prisoner, the palace and all the houses were plundered. After the capture, the British Government has taken control of the whole of Ashanti and for these reasons it means different punishment for a single offence.

The petition was sent to the King and Chiefs through a Commissioner to be signed in the Castle.

The Governor having received the said petition ordered Kwaku Fokuo and Boatin to be arrested and were sent to Accra. And a reply was sent to King Prempeh re on the petition that he will be removed to Sierra Leone.

---

[10] A typographical error for Ogua, that is, Cape Coast.

King Prempeh and his followers remained one year at Elmina and on the very day they were leaving to Sierra Leone, the 2 arrested Chiefs were sent to meet the gang.

After 3 years and 10 months that King Prempeh and his people had been at Sierra Leone, the Govenor of Sierra Leone paid his first visit to the Ashanti camp and announced to King Prempeh that war has broken out in Ashanti and that Asibi the Omanhini of Kokofu had been taken prisoner and will soon be sent to Sierra Leone to meet the gang. And after 8 days of the arrival of Asibi, every Ashanti political prisoner in Sierra Leone will be set at liberty to go wherever they please.

King Prempeh and his ex chiefs were quite ignorant of the war at Ashanti, and had they been more clever they would have proceeded to sign before the Governor a document showing their ignorancy and that they be exempted from every blame and punishment that might result from the cause of the war.

8 days after the arrival of Asibi to Sierra Leone, instead of being set at liberty, the King and the gang were removed to Seychelles in September 1900. 8 months after 15 more ex chiefs were sent from Kumasi to meet King Prempeh that is in or about June 1901.

During the detention at Seychelles several petition respecting to their release has been submitted but no favourable reply was received to any of the petition.

In November 1922 the remainder of the 15 chiefs sent in 1901 were released and sent to Kumasi.

In December 1923 Asibi was released and sent to Kumasi.

The reason why the Ashanti army did not fight before or after the capture of King Prempeh was due to the following reasons.

(a) Before the English army entered Kumasi, everybody in Kumasi knew that they were coming to capture King Prempeh. The Ashanti Chiefs were in opinion to fight the English to defend their King and if they were not successful, then it would not be their fault.

The Chiefs then requested King Prempeh and Queen Ya Echia to retire from Kumasi to Breman village and to remain only the chiefs in the town to wait for the arrival of the English Army.

King Prempeh thanked them for their kind offer and then addressed them as follows:—

> "My Chiefs, I would ask you to remember in the past days of Civil War in Kumasi, how it was very difficult to restore peace.
>
> The Chiefs finding themselves much handicapped, Queen Yachia, Asafu Boachie and other chiefs sent an ambassador to the English Governor at the Coast asking the Governor to help to restore peace at Kumasi and to put some one on the throne.

The Governor sent 3 English Officers and soldiers to Kumasi and when peace was restored, the Officers asked the Chiefs whom they wish to be made King and all the Chiefs asked for me (Prempeh). The Officers also adjoined to the choice and I was thus proclaimed King of Ashanti.

And through this favour received in the hands of the English Government, I was not prepared to fight the British troops in spite I am to be captured by them— secondly I would rather surrender to secure the lives and tranquility of my people and countrymen."

The Chiefs and people were deeply touched with the speech of King Prempeh and which Kwami Apia of Mampon seconded and so there was no war.

Plate 11: 'Palaver and Submission of King Prempeh.' The arrest of Asantehene Agyeman Prempeh by Governor Maxwell in Kumase, 20 January 1896. (Source: R.S.S. Baden-Powell *The Downfall of Prempeh: A Diary of Life with the Native Levy in Ashanti 1895–96* London 1896 opposite p. 124)

Plate 12: 'Embarkation of King Prempeh.' Asantehene Agyeman Prempeh preparing to board H.M.S. *Racoon* for transit to prison in Elmina Castle, 5 February 1896. (Source: R.S.S. Baden-Powell *The Downfall of Prempeh: A Diary of Life with the Native Levy in Ashanti 1895–96* London 1896 opposite p. 149)

Plate 13: Asantehene Agyeman Prempeh seated between his father Kwasi Gyambibi and mother Yaa Kyaa in Elmina Castle, 1896. (Source: Kumase Fort Museum Photographic Collection)

Plate 14: The Asante exiles in the Seychelles. Edwesohemaa Yaa Asantewaa, Seychelles Governor E.B. Sweet-Escott, Asantehene Agyeman Prempeh and Asantehemaa Yaa Kyaa seated front row left to right, 1904. (Source: Information Department, Ministry of Education and Culture, Republic of Seychelles)

Plate 15: 'On his way home.' Asantehene Agyeman Prempeh boarding R.M.S. *Abinsi* at Liverpool on his way home from the Seychelles to Asante, 1924. (Source: *West Africa* London VIII 406 November 8 1924 p. 1243)

Plate 16: 'Chief Boadje, a fine old Ashanti patriot, who has reached the great age of 95.' Kumase Akwamuhene Asafo Boakye, a son of Asantehene Kwaku Dua Panin, at Liverpool on his way home from the Seychelles to Asante, 1924. (Source: *West Africa* London VIII 406 November 8 1924 p. 1242)

Plate 17: 'Mr. Frederick Prempeh, who was born at Coomassie, and went into exile at the age of two with his father.' Frederick Prempeh on board R.M.S. *Abinsi* at Liverpool on his way home from the Seychelles to Asante, 1924. (Source: *West Africa* London VIII 406 November 8 1924 p. 1242)

Plate 18: 'Nana Prempeh in Ashanti after his return from exile.' Agyeman Prempeh at his installation as Kumasihene standing between Governor Guggisberg and Chief Commissioner of Asante Maxwell, 1926. (Source: Royal Commonwealth Society, Smyly Gold Coast Photographic Collection, Plate Y30448L/41)

CHAPTER NINE

Reporting to the Living, Accounting for the Dead

AGYEMAN PREMPEH'S REPORT OF 1925

In 1924 Agyeman Prempeh returned to Asante after nearly twenty-nine years in exile. The British repatriated him as the private citizen Mr. Edward Prempeh, but to the great majority of his people he remained the Asantehene. As such he was bound by the norms that made an Asante ruler both responsible *for* and *to* the nation. Among other things this placed an obligation upon him to account for his stewardship of those who had shared his exile. Kingship entailed guardianship of the living. It also imposed a duty to preside over their increase. Ever expanding numbers of people was central to the Asante conception of good government. Thus on his return Agyeman Prempeh took immediate steps to compile a full report to the Asanteman about the people who had been detained with him in the Gold Coast, Sierra Leone and the Seychelles, as also about those additions to the nation who had been born under his care in exile. On 13 April 1925, five months after his return to Asante, Agyeman Prempeh convened a meeting at his temporary residence at Asafo in Kumase. Present at this gathering were numbers of Amanhene, members of the Kumase Council of Chiefs, and office holders of the Asante Kotoko Union Society. At this meeting Agyeman Prempeh's son and secretary Robert issued to all those present typed copies of a document which he had prepared on his father's instructions. These "were handed out to the chiefs to read to their people at home." According to slightly inaccurate reports reaching the British this document was entitled "A History of Prempeh and his Followers from the date of their exile to the present date." It was in fact entitled "A History of Nana Prempeh's Adventure during his 30 Years Captivity, namely, Elmina, Sierra Leone and Seychelles." In it Agyeman Prempeh accounted for his fellow detainees and further reported that, deaths notwithstanding, he had returned home with an additional sixty-four persons who had been born to the exile community. Several copies of this document have survived. That reproduced below is one of the original typescript copies distributed at the meeting at Asafo in 1925. It is the only one located thus far that includes the appended list of people who were with Agyeman Prempeh in exile. It is presently deposited in the Manhyia Record Office, Kumase.[1]

A HISTORY OF NANA PREMPEH'S ADVENTURE DURING HIS 30 YEARS CAPTIVITY, NAMELY, ELMINA, SIERRA LEONE AND SEYCHELLES

TO AMANHIN, CHIEFS, ELDERS AND PEOPLE OF ASHANTI
1. This is to inform and announce to you all today the most important adventures during the last 30 years of my captivity.

[1] This paragraph is condensed from T.C. McCaskie, "Asantehene Agyeman Prempe's Account to the Asanteman of His Exile from Kumase (1896–1924): A Document with Commentary" in *Asantesεm: The Asante Collective Biography Project Bulletin*, 7, June 1977: 32–42.

Chapter Nine

Firstly, as you all know, I was sent to Elmina Castle together with my followers namely, Queen Yaa Achia, Kwami Appia (Mamponhin), Chiefs Kwajoe Appia, Kofi Afrani, Adjaikoom, Kwami Amankwatia, Asafu Boachi, Kwami Subri, Agyeman Badu (my brother), Kwasi Gyembibi (my father), Chiefs Boachi Attonsa, Akorku, Kweku Wusu; (Women)—Amah Kwahan, Abina Kwadua, Akosua Cherm, Adjua Kutua-Poa and Juabin Serwah; (Children)—Kwasi Gyembibi, Kofi Mensah, Kwaku Duah, and Osei; (Servants)—Tontoe, Yaw Suajua, Yaw Boaten, Achampontia, Kweku Afriyie, Yeboa, Yaw Antwi, Kofi Osei, Kwami Ottin, Yaw Bampoe, Yaw Dabre, Kweku Fokuo, Batafuorja, Kachirie, Nuboa, Kweku Duah, Yaw Sraha, Achanou, Yaw Bimper, Amponsah, Yaw Dankwa, Kwami Abu and Boaten.

2. In the Castle, we stayed for a year during which time some efforts were made by the Ashantis represented by Chiefs Kwami Boaten and Kweku Fokuo for my repatriation which resulted in vain; and further there ensued the arrest of the said Boaten and Kweku Fokuo to join me in the Castle. At Elmina there we lost one Amponsah, the Chief Treasurer of Bantamahin.

3. For embarkation to Sierra Leone, 3 women and 18 servants were ordered to return back to Kumasi and one chief died. And so there remained 13 chiefs, 2 women, 6 servants and 1 child. Whilst leaving for Sierra Leone, two chiefs that is Kwami Boaten and Kweku Fokuo also came; 11 women were sent for from Kumasi together with 3 children and five servants, making a total of 15 chiefs, 13 women, 4 children and 11 servants to leave for Sierra Leone.

4. At Sierra Leone, 12 persons came to join me from Kumasi, while 10 persons were also sent back to Kumasi. On that very day when I was leaving for Sierra Leone, Chief Adjaikoom (Wikuhin) died.

5. At Sierra Leone I remained for 3 years and 10 months.

6. A week before my removal from Sierra Leone to Seychelles, Asibi (Kokofuhin) was sent to join me. But before he came the Governor himself came to ask me whether I would accept him and I willingly agreed. One Akorku who was unable to take the voyage through illness was left at Sierra Leone. I reached Seychelles on the 11th September 1900, that is 24 years and 3 months ago. From Sierra Leone to Seychelles I was with 14 Chiefs, 14 women, 13 children and 12 servants.

7. One year after our arrival at Seychelles, Yah Asantiwa and other Chiefs were also deported to Seychelles. Yah Asantiwa's Gang consisted of 15 Chiefs, 2 women and 4 servants. These were also given under my care by the Government. We all put heads together and formed one opinion in all matters concerning our common interests. On all together we arrived at Seychelles with 53 persons and 21 more with Yah Asantiwa, total 74 persons. On 29th May 1904, myself and the Gang were baptised by Rev. Johnson. 17 years ago, 34 persons including men, women and children were sent back from Seychelles to Kumasi. It remained therefore 40 persons there.

Reporting to the Living 177

8. Several years ago, 7 persons imigrated. One son of Asibi escaped from his father's house. 5 years ago, 35 persons, that is the family of the late Chief Boaten and the last Gang of Yah Asantiwa came to Kumasi. From that I see that if to be taken in number, I have returned the total amount of people taken from Kumasi and I have got 2 people in surplus. In November 1923, 7 persons were sent to Kumasi, that is Asibi and his family. In 1924 I came with 64 persons, and 3 still remaining in Seychelles, and in Mauritius studying clergy of which 6 are natives of Seychelles married to my followers and 58 Ashantis. I am pleased to tell you that omitting those who are dead, both old and young, I have returned to Kumasi the amount of people taken and I have got 64 persons in surplus which I brought with me to Kumasi.

9. 55 persons are interred or buried in foreign countries, that is one at Elmina, 5 at Sierra Leone and 49 at Seychelles.

10. You will also be pleased to hear that during these long 30 years that I have been away, myself and followers had always been carefully looked after by the Government. We were given allowances for our maintenance, quarters, water supply and medical treatment, and again the training of our children and free privileges.

11. The following is the list of Queen Yaa Achia, Chiefs and followers who died at Seychelles arranged according to periods of death.

List

1	Chief Kweku Fokuo	died 17/9/1900 that is 24 yrs 3 ms ago
2	Chief Kofi Subri	died 11/3/1901 that is 21 yrs 9 ms ago
3	Chief Asamoa Kwami	died 17/3/1903 that is 20 yrs 4 ms ago
4	Chief Kwesi Gyembibi	died 1/8/1903 that is 20 yrs 3 ms ago
5	Chief Kofi Kumah	died 20/1/1904 that is 19 yrs 10 ms ago
6	Chief Kojo Antwi	died 17/31906 that is 18 yrs 10 ms ago
7	Chief Buachi Atonsah	died 26/12/1906 that is 18 yrs – ms ago
8	Chief Kwami Afrifa	died 10/3/1907 that is 17 yrs 7 ms ago
9	Chief Kwami Amankwatia	died 14/7/1907 that is 17 yrs 2 ms ago
10	Chief Kwasi Adari	died 12/3/1908 that is 16 yrs 9 ms ago
11	Chief Kweku Nantwi	died 17/61908 that is 16 yrs 5 ms ago
12	Chief Kojo Antwi-Adjai	died 31/7/1908 that is 16 yrs 2 ms ago
13	Chief Kweku Nsia	died 30/6/1911 that is 14 yrs – ms ago
14	Chief Kwami Appia	died 27/10/1911 that is 13 yrs 9 ms ago
15	Chief Osei Kojo-Krome	died 28/9/1913 that is 11 yrs – ms ago
16	Chief Kofi Afrani of Ejisu	died 4/11/1915 that is 10 yrs – ms ago
17	Chief Elizabeth Yaa Achia	died 2/8/1917 that is 8 yrs 10 ms ago
18	Chief Albert Agyeman Badu	died 28/9/1917 that is 8 yrs 9 ms and 2 days ago
19	Chief Henry Kwami Boaten	died 19/11/1918 that is 8 yrs 8 ms ago
20	Chief Edu Kofi	died 5/3/1921 that is 5 yrs–ms ago
21	Chief Yah Asantiwa	died 5/10/1921 that is 4 yrs–ms ago
22	Chief Kojo Appia	died 5/7/1922 that is 2 yrs 11 ms ago

23	Chief Kwami Gyansah	died 4/5/1923 that is 2 yrs 7 ms ago
24	Chief Kofi Fofea	died on the sea when voyaging back to Kumasi

12. When a Chief dies Government always took measures to repatriate his wife and children to Kumasi. There was one woman called Affua Affie, wife of Nkwanta-Bissa of Adansi one of my chiefs, who got lost and every measure was taken for her search but it resulted in vain.

13. The graves of all the deceased were purchased by us and notwithstanding 4 years after the death of the Queen we all subscribed and purchased a large plot of ground where a vault was built. In the vault we placed the remainings of all our deceased, that is those bodies which have got five years and upwards and not below five years. For the present there still remain 10 respective bodies which are awaiting five years exhumation. But before my leaving Seychelles I took all necessary precautions in order that the graves will never get lost till one day you will give me your assistance to send one to Seychelles to exhume them and place them in the vault. After the death of Yah Asantiwa the remaining Chiefs who went with her made a separate petition to be repatriated and they were allowed; and a year after their repatriation, Asibi also petitioned stating that he was included in Yah Asantiwa's war and so he was thus allowed to come here.

14. A year after Asibi's repatriation, I learnt with great pleasure that through your combined efforts I am allowed to return to my country, for which I thank you most heartily. The Government sent the Provincial Commissioner, Mr. A. Duncan-Johnstone to meet me at Seychelles to escort me to Kumasi, and during the voyage I have had the best treatment and chance to see novels of the outer world.

Signed, EDWARD PREMPEH
Typed by, and
Signed by, ROBERT F.A. PREMPEH (Secretary)
Kumasi 13th April 1925

Names of the People who Accompanied Nana Prempeh to Seychelles

1	Nana Prempeh or Kwaku Duah III	Ashantihene
2	Yaa Achia	Ashantihemaa
3	Agyeman Badoo	Adoomhene
4	Kwami Appia	Omanhene of Mampong
5	Kojo Apiah	Omanhene of Offinsu
6	Kofi Afrani	Omanhene of Ejisu
7	Kwami Amankwatia	Krontihene of Kumasi
8	Asafu Boachie	Akwamuhene of Kumasi
9	Kwabena Ejukum	Yookuhene of Kumasi
10	Kofi Subri	Achempehene of Kumasi
11	Kwasi Akokoo	Head Linguist of Kumasi
12	Kweku Wusu	Linguist of Kumasi

13	Kwasi Gyembibi	Ayibiachilehene and the Ashantihene's Father
14	Boachie Atonsa	Akonfruhene of Kumasi
15	Kwami Boaten	Dominasihene of Kumasi
16	Kweku Forkuo	Linguist of Kumasi
17	George Asibi	Omanhene of Kokofu
18	Yah Asantiwa	Queen Mother of Ejisu
19	Kofi Fofieh	Nkonsonhene of Kumasi
20	Asamoah Kwami	Chief Executioner of Kumasi
21	Akwasi Adali	Hiahene of Kumasi
22	Kweku Nsia	Akroponhene of Kumasi
23	Kweku Nantwi	Linguist of Kumasi
24	Osei Kojo-Krome	A Chief in Kronti Clan of Kumasi
25	Antwi Adjaye	Nkwaiehene of Kumasi
26	Kwami Afrifah	Toasehene of Kumasi
27	Edu Kofi	Nkwantahene of Kumasi
28	Kwami Jansa	A Chief in Kronti clan of Kumasi
29	Kojo Antwi	Chief of Offinsu
30	Paul Akromah	Terchiehene
31	Kofi Kumah	Chief of Techimantia
32	Kwabina Nkwantabissa	Adansi-Odumassihene

List of People Who Came to Meet Ashantihene at Elmina

33	Amah Kwahan	Ashantihene's Wife
34	Abina Amiloa	Ashantihene's Wife
35	Frederick Prempeh	Son of Ashantihene
36	Yaw Suagyua	Ashantihene's Stool Bearer
37	Kweku Tontoe	Ashantihene's Stool Bearer
38	Kweku Afreh	Native Doctor
39	Kwami Yeboah	Native Doctor
40	Yaw Anohu	Ashantihene's Umbrella Holder
41	Kofi Sey	Ashantihene's Hammock Carrier
42	Kofi Sechire	Ashantihene's Hammock Carrier
43	Kwami Tin	Ashantihene's Hammock Carrier
44	Yaw Bampoh	Ashantihene's Hammock Carrier
45	Yaw Dabiler	Ashantihene's Hammock Carrier
46	Batafuoaja	
47	Kerchilai	
48	Nobila	
49	Kweku Forkuo	
50	Achampontia	
51	Yaw Boatin	
52	Akosua Kyem	Queen Mother's Servant
53	Adjua Kortupua	Queen Mother's Servant
54	Yah Yanoh	Adoomhene's Wife
55	Kwami Abu	Adoomhene's subject

56	Yaw Dankwa	Adoomhene's subject
57	Akroma	Adoomhene's subject
58	Boaten	Ashantihene's Father's subject
59	Kwaku Duah	Mamponghene's subject
60	Yaw Sraha	Mamponghene's subject
61	Kwami Achaou	Offinsuhene's subject
62	Kumpaou	Ejisuhene's subject
63	Amponsah	Krontihene's subject
64	Kofi Mensah	Akwamuhene's subject
65	Juaben Serwah	Achempehene's Wife
66	Kwaku Duah	Achempehene's Son
67	Osei	Head Linguist's subject

List of Subjects Who Came and Met Ashantihene at Sierra Leone

68	Akwa Morbi	
69	Affua Sapon	
70	Asante	
71	KojoTufuor	
72	Kwami Wura	
73	Achampon	
74	Affua Mansah	Servant of the Queen Mother
75	Amah Kotia	Servant of the Queen Mother
76	Ekua Antiae	Servant of the Queen Mother
77	Boatemaa	Wife of Mamponghene
78	Kwami Wan	Son of Mamponghene
79	Kweku Forkuo	Servant of Mamponghene
80	Kweku Sarkodie	Brother of Offinsuhene
81	Akwa Jewar	Wife of Offinsuhene
82	Oklayami	Servant of Offinsuhene
83	Mensuo	Servant of Ejisuhene
84	Dartano	Servant of Ejisuhene
85	Achamar	Wife of Chief Amankwatia
86	Yar Sukwa	Wife of Chief Amankwatia
87	Kwabena Nkatia	
88	Anowuo	
89	Darkuwar	
90	Kwesi Bonkoo	
91	Boaten Panin	
92	Boaten Kumar	
93	Yar Kudae	
94	Amah Asrewar	
95	Oti	
96	Kwabena Kufuor	
97	Kusi	
98	Kwaku Wia	

List of People Who Came and Met Ashantihene at Seychelles

99	Kwaku Fin	Servant of Chief Edu Kofi
100	Affua Affie	Wife of Adansi-Odumassihene
101	Alfred Prempeh	Ashantihene's Child born at Sierra Leone
102	James Prempeh	Ashantihene's Child born at Sierra Leone
103	Hannah Prempeh	Ashantihene's Child born at Sierra Leone
104	Kwami Subri	
105	Lucy Prempeh	
106	Marthe Appiah	Offinsuhene Kojo Appia's Child born at Seychelles
107	Afraniwar	Offinsuhene's Child born at Seychelles
108	Frederick Appia	Offinsuhene's Child born at Seychelles
109	William Appiah	Offinsuhene's Child born at Seychelles
110	Kojo Mensah	
111	Yar Santewar	Offinsuhene's Child born at Seychelles
112	Affua Nsia	Offinsuhene's Child born at Seychelles
113	Akua Mansah	
114	Addison	
115	Nkrooma	Offinsuhene's Grandchild born at Seychelles
116	Akosua	Offinsuhene's Grandchild born at Seychelles
117	Akua	Offinsuhene's Grandchild born at Seychelles
118	Amah	Offinsuhene's Grandchild born at Seychelles
119	Kwesi Broni	Offinsuhene's Grandchild born at Seychelles
120	Akwasi Gyembibi	
121	Yaw Kusi	Offinsuhene's Grandchild born at Seychelles
122	Philip	Offinsuhene's Grandchild born at Seychelles
123	Mensah	Offinsuhene's Grandchild born at Seychelles
124	Poku	Offinsuhene's Grandchild born at Seychelles
125	Tenten	Offinsuhene's Grandchild born at Seychelles
126	Amah	Offinsuhene's Grandchild born at Seychelles
127	Amanquah	Offinsuhene's Grandchild born at Seychelles
128	Akosua	Offinsuhene's Grandchild born at Seychelles
129	Alice Kuofuor	Offinsuhene's Grandchild born at Seychelles
130	Isaac Sarkodie	
131	Yar Nimo	Kontihene's Child born at Seychelles
132	Yar Nika	Kontihene's Child born at Seychelles
133	Akwasi Agyeman	
134	Kwabena Pon	
135	Maxime Dabre	Yaw Dabre's Child born at Seychelles
136	Kwami Dabre	Yaw Dabre's Child born at Seychelles
137	Abina Pokuwa	
138	Sarah Kwantabisa	Adansi-Odumassihene's Child born at Seychelles
139	Pierre Edu Kofi	
140	Julia Edu Kofi	
141	Julie Kwantabisa	
142	Gabriel Kwantabisa	
143	Willie Kwantabisa	

144	Yaw Kwantabisa	
145	Paul Akromah Jr.	Terchiehene's Child born at Seychelles
146	Adjua Akromah	Terchiehene's Child born at Seychelles
147	Beau Akromah	
148	Ticoeur Akromah	
149	Fernande Akromah	
150	Kwabena Akromah	
151	Prempeh	Frederick Prempeh's Child born at Seychelles
152	Frank Prempeh	Alfred Prempeh's Child born at Seychelles
153	Nell Prempeh	Alfred Prempeh's Child born at Seychelles
154	Huguette Prempeh	James Prempeh's Child born at Seychelles
155	Francis Prempeh	James Prempeh's Child born at Seychelles
156	May Prempeh	James Prempeh's Child born at Seychelles

THE DISPOSITION OF THE DEAD

When Agyeman Prempeh returned to Kumase he found a different town from the one he had last seen nearly twenty-nine years before. Colonial building overlay the old Asante capital and its historic landmarks and sacred sites had disappeared or were under threat from development. The Bantama mausoleum, burial place of the Asantehenes, was looted and destroyed by the British in 1896. Its royal coffins had already been removed and hidden at Breman, but the famous "brass pan" [*aya kɛsɛ*, see below] that stood before the old mausoleum was taken as a trophy to London. Other royal burial sites at Adwama, Adum, Akyeremade, Bampanase and Heman were located in the commercial heart of colonial Kumase and were damaged or dilapidated beyond repair. Agyeman Prempeh was appalled and mounted a campaign that lasted the rest of his life to restore appropriate respect and dignity to his own and the nation's royal ancestors. In 1927 he effected an exhumation of Oyoko and Dako remains buried at Heman and Adwama respectively. The Oyoko royals were reinterred in a section of the Kumase Government Cemetery set aside for that purpose while their Dako counterparts were reburied at Nsuta. The letter reproduced below lists the deceased and shows Agyeman Prempeh's strong feelings about this matter. It is to be found among his personal correspondence, examined in the Old Manhyia Palace (since 1995 the Manhyia Palace Museum).

Manhyia
Kumasi
27th November 1927
My good friend,
Be so kind as to receive these names of the Hallowed Dead for exhuming and burying by your kind permission. When I was taken away along with my Brother nobody was left to look after same. I find now as I wrote to you that cemeteries at Hemanho and Adjwama burial grove are unsuitable by reason of long years [of] neglect. The Hemanho in particular is encroached by the Court Building and is not suitable at all. It is a shaming thing to see that our Hallowed Dead are overlooked. We CANNOT FORGET them. They are our HEROES and HEROINES of Ashanti. I signed as requested on the order as you asked

me [MP. 10/18 (1928), Kumasi Exhumation Order, under provision of the Births, Deaths and Burials Ordinance (1925)]. I thank you for your kind assistance to help save the Hallowed Dead from a further harm.

I have the honour to be,
Your good Friend,
    E.P.
                    Kumasihene
Witness to signature and mark,
J.W.K. Appiah
Chief Clerk
His Worship,
The District Commissioner,
Kumasi.

Persons at Hemanho or Adjwama

At Hemanho:	At Adjwama grove:
Affuah Serwah (royal woman)	Yitaa (queen mother Dako tribe)
Achian (royal woman)	Danso Abiam
Behmma Dar (royal woman)	Gyakye Amooh
Juaben Serwah (Princess)	Ado Akyeapong
Akua Kabontiyeh (Princess)	Amie Adjoa
Chenchehene (royal man)	Obu Akwatia
Kwabena Enim (royal man)	Adjoa Firema
Kwamin Boaten (royal man)	Tutu Pim
Kweku Doum (Prince)	
Kojo Tufour (Prince)	

This accomplished, Agyeman Prempeh turned his thoughts to his kin and all those others buried in the distant Seychelles. In 1928 he decided that these remains should be exhumed and brought back to Asante where customary funeral rites might be performed by relatives and the dead reburied in their own lineage cemeteries. Arranging this was difficult and protracted. The Governor and the British administration in Asante were sympathetic from the outset, but there were delays until the Legislative Council in Accra agreed to meet the transportation costs and then further delays while the Seychelles authorities organized exhumation, packing and shipping. Agyeman Prempeh arranged for a "Great Funeral Custom" for his mother, father, brother and others to be held over fifteen days beginning on 14 March 1931, and then wrote a series of increasingly concerned reminders to British officialdom as over a year passed with the remains still in the Seychelles.

At last, on 9 October 1929 those remains recoverable by the Seychelles Administration were shipped from the Seychelles via Bombay and the Suez Canal to the Crown Agents in London, who arranged onward passage via Takoradi to Kumase. There were two packing cases. The first contained the remains and burial goods of twenty persons who had been interred in four repositories in the dedicated Asante vault in the Seychelles (see Para. 13 of the document of 13 April 1925 reproduced above). The second held nine persons who had been exhumed from clearly marked graves in the Seychelles Government Cemetery at Victoria. The Seychelles authorities feared that the remains of individuals could not be distinguished and identified. But when the two cases were opened in Kumase on 27 January 1930 Agyeman Prempeh and those with him were able to identify each of the bodies from its remains and burial goods. Agyeman Prempeh's own handwritten list of those returned to Asante is on a single sheet of paper that was, when examined, in the possession of the Asantehene Otumfuo Opoku Ware II (1970–1999).

O.H.M.S. Cases 1 and 2, Bones of All Those Died in Seychelles Restored to Ashanti for Burial 1930

Case 1
Yaa Achia (my mother)
Agyeman Badoo (my younger brother)
Akwasi Gyembibi (my father)
Kwami Amankwatia of Bantama
Anchi Adjaye of Nkawie
Osei Kojo-Krome of Achuma
Kwami Afrifa of Toasi
Assamoah Kwami of Adoom
Kofi Subri Achempehene
Akwasi AdalIi Hiahene
Kweku lnsia of Akropong
Kweku Forkuo Linguist
Kweku Nanchu Linguist
Kofi Kuma of Techimantia
Boachie Attonsah Akonfrohene
Kwami Appiah Mamponghene
Afrani Ababio Ejisuhene
Kwami Yeboah King's servant
Kwabena Kuffour Servant of Kofi Fofie Nkonson
Akwasi Bonkoo Servant of Asafu Buachie of Akomu

Case 2
Edu Koffi of Berekum
Kwami Jamsaah of Apimanim
Hry. Boaten of Dominasi
Kojo Appiah of Offinsu
Kojo Anchwi Sub-Chief of Offinsu
Kweku Sarkordie Brother of Offinsu Chief
Yah Asantiwa Queen Mother Ejisu
Kojo Tufour King's servant
Darkouwar Maid servant

Agyeman Prempeh continued to be vexed by the sad condition of the cemeteries in Kumase. He was especially troubled about Bampanase, where in former days his mother and brother would have been buried but which was now encroached upon and overlooked by private dwellings. The resiting of Bampanase to another location was linked to the need to rescue the coffins of the Asantehenes from their temporary shelter at Breman and restore them to a rebuilt Bantama mausoleum. On 10 September 1929, as he awaited news of the remains from the Seychelles, Agyeman Prempeh raised his concerns with British officials. The following letter was addressed to the D.C. (Kumase). It is deposited in Ghana National Archives, Kumase, ARG 1/2/25/8 (which also contains a variant version of 12 September 1929 that was copied to the Chief Commissioner).

Manhyia
Kumasi
10th September 1929
My friend,
    I have been discussing with my Chiefs a subject which is sacred to all Ashantis. The Ashantiman has as you know two National Monuments which

embody for us all that is most sacred in our lives and all that we revere most deeply. These monuments are known as BAMPANASI EBAM and BANTAMA DAN KESSIE and are the burial places of our Ashanti Kings and have for us a meaning which is the basis of our religion and our reverence for the dead. Today we are finding that our own houses are improved but these sacred places are in disrepair. They are no longer an honour but are a source of shame instead. In these days elaborate tombstones for the deceased relatives are rising up all over the countryside; not a village but has some special reminder of its dead. Our dead Kings deserve no less of us and we want now to restore these holy places. There remains then only a question of financial help. Buildings for both cemeteries will cost £5,500. Kumasi will give to it £1,000 and Kokofu and Bekwai and Kumawu will assist us. We are requesting to Government to help us with the rest. Be assured I remain always
Your good friend
Agyeman Prempeh Kumasihene
Witness by,
I.K. Agyeman
Tribunal Clerk
His Honour,
The District Commissioner,
Kumasi.

THE MATTER OF THE "BRASS PAN"

Government gave its approval and financial support for work to begin on building a new Bampanase cemetery at Breman and a replacement for the destroyed Bantama mausoleum complex close to its original site. Chief Commissioner of Asante Maxwell laid the foundation stone at Bantama on 13 February 1930. Both projects were completed by July of that year and scheduled to be opened officially on 30 March 1931 at the close of the "Great Funeral Custom" for those whose remains had been returned from the Seychelles. But there was a problem. Agyeman Prempeh was determined that the "brass pan" looted from the old Bantama mausoleum should be restored to the new one. To this end he petitioned the Chief Commissioner of Ashanti, then H.S. Newlands, for its return.[2] Newlands was aware that in 1817 T. E. Bowdich had referred to the pan as being used for "human sacrifices." He also knew that, in his *Religion and Art in Ashanti*, R. S. Rattray, head of Asante's Anthropological Department, had challenged the truth of Bowdich's testimony. Newlands therefore asked Agyeman Prempeh to let him have an account of the history of the pan, and of its uses.[3] On 29 August 1930 Edward Prempeh signed a document entitled "History of the Bantama Brass Pan." It was witnessed by J. B. Prempeh, as "Secretary." This was his son, the Reverend John Prempeh, who had recently returned from Mauritius where he had trained for the Anglican priesthood.

The "History of the Bantama Brass Pan" [*BBP*] is a short work in five pages. McCaskie found an autograph copy of the document among the papers of the late Meyer Fortes, and in 1983 located

---

[2] NAG (Accra) ADM 11/1/1370, E. Prempeh to Chief Commissioner, 17 July 1930.
[3] NAG (Accra) ADM 11/1/1370, Newlands to Colonial Secretary, 14 November 1930.

a photocopy among unclassified papers in the Old Manhyia Palace. This text is reproduced below. The copy actually sent to the Chief Commissioner was retyped with only minor changes, and is preserved in the National Archives of Ghana, Accra, ADM 11/1/1370. It is clear that Edward Prempeh based *BBP* on a re-reading of the opening pages of *HAK* (see Chapter Five), and it is of considerable interest to see how, in 1930, he interpreted some of the more difficult passages in the latter.

HISTORY OF THE BANTAMA BRASS PAN

At Akyim there is a village called Asiakwa, that has the following explanation viz—,

A hunter went once went out with his gun to hunt, and when he saw an antelope he wanted to shoot her, but she shouted out – "Do not kill me, because tomorrow (meaning the next day) I shall be accompanying a very big thing that will come. The hunter on hearing these words did not shoot her, but returned to report the news to the people in the village.

On the next morning there was a terrible Thunderstorm and the Court Crier wearing a monkey-skin on his head descended from heaven beating a Gong-Gong in his hand saying "Doncouma se obobo Adie" meaning Creation was to be made, and on arriving on the earth he took a seat. The descendants of the Court Crier are now at Kantikrono few miles from Kumasi, and they are the present Gong-Gong beaters.

Another terrible Thunderstorm was heard afterwards and the Big Brass Pan, together with the Gold Chain came down from Heaven the Chain hung in the Pan.

At this stage a woman by name "Adoofa" holding a white stool came down from Heaven by the Chain and laid the stool in the Pan and sat behind it. Her descendants are now at Gyakyi, Kumasi, and they serve the Queen Mother.

What was seen afterwards, was that that the "Obar Panyin" meaning the Old Lady by name "Anchiwar Nyame" came down from Heaven by the Gold Chain and took her seat on the Stool in the Pan.

At this juncture all, the people in the village came and surrounded her and said – "Nana what do you require please?"

She made signs with her hands, as if she was holding a very big thing with her two hands, and then she pointed her finger to her mouth meaning "Kill a fowl and prepare food for me first, and after eating some, I will speak."

When her wishes were accomplished and she had tasted the food her mouth at once opened and she said – "What I am bringing to you is very great, but I did not mean to land here,—I came here for nothing, and so I am going." The above is the explanation of Akyim [Abuakwa.] Asiakwa. After these words were spoken, the Old Lady, the Brass Pan, the Gold Chain, the Court Crier, disappeared and the people there did not see them again.

They went to "Assumanya Asantimansoo" and landed just under a tree called "Atouar" that is still there.[4] The tree itself has died out but grows again in the same place.

When the Old Lady arrived there she said, "This is where I am going to settle," and she told the people there, "I have brought you Asantiman". This is the explanation for Asantimansoo, and the word Asantiman was named by the Old Lady Anchiwar Nyame.

The hole from which the Asantiman came, can be found to-day at Asantimansoo.

Close to the tree above mentioned, there is a stone called "Abohenbuo"[5] at Assumanya and by that Stone a Silver Chain from Heaven came and pitched near it, hanging. At this stage the Abohen people such as Kenyassehene, Mampontinhene, Yookoohene came from Heaven by the Silver Chain and took their seats by the Old Lady, and they wore Tiger Skins as their hats, There is also a hole from which all the Yookoo [people] and the Dako family came and sat by the Obar Panyin

Some of the Yookoos from Akyim on hearing of the Old Lady came and served her— and also some other Yookoos came and served her at Asantimansoo.

There are also other families called the Abousoua-Ban-Ensoo[6] that came from an Adansi village called "Ahinsan". They are

1. Braituo
2. Atina
3. Agona and Asokore
4. Jume
5. Asona
6. Aduana
7. Asechire.

There is an explanation for the Adansi Ahinsan i.e. the hole from which these people came to serve the Old Lady.

Now, the Obar Panyin was in family way when she landed, and gave birth to a female child at Asantimansoo, and she was named "Obiriponmar Piasiai."

Anchiwar Nyami was the head of the Yookoos, Dakos, and the Abousoua-Ban-Ensoo, in other words the Head of the Family.

When she died at Assumanya Asantimansoo, her daughter Obiriponmar Piaisiai succeeded her—and she gave birth to 10 children: 3 men, and 7 women.

---

[4] Twi *atoaa*, a species of cashew.
[5] Twi *Abohyenbɔɔ*, "Abohyen Stone," see Twi *ɔbɔɔ*, "stone."
[6] Twi *abusuabansu*, untranslatable, but approximating to an English "configuration of families."

The first born was "Achampon Tintin," who succeeded her mother Obiriponmar Piaisiai when she died, was the first man to be the head of the family over the Asantiman. After his death at Asantimansoo, his younger brother Chume succeeded him; and after Chume's death at Asantimansoo, his brother Antwi succeeded him.

When Antwi died, one of the grandsons (7 grandsons) of Obiriponmar Piaisiai called "Kobia Awuanfi" succeeded.

When he got to the Stool — he had a servant called Kokor who owned a farm (afuo) – that he used to inspect now and then, and each time he (Kobia Awuanfi) wished to inspect same he said, "I am going to Kokor-Afuome i.e. Kokor's farm.

Then he afterwards told the Asantiman, "We are too overcrowded here at Asantimansoo, so we must remove to a much wider place, and he accordingly brought his family to Kokor-Afuome, that is now called "Kokofoo." When removing to Kokor-Afuome, he brought with him the Gold Chain and the Brass Pan.

After his death — his younger brother – Oti-Akenten — succeeded him, and his sister's name was "Ofaibi-Odi-Nihoo".

She married to one Adu Gyanfi at Asantimansoo. When every one scattered to various places, her husband told her that he was going to find a suitable place to settle, and then he would send for her.

When the husband went, and had kept long in sending for her so she sent a bearer to go and find his whereabouts. The bearers name was Nyam Panyin. He started the journey via Kumasi, and after some days walk he at last met the husband at Onoh—From Onoh he the husband went to Jamarsi, and on this account one hears of Jamarsihene.

The messenger on meeting the husband at Onoh said, "I was sent by my master Ofaibi-Odi-Nihoo to find your whereabout." He replied, "I am here go and fetch her."

When the messenger arrived and delivered the message of the husband to her—she begged leave of her brother Oti-Aken-Ten who gave her leave to go and meet her husband.

On her arriving at Kumasi—she said "God is great here—and she sent a bearer to go and tell her brother Oti-Aken-Ten, that Kumasi was a much better place than Kokofoo, and advised him to come and settle there and when she sent the messenger with that message to her brother at Kokofoo she continued on her journey to meet her husband.

Oti-Aken-Ten accordingly came and settled at Kumasi, and he brought with him whilst coming, the Chain and the Brass Pan.

When he arrived at Kumasi, he met a woman called Adowar Nkrawri staying at Jabraim at a place called Kuma – where the present Post Office is, and that land belonged to her. Oti-Aken-Ten asked her to buy that land from her which she agreed to. She sold same for 30 preguans i.e. £240.0.0. and he Oti-Aken-Ten settled there.

Before Oti-Aken-Ten left Kokofoo, he left his younger brother Gembi there to look after the family that had been left behind – in other words Gembi was appointed Head of the family at Kokofoo, and at that time the other Oman had scattered to other places, and there was no peace amongst them at all, one Oman would fight against another and the victorious killed the other, and took away all the properties.

When all the Oman saw that peace could not exist amongst them so they all resolved and said,—"When the Old Lady (Obar Panyin) was at Asantimansoo, we served her quite well, and there was peace amongst us all always, but as we are now scattered, we see that there is no peace amongst us; and as the grandson of Anchiwar Nyame who is Oti-Aken-Ten is at Kumasi, so we should all go back and serve as our King, in order that peace will exist amongst us, and that he will also settle disputes amongst us.

When they all met at Kumasi, they unanimously appointed Oti-Aken-Ten as their King, and in return Oti-Aken-Ten thanked them, and gave them 30 preguans or £240.0.0. as Aseda — and since then Asantehene existed till 1896, when they all scattered again.

After the death of Oti-Aken-Ten, his younger brother Obiri Yeboa succeeded, and after his death King Osei Tutu succeeded.

When King Osei Tutu took up the Stool he said that the Brass Pan was a very great thing for the Asantiman; and therefore same should be placed where he was to be buried and also at the late Asante Kings burial place i.e. Bantama, and the Pan was accordingly placed at the place aforesaid, and it remained there till 1896 when it was removed to England.

As regards the Gold Chain – When any Asante King or Asante Hemar died, a link of it was removed and buried with him or her always, and this system had always existed until the time of King Kussi Oboadum, who for some special reasons buried the rest under the ground until they got spoilt.

I also wish to add that the Brass Pan had always remained unchanged since it came to the Earth, and all the Asantimans souls are within it.

In conclusion, I wish to make it clear, that the allegation that human beings were killed in the Brass Pan is not a fact at all and therefore it is not correct, and the above explanation is the real and the correct one.

Notwithstanding the petition, the colonial authorities refused to return it, still convinced that the pan was inseparably bound up with human sacrifice. Agyeman Prempeh pressed his case repeatedly in letters to colonial officials. On 22 February 1931 he set out his position once again in a last ditch effort to persuade the British to return the "brass pan" before the "Great Funeral Custom" was celebrated concurrently with the removal of the royal coffins to the new Bantama mausoleum. This letter is reproduced below. It is from Agyeman Prempeh's personal correspondence, examined in the Old Manhyia Palace, but the "Ashanti Families" file in which it is deposited has now been transferred to the Manhyia Record Office, Kumase, where its reclassification is pending.

KUM APIM A APIM BEBA

Nana Prempeh
Omanhene-Panyin of
Ashanti-Kumasi
Ohinba P.K. Prempeh
Private Secretary

Menhia
Kumasi
Ashanti
Gold Coast
West Coast Africa

22nd February 1931

My good friend,

I take this opportunity to say it is most important that the Brass Pan is put in the Mausoleum before the late Ashanti Kings' remains are put in. This Brass Pan was not ever used for any one thing in particular but is a sacred thing to Ashantis. All [the] souls of Ashantis are within it. If it is not put in the Mausoleum is lacking something and is not what was planned. The Ashanti Kings are not contented when it is gone away from them. I send you this my plea to return the Brass Pan to its resting place. Forever if it is gone away the steps I have taken with your assistance cannot be said to be completed. The spiritual fact is the Brass Pan is needful to those who dwell forever in the Mausoleum and if not they will keenly feel its loss to them. I know well that you have our best interest at heart so I send you this to answer my prayers to return the Brass Pan to stop the plans becoming spoiled. It is the best thing for the Ashantis if their sacred Brass Pan is put back and will make every one glad. I remain once more Your Friend

Agyeman Prempeh
Kumasihene

His honour the District Commissioner
Kumasi.

But the British were unmoved and the "brass pan" stayed in London. The "Great Funeral Custom" went ahead as planned, and when it closed Chief Commissioner Newlands carried out the official opening of the new Bantama Mausoleum. The new Bampanase at Breman was declared open at the same time. In the event the coffins of the Asantehenes remained at Breman where they were put into the Bampanase. The Bantama Mausoleum stood empty and remains so today. We can only speculate that the absence of the "brass pan," as Agyeman Prempeh suggested to the British, left the building somehow incomplete and unusable for its designated purpose. Be that as it may, when the "Great Funeral Custom" was completed the remains that had been returned from the Seychelles were finally at rest. Agyeman Prempeh ordered that the reburied dead be informed that their funeral customs had been performed. Accordingly, messengers were sent to the lineage cemeteries where each of the bodies now lay. Agyeman Prempeh had drawn up a list of these cemeteries in February 1930 for the information of the Chief Commissioner of Asante and his Medical Officer of Health. This is reproduced below. It is an enclosure in Agyeman Prempeh to C.C.A., dd. 5 February 1930, in Ghana National Archives, Kumase, ARG 6/2/8.

The following were Buried as follows

Yaa Achia at Breman, Kumasi [Division]
Agyeman Badoo at Breman, Kumasi [Divisionl
Kwesi Gyembibi at Breman, Kumasi [Division]
Kwame Amankwatia at Asirimaso on Nkawe Rd., Kumasi [Division]
Anchu Adjaye at Nkawe, Kumasi [Division]
Osei Kojo-Krome at Techiman, Kumasi [Division]
Kwame Afrifra at Toase, Kumasi [Division]
Edu Kofi at Nkwanta, Brekum [Division]
Kwame Jansah at Apimanim, Kumasi [Division]
Asamoah Kwame at Quangman, Kumasi [Division]
Kofi Subri at Boarso, Kumasi [Division]
Henry Boaten at Ankarse, Kumasi [Division]
Akwassi Adalli at Kunsoo, Kumasi [Division]
Kweku lnsia at Akropong, Kumasi [Division]
Kweku Fokuo at Ajumame, Kumasi [Division]
Kweku Nanchu at Darban, Kumasi [Division]
Kofi Kumah at Techimentia, Brekum [Division]
Boachie Attensa at Kentenchirai, Kumasi [Division]
Kwame Apia at Mampong
Kojo Apia at Ofinso
Kojo Anchu at Ofinso
Kweku Sakodier at Ofinso
Afrani Ababio at Ejisu
Yar Santewar at Ejisu
Kwame Yeboa at Mojisu, Kumasi [Division]
Kojo Tufour at Kropo, Kumasi [Division]
Kwabena Kuffor at Bare Kessie, Kumasi [Division]
Kwasi Bonkoo at Satiasi, Kumasi [Division]
Darkowar at Satiasi, Kumasi [Division]

PART III
WORKS CITED

Addo-Fening, R. "The Background to the Deportation of King Asafo Agyei and the Foundation of New Juaben," in *Transactions of the Historical Society of Ghana*, 14, 2, 1973: 213–228.
—— *Akyem Abuakwa 1700–1943 from Ofori Panin to Sir Ofori Atta*, Trondheim, 1997.
Adjaye, Joseph K. *Diplomacy and Diplomats in Nineteenth Century Asante*, Lanham, 1984.
—— "*Asantehene* Agyeman Prempe I, Asante History, and the Historian," in *History in Africa*, 17, 1990: 1–29.
Agyeman-Duah, J. "Mampong, Ashanti: A Traditional History to the Reign of Safo Kantanka," in *Transactions of the Historical Society of Ghana*, 4, 2, 1960: 21–25.
Arhin, Kwame "The Asante Praise Poems: The Ideology of Patrimonialism" in *Paideuma*, 32, 1986a: 163–197.
—— "A note on the Asante Akonkofo: a non-literate sub-elite, 1900–30," in *Africa*, 56:1, 1986b: 25–31.
Akyeampong, Emmanuel "Asante Medicine in the Seychelles," in *Ghana Studies Council Newsletter*, 12, 1999a: 5–6.
—— "Christianity, Modernity, and the Weight of Tradition in the Life of Asantehene Agyeman Prempeh I, c.1888–1931," in *Africa*, 69, 2, 1999b: 279–311.
Baesjou, René (ed.) *An Asante Embassy on the Gold Coast. The mission of Akyempon Yaw to Elmina 1869–1872*, Leiden and Cambridge, 1979.
Bellis, James O. "Archeology and the Culture History of the Akan of Ghana: a case study," Ph.D. Dissertation, Indiana University, 1972.
Boahen, A. Adu "Prempeh in Exile," in *University of Ghana Institute of African Studies Research Review*, 8:3, 1972: 3–20.
—— "When did Osei Tutu die?", in *Transactions of the Historical Society of Ghana*, 16, 1, 1975: 87–92.
—— "A Nation in Exile: the Asante on the Seychelles Islands, 1900–24," in Enid Schildkrout (ed.), *The Golden Stool: Studies of the Asante Center and Periphery*, Washington, D. C., 1987: 146–60.
—— *African Perspectives on Colonialism*, Baltimore, 1987.
Bosman, W. *A New and Accurate Description of the Coast of Guinea*, London, 1705.
Bowdich, T. E. *Mission from Cape Coast Castle to Ashantee*, London, 1819.
Bradley, J. *A History of Seychelles*, 2 vols, nd, Victoria, Seychelles.
Brown, James Wilson "Kumasi, 1896–1923: urban Africa during the early colonial period," Ph.D. Dissertation, University of Wisconsin at Madison, 1972.
Busia, K. A. *The Position of the Chief in the Modern Political System of Ashanti*, London, 1951.
Crowder, Michael, and Ikime, Obaro (eds.) *West African Chiefs: Their Changing Status under Colonial Rule and Independence*, Ile-Ife and New York, 1970.

Daaku, K. Y. "Pre-Ashanti States," in *Ghana Notes and Queries*, 9, 1966: 10–13.
—— *Trade and Politics on the Gold Coast 1600 to 1720*, Oxford, 1970.
DeCorse, C. R. *An Archaeology of Elmina: Africans and Europeans on the Gold Coast, 1400–1900*, Washington, D. C., 2001.
Denteh, A. C. "Ntorɔ and Ntɔn," in *University of Ghana Institute of African Studies Research Review*, III, 3, 1967: 91–96.
Dupuis, J. *Journal of a Residence in Ashantee*, London, 1824.
Fuller, Francis *A Vanished Dynasty: Ashanti*, London, 1921.
Fynn, J. K. "The Reign and Times of Kusi Obodum, 1750–64," in *Transactions of the Historical Society of Ghana*, 8, 1965: 24–32.
Hagan, George P. "Ashanti Bureaucracy: A Study of the Growth of Centralised Administration in Ashanti from the Time of Osei Tutu to the time of Osei Tutu Kwamina Esibe Bonsu," in *Transactions of the Historical Society of Ghana*, 12, 1971: 43–62.
Kea, R. A. "Trade, State Formation and Warfare on the Gold Coast, 1600–1826," Ph.D. Dissertation, University of London, 1974.
Kimble, D. *A Political History of Ghana, 1850–1928*, Oxford, 1963.
Kyerematen, A. A. Y. "Ashanti Royal Regalia: Their History and Functions," D. Phil. Thesis, Oxford, 1966.
Lewin, T. J. *Asante before the British: The Prempean years 1875–1900*, Lawrence KS, 1978.
Martin, B. G. "Arabic materials for Ghanaian history," in *University of Ghana Institute of African Studies Research Review*, II, 1, 1965: 74–83.
McCann, James C. *Green Land, Brown Land, Black Land. An Environmental History of Africa, 1800–1990*, Portsmouth NJ and Oxford, 1999.
McCaskie, T. C. "Innovational Eclecticism: the Asante Empire and Europe in the Nineteenth Century," in *Comparative Studies in Society and History*, 14, 1, 1972: 30–45.
—— "The Paramountcy of the Asantehene Kwaku Dua (1834–1867): A Study in Asante Political Culture," Ph.D. Dissertation, Cambridge, 1974.
—— "Asantehene Agyeman Prempe's Account to the Asanteman of His Exile from Kumase (1896–1924): A Document with Commentary" in *Asantesɛm*, 7, 1977: 32–42.
—— "Anti-witchcraft Cults in Asante: An Essay in the Social History of an African People," in *History in Africa*, 8, 1981: 125–54.
—— "*Ahyiamu*—"A place of meeting": an essay on process and event in the history of the Asante state", in *Journal of African History*, 25, 2, 1984, 169–88.
—— "Power and Dynastic Conflict in Mampon," in *History in Africa*, 12, 1985: 167–85.
—— "Komfo Anokye of Asante: Meaning, History, and Philosophy in an African Society," in *Journal of African History*, 27, 2, 1986: 315–39.
—— *State and Society in Precolonial Asante*, Cambridge, 1995a.
—— "*Konnurokusɛm*: Kinship and Family in the History of the *Oyoko Kɔkɔɔ* Dynasty of Kumase," in *Journal of African History*, 36, 1995b: 357–389.
—— "Asante and Ga. The History of a Relationship," in Paul Jenkins (ed.), *The Recovery of the West African Past. African Pastors and African History in the Nineteenth Century*, Basel, 1998: 135–153.
—— "Cultural Encounters: Britain and Africa in the Nineteenth Century", in A. Porter

(ed.), *The Oxford History of the British Empire. Volume III. The Nineteenth Century*, Oxford, 1999: 665–89.
— *Asante Identities: History and Modernity in an African Village 1850–1950*, Edinburgh and Bloomington IN, 2000.
Nketia, J. H. K. *Apaee (poems recited by the Abrafo of the Asantehene on state occasions)*, Institute of African Studies, University of Ghana, 1966.
Owusu-Ansah, D. *Islamic Talismanic Tradition in Nineteenth-century Asante*, Lewiston MD, 1991.
Priestley, M. and Wilks, I. "The Ashanti Kings in the eighteenth century: a revised chronology," *Journal of African History*, I, I, 1960: 83–96.
Rattray, R. S. *Ashanti*, Oxford, 1923.
— *Religion and Art in Ashanti*, Oxford, 1927.
— *Ashanti Law and Constitution*, Oxford, 1929.
Reindorf, C. C. *History of the Gold Coast and Asante*, Basel, 1895.
Shinnie, Peter "Early Asante: Is Wilks Right?", in J. Hunwick and N. Lawler (eds.), *The Cloth of Many Colored Silks*, Evanston IL, 1996: 195–204.
Shinnie, Peter and Ama, *Early Asante*, Dept. of Archaeology, Calgary, 1995, reprinted, Kumasi, 1998.
Smith, E. W. *The Golden Stool*, London, 1926.
Tordoff, William "The exile and repatriation of Nana Prempeh I of Ashanti, 1896–1924", in *Transactions of the Historical Society of Ghana*, 4, 2, 1960: 33–55.
— *Ashanti under the Prempehs 1888–1935*, Oxford, 1965.
Vivian, B. C. "Origins of the Asante Research Project: 1989–90. Excavations at Asantemanso," in *Nyame Akuma*, 34, 1990: 19–22.
Wilks, Ivor "Aspects of Bureaucratisation in Ashanti in the Nineteenth Century," in *Journal of African History*, 7, 2, 1966: 215–33.
— *Asante in the Nineteenth Century: the structure and evolution of a political order*, Cambridge, 1975.
— "A Note on Career Sheet ACBP/28: Kwaadu Yaadom," in *Asantesɛm*, 11, 1979: 54–56.
— *Asante in the Nineteenth Century: the structure and evolution of a political order*, (reprinted with a new Preamble), Cambridge, 1989.
— *Forests of Gold. Essays on the Akan and the Kingdom of Asante*, Athens, OH, 1993.
— *One Nation, Many Histories. Ghana Past and Present*, Accra, 1996.
— "An Asante Pharmacopeia?," in *Ghana Studies Council Newsletter*, 11, 1998: 4–5.
— "Asante Nationhood and Colonial Administrators, 1896–1935," in C. Lentz and P. Nugent (eds.), *Ethnicity in Ghana. The Limits of Invention*, London, 2000: 68–96.
— *Akwamu 1640–1750. A Study of the Rise and Fall of a West African Empire*, Trondheim, 2001.
Wilks, I., Levtzion, N., and Haight, B. M. *Chronicles from Gonja: A Tradition of West African Muslim Historiography*, Cambridge, 1986.
Yarak, Larry W. "Kwasi Boakye and Kwame Poku: Dutch-Educated Asante 'Princes'," in Enid Schildkrout (ed.), *The Golden Stool: Studies of the Asante Center and Periphery*, Washington, D.C., 1987: 131–45.
— *Asante and the Dutch 1744–1873*, Oxford, 1990.

PART IV
CONCORDANCE

INTRODUCTION

The Concordance indexes all references to people and places in Asantehene Agyeman Prempeh's writings in Chapters Five to Eight, and selectively in Chapter Nine (children, grandchildren, and unidentified "servants" being for the most part omitted). All spellings of names as they appear in the texts are recorded within quotation marks, and are cross-referred to an acceptable present day form, for example: "Ignarsi," see Anyinase. There is no agreed Twi orthography and so there are no mandated rules for rendering Akan names into English. Thus we have aimed for no more than a consistent measure of internal standardisation. Orthographic difficulties are compounded by two features. First, Akan Twi has a wide range of dialects and, within these, spoken registers that have evolved over time and are continuing to do so at varying rates. Second, Akan Twi has a tendency to syncope, the process of losing sounds or letters from words over time. Thus we have, in general, preferred to use emerging forms, for example, "*konti*" (the military formation), rather than the earlier "*kronti*," and still earlier "*kurontiri*," or "*fo*" (people), rather than the earlier "*foɔ*" and "*forɔ*." That said, the reader may detect a certain indecision on our part between use of, for example, the Twi ending "eɛ" and the corresponding English "ie." Thus we have generally preferred the less accurate "Afriyie" to the more accurate, but keyboard unfriendly, "Afriyeɛ." Conversely, however, we have recognized that such a key Twi term as *ntɔrɔ* cannot happily be rendered "*ntoro*."

Many entries in the Concordance include information about persons and places that is not found in Agyeman Prempeh's texts. It is constructed to enable the reader to relate the writings to the broader corpus of work in Asante Studies. In this respect we have been fortunate to be able to draw upon the resources of the Asante Collective Biography Project (ACBP), in which information on persons, places, and offices is compiled from a myriad of both written and oral sources. This Project was directed by Wilks and McCaskie in the 1970s.[1] Much of its working material is now on deposit in the archives of the

---

[1] See I. Wilks, *Asante in the Nineteenth Century: the structure and evolution of a political order*, Cambridge, 1989: xxxii–xxxiii, and T. C. McCaskie, *State and Society in Precolonial Asante*, Cambridge, 1995: 466–67.

Herskovits Memorial Library, Northwestern University. More widely available are the Project's bulletins, *Asante Seminar*, 1–6, 1975–76, and *Asantesem*, 7–11, 1977–79.

The ACBP was in many respects a development from the three year Ashanti Research Project launched by the Institute of African Studies, University of Ghana, in May 1963.[2] Among its various objectives was one, directed by Wilks, to compile basic data on Asante stool histories. The late Joseph Agyeman-Duah, erstwhile Senior State Secretary of the Kumase Traditional Council, undertook by far the greater bulk of the research. In compiling this Concordance we have drawn heavily upon the extraordinarily useful corpus of material put together by Agyeman-Duah over the two decades 1963 to 1983.[3] Relevant items from this corpus have been noted in the entries below, using the notation, [AS/—].

ABBREVIATIONS, ETC.

aka	also known as	fl	floruit
b	born	dau	daughter
ca	circa	int al	*inter alia* or *inter alios*
C17	17th century	mat	maternal
C18	18th century	mls	miles
C19	19th century	pat	paternal
cf	consult	qv	cross-refer
d	died	temp	at the time of
dsp	died without issue		

Distances and directions are measured from Kumase, and are approximate. The former are in miles, and the latter follow the sequence:
N (0°), NNE (22° 30′), NE (45°), ENE (67° 30′),
E (90°), ESE (112° 30′), SE (135°), SSE (157° 30′),
S (180°), SSW (202° 30′), SW (225°), WSW (247° 30′),
W (270°), WNW (292° 30′), NW (315°), NNW (337° 30′).

---

[2] See J. H. Kwabena Nketia, A. S. Y. Andoh and Ivor G. Wilks, *Ashanti Research Project. First Conference May 17–May 20, 1963*, Institute of African Sudies, Legon, 1964.

[3] A schedule of Agyeman-Duah's "Stool Histories," nos. 1–215, held by the Institute of African Studies, University of Ghana, in 1966, will be found in *Ashanti Research Project, Progress Report No. 1, 1963–1966*, Institute of African Studies, Legon, 1966: 16–215. No schedule of later accessions has been seen. However, Agyeman-Duah continued to work with Wilks into the 1980s, and copies of "Stool Histories," nos. 1–303 will be found in the Wilks Papers, Herskovits Memorial Library, Northwestern University.

The following Twi terms are used.

abusua (plural, *mmusua*), the exogamous matrilineage characteristic of the Akan generally.

afenasoani (*afenasoafo*), traditionally swordbearers in the royal household, but also widely employed as official messengers.

fekuo, literally, a group of people, but used to refer to collectivities.

ntɔrɔ, cultic organisations defined by patriliny and concerned with the ritual cleansing of the *kra* or "soul."

obaa-panin, female head of a segment of a matrilineage.

ɔbirɛmpɔn (female *ɔbirɛmpɔmma*), literally "big man" or "big woman," with reference to socially recognised achievement.

odekuro (plural, *adekurofo*), village head.

ɔhene (plural, *ahene*), title denoting stool holders of various ranks and functions.

ɔkyeame (plural, *akyeame*), here denoting official counsellors and advisors, often referred to as "linguists."

ɔmanhene (*amanhene*), here denoting heads of the major Asante territorial divisions.

Diacritical marks used in the handwritten text of *HAK* and *OA/OY* are ignored for the purposes of indexing.

"Abboagi akumadoma," *see* Akomadoma
Abena, 136, dau of Yaa Afere (qv), and Kankam (qv).
Abena Akyampoma, 145, dau of Bimma Dehyeɛ (qv), and wife of Owusu Ansa Panin (qv).
Abena Gyapa, 130, 131, 145, dau of Birempomaa Piesie (qv); mother of, *int al*, Manu (qv).
"Abena Japa," *see* Abena Gyapa
Abena Kwadua, 176, exiled to Elmina with Agyeman Prempeh.
Abena Sapon, 142, dau of Akua Nansewaa (qv), and Apaw (qv) of Kumase Apeboso (qv).
Aberefi, 136, dau of Asantehemaa Afua Sapon (qv) and Apagyahene Owusu Afriyie (qv).
Aberefi Yaa, 133, 134, dau of Asantehemaa Akua Afriyie (qv); sister of Asantehene Osei Kwadwo (qv); mother of Asantehemaa Kwadu Yaadom (qv) and Sewaa Awukuwaa (qv); and wife of 1) Mamponhene Attakora Panin (qv); 2) Mamponhene Asumgyima (qv); and 3) Mamponhene Safo Katanka (qv).

Abesim, 101, 70 mls NW, settled by refugees from Domaa (qv).
"Abina Achempoma," *see* Abena Akyampoma
"Abina Japa," *see* Abena Gyapa
"Abina Kwadua," *see* Abena Kwadua
"Abina Sapon," *see* Abena Sapon
"Abinah," *see* Abena
"Abinah Achempoma," *see* Abena Akyampoma
"Abinah Japa," *see* Abena Gyapa
"Aboa-Dier," *see* Aboadeɛ
Aboadeɛ, **99, 116, 117**, Asante *ntɔrɔ*, associated with Bosompra.
"Aboagar," 100, unidentified.
Aboagye Asare, 99, made *odekuro* of Besease (qv) by Obiri Yeboa, in Domakwai *fekuo* (qv). [AS/105].
"Abohen," *see* Oyoko Abohyen
"Abohin," *see* Oyoko Abohyen
"Abontemu," *see* under Kaase
"Abontemuheni," *see* Kwasi Koɔ
"Abo-o," 121, unidentified.
"Abooakwah," *see* Abuakwa
Abradi, 134, town 10 mls NNE.

"Abrādie," 116, Asante ntɔrɔ.
"Abradie," see Abradi
"Abrafie," see Aberefi Yaa
"Abraefi," see Aberefi
Abrafoɔhene, 96, 97, head of the abrafoɔ, the law enforcement officers in the Adum fekuo of Kumase.
"Abrafuor," see Abrafoɔhene
"Abrafuorheni," see Abrafoɔhene
"Abranie," 116, Asante ntɔrɔ.
"Abrèfa Panir," see Abrefa Panin
Abrefa Panin, 99, head of Kwadwokrom (qv), late C17 to early C18. Took title "Soadurohene" after earlier Soaduro transformed into Kumase Akwamu (qv). [AS/191].
"Absim," see Abesim
Abrenkese Nyameani, 99, 133, 136, 15 mls SE. Cf Amponsen, Owusu Panin, Kankam. [AS/224].
Abu, 136, Nkonsonhene in Kumase Apeboso (qv), in succession to Apaw (qv) whose widow, Odɛɛ (qv), he married. Killed in civil wars, mid-1883.
Abu, aka Owusu Penemo, 142, Nkonsonhene in Kumase Apeboso (qv). Husband of Asantehemaa Yaa Dufie (qv), and father of Kwaku Pimpim (qv). Led Nkonson fekuo at battle of Katamanso, 1826 [Reindorf, 1895: 352].
"Abuadiae," see Aboadeɛ
"Abuadie," see Aboadeɛ
Abuakwa, 124, village 7 mls W, centre of potmaking.
"Abuhen," see Oyoko Abohyen
"Accrofunsu," see Mampon Akrofonso
"Achamar," see Akyaama
"Achampon Kofi," see Akyampon Kofi
"Achampon Tintin," see Akyampon Tenten
"Achar," see Akyaa
"Achar Kesie," see Akyaa Kese, dau of Akua Fokuo
"Achempem," see Akyempem
"Achempem Afriae," see Owusu Afriyie
"Achempom Akwasi," see Akyampon Kwasi
"Achempontintin," see Akyampon Tenten
"Achia Kesie," see Akyaa Kese, dau of Kwadu Yaadom
"Achim," see Akyem
"Achim Abuadie," see Aboadeɛ
"Achimadie," see Akyeremade
"Achimpim," see Akyempem
"Achinpimheni," see Akyempem
"Achrer-kūn Kojan," see Akyereko
"Achua," see Atwea
"Achule Boanah," see Yaw Twereboanna
"Achundie," 116, Asante ntɔrɔ.
"Acrafordier," 99, unidentified.

"Acra-fuor," see Yam Panir
"Acrudie," 116, Asante ntɔrɔ.
Adakwa Yiadom, 104, 106, 109, Dwabenhene; commanded right flank of the vanguard in the war of liberation against Denkyira, 1701 [Reindorf, 1895: 52–6].
"Adan Chimansu," see Adenkyemenaso
Adanse, 87, 89, 93, 103, 110, 115, 120, 121, 122, 178, 187, one of the early Akan polities, centred on Adansemanso (qv). Dominant regional power until mid-C17, when Denkyira (qv) became ascendant.
Adanse Ahensan, 87, 89, 187, apparently nickname ("the king has gone back") used to refer to Adansemanso (qv). The name is preserved in the present village Ahensan, 3 mls E of the old site.
Adansemanso, 87, abandoned site, 25 mls S, near Adubiase, where several Asante "clans" (mmusua), including the Bretuo (qv), locate their origins. Cf Adanse Ahensan.
"Adansi," see Adanse
"Adansi Ahinsan," see Adanse Ahensan
"Adansimansu," see Adansemanso
"Adar Kussi, see Adom Kusi
"Adarkwar," see Adakwa Yiadom
"Adar Kwar Yardum," see Adakwa Yiadom
"Adar Kwar Yia Dom," see Adakwa Yiadom
"Adduanah," see Aduana
"Adébilayua," 145, dau of Amma Adedeɛ (qv).
"Adenchimansu," see Adenkyemenaso
Adenkyemenaso, 87, 111, section of Kumase, seat of Oyoko Atutuehene (qv). [AS/32].
"Aderkwar Yardom," see Adakwa Yiadom
"Adjaikoom," see Kwabena Agyeikum
"Adjiman Badoo," see Agyeman Badu
"Adjua Chilé", see Adwowa Kyire
"Adjuah," see Adwowa
"Adjua Kutu," see Adwowa Kutu
"Adjua Kutua-Poa," 176, among deportees to Elmina 1896.
"Adjuan Pon Awukuo," see Adwampon Awukuo
"Adjua Sewah," see Adwowa Sewaa
"Adoa Inkra Youli," see Adowaa Nkrawiri.
Adom Kusi, 101, leader of Domaa (qv). Fought 1st Domaa war against Oti Akenten (qv), 2nd against Obiri Yeboa (qv), and was slain in 3rd by Osei Tutu (qv).
Adoma Akosua, 128, 135, dau of Sewaa Awukuwaa (qv) and Owusu (qv). Married another Owusu (qv) and mother of Akua Sewaa (qv), Osei Kwasi (qv), and Osei Kwadwo Kumaa. Made Asantehemaa ca 1809. Purchased Apa (qv), her father's town. Destooled ca 1819 by Asantehene

Osei Tutu Kwame (qv), for conspiracy, and d 1838. [*Asantesɛm*, 11: 14–17].
Adonten, 106, 137, 139, main body of Kumase army. [AS/95].
Adonten Boaten, 137, Kumase Adontenhene temp Asantehene Mensa Bonsu (qv). Husband of Afua Sewaa (qv).
"Adontin," *see* Adonten
"Adontini," *see* Adonten
"Adoofa," 186, woman with white stool who arrived at Adansemanso (qv) to usher in Ankyewa Nyame (qv). At *HAK* 5.3 "Dufua" is treated as the name of the stool.
"Adoom," *see* Adum, section of Kumase
Adoom Aoawina, 95, servant of Osei Tutu (qv), otherwise unidentified.
"Adoom Asamua," *see* Adum Asamoa
"Adooms," *see* Adum, section of Kumase
"Adoonkoo," *see* Adunku
"Adou," *see* under Adu, husband of Ata Sewaa
"Adoùn-Coo-diclo," *see* Adunku
Adowaa Nkrawiri, 92, original owner of land on which Kumase was built.
"Adowar Nkrawri," *see* Adowaa Nkrawiri
Adu, 142, husband of Adwowa Sewaa (qv), otherwise unidentified.
Adu, 143, husband of Ata Sewaa (qv), and father of Opoku (qv). Probably Kumase Atene Akotenhene Adusei Kra, d 1838, son of Asantehene Opoku Fofie (qv).
Adu, 144, husband of Opokuwaa (qv), dau of Ata Sewaa (qv), otherwise unidentified.
Adu, 145, husband of Yaa Manfu (qv), otherwise unidentified.
Aduana, 87, a major *abusua*, "clan," in Asante.
"Adu Atah," *see* Adu Atta
Adu Atta, 135, last child of Amma Sewaa (qv), dau of Adoma Akosua (qv).
"Adu Chum," *see* Adu Twum
"Adufodier," 116, Asante *ntɔrɔ*, *see* Bosommuru.
Adu Gyamfi, 91, Bretuo founder of Wono, who moved to Gyamase (qv). Married to Ofebiri Odeneho (qv). [AS/161, 162].
"Adu Janfi," *see* Adu Gyamfi
"Aduku," *see* Adunku
Adum, 103, section of Kumase, seat of the Asantehene's executioners under Adumhene. Cf. Adum Asamoa; Asamoa Kwame.
Adum, 122, 123, seat of Abakomdwahene in the Kumase Nkonson *fekuo*, custodian of heirs-apparent to the Golden Stool.
"Adumakundie," 116, Asante *ntɔrɔ*.
Adum Asamoa, 101, 103, accompanied Osei Tutu on his return to Asante from Akwamu (qv). Made Adumhene under Kumase Akwamuhene Awere (qv). [AS/5].
"Adum Asamua," *see* Adum Asamoa
"Aduma Akosua," *see* Adoma Akosua
Adunku, 100, 108, 10 mls SSE. Placed in Domakwai (qv) by Obiri Yeboa. Cf. Akura Ameyaw.
Adunnya Safie, 103, Denkyira refugee in Adanse. Given to Asantehene Osei Tutu, who appointed him "crown prosecutor", i.e. Akyeamehene, in place of Boansi Kofo (qv), and also head of the reorganized Domakwai Nifa *fekuo* in the Akyempem (qv). Said to have died in Denkyira war of 1700–01.
Adu Twum, 134, son of Asantehene Opoku Ware (qv). 2nd wife was Asantehemaa Kwadu Yaadom (qv), and children included Asantehene Opoku Fofie (qv) and Asantehemaa Yaa Dufie (qv). Served in the Akyamfo-Dumienu *fekuo* in Kumase. Later given the Akankade *ɔkyeame* stool, created by Osei Kwame; died ca 1776. [AS/75. *Asantesɛm*, 10: 46–8].
Adwaa, 142, section of Kumase.
Adwaase, 88, 106, town, 5 mls E, belonging to the Dako *abusua*. [AS/88].
Adwowa, 136, dau of Yaa Afere (qv) and Asabi Boakye (qv). Younger full sister, therefore, of Yaw Twereboanna.
Adwowa Jantuo, 137, 5th dau of Asantehemaa Yaa Kyaa (qv) and Kwasi Gyambibi (qv). Apparently unmarried in 1896.
Adwowa Kutu, 143, dau of Ata Sewaa (qv) and Adu (qv). Mother of Osei (qv) and Sewaa (qv) by her marriage to Owusu (qv).
Adwowa Kyire, 143, dau of Ata Sewaa (qv) and Adu (qv). Married Owusu (qv).
Adwowa Sewaa, 142, dau of Asantehemaa Yaa Dufie (qv) and Owusu (qv). Married Adu (qv).
Adwowa Sewaa, 142, dau of Pokuwaa (qv) and Apea Kɔ (qv). Married Kwadwo Adɛe (qv).
Adwuampon, 90, early capital of the Dwaben people.
Adwuampon Awukuo, 121, old Denkyira trading centre, otherwise unidentified.
Adwumakaase, 106, 10 mls NE. Founded by Asenso Kofo (qv). [AS/111].
Afarkwa, 142, 2nd husband of Akua Nansewaa (qv). Possibly the Akrofuomhene Afarkwa, who took refuge in Akyem Kotoku in the civil wars, 1883–88.
"Affiguarsy," *see* Effiduase
"Affoi Kwah," *see* Afarkwa
"Affua Sewah," *see* Afua Sewaa
"Afoanpon," 109, town unidentified, men said to have killed Ntim Gyakari (qv).

"Afrani Ababio," *see* Kofi Afrani
"Afriae," *see* Owusu Afriyie, Apagyahene
"Afriae," *see* Yaw Afriyie, Otikromhene
"Afua Cobbi," *see* Afua Kobi
"Afua Cobi," *see* Afua Kobi
"Afua Gobbi," *see* Afua Kobi
"Afua Inpla Chilé," *see* Afua Mprakyere
"Afua Kobbi," *see* Afua Kobi
Afua Kobi, 122, 136, 137, 140, 141, dau of Asantehemaa Afua Sapon (qv) and Apagyahene Owusu Afriyie (qv). Asantehemaa, removed from office 1884, d 1900. Mother of Asantehenes Kofi Kakari (qv) and Mensa Bonsu (qv), and Asantehemaa Yaa Kyaa (qv). *See* McCaskie, 1995b: passim.
Afua Mprakyere, 141, dau of Akosua Berenya (qv) and Ntim (qv). Married 1) "Yaw Berkun" (qv), and 2) an unnamed Adanse man.
"Afuardie," 116, Asante *ntɔrɔ*.
Afua Sapon, 122, 128, 135, 136, 137, 141, 142, dau of Asantehemaa Amma Sewaa (qv) and Apaw Panin (qv). Married Apagyahene Owusu Afriyie (qv), and gave birth to, *int al*, heir apparent Osei Kwadwo (qv) and Asantehemaa Afua Kobi (qv). Asantehemaa temp Asantehene Kwaku Dua Panin (qv), but executed (with Osei Kwadwo) in 1859 on the supposition that both were plotting to overthrow the Asantehene. *See* McCaskie, 1995b: 363–73.
Afua Sapon, 142, dau of Akosua Berenya (qv) and Kwame Boakye (qv).
Afua Sewaa, 136, 137, younger dau (born ca 1824) of Afua Sapon (qv) and Apagyahene Owusu Afriyie (qv). Married Adonten Boaten (qv). Dsp.
"Agimadie," 116, Asante *ntɔrɔ*, aka Bosomtwe.
Agona, 87, 89, major *abusua* of Asante, linked at **87** with Asokore (qv).
Agona, 98, town, 25 mls NE, home of Okomfo Anokye (qv).
"Agonah," *see* Agona, *abusua*
"Agona Yamua," *see* Yamoa
"Aguanpon," *see* Adwuampon
"Agumakarsi," *see* Adwumakaase
"Agunār," *see* Agona, *abusua*
Agyeibi, 107, 146, Denkyira *ɔbirɛmpɔn*, defected to Osei Tutu prior to Denkyira war of 1701. Resettled at Kwadwokrom (qv), and became Atwomahene. [AS/184]. Married Akua Ago (qv), and was father of Daako (qv). Cf Kwakwa Bene; Yim Awere.
Agyeikum, 142, 1st son of Pokuwaa (qv) and Kwaku Tawia (qv). May be identical with Kumase Oyokohene Kwabena Agyeikum (qv).

Agyeman Badu, 123, 137, 176, 177, 191, son of Asantehemaa Yaa Kyaa (qv) and Kwasi Gyambibi (qv). Born 1874. Made heir-apparent to his brother, Asantehene Agyeman Prempeh. Exiled to Seychelles, baptised Albert, d. 1917.
Agyeman Prempeh, 128, 137, 147–66, passim. Son of Asantehemaa Yaa Kyaa (qv) and Kwasi Gyambibi (qv). Born 1872. Enstooled as Asantehene Kwaku Dua III in 1888, but became better known as Agyeman Prempeh. Abducted by Gov. Maxwell of the Gold Coast in 1896, repatriated 1924, styled "Kumasihene" 1926, d. 1931.
Ahenkuro, 88, immigrants attached to Oyoko Atutuo (qv) by Asantehene Osei Tutu (qv).
"Ahensan," *see* Adanse Ahensan
"Ahinkulo," *see* Ahenkuro
"Ahinsan," *see* Owusu Ansa, John
"Ahoom-fuor," 96, unidentified.
"Ah Poon Sem," *see* Amponsem
"Ah-Same," 101, unidentified village.
"Ajae Bi," *see* Agyeibi
"Ajaeby," *see* Agyeibi
"Ajae Kum," *see* Agyeikum
"Ajoar," *see* Adwaa
"Ajuabumoa," *see* Dwabenmma
"Ajuabumoar," *see* Dwabenmma
"Ajua Jantu-O," *see* Adwowa Jantuo
"Ajummah moo," *see* Kokofu Adwamamu
"Ajuan Pon Awukuo," *see* Adwampon Awukuo
"Ajuarsi," *see* Adwaase
"Ajusou," *see* Kokofu Adweso
Akanase, 143, section of Kumase.
"Akanasi," *see* Akanase
"Akenten," *see* Oti Akenten
"Akim," *see* Akyem
"Akim," *see* Asante Akyem
"Akim Aboadie, *see* Aboadeɛ
"Akimadoma," *see* Akomadoma
"Akim Asiakwa," *see* Asiakwa
"Akodam," *see* Akwadan
"Akōkofae," *see* Akokofe
Akokofe, 88, 106, Oyoko town south of Kumase. [AS/151].
"Akokofer," *see* Akokofe
"Akom," 116, Asante *ntɔrɔ*, aka "Busukony."
"Akom," *see* Akwamu, kingdom
"Akom," *see* Akwamu, Kumase *fekuo*
Akomadoma, 98, 130, 131, dau of Birempomaa Piesie (qv) and mother of Asantehene Obiri Yeboa (qv).
Akomfode, 179, 184, stool in Kumase Manwere created by Kwaku Dua Panin (qv) for his son Boakye Attansa (qv). [AS/222].

Concordance

"Akomheni," *see* Akwamu, kingdom
"Akompondiawuo," *see* Kwapon Odeawuo
"Akonfrohene," *see* Akomfode
"Akonfruhene," *see* Akomfode
"Akorku," *see* Kwasi Akoko
"Akorsa Yiadom," *see* Akosa Yiadom
"Akorsan Yiadom," *see* Akosa Yiadom
Akosa Yiadom, 105, 106, 112, prior to the Denkyira war of 1700, purchased command of the Kumase Adonten troops. Became 1st ɔhene of Amakom (qv). Given Nyaako Kusi Amoa (qv) in marriage by Osei Tutu (qv), but in a subsequent conflict with him, Akosa Yiadom is said to have been slain. [AS/77].
Akosua Aberewaa, 139, 1st child of Amma Mansa (qv) and Kwabena Safo (qv), b 1894. Sister of Kwadwo Owusu Ansa.
"Akosua Abruãh," *see* Akosua Aberewaa
"Akosua Begran," *see* Akosua Berenya
"Akosua Braegua," *see* Akosua Berenya
Akosua Berenya, 136, 141, according to *HAK*/11–12, offspring of an illicit affair between Yaa Afere (qv), dau of Afua Sapon (qv), and the ɛsɛn Boadi (qv). *HAK*/18–19, however, erroneously has her as dau of Asantehemaa Afua Sapon (qv). Married 1) Ntim (qv) and Afua Mprakyere born. Married 2) Owusu (qv), and Amma Sewaa born. Married 3) Kwame Boakye (qv), and four children survived. In 1891 was accused of adultery with Asoamfohene Kwasi Agyei, and both were executed for having violated Agyeman Prempeh's recent edict against having sexual relationships with any of the uterine sisters of Yaw Twereboanna (qv). See supra, Ch 1:**14**.
"**Akosua Cherm," 176**, among deportees to Elmina 1896.
"Akosua Insia," *see* Akosua Nsia
"Akosua Manhya," *see* Akosua Manhyia
Akosua Manhyia, 137, 141, younger dau of Akua Afriyie (qv) and Kyidomhene Krapa (qv). Married Yaw Daani (qv), but *see supra*, Ch 1: **9**. Mother of Yaw Sanhene (qv) and Kwabena (qv), b ca 1895.
Akosua Nsia, 137, 140, 2nd dau of Akua Afriyie (qv) and Krapa (qv). Married Atta (qv), possibly Anowuhene.
Akoto, 126, Akwamuhene said to have given refuge to Osei Tutu (qv). The ruler in question is usually named as Ansa Sasraku.
"Akoulah mi Yaw," *see* Akura Ameyaw
Akradware, 98, 117, "Soul-Washers" organisation in the palace, dedicated to the service of the *kra* of the reigning Asantehene. *See* McCaskie, 1995a: 293.

"Akraguãdie," *see* Akradware
Akua Abakoma, 137, 139, 2nd dau of Asantehemaa Yaa Kyaa (qv) and Kwasi Abayie (qv). Married Kwaku Owusu, and mother of, *int al*, Asantehene Osei Agyeman Prempeh II.
Akua Adɛ, 136, 141, apparently 3rd dau of Yaa Afere (qv) and Kankam (qv), but misdescribed in 141 as 5th (surviving) child of Afua Sapon perhaps by confusion with Odɛe (qv). Dsp.
"Akua Ader," *see* Akua Adɛ
Akua Afriyie, 110, 128, 133, dau of Asantehemaa Nketewa Ntim Abamu (qv), and sister of Asantehene Kusi Obodum (qv). Married 1) Kwasi Koɔ (qv); 2) Abradehene Opoku Tia (qv), father of Aberefi Yaa (qv); 3) Akyempemhene Owusu Afriyie (qv), father of Asantehene Osei Kwadwo (qv). Asantehemaa mid-C18.
Akua Afriyie, 136, dau of Afua Sapon (qv) and Apagyahene Owusu Afriyie (qv), and sister, *int al*, of Afua Kobi (qv). Wife of Boakye Dankwa (qv).
Akua Afriyie, 136, 137, 138, 140, 141, 1st dau of Asantehemaa Afua Kobi (qv) and Kwasi Abayie (qv). Married 1) Krapa (qv), 2) Asafo Boakye (qv). Gave birth to 20 children in all; d Kumase 1921.
Akua Afriyie, 137, 139, 3rd dau of Yaa Kyaa (qv) and Kwasi Abayie (qv). Married Boaten (qv) of the Adonten. Recognised by British as successor to her mother, but only as "Kumasihemaa." Succeeded by Amma Adusa (qv).
"Akuafiae," *see* Akua Afriyie, dau of Afua Sapon
"Akuafiae," *see* Akua Afriyie, dau of Nketewa Ntim Abamu
Akua Ago, 130, 146, dau of Birempomaa Piesie (qv). Married Atwomahene Agyeibi (qv). Mother of Daako (qv).
"Akua Akrũkru," *see* Akua Akrukruwaa
Akua Akrukruwaa, 134, 143, 144, dau of Asantehemaa Kwadu Yaadom (qv) and Adu Twum (qv). Full sister of, *int al*, Asantehemaa Yaa Dufie (qv) and Asantehene Opoku Fofie (qv). Married Owusu (qv); d 1807, from smallpox.
Akua Akyaa, *see* Yaa Kyaa dau of Ohene Afrewo
"Akua Badoo," *see* Akua Badu
Akua Badu, 137, 141, dau of Akua Afriyie (qv). Married the *afenasoani* Atta Kwasi who became Abanasehene in 1914.
"Akua Bakumma," *see* Akua Abakoma
"Akua Der," *see* Akua Adɛ

Akua Fokuo, 137, 139, b 1861, dau of Asantehemaa Yaa Kyaa (qv) and Kwasi Abayie (qv). Married 1) Mamponhene Kwabena Dwumo (qv); 2) ɔkyeame Kwame Dwuben (qv); 3) Akyempemhene Osei Tutu (qv), giving birth to Owusu Nkwantabisa (qv), Owusu Ansa (qv) and Akyaa Kese (qv).
"Akuafriae," see Akua Afriyie, dau of Nketewa Ntim Abamu
"Akua Friae," see Akua Afriyie, dau of Afua Sapon
"Akua Friae," see Akua Afriyie, dau of Afua Kobi
"Akua Friae," see Akua Afriyie, dau of Yaa Kyaa
"Akua Gu," see Akua Ago
"Akua Guarkun," see Akua Nyaako
"Akua Krukru, see Akua Akrukruwaa
"Akua Intim," see Akua Ntim
"Akua Intimi," see Akua Ntim
Akua Nansewaa, 142, dau of Adwowa Sewaa (qv) and Adu (qv). Married 1) Apaw of Kumase Apeboso (qv), and 2) Afarkwa (qv).
"Akua Nansiwar," see Akua Nansewaa
Akua Ntim, 144, dau of Sewaa, granddaughter of Adwowa Kutu. Married "Kodjoe Konson Kwar" (qv).
Akua Nyaako, 140, daughter of Akosua Nsia (qv) and Atta (qv). Dsp.
Akua Sewaa, 135, 1st child of Asantehemaa Adoma Akosua (qv). Sister of Osei Kwasi (qv) and Osei Kwadwo Kumaa (qv).
"Akua Sewah," see Akua Sewaa
Akuamoa Panin, 135, Dwabenhene, fl 1760s to 1770s. Father of Okyere Kotoku (qv), 3rd husband of Asantehemaa Amma Sewaa (qv).
"Akuamua Pani," see Akuamoa Panin
"Akudan," see Akwadan
"Akumadoma," see Akomadoma
Akumanten, 103, fekuo created by Osei Tutu (qv) for his servant Tonto Diawuo (qv) of Sepe, and placed in the Hia group (qv) under Akyempemhene Owusu Afriyie (qv). [AS/80].
"Akumantrae," see Akumanten
"Akumantre," see Akumanten
Akura Ameyaw, 100, made odekuro of Adunku (qv), under Domakwai (qv), by Obiri Yeboa. Ca 1700 fought first engagement in the Denkyira war.
"Akroponhene," see Akuropon
Akuropon, 179, town 9 mls NW, in Kyidom Division of Kumase [AS/199]. Cf Kwaku Nsia.
Akwadan, 108, Kumase Asokwahene, brother of Nuamoa (qv), and cf Asokwa.

Akwamu, 98, 100, 101, 125, 126, kingdom in late C17 and early C18 based on Nyanawase, about 25 mls NW of present day Accra. See Wilks, 2001, passim.
Akwamu, 102, 119, 123, 124, 125, Kumase fekuo, first called Soaduro (qv), ranking after Konti (qv). Seat in Asafo in Kumase. [AS/38]. Cf Awere, Asafo Boakye.
"Akwasi," see Kwasi, son of Akua Fokuo
"Akwasi," see Kwasi, son of Ohene Afrewo
"Akwasiasy," 99, unidentified place. Odekuro Tabiri (qv) given office in the Twafuo fekuo (qv).
"Akwasi Abayae," see Kwasi Abayie
"Akwasi Ader," see Kwasi Adɛ
"Akwasi Ajim," see Kwasi Agyeim
"Akwasi Berkun," see Kwasi "Berkun"
"Akwasi Bonkoo," 184, 'servant' of Asafo Boakye (qv).
"Akwasi Chiu," see Kwasi "Chiu"
"Akwasi Gembibi," see Kwasi Gyambibi
"Akwasi Gembili," see Kwasi Gyambibi
"Akwasi-Kor," see Kwasi Koɔ
"Akwasi Prah," see Kwasi Pra
"Akwasi Tobo," see Kwasi "Tobo"
Akyaa, 140, dau of Asantehemaa Yaa Kyaa (qv); married Kwame Gyansa of Bantama (qv).
Akyaa Kese, 134, dau of Asantehemaa Kwadu Yaadom (qv) and Mamponhene Safo Katanka (qv).
Akyaa Kese, 139, dau of Akua Fokuo (qv) and Akyempemhene Osei Tutu (qv).
Akyaama, 180, wife of Bantamahene Kwame Amankwatia (qv).
Akyampon Kofi, 93, said to be son of Oti Akenten (qv). One of the 7 gunmen (Konti Atuo Nson) who accompanied Osei Tutu into exile in Denkyira. Later made Afarihene in the Konti fekuo.
Akyampon Kwasi, 135, son of Asantehemaa Amma Sewaa (qv), and Boakye Yam Kumaa (qv). Full brother of Asantehene Kwaku Dua Panin (qv). Killed ca 1800. See McCaskie, 1995b: passim.
Akyampon Tenten, 90, 127, 130, 131, 188, son of Birempomaa Piesie (qv); first ruler at Asantemanso (qv).
Akyem, 88 115, 119, term used loosely and may refer to Asante Akyem (qv), Akyem Abuakwa (qv), or Akyem Kotoku (qv).
Akyem Abuakwa, state, became province of Asante by Asantehene Opoku Ware's victory of 1742. Became part of British Protected Territory of the Gold Coast in 1831. See Addo-Fening, 1997: passim.
Akyem Kotoku, 142, state, capital moved south after defeat by Asantehene Opoku

Ware (qv) in 1742. After 1831, claimed by British as part of the Protected Territory of the Gold Coast. Destination of many Asante refugees during civil wars, 1883–88.

Akyempem, 102, 103, 124, 134, Kumase *fekuo* created by Osei Tutu for Saben (qv). [AS/106]. Cf Owusu Afriyie.

Akyereko, 99, Twi *kyerɛ ɔko,* "battle leader." Title used by Ohwimhene Ntiamoa temp. Obiri Yeboa and Asantehene Osei Tutu. [AS/18].

Akyeremade, 122, section of Kumase, seat of Akyempemhene (qv).

"Akyim," *see* Asante Akyem

"Akyim," *see* Asiakwa

"Ama Come," *see* Amakom

"Amah Aduesan," *see* Amma Adusa

"Amah Come," *see* Amakom

"Amah Kwahan," *see* Amma Kwahan

"Amah Mansah," *see* Amma Mansa

"Amah Sewah," *see* Amma Sewaa

Amakom, 112, town, now E suburb of Kumase, belonging to the Adonten group. [AS/77]. Cf Akosa Yiadom.

"Amanchia," *see* Manhyia

Amaniampon, 113, 1st Mamponhene in late C17. In conflict with Twetwerudu (qv), and sought help from Osei Tutu (qv). Supporter of war of liberation from Denkyira, but died before start of campaign. Succeeded by Boahen Anantuo (qv).

"Amani Anpon," *see* Amaniampon

Amankwatia, 148, 151, Bantamahene (qv) and Kumase Kontihene (qv) under Asantehene Kofi Kakari (qv). Killed battle of Amoafo, 1874. *See* Wilks, 1993: 271–74.

Amankwatia Kwame, 154, 160, 176, 177, 178, 184, 191, became Bantamahene (qv) and Kumase Kontihene (qv) in 1888/9. Deported with Asantehene Agyeman Prempeh (qv) in 1896; d Seychelles 1907. *See* Wilks, 1993: 277 and 279.

Amankwatia Panin, 93, 101, 102, fl late C17 and early C18. *Akonnwasoani,* or stool carrier, to Osei Tutu (qv). Later made Bantamahene (qv) and Kumase Kontihene (qv). *See* Wilks, 1993: 243–55.

"Amanquatchia," *see* Amankwatia Panin

"Amanquatchia," *see* Amankwatia

"Amanquatchia," *see* Amankwatia Kwame

"Ambah," *see* Amma

"Ambah Abror," *see* Amma Abrɔɔ

"Ambah Adéder," *see* Amma Adedeɛ

"Ambah Adider," *see* Amma Adedeɛ

"Ambah Adjiman," *see* Amma Agyeman

"Ambah Akom," *see* Amma Kom

"Ambah Intoboo," *see* Amma Ntobu

"Ambah Intubu," *see* Amma Ntobu

"Ambah Kom," *see* Amma Kom

"Ambah Mansah," *see* Amma Mansa

"Ambah Sewah," *see* Amma Sewaa

Amma, 141, dau of Amma Kom (qv) and Kwasi Pra (qv); b ca 1894.

Amma Abrɔɔ, 140, dau of Ohene Afrewo (qv) and Kofi Kyem (qv).

Amma Adusa, 137, 6th dau of Yaa Kyaa (qv) and Kwasi Gyambibi (qv). Made Asantehemaa in 1927, as Kwadu Yaadom II.

Amma Adedeɛ, 145, 1st dau of Yaa Manfu (qv) and Adu (qv).

Amma Agyeman, 138, 141, 2nd dau of Akua Afriyie (qv) and Asafo Boakye (qv). Unmarried in 1896.

Amma Kom, 138, 141, 1st dau of Akua Afriyie (qv) and Asafo Boakye (qv). Married Kwasi Pra (qv).

Amma Kwahan, 176, 179, wife of Agyeman Prempeh.

Amma Mansa, 137, 139, 1st dau of Asantehemaa Yaa Kyaa (qv) and Kwasi Gyambibi (qv). Married 1) Kwaku Asokwa (qv), and 2) Kwabena Safo (qv).

Amma Ntobu, 142, dau of Opokuwaa (qv) and Apea Kɔɔ (qv).

Amma Sewaa, 128, 134, 135, according to *HAK* dau of Asantehemaa Kwadu Yaadom (qv) and Mamponhene Safo Katanka (qv). This, however, is queried in Wilks, 1975: 336–43, and McCaskie, 1995a: 180–83. Became Asantehemaa ca 1819. Married 1) Apaw Panin (qv), 2) Boakye Yam Panin (qv), 3) Okyere Kotoku (qv). Mother of, *int al,* Asantehemaa Afua Sapon (qv) and Asantehene Kwaku Dua Panin (qv).

"Ammaddie," 116, Asante *ntɔrɔ.*

Amoako, 99, village 20 mls NW. Placed under Domakwai by Obiri Yeboa [AS/134].

"Amoakùn," *see* Amoako

"Amo Come," *see* Amakom

Amponsa, 176, 180, Sanaahene, or treasurer, to Kumase Kontihene. Deported with Agyeman Prempeh (qv); died Elmina Castle, 1896.

"Amponsah," *see* Amponsa

Amponsem, 99, made Abrenkese Nyameanihene (qv) by Obiri Yeboa and placed in Domakwai (qv) under Saben (qv), late C17.

Amuamo Kyekye, 98, servant (tobacco pipe filler) of Akomadoma (qv), and mother of Awere (qv), whom Akomadoma gave to her son Obiri Yeboa (qv).

"Amuamochaichai," *see* Amuamo Kyekye

Anamenako, 145, section of Kumase, in Ankobea *fekuo*. Cf Owusu Ansa Panin. [AS/42].
Ananta, 139, military office created by Asantehene Opoku Ware (qv). [AS/3]. Cf Kwabena Safo.
"Anchi Adjaye," *see* Antwi Agyei Kumaa
"Anchiayami," *see* Ankyewa Nyame
"Anchioyami," *see* Ankyewa Nyame
"Anchiwar Nyame," *see* Ankyewa Nyame
"Anchoyami," *see* Ankyewa Nyame
"Anchu Adjaye, *see* Antwi Agyei Kumaa
"Anchuanyami," *see* Ankyewa Nyame
"Anchui," *see* Antwi, son of of Birempomaa Piesie
"Anchui," *see* Antwi, son of Bimma Dehyeε
Anim Kokobo, 93, 120, 122, Denkyirahene, fl 1650s and 1660s. Overlord of Oti Akenten (qv). Succeeded by Boa Amponsem (qv).
"Ankamady," 116, Asante *ntɔrɔ*.
Ankobea, 142, Kumase *fekuo* created by Asantehene Osei Kwadwo (qv). [AS/2]. Cf Kwaku Tawia.
"Ankobia," *see* Ankobea
Ankyewa Nyame, 85, 86, 87, 88, 89, 127, 146, 186, 187, apical ancestress of the Oyoko royals of Asante.
"Annamarkun," *see* Anamenako
"Annamil-ankum," *see* Anamenako
"Anni Cocobro," *see* Anim Kokobo
"Anni Kokobu," *see* Anim Kokobo
"Annifidier," 116, Asante *ntɔrɔ*.
"Annochi," *see* Okomfo Anokye
"Annowuo," *see* Anowu
"Annoyu," *see* Anowu
Anowu, 135, section of Kumase; cf Owusu Yaw; Atta.
"Anpon," *see* Amaniampon
Antoa, 90, 100, town, 8 mls NE, belonging to Kumase Adonten (qv). [AS/34]. Cf Saakodie Date.
"Antoi," *see* Antoa
Antwi, 145, 1st son of Bimma Dehyeε (qv) and Ntim (qv).
Antwi, 90, 127, 130, 188, son of Birempomaa Piesie (qv). Regarded as having ruled at Asantemanso (qv), and as younger brother of Akyampon Tenten (qv) and Twum (qv).
"Antwi Adjaye," *see* Antwi Agyei Kumaa
Antwi Agyei Kumaa, 179, 184, 191, Nkawiehene (qv). Deported to Seychelles; d 1908.
Anyim Panin, 91, 188, servant or bearer of Ofebiri Odeneho (qv), otherwise unidentified.
Anyinase, 88, Oyoko group, settled at Kokofu Adweso (qv), later establishing the Anyinase section of Kumase [AS/78].

Apa, 134, 135, Mampon town, 25 mls NE. Purchased by Asantehemaa Adoma Akosua early C19. Cf Owusu.
"Apaga," *see* Apagya
Apagya, 135, stool created by Asantehene Osei Kwame (qv) for Owusu Afriyie (qv), son of Asantehene Osei Kwadwo (qv). [AS/147].
"Apaou," *see* Apaw, husband of Odεe
"Apaou Pani," *see* Apaw Panin
"Apar," *see* Apa
Apaw, 142, Nkonsonhene at Kumase Apeboso (qv). Married Akua Nansewaa (qv); divorced.
Apaw, 136, Nkonsonhene at Kumase Apeboso, fl late C18 to early C19. Married Odεe (qv), dau of Asantehemaa Afua Sapon (qv), dsp. Succeeded by Abu (qv).
Apaw Panin, 135, son of Asantehene Kusi Obodum (qv). Made Nkonsonhene at Kumase Apeboso (qv). Married Asantehemaa Amma Sewaa (qv), and father of, *int al*, Asantehemaa Afua Sapon (qv).
Apea Koɔ, 142, 2nd husband of Opokuwaa (qv), otherwise unidentified.
Apeanin Kramo, 110, 120, Adansehene, attacked Kumase when army on campaign, and took captive, among others, Asantehemaa Nketewa Ntim Abamu (qv).
Apeboso, 135, 136, 142, section of Kumase, seat of Nkonson stool created by Asantehene Kusi Obodum (qv). Cf Abu, Abu (aka Owusu Penemo), Apaw, Apaw, Apaw Panin.
"Apia Kor," *see* Apea Koɔ
"Apiani Clamo," *see* Apeanin Kramo
"Apiani Cramo," *see* Apeanin Kramo
"Api Buoso," *see* Apeboso
"Appau," *see* Apaw, husband of Akua Nansewaa
"Appipladydie," 116, Asante *ntɔrɔ*.
"Apy Buosu," *see* Apeboso
"Arso Dagi, *see* Aso Daagye
"Arso Dāgifuor," *see* Aso Daagye
Asaaman, 87, 88, 92, 100, section of Kumase, former seat of Gyaasehene (Gyaase, qv) and of Oyoko Abohyenhene (qv).
Asaaman Kwadane, 146, section of Kumase, former seat of Oyoko Bremanhene (qv).
"Asabia Enchui," *see* Asabi Antwi
Asabi Antwi, 152, son of Asantehene Kwaku Dua Panin (qv). *Afenasoani*, promoted Asabihene in the Manwere *fekuo* by Asantehene Kofi Kakari (qv), ca 1872. Skilled negotiator. Killed 1889. [*Asante Seminar*, 6, 1976: 14–20].
"Asabie Boachie," *see* Asabi Boakye
Asabi Boakye, aka Kwame Serebo, 136, 137, son of Asantehene Kwaku Dua Panin (qv).

First occupant of the Asabi stool, added to the Manwere *fekuo* by his father. 3rd husband of Yaa Afere (qv), and father *int al* of Yaw Twereboanna (qv). Destooled, and banished, ca 1871, for adultery with wife of Manwerehene Brantuo (qv).

Asafo Agyei, 151, Dwabenhene, ca 1858–75, led migration into Gold Coast Colony in 1875, after attack by Asantehene Mensa Bonsu (qv); d 1876. *See* Wilks, 1975: 511–16, 606–608; Addo-Fening, 1973, passim.

Asafo Boakye, 138, 153, 154, 156, 157, 160, 163, 165, 176, 178, son of Asantehene Kwaku Dua Panin (qv). Married Akua Afriyie (qv), dau of Asantehemaa Afua Kobi (qv). Kumase Akwamuhene. Exiled in Seychelles; d Kumase 1925. *See Asantesɛm* 9, 1978: 15–27.

"Asafu Boachie," *see* Asafo Boakye
"Asafu Buachie," *see* Asafo Boakye
"Asafu Egay," *see* Asafo Agyei
Asakyiri, 87, a major Asante *abusua*.
"Asaman," *see* Asaaman
"Asaman Kwadan," *see* Asaaman Kwadane
Asamoa Kwame, 177, 179, 184, 191, Kumase Adumhene. Deported to Seychelles after 1900 war; died in exile, 1903.
"Asamoah Kwame," *see* Asamoa Kwame
"Asamoa Kwami," *see* Asamoa Kwame
"Asamoah Kwami," *see* Asamoa Kwame
Asante Akyem, 89, 103, northern lands of the Akyem incorporated into Asante in course of C18, and placed under various Kumase stools. Cf Dwansa, Asiedu Papaa Kese.
Asantemanso, 87, 88, 89, 90, 91, 115, 127, 131, 187, 188, 189, 15 mls SSE. Revered as place of origin of, *int al*, the Oyoko. *See* Shinnie and Shinnie, 1995 (1998), passim.
"Asarman," *see* Asaaman
"Asechire," *see* Asakyiri
Asenso Kofo, 106, 107, royal of Dwaben Annowo stool, migrated to Kumase as result of dispute. Given land and founded Adwumakaase (qv); aka Asenso Panin by contrast with his successor, Asenso Kuma. [AS/111].
"Asenso Pani," *see* Asenso Kofo
Asiakwa, 85, 186, Oyoko town now the capital of the Nifa Division of Akyem Abuakwa.
Asibi, 177, 179, Kokofuhene, succeeded Asibi I during early part of reign of Agyeman Prempeh. Deported to Seychelles after 1900 war. Baptised "George," repatriated 1924.
"Asibi, George," *see* Asibi
"Asie Bragnar," *see* Asiebrenya
"Asie Bragnare," *see* Asiebrenya

Asiebrenya, 112, 113, servant of Amakomhene Akosa Yiadom (qv). Executed for fostering hostility between Asantehene Osei Tutu (qv) and Amakomhene Akosa Yiadom.
Asiedu Papaa Kese, 103, 104, ruler of Hwereso, a town in Asante Akyem 18 mls E. Attacked and slain by Asantehene Osei Tutu (qv).
"Asin," *see* Assin
Asoamfo, 96, 97, 123, 124, hammock bearers to the Asantehene, belonging to the Suame section of Kumase. Cf Yaw Daani.
"Asoam-fuor", *see* Asoamfo
"Asocat," 107, unidentified place.
Aso Daagye, 131, dau of Birempomaa Piesie (qv).
Asokore, 87, 89, Asante *abusua*, here linked with Agona (qv).
Asokore, 140, town, 25 mls NE. Cf Gyima.
Asokore Mampon, 135, 4 mls ENE, seat of Kumase Nifahene. Cf Owusu Ansa. [AS/79].
Asokwa, 136, section of Kumase occupied by the Asantehene's hornblowers and traders, founded by defectors fron Denkyira ca 1700, cf. Nuamoa; Akwadan. [AS/1].
Asona, 87, a major Asante *abusua*.
"Assabidie," 116, Asante *ntɔrɔ*.
"Assachily," *see* Asakyiri
"Assafodie," 116, Asante *ntɔrɔ*, *see* Bosommuru.
"Assaman," *see* Asaaman
"Assamoah Kwami," *see* Asamoa Kwame
"Assani," 116, Asante *ntɔrɔ*.
"Assensoo Pani ," *see* Asanso Panin
"Assié dū Pāpā Kesié," *see* Asiedu Papaa Kese
Assin, 104, 115, 120, old Akan peoples of Pra valley region. Tributary to Denkyira (qv) in C17, and to Asante in C18. In dispute between Asante and British in C19, and finally became part of Gold Coast Colony in 1874.
"Assonchui," 139, unidentified place.
"Assokole," *see* Asokore
"Assokoli Mampon," *see* Asokore Mampon
"Assum Milamu," 144, unidentified, presumed section of Kumase.
"Assumanya Asantimansoo," *see* Asantemanso
"Assumgimmah," *see* Asumgyima
"Assumi Santimansu," *see* Asantemanso
"Assumya," *see* Asumenya
"Assumya Ashantimansu," *see* Asantemanso
"Assumya Ashanti-Mansuo," *see* Asantemanso
"Assunnāh," *see* Asona
Asukwa," *see* Asokwa
Asumenya, 90, old Asante division within which lies Asantemanso (qv).
Asumgyima, 134, 5th Mamponhene, fl mid-C18. 2nd husband of Aberefi Yaa (qv), and father of Asantehemaa Kwadu Yaadom (qv).

"Asumyia," *see* Asumenya
"Asumyia Ashantimansu," *see* Asantemanso
"Asumyia Santimansu," *see* Asantemanso
"Atar Sewah," *see* Ata Sewaa
Ata Sewaa, 143, dau of Akua Akrukruwaa (qv) and Owusu (qv). Married Adu (qv).
"Atina," *see* Tena
"Atnah," *see* Tena
Atta, 140, married Akosua Nsia (qv). Possibly ɔhene of Anowu (qv).
Atta Akwasi, 141, *afenasoani*, husband of Akua Badu (qv). Probably the Atta Kwasi who became Abanasehene in 1914.
"Atta Kular," *see* Attakora Panin
Attakora Panin, 134, 4th Mamponhene, fl early 1740s. 1st husband of Aberefi Yaa (qv). No children.
"Attinār," *see* Tena
"Attrah," *see* Tra
"Atutuo," *see* Oyko Atutuo
Atwea, 87, an Asante *abusua*, usually linked with Aduana as "Aduana ne Atwea."
Atwoma, 107, 108, district W and SW of Kumase.
"Awelli," *see* Awere
Awere, 98, 99, 102, 119, son of Amuamo Kyekye (qv). Given to Obiri Yeboa (qv), and made head of the new Soaduro *fekuo* (qv), subsequently renamed "Akwamu" (qv). Fought in 1st Domaa campaign in which Obiri Yeboa was slain.
Awere Gyamfuo 99, occupant of the Gyamfuo stool as head of the *Akrafoɔ*, i.e., "soul-washers," apparently then under Ohwimhene (qv). Cf Akradware.
Awiam, 87, town in the Oyoko Atutuo *fekuo* (qv).
"Awor-soum-marn," *see* Owusu Mmara
Awua Kokonin, 93, one of the 7 gunmen (*Konti Atuo Nson*) who accompanied Osei Tutu into exile in Denkyira. Later headed group of royal hornblowers.
"Awucolonilly," *see* Awua Kokonin
Aya Keseho, 102, 186, 187, 188, 189, 190, the royal mausoleum at Bantama, sacked by the British in 1896. It took its name from the Aya Kese, the large brass pan that stood outside it.
"Aya Kesihum," *see* Aya Keseho
"Aya Kesihun," *see* Aya Keseho
"Ayulis," *see* Awere
"Ayuomo," *see* Awiam

"Badoo," *see* Badu, dau of Pokuwaa
"Badoo," *see* Badu, dau of Akua Akrukruwaa
Badu, 142, 143, dau of Opokuwaa (qv). Married Yaw Afriyie (qv), Otikromhene; their son was Osei Kwadwo (qv), unsuccessful candidate for Golden Stool in 1931.
Badu, 143, 144, 3rd dau of Ata Sewaa (qv) and Adu (qv). Two children, father unknown.
"Banjahi," unidentified, but *see* Ofoase
Bantama, 102, 140, 185, 186, 187, 188, 189, 190, section of Kumase containing the royal mausoleum, and seat of the Bantamahene who was also Kumase Kontihene (qv) [AS/39, 40]. *See* Wilks, 1993: 241–92.
"Bantuo," *see* Brantuo
"Barū," 100, appointed by Obiri Yeboa (qv) to head the Gyaase (qv), otherwise unidentified.
"Bekwa," *see* Bekwai
Bekwai, 89, 90, 106, 124, 18 mls SSE, capital of the southern Asante Division of the same name.
"Bekwi," *see* Bekwai
Berayiye, 131, dau of Abena Gyapa (qv); sister of Gyeami (qv) and Manu (qv); mother of Adwowa Pinaman, 1st Kokofuhene.
Besease, 99, 15 mls SW. Town placed in Domakwai (qv) by Obiri Yeboa. Cf Aboagye Asare. [AS/105].
"Biletuo," *see* Bretuo
Bimma Dehyeε, 145, dau of Bimma Fita (qv). Married Ntim (qv).
"Bimafie," *see* Bimma Fie
Bimma Fie, 133, dau of Manu (qv); sister of, *int al*, Asantehene Osei Tutu (qv); and mother of Asantehemaa Nyaako Kusi Amoa (qv) and Otieku Atwedie (qv).
Bimma Fita, 145, dau of Abena Gyapa (qv) and mother of Bimma Dehyeε (qv).
"Bimma Dihie," *see* Bimma Dehyeε
Birago, 137, 140, 3rd dau of Asantehemaa Yaa Kyaa (qv) and Kwasi Gyambibi (qv). Married Hemanhene Kwabia (qv). Son Kwabena b 1896.
"Birempomaa Piecie," *see* Birempomaa Piesie
Birempomaa Piesie, 131, dau of Ankyewa Nyame (qv). Treated as mother of the four pre-Asante rulers, and as ancestress of all the subsequent Asantehenes and Asantehemaas.
"Bisay arsy," *see* Besease
"Blabu Ashanti," 89, named as "queen" of the clans (*mmusua*) said to have originated at Adansemanso (qv).
"Blae Blae," *see* Brebre
"Blaetuo," *see* Bretuo
"Blé Blé," *see* Brebre
Boa Amponsem, 93, 94, 104, Denkyirahene (d ca. 1694), succeeded Anim Kokobo (qv). Osei Tutu (qv), as a young man, was sent to his court as a security. *See* Wilks, 1993: 103–105, 109–111.

"Boachie," *see* Boakye Yam
"Boachi Attensa,", *see* Boakye Attansa
"Boachi Attonse," *see* Boakye Attansa
"Boachie Attansa," *see* Boakye Attansa
"Boachie Attonsa," *see* Boakye Attansa
"Boachie Dankua," *see* Boakye Dankwa
"Boachie Tin-Tin," *see* Boakye Tenten
"Boachie Yam Kuma," *see* Boakye Yam Kumaa
"Boachiwar," *see* Boakyewaa
Boadi, 136, ɛsɛn, or "crier" involved in illicit affair with Yaa Afere (qv). Father of Akosua Berenya (qv).
"Boadie," *see* Boadi
Boadu Akufu, 111, Denkyirahene in succession to Ntim Gyakari (qv).
"Boagy Assaillir," *see* Aboagye Asare
Boahen Anantuo, 106, 2nd Mamponhene, commander of Asante forces in invasion of Denykira, 1700. Said to have died of wounds.
"Boahin Nantuo," *see* Boahen Anantuo
"Boa Katia," *see* Boa Kwatia
Boa Kwatia, 113, 114, 145, described as both nephew of Obiri Yeboa (qv) and as son of Otwiwaa Keseɛ (qv). After the death of Osei Tutu (qv) in 1717, contested the succession with Opoku Ware (qv). See McCaskie, 1995a: 370 n. 10.
Boakye Attansa, 176, 177, 179, 184, 191, aka **Boakye Ansa**. Born ca 1848, son of Asantehene Kwaku Dua Panin (qv). Made Akomfodehene (qv). 2nd husband of Mamponhemaa Amma Sewaa Akoto. Exiled with Agyeman Prempeh in 1896. Died Seychelles 1906.
Boakye Dankwa, 136, 1st son of Asantehene Kwaku Dua Panin (qv). Adwomfuohene in Kumase, that is, head of the Mint at Eburaase, literally "under the forge." [Wilks 1975, 418–21]. Married ca 1855 Akua Afriyie (qv), dau of Afua Sapon (qv).
Boakye Tenten, 136, ɔkyeame on the Boakye Yam Panin Stool. 2nd husband of Asantehemaa Afua Kobi (qv). Adopted sons included Kwaku Fokuo (qv). [*Asante Seminar*, 6, 1976: 5–13].
Boakyewaa, 134, dau of Asantehemaa Akua Afriyie (qv) and Kwasi Koɔ (qv).
Boakye Yam, 100, appointed ɔhene of Nkwanta (qv) by Obiri Yeboa (qv). Said to have been an immigrant from Denkyira [AS/136].
Boakye Yam Kumaa, 135, Kumase Nkwantananhene and Hemanhene, d ca 1798. Son of Anyinasehene Akyampon Kwasi, and grandson of Nkwantananhene Boakye Yam (qv). 2nd husband of Asantehemaa Amma Sewaa (qv), and father of *int al*, Nkwantananhene Akyampon Kwasi (qv) and Asantehene Kwaku Dua Panin (qv). See Wilks, 1975: 366; Yarak, 1990: 254–268; McCaskie, 2000: 26–30.
Boansi Kofo, 111, Akyeamehene, but later made Oyoko Atutuohene, resident in the Adenkyemenaso section of Kumase (qv). Member of delegation to Akwamu to escort Osei Tutu to Kumase. Held a high military command in Osei Tutu's campaign against the Domaa.
"Boansi Kufu," *see* Boansi Kofo
"Boansy Kuffu," *see* Boansi Kofo
"Boapunsem," *see* Boa Amponsem
Boaten, 139, husband of Akua Afriyie (qv). From the Kumase Adonten, otherwise unidentified.
Boaten, 142, son of Akosua Berenya (qv) and Kwame Boakye (qv).
"Boatin," *see* Adonten Boaten, Adontenhene
"Boatin," *see* Boaten, son of Akosua Berenya
"Bodu Acafun," *see* Boadu Akufu
"Boemtamah," *see* Bantama
"Boensu," *see* Mensa Bonsu
"Bonsu," *see* Osei Tutu Kwame
Bonwire, 97, weaving centre 12 mls E. Cf Kan. [AS/148].
"Bon-you-ler," *see* Bonwire
Bosommuru, 116, major Asante ntɔrɔ, containing Adufudeɛ and Asafodeɛ. Among those belonging to the former were Asantehenes Osei Tutu, Osei Kwadwo, Osei Tutu Kwame, and Osei Yaw, and to the latter, Opoku Ware and Opoku Fofie.
Bosomtwe, 116, major Asante ntɔrɔ, here equated with "Agimadie."
"Bragnare," *see* Asiebreyaa
"Braituo," *see* Bretuo
"Brajoe," *see* Birago
Brantuo Kumaa, 136, Manwerehene. Cuckolded by Asabi Boakye (qv). Executed 1872. See McCaskie 2000: 58–62.
"Brayae," *see* Birago
"Brayiae," *see* Berayiye
Brebre, 120, 121, son of Adansehene Apeanin Kramo (qv). Reindorf, 1895: 52, has a story about a Berebere, wife of Denkyirahene Ntim Gyakari (qv), which has some common features.
Brefo Apaw, 93, one of the 7 gunmen (*Konti Atuo Nson*) who accompanied Osei Tutu into exile in Denkyira. Later made Akwaboahene. [AS/17].
"Bré Kuran, *see* Obirikoran
"Bremand," *see* Oyoko Breman
Bretuo, 87, 89, 187, a major *abusua* of Asante, and that of, among others, the

Mamponhenes. *See* McCaskie, 1985: passim.
"Brinpoma Piecie," *see* Birempomaa Piesie
"Bro Bay," *see* Brobi
Brobi, 140, Gyamasehene (qv), d in civil wars 1884–88. 1st husband of Ohene Afrewo (qv).
"Brofuapayou," *see* Brefo Apaw
"Bronkome," 135, part of Kumase Nkwantanan (qv).
"Broomaankama," *see* Burum Ankombra
"Buabodro," *see* Yamoa
"Bua Punsem," *see* Boa Amponsem
"Buachi Attansah," *see* Boakye Attansa
Burum Ankombra, 94, ruler of the Sehwi. Attacked and defeated by Denkyirahene Boa Amponsem (qv), with the aid of Osei Tutu (qv) and his followers who insisted on retaining the booty they acquired. Bowdich, 1819: 236–37, refers to the defeat of "the king Boomancumma" of Sehwi. If this is the same ruler, then Bowdich's chronology was in error.
"Busukony," 116, asante *ntɔrɔ*, aka "Akom."
"Busumchui," *see* Bosomtwe
"Busumulu Julah," *see* Kwaku Bosommuru Dwira

"Chen Chen Heni," *see* Kyenkyenhene
"Chen Chen Roo," *see* Twetwerudu
"Chen Chen Roulou," *see* Twetwerudu
"Chen Chen Rulu," *see* Twetwerudu
"Choom," *see* Twum
"Chromaclor," *see* Kyiroma
"Chum," *see* Twum
"Chumas," *see* Atwoma
"Chume," *see* Twum
"Chundroassi," *see* Twumaduase
"Chwa-fuor," *see* Twafuo
"Chwafuor Taby," *see* Tabiri
"Contanasi," *see* Kuntanase
"Contenasy," *see* Kuntanase
"Contile," *see* Konti
"Contileheni," *see* Konti

Daaboase, 124, section of Kumase.
Daako, 146, son(s) of Akua Ago (qv), and pat grandson(s) of Obiri Yeboa (qv). The text in *HAK* reads, "Dār Kun Dārkun," and tradition has it that Akua Ago had two sons of this name, both of whom contested the kingship on the death of Opoku Ware in 1750. The tradition was reported in Reindorf, 1895: 69. In the event Kusi Obodum was chosen and Daako, or the Daakos, took refuge in Baoule (present-day Côte d'Ivoire). *See* McCaskie, 1995a: 175–77.

Dadease, 89, 90, town, 11 mls NE, said to have formerly been province of Dwaben (qv), but later relocated to the Kokofu area (qv).
"Dadiasi," *see* Dadease
"Dadiesi," *see* Dadease
Dako, 87, 88, 125, 183, Akan *abusua* always linked with Oyoko (qv).
"Daku," *see* Dako (*abusua*)
"Dankira," *see* Denkyira
"Dāou Daou," 108, presumably the Awu Dawu, among the Denkyira who assisted Osei Tutu in the Asante war of liberation, 1700–01, and placed under Amankwatia Panin (qv). Cf Agyeibi, Kwakwa Bene, Yim Awere.
"Darboasy," *see* Daaboase
"Dar-boasy," *see* Daaboase
"Darkun," *see* Daako
"Dār Kun Dārkun," *see* Daako
"Denkera," *see* Denkyira
Denkyira, 93, 94, 95, 102, 103, 104, 105, 106, 107, 108, 109, 110, 111, 115, 120, 121, 122, dominant regional power NW and SE of Moinsi Hills from mid-C17 until war of 1700–01 when coalition led by Osei Tutu (qv) destroyed its power. Cf Anyim Kokobo, Boa Amponsem, Boadu Akufu, Ntim Gyakari.
"Dinkira," *see* Denkyira
"Docu," *see* Doku
Doku, 93, stool carrier to Manu (qv), and mother of Amankwatia Panin (qv).
"Doma," *see* Domaa
Domaa, the three Domaa wars: First, **96, 97**, Oti Akenten (qv) involved in boundary dispute with Domaahene Adom Kusi (qv), who abandoned his lands and resettled at Suntreso (qv). Second, **97, 98, 99, 105, 110**, Obiri Yeboa (qv) planned to drive Adom Kusi off the Suntreso lands. The attack failed and Obiri Yeboa was killed as predicted by Agonahene and priest Yamoa (qv). Third, **101, 102**, Osei Tutu (qv) swore to revenge the death of Obiri Yeboa. Adom Kusi was defeated and slain. His people dispersed, many settling far to the northwest at Abesim (qv), Drobo, etc, to become part of the new Gyaman state.
"Domāh-Kwaïr," *see* Domakwai
Domakwai, 99, 103, *fekuo* created by Obiri Yeboa and placed under his son, Saben (qv). After death of Obiri Yeboa, *fekuo* renamed Akyempem (qv), and Domakwai divided into Benkum and Nifa, both within Akyempem.
"Doma Kwayir," *see* Domakwai
Dominase, 137, section of Kumase, seat of Kyidomhene.

"Domar," *see* Domaa
"Dominasie," *see* Dominase
"Dommar," *see* Domaa
"Dorlit," **100**, *odekuro* appointed to position under Akyempem by Obiri Yeboa (qv).
"Dossam," **101**, unidentified.
Dwaaso, 103, 104, town, 37 mls ESE, in Asante Akyem.
Dwaben, 89, 90, 104, 105, 106, 135, 148, 151, 157, 163, 16 mls NE, capital of the Northeastern Asante Division of the same name. Cf Adakwa Yiadom, Akuamoa Panin, Asafo Agyei, Dwaben Sewaa.
Dwabenmma, 90, early settlement of the Dako (qv) who founded Nsuta (qv).
Dwaben Sewaa, 176, 180, wife of Kumase Akyempemhene Kofi Boakye (qv). Accompanied Agyeman Prempeh into exile in Elmina, 1896.
Dwaberem, 188, the Great Market of Kumase, centre of urban life.
Dwansa, 89, town in Asante Akyem (qv), 35 mls E.
Dwum, 87, Asante *abusua*, here paired with Asona (qv).

Edweso, 178, 179, 180, 184, town, 12 mls E, capital of powerful Kumase sub-division of the same name. Cf Kofi Afrani.
Effiduase, 91, district and town, 17 mls NE, seat of Mampon Nifahene.
"Efriyae," *see* Owusu Afriyie, son of Osei Tutu (qv)
"Eh-Hwim-diclo," *see* Ohwim
"Ekua Efriyae," *see* Akua Afriyie, Asantehemaa
Ekuona, 87, Asante *abusua*, linked with Asokore (qv).
"Ekuonah," *see* Ekuona
Elmina, 109, 110, 158, 164, 165, 176, 179, port on the Guinea Coast, involved in C15 in long distance trade with Europe and the Western Sudan. Tributary of Denkyira (qv) in C17, and of Asante in C18. In 1874 became part of the British Colony of the Gold Coast. Fort used to confine Asante political prisoners after 1896. See DeCorse, 2001.
Esereso, 88, 6 mls SSE, section of Oyoko Breman (qv).
"Essen," 86, heralded the arrival of Ankyewa Nyame (qv) from the sky at Asantemanso. See Twi *ɛsɛn*, "herald, messenger."

"Fa-Ba-Wa-li," *see* Fabaware
Fabaware, 88, 8 mls ENE. Old settlement of Oyoko Breman (qv). Land said to be given by Osei Tutu to his wife Ayodeneho, whose son Oti Awere founded Otikrom (qv). [AS/163].
Fafrahamoɔ, 123, Atwoma forest, SSW of Kumase.
Fante, 122, coastal peoples made tributary to Asante in 1807, but became part of the British Protected Territory of the Gold Coast in 1831.
"Fanti," *see* Fante
"Fantiheni," 96, possibly the Nfantihene, though this stool is regarded as having been created only in the mid-C18. [AS/68]
"Febredinhun," *see* Ofebiri Odeneho
"Febydinun," *see* Ofebiri Odeneho
Feyiase, 100, 108, town placed under Domakwai (qv) by Obiri Yeboa. [AS/74].
"Féyiasi," *see* Feyiase
"Fredua," *see* Fredua Agyeman, Kenyasehene
Fredua Agyeman, 100, 2nd *ɔhene* of Kenyase (qv). Considered as successor to Obiri Yeboa (qv), but his terms unacceptable. Fought in 2nd and 3rd Domaa wars (qv) and against Denkyira in 1700–01 [AS/110].
Fredua Agyeman, 138, son of Akua Afriyie (qv) and Asafo Boakye (qv).
"Fredua Ajiman," *see* Kwaku Dua Panin
"Fredua Ajiman," *see* Fredua Agyeman

"Gamby," *see* Gyeami
"Garmarsi," *see* Gyamase
"Gembi," *see* Gyeami
"Gharci," *see* Gyaase
"Gharsiwah Primcor," *see* Gyaasewa
"Gia buor Suor," 102, unidentified, possibly founded by Gyedu Kumanin (qv).
"Gimmah," *see* Gyima
"Glusuo," *see* Osei Kwaku Goroso
"Guansah," *see* Dwansa
"Guarcun," *see* Nyaako Kusi Amoa
"Guarcun Kussi Amua," *see* Nyaako Kusi Amoa
"Guarku Kussi Amua," *see* Nyaako Kusi Amoa
Gyaase, 100, 106, 125, literally "the hearth": Kumase *fekuo* under the titular leadership of the Saamanhene. [AS/52]. Includes the Gyaasewa (qv). Cf Baru.
Gyaasewa, 96, nicknamed Pinanko. Large organisation within the Gyaase (qv), comprising many of the administrative agencies of the state. *See* Wilks, 1975: 469–70; McCaskie, 1995a: 284. The development of the Gyaasewa is usually associated with Asantehene Opoku Ware (qv), but the implication here is that its origins are to be found in the reign of Oti Akenten (qv).

Gyakye, 186, town 10 mls SE, said to be home of descendants of "Adoofa," (qv).
"Gyakyi," *see* Gyakye
Gyamase, 91, 140, 146, 188, 24 mls NNE. Seat of Mampon Benkumhene. Cf Adu Gyamfi; Brobi; Yaw Sekyere.
Gyeami, 100, 131, 189, Kokofuhene, son of Abena Gyapa (qv), and brother of Manu (qv). Chosen to succeed Obiri Yeboa (qv), but declined.
Gyedu Kumanin, 93, 102, one of the 7 gunmen (*Konti Atuo Nson*) who accompanied Osei Tutu into exile in Denkyira. Later made Amakye Barihene. [AS/175].
Gyima, 140, ɔhene of Asokore (qv). Married Kwadu (qv), dau of Yaa Kyaa (qv).

Heman, 140, town, 14 mls NE, under the Kumase Benkum. [AS/170]. Cf Kwabia.
"Henry Boaten," *see* Kwame Boaten, Kyidomhene
"Henry Kwami Boaten," *see* Kwame Boaten, Kyidomhene
Hia, 103, *fekuo* created by Osei Tutu (qv) for Okra Saben Domse (qv), son of Obiri Yeboa (qv). Placed under Kumase Akyempemhene Owusu Afriyie (qv). [AS/154].
"Hiau," *see* Hiawu
Hiawu, 141, *fekuo* in the Kumase Gyaase, with responsibilities in the royal household.
"Himan," *see* Heman
"Hinar," *see* Hia
"Hry. Boaten," *see* Kwame Boaten, Kyidomhene

"Ignarsi," *see* Anyinase
"Incanphékesier," *see* Nkofe
"Inkatia," 116, Asante ntɔrɔ.
"Inkatia Otimabamu," *see* Nketewa Ntim Abamu
"Inkatiar Otim," *see* Nketewa Ntim Abamu
"Inkatiar Otim Abamu," *see* Nketewa Ntim Abamu
"Inkatiar Ottim," *see* Nketewa Ntim Abamu
"Inkransan," *see* Nkoransa
"Inkrunba," *see* Nkruma
"Inkukuah," *see* Nkukuwa
"Inkwanta Boachie," *see* Boakye Yam
"In-Kwa-Ta-Nan," *see* Nkwantanan
"Inkwayulaes," *see* Nkawie
"In-nua-soo," 96, unidentified.
"Insua," 86, unidentified, but cf Twi *asua*, a stream.
"Insuasie," *see* Nsuase
"Insuta," *see* Nsuta
"Insūtar," *see* Nsuta

"Intim," *see* Ntim Gyakari
"Intimi Jakale," *see* Ntim Gyakari
"Intimi Jakali," *see* Ntim Gyakari
"Intolly Awinsin," *see* Ntori Hwensin

"Jabraim," *see* Dwaberem
"Jaedukumanin," *see* Gyedu Kumanin
"Jamarsi," *see* Gyamase
"Jamasi," *see* Gyamase
"Jarsi," *see* Gyaase
"Jemmie," *see* Gyeami
"Juaben Serwah," *see* Dwaben Sewaa
"Juabin," *see* Dwaben
"Juabin Serwah," *see* Dwaben Sewaa
"Juarsi," *see* Dwaaso
"Jubin," *see* Kwame Dwuben
"Jume," *see* Dwum

Kaase, 96, 111, 134, town 3 mls SE, now within Kumase. Seat of the Kaasehene. Organised as Kumase *fekuo* by Oti Akenten (qv), apparently with the title "Abontemu." Town later ravaged by Asantehene Osei Tutu (qv) who accused Kaase royals of having insulted him. [AS/35]. Cf Kwasi Koɔ.
"Kakari," *see* Kofi Kakari
"Kām Kām," *see* Kankam
"Ka-n," *see* Kan
Kan, 97, of Bonwire (qv). Several later Bonwirehenes bore this name.
Kankam, 136, Abrenkese Nyameanihene (qv). Married Yaa Afere (qv), dau of Asantehemaa Afua Sapon (qv).
"Kantikrono," *see* Kantinkronu
Kantinkronu, 186, village, 5 mls E.
"Karkari," *see* Kofi Kakari
"Karsi," *see* Kaase
"Karsians," *see* Kaase
"Karsy," *see* Kaase
"Kenassie," *see* Kenyase
"Kenassy," *see* Kenyase
Kenyase, 87, 100, 187, town of the Oyoko Abohyen group, 6 mls NE. Cf Fredua Agyeman [AS/110].
"Kharsi," *see* Kaase
"Kidom," *see* Kyidom
"Kobia Amanphie," *see* Kwabia Anwafi
"Kobia Anguanfi," *see* Kwabia Anwanfi
"Kobia Awuanfi," *see* Kwabia Anwanfi
"Kobia Gwanfi," *see* Kwabia Anwanfi
"Kobia Kwanfi," *see* Kwabia Anwanfi
"Kobia wanphie," *see* Kwabia Anwanfi
"Kobinā Annae," *see* Kwabena Anni
"Kobina Asafu," *see* Kwabena Safo
"Kobina Chrechuae," *see* Kwabena Kyeretwe

"Kobinah," see Kwabena, son of Akosua Manhyia
"Kobinah Anni," see Kwabena Anin
"Kobinah Annii," see Kwabena Anin
"Kodjoe," see Kwadwo Tene
"Kodjoe," see Kwadwo Owusu Ansa
"Kodjoe Broenir," see Kwadwo Broni
"Kodjoe Fofie," see Kwadwo Fofie Baakompra
"Kodjoe Konson Kwar," 144, husband of Akua Ntim (qv), otherwise unidentified.
"Kodjoe Kroom," see Kwadwokrom
"Kodjoe Tufor," see Kwadwo Tufuo
Kofi Afrani, 176, 177, 178, 184, 191, aka Afrani Ababio, (i.e. Afrani II). Edwesohene. Taken captive with Agyeman Prempeh to Elmina in 1896. Died Seychelles 1915.
"Kofi Amanfun," 98, made head of the Akradware (qv) by Obiri Yeboa (qv), under Awere (qv).
"Kofi Chem," see Kofi Kyem
"Kofi Fofea," see Kofi Fofie Kaserepa
"Kofi Fofieh," see Kofi Fofie Kaserepa
Kofi Fofie Kaserepa, 178, 179, 184, Nkonsonhene (qv) in Kumase Gyaase. Fought in 1900 war. Exiled to Seychelles, died at sea 1924. [AS/47.].
"Kofi In-Tea," see Kofi Nti
Kofi Kakari, 110, 122, 128, 132, 136, 148, 151, 157, 2nd son of Asantehemaa Afua Kobi (qv) and Kofi Nti (qv), and brother of *int al* Mensa Bonsu (qv) and Yaa Kyaa (qv). Made Asantehene in 1867. Forced from office 1874. Succeeded by brother, Mensa Bonsu, on whose destoolment in 1883, Kofi Kakari again contested, but unsuccessfully, the Golden Stool. Kwaku Dua Kumaa (qv), 1st son of Yaa Kyaa, became Asantehene in April 1884, but died in early June. Kofi Kakari was assassinated on 24 June, thus opening the way for Yaa Kyaa to advance the candidacy of her younger son, Agyeman Prempeh. See Ch 1, *supra*, 9–11.
"Kofi Karkari", see Kofi Kakari
Kofi Kumaa, 177, 179, 184, 191, Takyimantiahene (qv). Fought in 1900 war, died in exile in Seychelles, 1904.
"Kofi Kumah," see Kofi Kumaa
Kofi Kyem, 140, Kumase *okyamfo* (shield-bearer) and Adumasahene at Ofuase Senfi. 2nd husband of Ohene Afrewo (qv). Their dau Amma Sewaa Nyaako became Asantehemaa, d 1977.
"Kofi Mansa," see Kofi Mensa
Kofi Mensa, 136, only surviving child of Akua Afriyie (qv) and Boakye Dankwa (qv). B ca 1857, d 1873, see McCaskie, 1974: 227.

"Kofi Mensah," 176, 180, child, subject of Kumase Akwamuhene, joined Asante prisoners in Elmina.
Kofi Nti, 136, grandson of Asantehene Osei Kwadwo (qv); 1st husband of Asantehemaa Afua Kobi (qv); and father of heir-apparent Kwabena Anin (qv), Asantehenes Kofi Kakari (qv) and Mensa Bonsu (qv), Asantehemaa Yaa Kyaa (qv), and Akua Afriyie (qv). Boakye Yam Panin *ɔkyeame*. [AS/73], and see Wilks, 1993: 337, 353–57.
Kofi Subri, aka Kofi Boakye, aka Boakye Yam, 154, 160, 176, 177, 178, 184, 191, son of Kwaku Dua Panin (qv), born ca 1836. Became Kumase Akyempemhene temp Mensa Bonsu. 1st husband of Mamponhemaa Amma Sewaa Akoto. Their son, Kwaku Dua Mampon supported British in 1900 war and was made Kumase Atipinhene in succession to Kwame Boakye (qv). Kofi Subri abducted with Agyeman Prempeh in 1896 (but wrongly referred to as "Kwame Subri" in Agyeman Prempeh's letter of 13 April 1925. See *supra* 176). Died in Seychelles 1901.
"Kojo Anchu," see Kwadwo Antwi
"Kojo Anchwi," see Kwadwo Antwi
"Kojo Antwi," see Kwadwo Antwi
"Kojo Antwi-Adjai," see Antwi Agyei Kumaa
"Kojo Apia," see Kwadwo Apea
"Kojo Apiah," see Kwadwo Apea
"Kojo Appia," see Kwadwo Apea
"Kojo Appiah," see Kwadwo Apea
"Kojokroemdiclo," 99, literally, *odekuro* of Kwadwokrom (qv).
"Kojokulom," see Kwadwokrom
"Kojo Tufour," see Kwadwo Tufuo
"Kokobin," see Kwakwa Bene
"Kokobinny," see Kwakwa Bene
"Kokofoo," see Kokofu
Kokofu, 89, 90, 91, 92, 96, 97, 100, 106, 124, 133, 159, 165, 176, 179, 188, 189, 15 mls SE. Capital of the Asante Division of the same name. Seat of Kokofuhene who belongs to same Oyoko lineage as Asantehene. Cf Asibi.
Kokofu Adwamamu, 100, placed by Obiri Yeboa under Domakwai (qv).
Kokofu Adweso, 88, village on outskirts of Kokofu (qv), settled by Oyoko group that later founded Anyinase (qv). [AS/78].
"Kokofu ajummah moo," see Kokofu Adwamamu
"Kokofuo," see Kokofu
"Kokor," see Kokofu
"Kokor Affuo," see Kokofu
"Kokor-Afuome," see Kokofu
Komfo Berewaa, 135, child of Akua Sewaa (qv).

Kona, 99, *odekuro*, placed by Obiri Yeboa in Domakwai *fekuo* (qv).
"Konfuōr Briwah," *see* Komfo Berewaa
Konti, aka Kronti, 96, 102, 103, 106, 124, 125, 178, title of top ranking military commander in Kumase. Seat in Bantama (qv). Cf Amankwatia Panin; Amankwatia; Amankwatia Kwame.
"Koobina Jummor," *see* Kwabena Dwumo
"Kotorku," *see* Akyem Kotoku
"Kragualier," *see* Akradware
"Kra Kohue," 140, dau of Ohene Afrewo (qv) and Brobi (qv).
"Kra Korhuer," *see* "Kra Kohue"
Krapa, 137, son of Asantehene Kwaku Dua Panin (qv). Married Akua Afriyie (qv). Kumase Kyidomhene, d 1874, at battle of Amoafo. Children included Ohene Afrewo (qv).
"Krapah," *see* Krapa
"Krapunsem," *see* Okra Amponsem
Kuntanase, 88, 106, old Oyoko town 16 mls SE above Lake Bosomtwe.
"Kūntror," 86, Asante *suman* associated with Ankyewa Nyame (qv) and Asantemanso (qv). Cf Kwabena.
Kusi Obodum, 110, 128, 133, 135, son of Nketewa Ntim Abamu (qv). Asantehene 1750, in succession to Opoku Ware. A dissolute life style and failing health led to his abdication in 1764. Died a few months later. *See* Fynn, 1965: passim.
"Kusiobordum," *see* Kusi Obodum
"Kussi," 141, 1st son of Kwadu (qv) and Subri (qv).
"Kussie," *see* Kusi Obodum
"Kussi Obodum," *see* Kusi Obodum
"Kussi Obordum," *see* Kusi Obodum
"Kutu," *see* Adwowa Kutu
Kwabena, 86, this passage is very difficult to read. Kwabena is the name of a *suman*, or spirit, obviously closely associated with Ankyewa Nyame and Asantemanso, and is presumably the "Santeman Kobina" known to Rattray [1923: 127, 129, 132; 1929: 144]. "The old Queen Mother [of Asantemanso]," Rattray wrote, "said it was the soul of the leaves and the trees and of the earth at that spot."
Kwabena, 141, 2nd son of Akosua Manhyia (qv) and Yaw Daani (qv); b ca 1895.
Kwabena Agyeikum, 176, 178, Kumase Oyokohene in Oyoko Atutuo group (qv). Went into exile with Agyeman Prempeh (qv) in 1896; d 1897.
Kwabena Anin, 122, 136, 183, 1st child of Asantehemaa Afua Kobi (qv) and Kofi Nti (qv). Made heir-apparent in succession to Osei Kwadwo (qv) but died before succeeding.
Kwabena Anni, 142, 1st son of Afua Mprakyere (qv) and "Yaw Berkun" (qv).
Kwabena Dwumo, 139, 15th Mamponhene. 1st husband of Akua Fokuo (qv). Supreme commander of Asante armies 1874; died ca 1881.
"Kwabena Kuffour," 184, 'Servant' of Kofi Fofie Kaserepa (qv).
Kwabena Kyeretwe, 137, 2nd son of Asantehemaa Yaa Kyaa (qv) and Kwasi Abayie (qv), b ca 1863. Candidate for Asantehene on death of elder brother Kwaku Dua Kumaa (qv), but rejected for abrasive personality.
Kwabena Safo, 139, Anantahene (qv). 2nd husband of Amma Mansa (qv). Father of Akosua Aberewaa (qv) and Kwadwo Owusu Ansa (qv).
Kwabia, 140, ɔhene of Heman (qv) 1890s. Husband of Birago (qv).
Kwabia Anwanfi, 90, 91, 92, 127, 188, said to have been son of Okyeremaa (qv), and elder brother of Oti Akenten, his successor. *Abusuatiri*, or "clan" head of the Oyoko of Asantemanso (qv) and Kokofu (qv). *See* Reindorf, 1895: 47, 346b.
"Kwabiah," *see* Kwabia
"Kwabinah," *see* Kwabena
Kwadu, 136, 141, dau of Yaa Afere (qv) and Nyameanihene Kankam (qv). Married Subri (qv).
Kwadu, 137, 140, dau of Yaa Kyaa (qv) and Kwasi Gyambibi (qv). Married Gyima (qv).
"Kwadu," *see* Kwadu Yaadom
Kwadu (Konadu) Yaadom, 122, 128, 134, 135, 142, 143, Asantehemaa, b ca 1752, d 1809. Dau of Aberefi Yaa (qv) and Mamponhene Asumgyima (qv). According to *HAK*, mother of 11 children including four Asantehenes, Osei Kwame (qv), Opoku Fofie (qv), Osei Tutu Kwame (qv), and Osei Yaw (qv); three who died as heir-apparents, Opoku Kwame (qv), Osei Kofi (qv), and Osei Badu (qv); and two Asantehemaas, Amma Sewaa (qv) and Yaa Dufie (qv). This, however, appears chronologically impossible; *see* Wilks 1975: 336–43; McCaskie 1995a: 180–83, and 1995b: 373–76; *Asantesεm*, 11, 1979: 5–13, 14–17, 54–56.
Kwadu (Konadu) Yaadom II, *see* Amma Adusa
"Kwadu Yadom," *see* Kwadu Yaadom
"Kwadua," *see* Kwaku Dua Panin
Kwadwo Antwi, 177, 179, 184, 191, Kontihene of Offinso (qv). Deported after 1900 war. Died Seychelles, 1906.

Concordance

Kwadwo Apea, 176, 177, 178, 181, 184, 191, Offinsohene (qv). Deported with Agyeman Prempeh in 1896. Died Seychelles, 1922.

Kwadwo Broni, 142, son of Pokua (qv) and Apea Kɔ (qv), otherwise unidentified.

Kwadwo Fofie Baakompra, 137, senior ranking ɔkyeame. Said to have given Agyeman Prempeh his nickname. See above, Ch 1, 7.

Kwadwokrom, 99, 107, section of Kumase; according to tradition [AS/191] founded temp Obiri Yeboa (qv) by a hunter, Kwadwo Tene, who was succeeded by his nephew, Abrefa Panin (qv). Cf Agyeibi; Otieku Atwedie.

Kwadwo Owusu Ansa, 139, aka Henry Owusu Ansa. Son of Amma Mansa (qv) and Kwabena Safo (qv); b 1895; served as secretary to Agyeman Prempeh on his return from exile in 1924; d 1978.

Kwadwo Tufuo, 135, son of Akua Sewaa (qv).

Kwadwo Tufuo, 155, 156, 161, 162, 180, 184, 191, member of embassy to London, 1895–96. Exiled to Sierra Leone. Died Seychelles. May be the Kwadwo Tufuo son of Akua Sewaa (qv).

"Kwajoe Appia," see Kwadwo Apea

"Kwajum," 144, husband of Yaa Dufie, dau of Adwowa Kutu (qv). Name presumed to be Kwadwom, but unidentified.

Kwakru, 95, perhaps Akua Kuru, "queen," presumably obaapanin, of Takyiman (qv) in Atwoma (qv). Married, and slain, by Osei Tutu (qv).

Kwaku Asokwa, 139, ɔhene of "Assonchui," (unidentified). 1st husband of Amma Mansa (qv).

"Kwaku Asukwa," see Kwaku Asokwa

Kwaku Bosommuru Dwira, 152, soul-washer (akradwareni), favourite of Asantehene Kofi Kakari and given charge of the Akomfode Stool in Manwere fekuo; died 1887.

"Kwakudua," see Kwaku Dua Kumaa

"Kwakudua," see Kwaku Dua

Kwaku Dua, 138, son of Akua Afriyie (qv) and Asafo Boakye (qv).

"Kwakudua I," 142, son of Akosua Berenya (qv) and Kwame Boakye (qv).

"Kwakudua II," 142, son of Akosua Berenya (qv) and Kwame Boakye (qv).

"Kwakudua II," see Kwaku Dua Kumaa

"Kwakudua III," see Agyeman Prempeh

"Kwakudua Asamu," 135, see Kwaku Dua Panin

"Kwakudua Asamu," 137, see Agyeman Prempeh

Kwaku Dua Kumaa, aka Agyeman Kofi, 123, 128, 137, 152, 155, 161, 1st son of Asantehemaa Yaa Kyaa (qv) and Kwasi Abayie (qv). Heir-apparent to Mensa Bonsu (qv), b ca 1861. Made Asantehene April 1884, but died early June, probably of smallpox.

Kwaku Dua Panin, aka Kwaku Dua Asamu, 88, 122, 128, 135, 137, son of Asantehemaa Amma Sewaa (qv) and Boakye Yam Kumaa (qv). Named Fredua Agyeman, but enstooled as Asantehene Kwaku Dua in 1834. Died in office 1867. Of the sons of Kwaku Dua Panin who married into the royal family, the following are noted: Asabi Antwi (qv), Asafo Boakye (qv), Boakye Attansa (qv), Boakye Dankwa (qv), Kofi Subri (qv), Krapa (qv), Kwame Boakye (qv), Kwasi Abayie (qv), and Kwasi Gyambibi (qv).

Kwaku Fokuo, 154, 155, 158, 159, 160, 161, 164, 176, 177, 179, 184, 191, ɔkyeame on the Boakye Yam Panin stool. Member of embassy to London 1895–96. Died in exile in Seychelles, 1900.

Kwaku Nantwi, 154, 160, 177, 179, 184, 191, ɔkyeame on the Akankade stool created for Adu Twum (qv). Died Seychelles, 1908.

Kwaku Nsia, 177, 179, 184, 191, ɔhene of Akuropon (qv). Fought in 1900 war, exiled to Seychelles, d 1911. [AS/199].

Kwaku Owusu, 139, 176, 178, ɔkyeame on the Bosommuru Fabem stool. Married Akua Bakoma (qv), and father, int al, of Asantehene Osei Agyeman Prempeh II (qv). Deported by British to Seychelles, 1896. [AS/174].

Kwaku Pimpim, 142, son of Asantehemaa Yaa Dufie (qv) and Nkonsonhene Abu aka Owusu Penemo (qv). Created first Mamesenehene by Asantehene Osei Tutu Kwame (qv) in reward for his services in the Gyaman campaign of 1818–19 [AS/172, 203]. See Wilks, 1975: 354–55; 358.

"Kwaku Pipim," see Kwaku Pimpim

"Kwaku Taeyua," see Kwaku Tawia

Kwaku Tawia, 142, Kumase Ankobeahene temp Asantehenes Kwaku Dua Panin (qv) and Kofi Kakari. Remembered for his wealth. Married Pokuwaa (qv), dau of Adwowa Sewaa (qv). 1st child Agyeikum (qv). [AS/2].

"Kwaku Ysu," see Kwaku Owusu

Kwakwa Bene, 107, Denkyira ɔbirɛmpɔn, defected to Osei Tutu prior to Denkyira war of 1701. Resettled at Kwadwokrom (qv), and became Atwoma Agogohene. [AS/135]. Cf Agyeibi; Yim Awere.

"Kwakwabin," see Kwakwa Bene

Kwaman, 104, name of the Kumase area before the establishment of the Asante capital there.

Kwame Afrifa, 177, 179, 184, 191, Toasehene (qv). Deported after 1900 war. Died Seychelles, 1907.
"Kwame Afrifra," *see* Kwame Afrifa
Kwame Amankwatia, aka Amankwatia Kwame, 154, 160, 176, 177, 178, 180, 184, 191, b late 1830s. Took office as Bantamahene/Kumase Kontihene ca 1888. Seized with Agyeman Prempeh in 1896 and exiled to Elmina. Joined by wives Akyamaa (qv) and Yaa Sukwa (qv) in Sierra Leone; d Seychelles 1907.
Kwame Apea Osukye, 166, 176, 177, 178, 184, 191, 21st Mamponhene. Abducted with Agyeman Prempeh 1896. Died in Seychelles 1911.
Kwame Boakye, 141, 162, 3rd husband of Akosua Berenya (qv). Presumably the Atipinhene of this name; b ca 1850, son of Asantehene Kwaku Dua Panin (qv). Fought in 1900 war, imprisoned in Elmina.
Kwame Boaten, 155, 158, 159, 161, 164, 176, 177, 179, 184, 191, Kumase Kyidomhene. Appointed head of 1895–96 embassy to London; arrested by British July 1896; deported to Sierra Leone; died in Seychelles, 1918. [AS/158]: *Asantesem,* 8, 1978: 12–21.
Kwame Boaten, 135, 183, royal, son of Asantehemaa Amma Sewaa (qv) and Okyere Kotoku (qv).
Kwame Dwuben, 139, made *ɔkyeame* on the Butuakwa Stool, 1873. 2nd husband of Akua Fokuo (qv). Opposed choice of Agyeman Prempeh as Asantehene. Executed 1887 for cruelty.
Kwame Gyansa, 140, 178, 179, 184, 191, Apemanimhene in the Kumase Konti. Husband of Akyaa (qv), dau of Asantehemaa Yaa Kyaa (qv). Fought in 1900 war. Exiled to Seychelles, d 1924.
Kwame Kusi, 135, 2nd son of Amma Sewaa (qv), dau of Kwadu Yaadom (qv), and Apeboso Nkonsonhene Apaw Panin (qv).
Kwame Poku Sawariso, 143, 3rd son of Ata Sewaa (qv) and Adu (qv). Member of Kumase Deboso group who displayed his wealth before Asantehene Kwaku Dua Panin (qv). See *Asantesεm,* 10, 1979: 37–41.
"**Kwami**," **139,** 4th child of Akua Bakoma (qv) and Kwaku Owusu (qv).
"Kwami Afrifa," *see* Kwame Afrifa
"Kwami Afrifah," *see* Kwame Afrifa
"**Kwami Ajim,**" **145,** 1st son of Yaa Pani (qv) and Saben of Nsuase (qv).
"Kwami Amankwatia," *see* Kwame Amankwatia
"Kwami Appia," *see* Kwame Apea Osukye
"Kwami Appiah," *see* Kwame Apea Osukye
"Kwami Boachie," *see* Kwame Boakye
"Kwami Boaten," *see* Kwame Boaten, Kyidomhene
"Kwami Boatin," *see* Kwame Boaten, royal
"Kwami Boatin," *see* Kwame Boaten, Kyidomhene
"Kwami Gyansah," *see* Kwame Gyansa
"Kwami Jamsaah," *see* Kwame Gyansa
"Kwami Jansah," *see* Kwame Gyansa
"Kwami Kussi," *see* Kwame Kusi
"Kwamin Boaten," *see* Kwame Boaten, royal
"Kwami Silibuo," *see* Asabi Boakye
"Kwami Subri," *see* Kofi Subri
"**Kwami Subri,**" **181,** joined Agyeman Prempeh in Seychelles, otherwise unidentified.
"Kwandu," *see* Kwadu, dau of Yaa Afere
"Kwandu Yardom," *see* Kwadu Yaadom
"**Kwanimar,**" **134,** child of Akua Afriyie (qv) and Kwasi Kɔ (qv).
"Kwankua II," *see* Kwaku Dua Kumaa
"Kwantannan," *see* Nkwantanan
Kwapon Odeawuo, 103, Oyoko Abohyenhene in Kumase, temp Asantehene Osei Tutu.
"Kwase Gyembibi," *see* Kwasi Gyambibi
"**Kwasem,**" **103,** given office in the Kyidom *fekuo* by Osei Tutu (qv); otherwise unidentified.
Kwasi, 139, son of Akua Fokuo (qv) and Kwame Dwuben (qv). Dsp.
Kwasi, 140, b ca 1896, son of Ohene Afrewo (qv) and Yaw Sekyere (qv).
Kwasi Abayie, 137, aka Kwasi Afriyie, son of Asantehene Kwaku Dua Panin (qv) and Takyiwaa (dau of Asantehene Osei Tutu Kwame). Made Kumase Somihene ca 1850. 1st husband of Yaa Kyaa (qv) and father of, *int al,* Asantehene Kwaku Dua Kumaa (qv) and Kwabena Kyeretwe (qv). Died 1867.
Kwasi Adε, 141, 1st son of Akua Badu (qv) and Atta Akwasi (qv). Dsp.
Kwasi Agyeim, 137, presumably the son of Odεe (qv) and Apeboso Nkonsonhene Abu (qv), who unsuccessfully contended for the Golden Stool in 1884. See Wilks, 1975: 368.
Kwasi Akoko, 176, 178, Akyeamehene and Kumase Domakwaihene. In exile with Agyeman Prempeh in Elmina and Sierra Leone, later joined him in Seychelles.
"Kwasi Akokoo," *see* Kwasi Akoko
Kwasi "Berkun," 137, 1st (surviving) son of Akua Afriyie (qv) and Krapa (qv).
Kwasi "Chiu," 142, 1st son of Akua Nansewaa (qv) and Afarkwa (qv).
Kwasi Gyambibi, 137, 143, 154, 160, 176, 177, 179, 184, 191, son of Asantehene Kwaku Dua Panin (qv). Became Kumase Ayebiakyerehene. Married 1st Yaa Ntia (qv).

After her death, married Asantehemaa Yaa Kyaa (qv) and was father of, *int al*, Asantehemaa Agyeman Prempeh (qv), heir-apparent Agyeman Badu (qv), and Amma Adusa (qv) who became Asantehemaa Kwadu Yaadom II. Deported by British, 1896. Died in exile in Seychelles, 1903.
"Kwasi Gyembibi," *see* Kwasi Gyambibi
Kwasi Kɔɔ, 134, first husband of Asantehemaa Akua Afriyie (qv). Kaasehene (qv) mid-C18.
Kwasi Pra, 141, apparently from the Hiawu (qv) *fekuo*; married Amma Kom (qv).
Kwasi "Tobo," 143, son of an unidentified *ɔkyeame*. Married Amma Ntobu (qv).
"Kweku Fokuo," *see* Kwaku Fokuo
"Kweku Nanchu," *see* Kwaku Nantwi
"Kweku Nantwi, *see* Kwaku Nantwi
"Kweku Nsia," *see* Kwaku Nsia
"Kweku Wusu," *see* Kwaku Owusu
Kyenkyenhene, 135, 183, eldest son of Asantehemaa Amma Sewaa (qv) and Apaw Panin (qv). Killed ca 1800 probably in internecine struggles between Asantehene Osei Kwame (qv) and Asantehemaa Kwadu Yaadom (qv).
Kyerema Di Abetia, 108, Denkyira head drummer, supporter of Osei Tutu. Became Kumase Nkukuwafohene.
Kyidom, 103, 106, 125, Kumase *fekuo* created as rear guard of army by Osei Tutu (qv) before 1700, and command given to Okra Amponsem (qv).
Kyiroma, 132, 133, given second name "Clor" in *HAK*, probably "Korɔ." 2ⁿᵈ dau of Manu (qv) and Owusu Panin (qv); sister of, *int al*, Osei Tutu; and mother of Nketewa Ntim Abamu (qv).

"Lamina," *see* Elmina
"Lanta," *see* Ananta

Mampon, 89, 90, 106, 113, 35 mls NNE, capital of the Mampon Division of Asante whose *amanhene* rank next to Asantehene, and were commanders-in-chief of the Asante army. Cf Amaniampon; Asumgyima; Attakora Panin; Boahen Anantuo; Kwabena Dwumo; Kwame Apea Osukye; Safo Katanka. *See* Agyeman-Duah, 1960: passim; McCaskie, 1985, passim.
Mampon Akrofonso, 90, early capital of the Mampon, moved to present location by Attakora Panin (qv).
Mamponten, 87, town, 7 mls N, part of Oyoko Abohyen group (qv).

Manhyia, 136, formerly royal country seat and now, incorporated into Kumase, location of Asantehene's palace.
"Manpon," *see* Mampon
"Manpon krofonso," *see* Mampon Akrofonso
"Manpontin," *see* Mamponten
Manu, 88, 93, 99, 100, 130, 132, 133, dau of Abena Gyapa (qv). Married Owusu Panin (qv), and mother of, *int al*, Osei Tutu (qv).
Manu, 144, dau of Adwowa Kyire (qv) and Owusu (qv).
"Manue," *see* Manu
"Marnoo," *see* Manu
"Mensah," *see* Mensa Bonsu
Mensa Bonsu, 122, 128, 136, 148, 149, 151, 152, 3ʳᵈ son of Asantehemaa Afua Kobi (qv) and Kofi Nti (qv), born ca 1838. Succeeded his brother Kofi Kakari (qv) as Asantehene in 1874. Removed from office 1883. Went into exile in the Gold Coast Colony, and died at Praso in 1896. Reinterred in Kumase, 1911.
Mpankronu, 101, town 5 mls N. Defeated by Amankwatia Panin (qv) in late C17 local wars.

"Nanchui," *see* Kwaku Nantwi
"Nitibansu," 134, unidentified place.
"Nkawe," *see* Nkawie
Nkawie, 108, 179, 184, 191, 13 mls WSW. Town in Kumase Konti (qv). Denkyira in origin, joined Osei Tutu (qv) before the war of liberation 1700–01. Founded Nkawie Kumaa. [AS/102].
Nketewa Ntim Abamu, 110, 128, 132, 133, dau of Kyiroma (qv). Became Asantehemaa. Captured during raid on Kumase by Adansehene Apeanin Kramo (qv), and died in exile. Mother of Asantehene Kusi Obodum (qv) and Asantehemaa Akua Afriyie (qv).
Nkofe, 96, *fekuo* of hornblowers to the Asantehene. [AS/145].
Nkonson, 179, 184, stool in the Kumase Gyaase, created by Asantehene Osei Kwadwo (qv) on his accession [AS/47]. Cf Kofi Fofie Kaserepa.
Nkoransa, 90, 154, 155, 161, town, 150 mls N, and capital of province of same name.
Nkruma, 136, 3ʳᵈ son of Yaa Afere (qv) and Asabi Boakye (qv).
Nkukuwa, 108, ward of Kumase.
"Nkwaiehene," *see* Nkawie
Nkwanta, 100, Nkwanta(kese), 12 mls N, town founded by Denkyira immigrants and later placed under Kumase Akwamuhene [AS/136]. Cf Boakye Yam.

Nkwantanan, 135, section of Kumase, seat of Nkwantananhene; cf Boakye Yam Kumaa; Akyampon Kwasi.

Nsuase, 145, seat of Domakwaihene and Akyeamehene.

Nsuta, 88, 90, 30 mls NE, capital of the Asante Division of the same name.

Ntim, 145, husband of Bimma Dehyeɛ (qv); otherwise unidentified.

Ntim Gyakari, 104, 111, ɔmanhene of Denkyira (qv). Slain in Asante war of independence against Denkyira, 1700–01. Succeeded by Boadu Akufu (qv).

Ntori Hwensin, 103, resident of Dwaaso (qv); betrayed Asiedu Papaa Kese (qv).

Nuamoa, 108, Kumase Asokwahene, brother of Akwadan (qv) and cf Asokwa.

"Nuamoah," *see* Nuamoa

Nunu, 92, relative of Adowaa Nkrawiri (qv).

Nyaako Kusi Amoa, 112, 128, 132, 133, 1st Asantehemaa. Dau of Bimma Fie (qv), given in marriage by her uncle, Osei Tutu (qv), to Amakomhene Akosa Yiadom (qv). On his death, said to have married successively, 1) Amakomhene Adu Panin; 2) Amakomhene Adu Manu; and 3) Amakomhene Adu Mensa, who was father of Opoku Ware (qv). [AS/77]. *See* McCaskie, 1995a: 405 n.65.

"Nyam Panyin," *see* Anyim Panin

"Obeny Fītār," *see* Bimma Fita

"Obina Japa," *see* Abena Gyapa

Obirikoran, 119, son of Kumase Akwamuhene. Brought the *suman* Apafram from "Akim" (qv) to Asante.

"Obiriponmar Piaisiai," *see* Birempomaa Piesie

"Obiriponmar Piasai," *see* Birempomaa Piesie.

Obiri Yeboa, 97, 98, 99, 100, 102, 105, 110, 117, 128, 130, 131, 189, son of Akomadoma (qv). Late C17 ruler of the Kumase people, slain in the 2nd Domaa war (qv). Succeeded by Osei Tutu (qv), then in Akwamu (qv).

"Obi Yaeboa," *see* Obiri Yeboa

"Obi Yaeboh," *see* Obiri Yeboa

"Oboa Kwatiar," *see* Boa Kwatia

"Occra Punsem," *see* Okra Amponsem

"Ochilé mah Dier Abaetiae," *see* Kyerema Di Abetia

"Ochilemar," *see* Okyeremaa

"Ochily Kotoku," *see* Okyere Kotoku

"Odācor," *see* Dako

"Odae," *see* Odɛe

"Oday," *see* Odɛe

Odɛe, 136, 137, 4th dau of Asantehemaa Afua Sapon (qv) and Apagyahene Owusu Afriyie (qv). Married 1) Apeboso Nkonsonhene Apaw (qv); 2) Apeboso Nkonsonhene Abu (qv). The child of the 2nd marriage was Kwasi Agyeim (qv).

"Odro Agin Samuo," *see* Oduro Agyensamu

"Odruo Aginsemuo," *see* Oduro Agyensamu

Oduro Agyensamu, 104, 111, Assin accused of poisoning Denkyirahene Boa Amponsem (qv).

"Ofaibi-Odi-Nihoo," *see* Ofebiri Odeneho

Ofebiri Odeneho, 91, 92, 130, 131, dau of Birempomaa Piesie (qv), sister of Oti Akenten (qv), and wife of Adu Gyamfi (qv). Her mausoleum, Ofebiri Odeneho Baamu, is in Kwadaso, now a Kumase suburb. [AS/246]. *See* McCaskie, 1995a: 405 n.65.

Offinso, 178, 184, 191, town 20 mls N, capital of powerful Kumase sub-division of the same name.

Ofoase, 100, town, 14 mls S. [AS/131]. Cf Okine.

"Offoonassy," *see* Ofoase

Oframu, 93, one of the 7 gunmen (*Konti Atuo Nson*) who accompanied Osei Tutu into exile in Denkyira. Later made Assuowinhene. Keeper of the Asantehene's percussion cap gun, and thus referred to as "Tufuor," (cf Twi *otuo*, "gun"). [AS/188].

"Oguar," 158, that is, Ogua, the Twi name for Cape Coast.

"O'guebrydinhun," *see* Ofebiri Odeneho

"Ohen Afraewuo," *see* Ohene Afrewo

"Ohen Afrae Yow," *see* Ohene Afrewo

"Ohenafré Ya," *see* Ohene Afrewo

Ohene Afrewo, 137, 140, dau of Akua Afriyie (qv) and Krapa (qv). Married 1) Gyamasehene Brobi (qv); 2) Kofi Kyem (qv); 3) Gyamasehene Yaw Sekyere (qv).

"Ohiem Dicko," *see* Ohwim

"Ohin Afrwo," *see* Ohene Afrewo

"Oh-kun-ah," *see* Kona

"Oh-kùn-ah-diclo," *see* Kona

Ohwim, 99, Kumase stool, [AS/18], *odekuro* appointed to office under Soaduro headed by Awere (qv). Cf Akyereko.

Okine, 100, appointed *odekuro* of "Banjahi" (unidentified) and Ofoase (qv) by Obiri Yeboa (qv).

"Okaïñ," *see* Okine

Okomfo Anokye, 98, 102, 103, 105, 106, 108, 109, 110, 111, 114, 126, late C17 and early C18 prophet, to whom many magical powers are attributed. Generally regarded as architect of Osei Tutu's political and military successes. *See* Rattray, 1929: 270–84; McCaskie, 1986: passim.

Concordance

Okra Amponsem, 94, 103, Denkyira, given as servant to Osei Tutu (qv), and later made Kumase Kyidomhene. [AS/158]. Said to have died in Denkyira war of 1700. See Wilks, 1993: 332–33.

"O'Kraodomsin," *see* Okra Saben Domse.

Okra Saben Domse, 103, Saben Kumaa, son of Obiri Yeboa (qv), and renamed when made head of new Hia *fekuo* (qv) by Osei Tutu. [AS/154]. Said to have died in Denkyira war of 1700.

Okyeremaa, 130, 131, dau of Birempomaa Piesie (qv), and mother of Kwabia Anwanfi (qv) and Oti Akenten (qv).

Okyere Kotoku, 135, son of Dwabenhene Akuamoa Panin (qv), married Asantehemaa Amma Sewaa (qv).

"Onoh," *see* Wono

Opoku, 143, 1st son of Ata Sewaa (qv) and Adu (qv). Seemingly the Opoku Ahom b ca 1818; given the unprecedented position of "second heir-apparent" by Asantehene Kwaku Dua Panin (qv) ca 1834—second, that is, to Osei Kwadwo (qv); executed early 1848. See McCaskie, 1974: 217–21; Wilks, 1975: 331, 353–54, 359, 362, 592; McCaskie, 1995b: 385.

Opoku, 143, son of Takyiwaa (qv).

"Opokua," *see* Opokuwaa, dau of Akua Sewaa

"Opokua," *see* Opokuwaa, dau of Adwowa Sewaa

"Opokua," *see* Opokuwaa, dau of Ata Sewaa

Opoku Ahom, *see* under Opoku son of Ata Sewaa

"Opoku Atia," *see* Opoku Tia

"Opoku Fofiae," *see* Opoku Fofie

Opoku Fofie, 122, 128, 134, 2nd son of Asantehemaa Kwadu Yaadom (qv) and Adu Twum (qv), and full brother therefore of Opoku Kwame (qv), Yaa Dufie (qv), and Akua Akrukruwaa (qv). Heir-apparent in succession to Opoku Kwame. Became Asantehene in 1803 or 1804; d 1804, probably of smallpox.

Opoku Kwame, 122, 134, b ca 1768, 1st son of Asantehemaa Kwadu Yaadom (qv) and Adu Twum (qv), and full brother therefore of Yaa Dufie (qv), Akua Akrukruwaa (qv), and Opoku Fofie (qv). Made heir-apparent by Asantehene Osei Kwadwo but died in 1797–poisoned on the instructions of Asantehene Osei Kwame (qv) so report had it.

"Opoku Kwami," *see* Opoku Kwame

Opoku Kyakya, 135, son of Akua Sewaa (qv), otherwise unidentified.

"Opoku Ofiae," *see* Opoku Fofie

Opoku Tia, 134, 2nd husband of Asantehemaa Akua Afriyie (qv), and father of Aberefi Yaa (qv). Abradehene.

"Opokutintin," *see* Opoku Ware

Opoku Tukɔ, 143, 4th son of Ata Sewaa (qv) and Adu (qv). Twi *tu kɔ* has the sense of "traveller," and Opoku Tukɔ may be the Kwame Poku b 1827, sent for education to the Netherlands 1837, entered the Delft Academy 1844, returned to the Gold Coast 1847, and died by suicide 1850. See Yarak, 1987: 131–36.

Opokuwaa, 135, dau of Akua Sewaa (qv). Mother of, *int al*, Osei Kwaku Goroso (qv).

Opokuwaa, 142, 143, dau of Adwowa Sewaa (qv) and Adu (qv). Married 1) Kumase Ankobeahene Kwaku Tawia (qv), and first of their six children was Agyeikum (qv). Married 2) Apea Kɔ (qv).

Opokuwaa, 143, 144, dau of Ata Sewaa (qv). Married Adu (qv).

Opoku Ware, aka Opoku Tenten, 113, 114, 128, 132, 133, 2nd Asantehene, ca 1720 to 1750. Son of Nyaako Kusi Amoa (qv) and by general report, Amakomhene Adu Mensa. See Wilks, 1975: 331. Architect of imperial Asante.

Osafo Akonton, 112, Tafohene, killed by Osei Tutu (qv).

"Osafoo Acontun," *see* Osafo Akonton

"Osafu Acontum," *see* Osafo Akonton

"Osafu Acontun," *see* Osafo Akonton

"Osai Kudjoe," *see* Osei Kwadwo, Asantehene.

"Osai Tutu," *see* Osei Tutu

Osei, 143, son of Adwowa Kutu (qv), otherwise unidentified.

Osei Du, 122, 135, 3rd son of Asantehemaa Kwadu Yaadom (qv) and Owusu Ansa of Asokore Mampon (qv). Heir-apparent, d. 1807, on campaign.

Osei Kofi, 122, 135, 1st son of Asantehemaa Kwadu Yaadom (qv) and Owusu Ansa (qv). Died late C18 as heir-apparent.

Osei Kofi, 145, son of Yaa Manfu (qv) and Adu (qv).

"Osei Kojo-Krome," *see* Osei Kwadwokrom

Osei Kɔkɔ, 133, son of Manu (qv) and Owusu Panin (qv). Only full brother of Asantehene Osei Tutu (qv).

Osei Kwadwo, 88, 128, 132, 134, son of Asantehemaa Akua Afriyie (qv) and Akyempemhene Owusu Afriyie (qv). Brother of Aberefi Yaa (qv). Father of Owusu Afriyie, Apagyahene (qv). Asantehene 1764–77.

Osei Kwadwo, 122, 136, b ca 1810, son of Asantehemaa Afua Sapon (qv) and Apagyahene Owusu Afriyie (qv). Heir-apparent under Asantehene Kwaku Dua Panin (qv), but executed with his mother in 1859 on the supposition that they had plotted to replace Kwaku Dua Panin by Osei Kwadwo. *See* McCaskie, 1995b: 363–73.

Osei Kwadwo, 143, son of Badu (qv) and Yaw Afriyie (qv). Unsuccessful candidate for the Golden Stool, 1931.

Osei Kwadwokrom, 177, 179, 184, 191, Atwoma-Takyimanhene (qv), fought in 1900 war, exiled to Seychelles, d 1913.

Osei Kwadwo Kumaa, 135, son of Asantehemaa Adoma Akosua (qv).

Osei Kwaku Goroso, 135, royal, mat descendant of destooled Asantehemaa Adoma Akosua (qv) through his mother Opokuwaa (qv) and grandmother Akua Sewaa (qv). Lacking support for claims to Golden Stool. Supported Yaw Twereboanna (qv) in civil wars, and took refuge in Gold Coast Colony. *See* Lewin, 1978: 124, 256 n. 61.

Osei Kwame, 122, 134, Asantehene, enstooled 1777, abdicated 1803 and committed suicide. According to *HAK* was son of Asantehemaa Kwadu Yaadom (qv) by her marriage to Mamponhene Safo Katanka (qv). This is queried in Wilks, 1975: 336–43, and McCaskie, 1995a: 180–83.

Osei Kwasi, 135, 1st son of Asantehemaa Adoma Akosua (qv) and Owusu (qv).

Osei Kwasi, 144, 1st son of Adwowa Kyire (qv) and Owusu (qv).

Osei Tutu, 88, 93–5, 98–114, 119, 125–6, 128, 130, 132–3, 189, son of Manu (qv) and Owusu Panin (qv). Leader of the movement for Asante independence from Denkyira (qv), 1700–01. Became 1st ruler, Asantehene, of the unified Asante nation – the Asanteman; d 1717, in the course of a southern campaign. *See* Boahen, 1975: passim.

Osei Tutu, 139, Akyempemhene; son of Owusu Ntobi and grandson of Asantehene Osei Tutu Kwame (qv). Married Akua Fokuo (qv), d 1925.

Osei Tutu Kwame, aka Osei Asibe Bonsu, 122, 128, 132, 135, Asantehene, 1804–23. Son of Asantehemaa Kwadu Yaadom (qv) and Owusu Ansa (qv).

Osei Yaw Akoto, 122, 128, 132, 135, b ca 1807, 1st child of Kwadu Yaadom (qv) and her 3rd husband, Owusu Yaw (qv). Heir-apparent by, or before, 1817. Made Asantehene while on campaign, 1824. Signed Anglo-Asante Treaty of 1831; d 1833.

"Ossafu Kantanka," *see* Safo Katanka
"Ossafu Kwantankan," *see* Safo Katanka
"Ossafu Passuanpah," *see* Safo Pasoampa
"Ossafuor," *see* Safo Katanka
"Ossai," *see* Osei
"Ossai Akoto," *see* Osei Yaw Akoto
"Ossai Akwasi," *see* Osei Kwasi, son of Adoma Akosua (qv)
"Ossai Akwasi," *see* Osei Kwasi, son of Adwowa Kyire (qv)
"Ossai Asibi," *see* Osei Tutu Kwame
"Ossai Bonsu," *see* Mensa Bonsu
"Ossai Bonsu I," *see* Osei Tutu Kwame
"Ossai Doo," *see* Osei Du
"Ossai Du," *see* Osei Du
"Ossai Kodjoe," *see* Osei Kwadwo, Asantehene
"Ossai Kodjoe," *see* Osei Kwadwo, heir-apparent
"Ossai Kodjoe Kuma," *see* Osei Kwadwo Kumaa
"Ossai Kofi," *see* Osei Kofi, son of Yaa Manfu
"Ossai Kudjoe," *see* Osei Kofi
"Ossai Kwakudua I," *see* Kwaku Dua Panin
"Ossai Kwami," *see* Osei Kwame
"Ossai Tutu," *see* Osei Tutu, Akyempemhene
"Ossai Yaw," *see* Osei Yaw Akoto
"Ossay Atu," *see* Osei Tutu
"Ossay Glusso," *see* Osei Kwaku Goroso
"Ossay Kofi," *see* Osei Kofi, son of Kwadu Yaadom
"Ossay Kojo," *see* Osei Kwadwo, Asantehene
"Ossay Kokor," *see* Osei Kɔkɔ
"Ossay Poku," *see* Opoku Ware
"Ossay Tutu," *see* Osei Tutu

Oti Akenten, 91, 92, 93, 96, 97, 128, 130, 131, 132, 188, 189, said to have been son of Okyeremaa (qv). *Abusuatiri* or "clan" head of the Oyoko of Kokofu (qv) and Kumase in succession to his elder brother Kwabia Anwanfi (qv). Succeeded by Obiri Yeboa (qv).

"Otiecu Achulier," *see* Otieku Atwedie
"Oti Kotia," *see* Oti Kwatia

Otikrom, 143, town, 8 mls ENE. [AS/163]. Cf Yaw Afriyie.

Otieku Atwedie, 107, 133, son of Bimma Fita (qv) and brother of Asantehemaa Nyaako Kusi Amoa (qv). Appointed by Osei Tutu to reside in Kwadwokrom (qv) with Agyeibi (qv) and other Denkyira defectors. [AS/184].

Oti Kwatia, 99, placed by Obiri Yeboa under Domakwai (qv). The name probably in error for Amoako Panin. [AS/134].

"Otiwa Kesie," *see* Otwiwaa Keseε

"Otti Akenten," *see* Oti Akenten
"Ottieku Achulie," *see* Otieku Atwedie
"Ottiwar Kesie," *see* Otwiwaa Keseɛ
Otwiwaa Keseɛ, 131, 146, dau of Birempomaa Piesie (qv), and mother of Boa Kwatia (qv).
"Oun . . .(?)," *see* Wono
"Ownano," *see* Wono
"Owoano," *see* Wono
"Owon . . .(?), *see* Wono
Owusu, 134, ɔhene of Apa (qv), husband of Sewaa Awukuwaa (qv).
Owusu, 135, husband of Adoma Akosua (qv), otherwise unidentified.
Owusu, 142, 2nd husband of Asantehemaa Yaa Dufie (qv), otherwise unidentified.
Owusu, 143, husband of Akua Akrukruwaa (qv), otherwise unidentified.
Owusu, 143, husband of Adwowa Kutu (qv), otherwise unidentified.
Owusu, 144, husband of Adwowa Kyire (qv), otherwise unidentified.
Owusu Afriyie, 102, 103, 134, Akyempemhene, d ca 1750. Son of Asantehene Osei Tutu (qv). 3rd husband of Asantehemaa Akua Afriyie (qv) and father of Asantehene Osei Kwadwo (qv). Trained by Saben (qv) as his successor. Still remembered for his generalship.
Owusu Afriyie, 135, Apagyahene, son of Asantehene Osei Kwadwo (qv), husband of Asantehemaa Afua Sapon (qv), and father of, *int al*, Asantehemaa Afua Kobi (qv). [AS/147].
Owusu Ansa, 135, of Asokore Mampon (qv), d ca 1784. Son of Asantehene Osei Kwadwo (qv), husband of Asantehemaa Kwadu Yaadom (qv), and father of Osei Kofi (qv), Osei Asibe (qv Osei Tutu Kwame,) and Osei Du (qv).
Owusu Ansa, 139, son of Akua Fokuo (qv) and Akyempemhene Osei Tutu (qv).
Owusu Ansa, John, 155, 161, 162, born 1851, son of Sarah Boxell of Cape Coast and Owusu Ansa, son of Asantehene Osei Tutu Kwame (qv). Mission educated, served in the Gold Coast Rifle Corps, and in the Gold Coast Civil Service as clerk. Was a trader on Lower Niger in 1887, thereafter entered Asante political service, becoming a powerful voice in government. Member of Embassy to London, 1895–6. Returned to London to work for restoration of Agyeman Prempeh. *See* Wilks, 1975: 632–60.
Owusu Ansa Panin, 145, son of Asantehene Osei Tutu Kwame (qv). Anamenakohene (qv). Husband of Abena Akyampoma (qv). [AS/42].

Owusu Mmara, 99, ɔhene of the Sodo (qv) in the royal household. Made chief of the Twafuo by Obiri Yeboa.
Owusu Nkwantabisa, 139, son of Akua Fokuo (qv) and Akyempemhene Osei Tutu (qv).
Owusu Panin, 99, 133, Abrenkese Nyameanihene (qv), father of Osei Tutu (qv).
Owusu Taseamandi, 152, son of heir-apparent Osei Kwadwo (qv) and Ampomahwene, a royal of Gyaman. Offended Asantehene Mensa Bonsu (qv) and took refuge in Gold Coast Colony. Apparently committed suicide at Elmina, 1881.
"Owusu Tassiah Marndier," *see* Owusu Taseamandi
Owusu Yaw, 135, of Anowo (qv). Son of Nkonsonhene Osei Yaw and grandson of Akyempemhene Owusu Afriyie (qv). Last husband of Asantehemaa Kwadu Yaadom (qv) and father of Asantehene Osei Yaw (qv).
"O'Yam Pani," *see* Anyim Panin
Oyoko, 87, 88, 89, 92, 124, 125, 131, 187, major Asante *abusua*, conceptualised as comprising the descendants and associates of Ankyewa Nyame (qv), and as divided into three principal segments, Oyoko Abohyen (qv), Oyoko Atutuo (qv), and Oyoko Breman (qv). [AS/28].
"Oyukun Abohen," *see* Oyoko Abohyen
Oyoko Abohyen, 87, 88, 100, 106, 187, branch of the Oyoko including Kumase Oyokohene (cf Asaaman), Kenyase (qv), Mamponten (qv), and Anyinase (qv). The royal lineage, the Oyoko Kɔkɔ, belongs to this group. [AS/28].
Oyoko Atutuo, 87, 88, 106, branch of the Oyoko including Adenkyemenaso (qv), Pampaso (qv), Ahenkuro (qv), Awiam (qv). Cf Boansi Kofo, 1st Atutuohene; Kwabena Agyeikum. [AS/32].
Oyoko Breman 87, 88, 106, branch of the Oyoko including the Asaaman Kwadane section of Kumase, and Esereso. [AS/56].
"Oyuku," *see* Oyoko
"Oyuku Abohen," *see* Oyoko Abohyen
"Oyukor," *see* Oyoko
"Oyusu," *see* Owusu, husband of Adwowa Kutu
"Oyusu," *see* Owusu, Apahene
"Oyusu," *see* Owusu, husband of Adoma Akosua
"Oyussi Pani," *see* Owusu Panin
"Oyusu Ansa," *see* Owusu Ansa, son of Akua Fokuo
"Oyusu Ansa Pani," *see* Owusu Ansa Panin
"Oyusu Kwantabisa," *see* Owusu Nkwantabisa

Paakuso, 96, village of hammock bearers, *asoamfo* (qv), 6 mls ENE.

Pampaso, 87, 114, Oyoko Atutuo section of Kumase, the *obaa-panin* of which controlled the Atinafo who served as nurses to young royals and princes.

"Panclon annu," *see* Mpankronu

"Panpasoo," *see* Pampaso

"Parkosoo," *see* Paakuso

"Pha-fra-hamoo," *see* Fafrahamoɔ

"Phiarsy," *see* Feyiase

"Pipim," 143, child of Yaa Ntia (qv) and Kwasi Gyambibi (qv).

Poku, 88, ɔhene of Anyinase (qv), temp Asantehene Kwaku Dua Panin (qv).

"Poku," *see* Opoku, son of Ata Sewaa (qv)

"Poku," *see* Opoku, son of Takyiwaa

"Pokua," *see* Opokuwaa, dau of Ata Sewaa

"Poku Cha Cha," *see* Opoku Kyakya

"Poku Fofie," *see* Opoku Fofie

"Poku Offiae," *see* Opoku Fofie

"Poku Tikor," *see* Opoku Tukɔ

"Poku Tintin," *see* Opoku Ware

Prempeh, Frederick A, 139, son of Agyeman Prempeh (qv); b 1894, accompanied father into exile, and returned with him to Asante in 1924. Served his father as amanuensis and, in this capacity, penned *HAK*.

"Prince Akwasi," *see* Prempeh, Frederick aka Kwasi Gyambibi

Saakodie Date, 100, said to be son of Adu Gyamfi (qv), and husband of Mamponhemaa Akyaama. Purchased lands at Adumanu from Boansi Kofo, to become first Antoahene in the Adonten *fekuo* of Kumase. Remembered for having proposed that Osei Tutu (qv) should be brought from Akwamu to become Asantehene. [AS/34].

"Sabbim," *see* Saben

Saben, 99, 100, 102, 103, son of Obiri Yeboa (qv), appointed early in his reign to a new *fekuo*, Domakwai (qv). Under Osei Tutu (qv) promoted to head new *fekuo*, Akyempem (qv). Trained Owusu Afriyie (qv), son of Osei Tutu, as his successor. Died in 2nd Domaa war.

Saben, 145, functionary of ɔhene of Nsuase. Married Yaa Pani (qv).

"Sabin," *see* Saben of Nsuase

"Saepae," *see* Sepe Tinponmu

"Saepaes," *see* Sepe Tinponmu

"Saffié," *see* Adunnya Safie

"Saffier," *see* Adunnya Safie

Safo Katanka, 134, fl 1750s to 1760s. Led campaign in eastern Gonja, 1751. 6th Mamponhene in succession to Asumgyima (qv). According to *HAK*, 3rd husband of Aberefi Yaa (qv) and father of Sewaa Awukuwaa (qv). Later married Kwadu Yaadom (qv) and was father *int al* of Asantehemaa Amma Sewaa (qv) and Asantehene Osei Kwame (qv). These data are, however, queried in Wilks, 1975: 336–43, and McCaskie, 1995a: 180–83.

Safo Pasoampa, 93, one of the 7 gunmen (*Konti Atuo Nson*) who accompanied Osei Tutu into exile in Denkyira. Later made Bantama Baamuhene, custodian of the royal mausoleum. [AS/54].

"Saguarsy," *see* Sanyaase

"Sakudie Dater," *see* Saakodie Date

"Santimansu," *see* Asantemanso

Sanyaase, 124, section of Kumase.

Sawua, 100, village, 7 mls SE. *Odekuro* (said to be Amoako) placed by Obiri Yeboa (qv) under Saben (qv) in the Domakwai group (qv). [AS/87].

"Sechile," *see* Yaw Sekyere

"Séoūah," *see* Sawua

"Seper," *see* Sepe Tinponmu

Sepe Tinponmu, 100, 101, 103, the references to "Seper," *see* 100, and to "the 7 Saepaes" are presumably to the Sepe district that was defeated by Amankwatia Panin (qv) in the late C17 local wars. Sepe Tinponmu, a village now in NE suburbs of Kumase, was founded by Akumantenhene Tonto Diawuo (qv) temp Osei Tutu.

"Sewah," *see* Sewaa, dau of Akua Ntim

"Sewah," *see* Sewaa, dau of Adwowa Kutu

"Sewah Awukooār," *see* Sewaa Awukuwaa

"Sewah Okua," *see* Sewaa Awukuwaa

"Sewah Okuwa," *see* Sewaa Awukuwaa

"Sewah Okuwar," *see* Sewaa Awukuwaa

Sewaa, 144, dau of Akua Ntim (qv).

Sewaa, 143, 144, apparently aka Yaa Dufie, dau of Adwowa Kutu (qv).

Sewaa Awukuwaa (Okuwa), 134, 135, dau of Aberefi Yaa (qv) and Safo Katanka (qv). Married to Owusu (qv), Apahene (qv); mother of Asantehemaa Adoma Akosua (qv).

"Silésu," *see* Esereso

"Soadre," *see* Soaduro

"Soadro," *see* Soaduro

Soaduro, 99, 102, top-ranking military *fekuo* created by Obiri Yeboa and placed under Awere (qv). After the death of Obiri Yeboa in the second Domaa war, Soaduro was renamed "Akwamu" by Osei Tutu, and the Konti *fekuo* was created under Amankwatia Panin (qv), who outranked Awere. Cf Kwadwokrom.

"Sobis," 108, unidentified Denkyiras who joined Osei Tutu (qv) before the war of liberation 1700–01.

Sodo, 99, division of the royal household comprising the cooks.

"Soedoe," see Sodo

"Sor-Asū-Dā," see Kwame Poku Sawariso

Subri, 141, husband of Kwadu (qv), dau of Yaa Afere (qv). There seems no reason to equate him with either Kofi Subri (qv) or Kwami Subri (qv).

Suntreso, 96, village now within Kumase. See under Domaa.

"Suntresoo," see Suntreso

Tabiri, 99, appointed to position in the Twafuo (qv) by Obiri Yeboa (qv).

"Taffoo," see Tafo

Tafo, 111, 112, 3 mls N. Attacked by Asantehene Osei Tutu and Tafohene Osafo Akonton (qv) slain.

"Takiau," see Takyiwaa

"Takiman," see Takyiman

Takyiman, 95, 146, 191, town in Atwoma (qv) in which Osei Tutu took refuge after his flight from Denkyira, cf. Kwakru; Osei Kwadwokrom.

Takyimantia, 179, 184, 191, 50 mls NW. [AS/287]. Cf Kofi Kumaa.

Takyiwaa, 142, 143, dau of Opokuwa (qv) and Apea Kɔ (qv). Bore 1 child, Opoku (qv), father unknown.

Tena, 87, 89, 187, a major Asante *abusua*, technically merged with Bretuo (qv). See Wilks, 1975: 105–06; McCaskie, 1985: 169–74.

Toase, 179, 184, 191, town, 14 mls W. Cf. Kwame Afrifa; Yim Awere. [AS/128].

"Toasi," see Toase

Tonto Diawuo, 103, name mistakenly corrected to "Toto Jassae" in *HAK* 64:13. Servant of Asantehene Osei Tutu, made head of the Akumanten (qv) in the Hia (qv). Said to have been an immigrant from Denkyira, late C17. [AS/80].

"Tortoduawoo," see Tonto Diawuo

"Toto Jassae," see Tonto Diawuo

"Tra," see Tena

"Tufuor," see Oframu

"Tutuo," see Oyoko Atutuo

Twafuo, 99, *fekuo* of the army scouts, under command of Kumase Akwamuhene (qv).

Twetwerudu, 113, not satisfactorily identified, but apparently chief in the area of Adwira (Ejura, 50 mls NNE). Came in conflict with Mampon, late C17. Mamponhene Amaniampon (qv) sought help from Asantehene Osei Tutu (qv) who, in response, sent forces under Boa Kwatia (qv) and Opoku Ware (qv). Adwira became seat of Mampon Adontenhene.

Twum, 90, 127, 130, 131, 188, son of Birempomaa Piesie (qv). Regarded as ruler in Asantemanso (qv), in succession to his brother Akyampon Tenten (qv), and predecessor of his younger brother Antwi (qv).

Twumaduase, 101, village 7 mls E. Defeated by Amankwatia Panin (qv) in late C17 local wars.

Wani, 114, from Pampaso (qv), nurse of Opoku Ware (qv).

"Wanni," see Wani

Wawase, 145, section of Kumase.

"Wawasie," see Wawase

"Worna," 98, unidentified *ɔhene*, in charge of royal household guards, presumably Gyaase (qv).

Wono, 91, 92, 11 mls NE. Founded by Adu Gyamfi (qv). Formerly in Benkum Division of Mampon, under Gyamasehene. [AS/162, 246].

"Wrer-Dan-fuor," see Awere Gyamfuo

"Yā Abah," see Yaaba

"Yaa Achia," see Yaa Kyaa dau of Afua Kobi

Yaa Afere, 136, 2nd dau of Asantehemaa Afua Sapon (qv) and Apagyahene Owusu Afriyie (qv). Four children born of marriage to Abrenkese Nyameanihene Kankam (qv). Divorced, late 1850s, after illicit affair with Boadi (qv), resulting in birth of Akosua Berenya (qv). Remarried to Asabi Boakye (qv), giving birth *int al* to Yaw Twereboanna (qv). Died 1883.

Yaa Anani, 144, 1st dau of Adwowa Kyire (qv) and Owusu (qv). Bore 2 children, father(s) unknown.

Yaa Asantewaa, 176, 177, 179, 184, 191, Edwesohemaa, central figure in resistance to British, 1900; died in exile in Seychelles, 1921.

Yaaba, 138, dau of Akua Afriyie (qv) and Asafo Boakye (qv).

Yaa Dufie, 128, 132, 134, 142, 1st dau of Asantehemaa Kwadu Yaadom (qv) and Adu Twum (qv), and full sister, therefore, of Opoku Kwame (qv), Akua Akrukruwaa (qv), and Opoku Fofie (qv). 1st husband Abu aka Owusu Penemo (qv), and gave birth to Kwaku Pimpim (qv). 2nd husband Owusu (qv), and gave birth to Adwowa

Sewaa (qv). Asantehemaa temp Osei Yaw (qv) and early Kwaku Dua Panin (qv).

Yaa Kyaa, 122, 123, 136, 137, 139, 140, 153, 163, 164, 165, 176, 177, 178, 184, 191, 1st dau of Asantehemaa Afua Kobi (qv) and Kofi Nti (qv), b early 1840s. Married 1st Kwasi Abayie (qv) and 2nd Kwasi Gyambibi (qv). Asantehene Agyeman Prempeh was 1st son of 2nd marriage. Became Asantehemaa 1883. Principal architect of Asante reconstruction after the end of the civil wars. Abducted by British, 1896. Died Seychelles, 1917. See *Asantesεm*, 11, 1979: 18–29.

Yaa Kyaa, 140, aka Akua Akyaa. Dau of Ohene Afrewo (qv) and Yaw Sekyere (qv), b ca 1894. Married Kwabena Poku, Gyakye Abontendomhene. Their son Kwaku Adusei (b 1919) became Asantehene, as Opoku Ware II, 1970–99.

"Ya Annany," *see* Yaa Anani

Yaa Manfu, 145, 1st dau of Bimma Dehyeε (qv) and Ntim (qv). Married Adu (qv).

Yaa Ntia, 142, last child of Opokuwaa (qv) and Ankobeahene Kwaku Tawia (qv). Divorced, then married Apea Kɔ (qv).

Yaa Pani, 145, dau of Bimma Dehyeε (qv), married Saben of Nsuase (qv).

Yaa Sokwa, 180, wife of Bantamahene Kwame Amankwatia (qv).

"Ya bah," 138, dau of Akua Afriyie (qv) and Asafo Boakye (qv).

"Yachia," *see* Yaa Kyaa

"Yachia," *see* Yaa Kyaa dau of Ohene Afrewo

"Ya Chi-a," *see* Yaa Kyaa

"Yà Difiae," *see* Yaa Dufie

"Ya Dufiae," *see* Yaa Dufie

"Ya Dufiae," *see* Sewaa, dau of Adwowa Kutu (qv)

"Yae du Kummini," *see* Gyedu Kumanin

"Ya Efriae," *see* Yaa Afere

"Yafilé," *see* Yaa Afere

"Ya Fraie," *see* Yaa Afere

"Yah Asantiwa," *see* Yaa Asantewaa

"Ya Intia," *see* Yaa Ntia

"Ya Manfu," *see* Yaa Manfu

"Ya Mānfui," *see* Yaa Manfu

"Yamir Annir," *see* Abrenkese Nyameani

"Yami Ani," *see* Abrenkese Nyameani

"Yami Anni," *see* Abrenkese Nyameani

Yamoa, 98, Agonahene, and priest of Boabeduru. Said to have been elder brother of Okomfo Anokye (qv).

"Yam Panir," 96, presumably Yam Panin. Created Abrafoɔhene (qv) by Oti Akenten (qv). Apparently in the Konti *fekuo* (qv).

"Yamua," *see* Yamoa

"Yā Nany," *see* Yaa Anani

"Yā Odifiae," *see* Yaa Dufie

"Yā Panîj," *see* Yaa Pani

"Yā Pany," *see* Yaa Pani

"Yar Santewar," *see* Yaa Asantewaa

"Yar Sukwa," *see* Yaa Sokwa

Yaw, 140, son of Kwadu (qv) and Gyima (qv).

"Yaw Afriae," *see* Yaw Afriyie, son of Ata Sewaa

Yaw Afriyie, 143, son of Ata Sewaa (qv) and Adu (qv).

Yaw Afriyie, 143, son of Asantehene Osei Yaw (qv). Married Badu (qv), dau of Opokuwaa (qv). Otikromhene (qv); destooled. [AS/163].

"Yaw Berkun," 142, husband of Afua Mprakyere (qv). Otherwise unidentified.

Yaw Daani, 141, Suamehene, i.e. head of the *Asoamfo* (qv). Destooled 1896, but subsequently reinstated by British, and d 1924. Husband of Akosua Manhyia (qv). *See* Ch. 1, *supra*, 7.

"Yaw Danie," *see* Yaw Daani

Yaw Sanheni, 141, 1st son of Akosua Manhyia (qv) and Yaw Daani (qv), otherwise unidentified.

"Yaw Sanheni," *see* Yaw Sanhene

"Yaw Séchilé," *see* Yaw Sekyere

Yaw Sekyere, 140, 3rd husband of Ohene Afrewo (qv). Gyamasehene (qv).

Yaw Twereboanna, 136, 1st son of Yaa Afere (qv) and her 3rd husband Asabi Boakye (qv); b ca 1860. Emerged as strong contender for the Golden Stool in 1886, but after the election of Agyeman Prempeh in 1888 took refuge in the Gold Coast Colony and d there, 1908. *See* Wilks, 1975: 368–70, 570–82; Ch. 1, *supra* **10–12, 17**.

Yim Awere, 107, Denkyira ɔbirεmpɔn, defected to Osei Tutu prior to Denkyira war of 1701. Resettled at Kwadwokrom (qv), and later became Toasehene. [AS/128]. Cf Agyeibi; Kwakwa Bene; Kwame Afrifa.

"Yookoo," *see* Oyoko

"Yookooheni," *see* Oyoko Abohyen

"Youdyayim," *see* Yim Awere

"Youkou," *see* Oyoko

"Youkou-heni," *see* Oyoko Abohyen

"Yuku," *see* Oyoko

"Yuku Atutuo," *see* Oyoko Atutuo

"Yuku Blaémarn," *see* Oyoko Breman

"Yusu," *see* Owusu, husband of Adwowa Kyire

"Yusu An Sa," *see* Owusu Ansa

"Yukun," *see* Oyoko

"Yusu Yaw," *see* Owusu Yaw

Printed and bound by CPI Group (UK) Ltd, Croydon, CR0 4YY